CALLED TO HOLINESS
AND COMMUNION:
Vatican II on The Church

CALLED TO HOLINESS AND COMMUNION:
Vatican II on The Church

Edited by
Fr. Steven Boguslawski, O.P. and Robert Fastiggi

UNIVERSITY OF SCRANTON PRESS
Scranton and London

Library of Congress Cataloging-in-Publication Data

Called to holiness and communion : Vatican II on the church / edited by
Robert Fastiggi and Steven Boguslawski.
    p. cm.
Proceedings of a conference held Nov. 12-15, 2003 at Sacred Heart Major
Seminary.
Includes bibliographical references and index.
ISBN 978-1-58966-158-5 (pbk.)
1. Church--History of doctrines--Congresses. 2. Vatican Council (2nd
: 1962-1965)--Congresses. 3. Catholic Church--Doctrines--History--
Congresses. I. Fastiggi, Robert L. II. Boguslawski, Steven C.
BX1746.C253 2008
262'.52--dc22

    2008049196

Distribution:
UNIVERSITY OF SCRANTON PRESS
Chicago Distribution Center
11030 S. Langley
Chicago, IL 60628

TABLE OF CONTENTS

FOREWORD

EVERY ONCE IN A WHILE, we experience a providential coming together of people and events in such a profound, often unexpected way that the Holy Spirit was clearly at work making it all happen. Those of us who lived through the exciting days of Vatican II look back to those years as one of the "defining moments" for the Church Universal during the last half-century. The late Pope John Paul II and Pope Benedict XVI—themselves both participants in the conciliar experience—each in his own way have affirmed the unique blessing Vatican II has represented for our Church, especially for the ministry of evangelization.

Again, because of a confluence of various factors and the mysterious hand of the Holy Spirit, over the past decade, Sacred Heart Major Seminary in Detroit and the Pope John Paul II Cultural Center in Washington, D.C., have shared many resources and common experiences. Both of these institutions have a deep abiding commitment to the message and witness of the late Pope John Paul II, especially his understanding of the necessary connection of faith and culture in the work of the New Evangelization.

November 12-15, 2003, Sacred Heart Major Seminary, in conjunction with the Pope John Paul II Cultural Center, sponsored a special conference, *"Called to Holiness and Communion"* which included a number of cardinals, theologians, and philosophers of international reputation. I am pleased to share with you the work of this conference, now available as *"Called to Holiness and Communion: Vatican II on the Church,"* published by University of Scranton Press.

The editors, Father Steven Boguslawski, O.P. and Dr. Robert Fastiggi of Sacred Heart Major Seminary are to be commended for their diligence and wise perspective in bringing the project from conception to completion. I trust the reader will find the mysterious yet powerful hand of the Holy Spirit at work in these inspiring and insightful essays.

+ Adam Cardinal Maida, Archbishop of Detroit

IX

INTRODUCTION
Robert Fastiggi

DECEMBER 8, 2005 marked the fortieth anniversary of the solemn conclusion of Vatican II, the twenty-first ecumenical council of the Catholic Church. Looking back from the vantage point of over four decades, theologians are still trying to assimilate the doctrine of the Church presented by the council.

In many respects, Vatican II was the council *par excellence* of ecclesiology, the systematic study of the nature and mission of the Church. Two of the four conciliar constitutions, *Lumen gentium* (the dogmatic constitution) and *Gaudium et spes* (the pastoral constitution) deal *ex professo* with the mystery of the Church and her role in the modern world. The decrees, *Orientalium ecclesiarum* (on the Eastern Catholic Churches) and *Unitatis redintegratio* (on ecumenism), provide further insights on the catholicity of the Church and her commitment to Christian unity. The other 12 documents of Vatican II touch on ecclesiological topics either explicitly — such as *Ad gentes* (on the missionary life of the Church) — or implicitly — such as *Dei verbum* (on divine revelation).

The present volume consists of 16 chapters that were originally delivered at a symposium on the ecclesiology of Vatican II sponsored by Sacred Heart Major Seminary of Detroit, MI. on November 12-15, 2003. Leading scholars from the USA and abroad gathered at the John Paul II Cultural Center, Washington, D.C. to reflect on Vatican II's vision of the Church and the implications of this vision for the third Christian millennium. The talks given at that symposium have been revised and updated to constitute the 16 chapters of this volume.

These 16 chapters highlight the call to holiness and communion that is at the heart of Vatican II's ecclesiology. As the Mystical Body of Christ, the Church exemplifies the communion of the Catholic faithful, organically united to Christ, the Head. This Mystical Body is vivified by the Holy Spirit, the soul of the Church, who sanctifies and guides the faithful, anointing them with the special graces needed for their witness to the world and their communion with Christ.

In chapter one, the esteemed theologian, Avery Cardinal Dulles, S.J., provides a rich synthesis of the major themes that have emerged in discussions of Vatican II's ecclesiology. Using the 1985 Extraordinary Synod of Bishops as a point of departure, Cardinal Dulles demonstrates that many of the ecclesiological tensions that have emerged since Vatican II are, in reality, based on misunderstandings of the council.

In chapter two, Angelo Cardinal Scola, the Patriarch of Venice, draws upon the profound theology of Hans Urs von Balthasar to explore the theme of the Church as the spouse of Christ. In the process, he brings into focus the special Marian dimension of ecclesial communion.

Chapter three is by Francis Cardinal George, the Archbishop of Chicago. Making use of his erudition in both philosophy and theology, the Cardinal provides a lucid critique of various attempts to ground revelation in human subjectivity, with special attention given to the theologies of Schleiermacher, Tillich and Rahner. An authentic inculturation of the Gospel, however, must be rooted in the objective revelation of Christ, the universal norm of truth, and also in the Church, the universal sacrament of salvation.

In chapter four, Fr. Richard Schenk, O.P., offers many insights into the context and meaning of *Gaudium et spes*, the *Pastoral Constitution on the Church in the Modern World*. In particular, Fr. Shenk examines proper and improper meanings of discerning the "signs of the times."

Vatican II highlighted the importance of the Eucharist as "source and summit of the entire Christian life." In chapter five, Fr. Jeremy Driscoll, OSB, discusses the centrality of the Eucharist for ecclesial communion.

In chapter six, Msgr. Robert Sokolowski draws upon his expertise in phenomenology to explore the identity of the episcopal office. In particular, the role of the bishop as teacher is discussed, making use of a "theology of disclosure."

In chapter seven, Robert Fastiggi discusses the hierarchical constitution of the Church with special attention to the Petrine office. By means of historical and theological analysis, he argues that the indefectibility of the Catholic Church is intrinsically connected to ministry of the Roman Pontiff as the sign and instrument of ecclesial communion.

In chapter eight, Bishop Allen Vigneron, like Msgr. Sokolowski, makes uses of a theology of disclosure to examine the priestly office. Drawing upon both Vatican II and John Paul II's 1992 Apostolic Exhortation, *Pastores dabo vobis*, Bishop Vigneron underlines the mystery of the priest as a man of communion who is configured to Christ.

In chapter nine, Fr. Gabriel O'Donnell, O.P., discusses the renewal of religious life taught by Vatican II. In the process, he shows that many religious congregations failed to properly implement this renewal as envisioned by the council.

In chapter ten, Peter Casarella provides a comprehensive overview of the theology of the lay vocation as taught by Vatican II. In particular, he explores how the lay faithful are meant to collaborate in the sacred ministry of priests.

In chapter eleven, Carl Anderson examines the role of the family in the life of the Church. In his discussion, he shows how the renewal of the Church and her evangelizing mission cannot be separated from the "domestic church" of the family.

In chapter twelve, Pia de Solenni, offers many valuable insights into the authority of women in the Catholic Church. Manifesting full support of the Catholic Church's teaching on the all-male priesthood, she nevertheless shows how women have an irreplaceable authority grounded in the Church as the spouse of Christ.

In chapter thirteen, Janet Smith takes up the question of *sensus fidelium* in relation to the teaching of Pope Paul VI's encyclical, *Humanae vitae*. Making use of overlooked criteria for discerning the consensus of the *truly* faithful, she argues that the teaching of Paul VI against contraception authentically reflects the mind of the Church.

Fr. J. Augustine Di Noia, O.P., in chapter fourteen, discusses the vocation of the Catholic theologian in Catholic higher education. With passion and insight, he explains how fidelity to the Magisterium is essential to the true mission of theology in Catholic colleges and universities.

In chapter fifteen, Fr. Francis Martin examines the importance of biblical studies in both theology and the life of the Church. With special attention to *Dei Verbum* of Vatican II, he sheds light on

how the full meaning of God's Word must be discerned by both critical scholarship and the life of faith. In his emphasis on the centrality
of Christ to human history, Fr. Martin anticipates many of the themes
recently expressed in Pope Benedict XVI's book, *Jesus of Nazareth*.

In chapter sixteen, George Weigel links Vatican II's doctrine
on human dignity and communion to the concrete realities of the
American scene. He reflects on how the social teachings of the Catholic Church present a challenge to the expressions of democracy and
freedom in the USA.

The essays presented in this volume give special attention to
some of the more controversial issues of ecclesiology that have arisen
since Vatican II. In recent years, various schools of interpreting the
Council have arisen. Some emphasize the *discontinuity* of Vatican II
with prior tradition, and others stress the *continuity* of the Council
with traditional Catholic perspectives. The five-volume *History of Vatican II* (1995-2006), edited by G. Alberigo and J. Komonchak, in the
opinion of some, represents the *discontinuity* school, along with the
journal, *Concilium*. The international journal, *Communio*, founded by
Hans Urs von Balthasar, Henri de Lubac, S.J., and Joseph Ratzinger
is linked by many to the *continuity* school, as is the book by Bishop
Agostino Marchetto, *Il Concilio Ecumenico Vaticano II: Contrappunto
per la sua storia* (2005). If we were to use labels, the authors of this
present volume would probably represent the *continuity* school, but
it's unfair to generalize about the rich and nuanced perspectives of the
contributors. Certainly, the authors understand the teachings of Vatican II in continuity with the great Catholic tradition, but they are also
mindful of new insights and emphases brought by the Council to the
life of the Church.

Much has been said about the "spirit" of Vatican II. What
has often been neglected is the call to interior conversion that is at
the heart of the *aggiornamento* demanded by the Council. As *sancta
simul et semper purificanda* (LG, 8), the Church is called to an authentic
renewal in holiness and communion, grounded in fidelity and truth.
Only in this way can the light of Christ shine with greater splendor
before the nations of the earth.

CHAPTER 1

TRENDS IN ECCLESIOLOGY

Avery Cardinal Dulles, S.J.

CATHOLIC ECCLESIOLOGY in the past forty years has taken its main orientations from the Second Vatican Council. Much of the debate focuses on the Council itself. Did it demonstrate that doctrines deemed irreformable can in fact be reformed? If so, there would be no need to cling to the teachings of Vatican II itself. Just as Vatican II reformed the teaching of Trent and Vatican I, it is argued, theologians preparing for Vatican III are entitled to question the teachings of Vatican II, carrying on, no doubt, in the spirit of that Council but not binding themselves to the letter. If doctrines were continually subject to change, they would have no real binding force and consequently would be devoid of interest. Who would care what a nonbinding definition said?

Beginning with Paul VI, the Roman magisterium has called for faithful adherence to the actual teaching of Vatican II on points that it intended to settle. In order to correct widespread misinterpretations, Pope John Paul II convoked in 1985 an extraordinary session of the Synod of Bishops. In its very helpful Final Report this Synod advocates a hermeneutics of continuity, so that the Council documents may be read in conformity with earlier official teaching. Without ignoring the important developments of Vatican II, it cautions against depicting the Council as a doctrinal revolution. Focusing attention on the four great constitutions of Vatican II, the Report summarized the Council's teaching under four headings, of which the first and the third are of special interest for the purposes of the present volume, which is concerned with "the call to holiness and communion."

The first section, on the Mystery of the Church, elaborates on the teaching of *Lumen gentium* that the Church is a sacrament, that is to say, a sign and instrument of communion with God and of communion and reconciliation among human beings. In other words the Church is the sacrament of the communion of saints. Sacrament is, so to speak, the visible aspect of mystery of the triune God as he makes himself present in salvation history through the missions of the Word and the Holy Spirit. The concept of communion is further elaborated in the third section of the Report, which deals both with the full communion that exists among members of the Catholic Church and with the partial or imperfect communion that exists among all Christians.

The excellent principles set forth by the 1985 Synod have been generally neglected in recent theological literature. Some attention, however, has been given to its statement: "The ecclesiology of communion is a (or: the) central and fundamental idea in the documents of the council."[1] Some authors have said that the Church must be understood as a communion.[2] But it is important to bear in mind that Vatican II never calls the Church a communion.[3] Rather, it teaches that the Church is a sacrament that brings people together into communion with God and with one another. In other words, the Church is a sacrament of communion. Thus an ecclesiology of communion in conformity with Vatican II would hold that the Church as sacrament signifies and brings about spiritual communion among human beings and between them and God. This communion preeminently includes the members of the Church.

Postconciliar theology has been oscillating between two basic mentalities, which might be called the sacral and the secular. The difference between them may be symbolically expressed by contrasting

---

[1] *Final Report*, II C 1. Xavier Rynne, in his *John Paul's Extraordinary Synod* (Wilmington, Del.: Michael Glazier, 1986), uses the indefinite article "a" but the translation in *Origins* 15 (December 19, 1985): 444-50, at 448, reads: "the." In the original Latin, of course, no article is used.

[2] Dennis M. Doyle, *Communion Ecclesiology* (Maryknoll, N.Y.: Orbis, 2000). While insisting that the Church must be understood as a communion, Doyle recognizes many varieties of communion ecclesiology.

[3] In some English translations *Lumen gentium* 9 might seem to provide an exception. The Flannery translation reads: "Established by Christ as a communion of life, love, and truth, it is taken up by him also as the instrument for the salvation of all." But the original Latin *"in communionem vitae..."* means "for the sake of a communion of life..." Several sentences later LG 9 calls the Church "the visible sacrament of this saving unity."

two international reviews. *Concilium,* founded in 1964, has interpreted the Council in a very liberal sense, as favoring democratization in the Church and adaptation to the cultural trends of the day. *Communio,* founded in 1972, puts the accent on the stability and authority of Catholic tradition and on the opposition between the Church and the world. *Concilium* has been dominated by authors such as Edward Schillebeeckx and Hans Küng; *Communio* by its founders Henri de Lubac, Hans Urs von Balthasar, and Joseph Ratzinger. The two schools of interpretation give rise to accusations from each side that the other side is betraying the true intent of the Council.

As applied to the Church, the sacral mentality prefers a high ecclesiology, an ecclesiology from above, a descending ecclesiology, a vertical ecclesiology: one grounded on the Church as a revealed mystery or sacrament. The Church in this perspective appears as the visible sign and bearer of God's invisible grace. The authors speak of the *Ecclesia de Trinitate,* insofar as they see the Church in relation to the divine persons: the new People of God the Father, the body of Christ, and the Temple of the Holy Spirit. The focus is on the formal aspects of the Church, those given by divine institution.

The secularist mentality leans toward an ecclesiology from below, a low ecclesiology, an ascending ecclesiology: one that is horizontal. The focus is on the empirical aspect. The Church appears as an institution of human beings here on earth, always falling short of the divine ideal. This type of ecclesiology focuses on what may call the material rather than the formal elements of the Church--especially the members, all of whom exist in concrete sociocultural situations, and are subject to the limitations due to their respective personalities and the society in which they live.

Ecclesiology from below emphasizes the reformability of the Church and even the possibility of "remaking" the Church (to borrow the title of a book by Richard McBrien).[4] These authors make extensive use of social sciences, which, in their view, have a legitimate place in ecclesiology. Joseph Komonchak, for instance, calls for "a recognition that an ecclesiology remains merely formal and abstract as long as

---

[4]Richard McBrien, *The Remaking of the Church: An Agenda for Reform* (New York: Harper & Row, 1973).

it remains at the level of the merely theological and the universal, ignoring the human subjects and local communities in and out of which the Church exists and realizes itself in mission."[5]

Both mentalities can find support in the documents of Vatican II, which strike a careful balance between the two. The magisterium since the Council, reacting against unilateral versions of secular ecclesiology, has emphasized the divine and sacred aspects of the Church. In the light of this duality of approaches, I should like to take up ten problem areas that continue to be subjects of dispute among theologians.

1. The Church: Holy and Sinful.

Looked at from below, the Church appears to consist of imperfect members. Considered simply as a congregation or gathering of believers, the Church must be regarded as both holy and sinful. Küng puts the matter very crisply:

> Looking at the Church from above, so to speak, we see only the holiness of God and fail to take into account the men who compose it and who are constantly weak and tempted. ... In reality the Church is the battleground between God's Spirit and evil .... There are not two Churches.... There is only one Church, holy and sinful at the same time, *casta meretrix*, as it has often been called since patristic times, echoing Old Testament imagery.[6]

This would not be the place to review the whole controversy about the sinfulness in the Church, which has been explored with great erudition and subtlety by Hans Urs von Balthasar and Karl Rahner. It is noteworthy that official documents refrain from speaking of the Church herself as sinful. Vatican II declared: "The Church ... is held, as a matter of faith, to be unfailingly holy" (LG 39). Elsewhere it states: "The Church, however, clasping sinners to her bosom, at once holy and always in need of purification, follows constantly the path of penance and renewal" (LG 8). In other words, the Church herself is unfailingly holy, but because her members are sinful, the Church needs to be purified. The sins of the members, although they cannot be imputed to the Church herself, somehow defile her so that she needs to be purified.

[5]Joseph A. Komonchak, "Conceptions of Communion, Past and Present," *Cristianesimo nella storia* 16 (1995): 321-40, at 337-38.
[6]Hans Küng, *The Church* (New York: Sheed & Ward, 1968), 328.

John Paul II, while he strongly urges Catholics to repent for the past and present sins of Christians, has never apologized for the sins of the Church. Instead, he apologizes for the sins of the children of the Church. This distinction between holy Church and her sinful members may strike some critics as artificial, but it rests on a solid theological foundation. The Church is related in different ways to holiness and sinfulness. To be holy is to conform to the essential nature and mission of the Church, but to be sinful is to contradict the Church's nature and mission. She is indefectibly holy in her formal elements: her apostolic faith, sacraments, and ministry.[7] To the extent that her members sin, they distance themselves from her and are in need of reconciliation. Absolution from sins and censures overcomes the impairment of communion.

2. The Universal and the Particular Church.

Joseph Komonchak, in an article for *Concilium*, contrasted the two kinds of ecclesiology on this point. In an ecclesiology from above, he wrote, the universal Church is regarded as prior to its parts, but in the second, the "ascending" view, the whole is constituted by its components, which therefore precede it. The Church universal comes into being through the communion of the local churches.[8] The Church is seen as consisting of congregations, each of which is particular. The universal Church is regarded as an abstraction, formed by conceptually isolating what is common to each of the constituent congregations.

The priority of the local or particular church seems to be implied in the formula of J.-M. R. Tillard, who maintains that the universal Church is a "church of churches," a "communion of communions," that is to say, "a communion of local communities." His ecclesiology begins from below, with the particular eucharistic community, but he

---

[7]Cf. Pius XII, in his encyclical *Mystici corporis Christi,* states that the Church is spotless in her sacraments, in her sacred laws, in her evangelical counsels, and in the gifts and graces whereby she generates saints. "It cannot be laid to her charge if some members fall, weak or wounded"--cited from Claudia Carlen, ed., *The Papal Encyclicals 1939-1958* (Wilmington, N.C.: Consortium, 1981), no. 68, p. 50.

[8]Joseph A. Komonchak, "The Church Universal as the Communion of Local Churches," in G. Alberigo and G. Gutierrez, *Where Does the Church Stand? Concilium* 146 (New York: Seabury, 1981), 30-35.

recognizes that no such community may cut itself off from communion with all the others.[9]

The CDF produced a shock in some circles by its Declaration *Communionis notio* (1992), which asserts that the universal Church "is not the result of the communion of the churches, but in its essential mystery it is a reality ontologically and temporally prior to every individual particular church."[10]

About the year 2000 a well-publicized debate between Cardinal Walter Kasper and Cardinal Ratzinger occurred. Kasper asserted that the priorities between the universal and the particular church are mutual, inasmuch as they inhere in each other, but Ratzinger continued to defend the priority of the universal over the particular. His main contention was that the Church founded by Christ and animated by the Holy Spirit at Pentecost was universal, and that the sacraments impart communion with the universal Church. The essential effect of baptism, for example, is membership in the Church of Christ as a whole. The division into particular churches is secondary.

Ratzinger's position enjoys considerable support from Vatican II. According to LG 23 particular churches are "fashioned after the model of the universal Church." Once constituted, however, the particular churches offer the material, so to speak, from which the universal Church draws its membership. Thus the universal Church exists both in the particular churches and out of them. The Decree on the Bishops' Pastoral Office states that the "one holy catholic and apostolic Church of Christ is truly present and operative" in each particular church (CD 11). This, again, seems to indicate the priority of the universal Church.

3. Subsidiarity.

There has been a rather fierce debate over the past quarter of a century about the applicability of the principle of subsidiarity to the Church.[11] The problem stems from the encyclical *Quadragesimo*

---

[9]J.-M. R. Tillard, *Church of Churches: The Ecclesiology of Communion* (Collegeville, Minn.: Liturgical Press, 1992), 29-33.

[10]CDF, "Some Aspects of the Church Understood as Communion," 8-9; *Origins* 22 (June 25, 2992): 108-12, at 109.

[11]Jean Baptiste Beyer argues forcefully that while the principle of subsidiarity is valid for civil society, in which the structures of government rest upon the will of the governed, it does

anno, in which Pius XI declared that the principle of subsidiarity, or of "subsidiary function" (*"subsidiarii" officii principium,* DS 3738) required that the State should do only what it alone could do, leaving lower-level agencies free to accomplish what they could by their own powers. Pius XII said in 1946 that subsidiarity holds in the Church, without prejudice to her hierarchical structures. From reading his allocution I have the impression that he was talking about allowing free initiatives to arise within the Church without undue interference from the hierarchy. He was not talking about the distribution of power among different hierarchical agencies.

The Extraordinary Synod of 1985 recommended a study "of the question whether the principle of subsidiarity that has force in human society can be applied in the Church, and at what level and in what sense such application could or ought to take place."[12] Pope John Paul II encouraged discussion of the subject but did not commission an official study.

The question resurfaced at the Synod on Bishops, held in 2001. According to the recent apostolic exhortation *Pastores gregis,* "the Synod Fathers considered that, as far as the exercise of episcopal authority is concerned, the concept of subsidiarity has proved ambiguous, and they called for a deeper theological investigation of the nature of episcopal authority in the light of the concept of communion" (PG 56).

I personally believe that subsidiarity is not a felicitous way of describing the relations among hierarchical agencies in the Church. In English dictionaries the adjective "subsidiary" is defined as meaning "auxiliary," or "of secondary importance." If this is the intended meaning, the principle does not hold without modification for the Church, in which the universal authority was divinely instituted before there were any local or regional bodies. The apostolic college and the Pope should undoubtedly allow local agencies to do without interference what is best done on the local level, but the authority of the universal

---

not apply to the Church, which rests upon the self-impartation of the divine trinitarian life. He does, however, favor what he calls the "rightful autonomy of the local church." See his "Principe de subsidiarité ou `juste autonomie'," *Nouvelle Revue théologique* 108 (1986): 801-22. Joseph Komonchak, "Subsidiarity in the Church: The State of the Question," *The Jurist* 48 (1988): 298-349, is a full and balanced discussion. I have treated the question briefly in *The Reshaping of Catholicism* (San Francisco: Harper & Row, 1988), 201-5.

[12]Extraordinary Synod of 1985, Final Report, II C 8.

agencies is plenary and does not derive from the insufficiency of local agencies.

4. The Church: Hierarchical and Democratic.

In response to the Protestant Reformation the Catholic Church placed strong emphasis on her hierarchical structures, creating a certain risk that all initiative would be attributed to the clergy, lording it over a passive laity. Vatican II, building on the theological insights of Yves Congar and others, retrieved the concept of the royal priesthood of all the baptized, which had been nearly forgotten in post-Tridentine ecclesiology. The Constitution on the Church presents a general discussion of the Church as People of God before entering into the theme of its hierarchical structures.

In countries like the United States this shift of emphasis gave rise to the idea that the Council was in favor of Church government from below. Books began to appear with titles such as *Democratization of the Church*[13] and *A Democratic Catholic Church*.[14] These voices raised a serious question: Did Vatican II make a shift toward a democratic form of polity for the Church?

As I have said, Vatican II was anxious to clarify the active role of the laity in worship and in the apostolate. It particularly emphasized the vocation of laypersons to bring the leaven of the gospel into the family, the neighborhood, the market place, the public square, and the various professions. It strongly recommended that pastors draw on the talents of laypersons. At several points the Council urged pastors to consult with the laity and to listen to them when they speak on matters in which they enjoy competence (LG 37; GS 43, 62). But nowhere does the Council state that the laity have power in the governance of the Church. The episcopal order, with and under the Pope, is said to be "the subject of supreme and full power over the universal Church" (LG 22). Bishops "take on in an eminent and visible way Christ's own role as Teacher, Shepherd, and High Priest" (LG 21). The power that dioc-

---

[13] Alois Müller, ed., *Democratization of the Church*, Concilium 63 (New York: Herder and Herder, 1971).

[14] Eugene C. Bianchi and Rosemary Radford Ruether, ed., *A Democratic Catholic Church: The Reconstruction of Roman Catholicism* (New York: Crossroad, 1993).

esan bishops exercise in Christ's name cannot be circumscribed except by the supreme authority in the Church (LG 27).

It may still be asked whether the Council should have given governmental, liturgical, or magisterial authority to the laity. This question is a subject of lively debate in the United States and elsewhere today, as witnessed by Paul Lakeland's recent book, *The Liberation of the Laity*.[15]

To judge from Vatican I and Vatican II, Christ himself established the Church as a hierarchical society and intended the apostolic succession to continue in the episcopate until the end of time. We can only speculate on the reasons why God made the hierarchical form of government as a matter of divine law. For a secular society, which does not depend upon the preservation of any divine deposit, a democratic form of government may well be desirable. But the hierarchical form of polity, I would think, is better suited for the preservation of a revealed deposit, especially when the secular culture is predominantly hostile, as is the case in the United States today. The bishops, thoroughly schooled in the tradition and socialized in the community of faith, receive special graces to carry out their mission. Jesus promised to be with the apostolic leaders to the end of the age (Mt 28:20). Bishops alone are qualified to co-opt others into the episcopal order.

Hierarchical power is difficult to defend in our time, when the term "hierarchical" is generally used in a pejorative sense, even grotesquely caricatured. Bishops are suspected of promoting an ideology in order to defend their privileged status as a ruling class. To counter this charge some theologians are trying to redefine hierarchy in participatory terms that would involve a sharing of power with the laity.[16] These efforts may be praised provided that they do not infringe on the powers given by the Lord exclusively to the Pope and the bishops. The times surely call for efforts to build collaborative relationships in which talents of laypersons are fully utilized.

---

[15]Paul Lakeland, *The Liberation of the Laity: In Search of an Accountable Church* (New York: Continuum, 2003).

[16]Terence L. Nichols, *That All May Be One: Hierarchy and Participation in the Church* (Collegeville: Liturgical Press, 1997). See also Richard Gaillardetz, "Vatican II's Liturgy Constitution: The Beginnings of a Liturgical Ecclesiology," *Origins* 33 (October 30, 2003): 347-52, esp. 347-48.

5. Primacy and Collegiality.

In the political climate of the Western world, it was almost inevitable, I suppose, that the doctrine of collegiality should be misunderstood. Many partisans of democracy, looking on the Church in political terms, imagined that Vatican II was making a shift from a strictly monarchical to something like a parliamentary system of government. This move, while falling short of government from below, would at least raise the bishops from a position of subordination to one of virtual equality with the first bishop, the bishop of Rome.

The official teaching on collegiality is most compactly set forth in the Prefatory Note of Explanation that was distributed to the Council Fathers as the official interpretation of the text of *Lumen gentium*, chapter 3, before they took their final vote. By order of Paul VI, the Note was appended to the Council documents as an authentic norm of interpretation. This Note, together with the relevant passages in *Lumen gentium* itself, makes it clear that the principle of collegiality does not in any way reduce the powers of the Pope as defined by Vatican I. He retains full authority in and over the college. Only he can call the other members to collegiate action, and any action that they might take without his approval would be null and void. When the college acts, it includes the Pope not simply as a member but as its responsible head. His position is analogous to that of Peter, who spoke for the apostles in his confession of faith at Caesarea Philippi and in his sermon on Pentecost. It would seem to follow that when the Pope discerns a sufficient consensus, he can speak for the whole body of bishops without summoning a council or conducting a head count.

Joseph Ratzinger makes the point that community leadership cannot be in the first instance collegial. It is inseparable from personal responsibility. The principle of "one responsible person," he writes, is "anchored fast in the trinitarian belief in God himself, since the trinity becomes meaningful and in fact recognizable for us through the fact that in his Son as man God himself has become witness to himself."[17] Early Church Fathers, such as Ignatius of Antioch, taught that the bishop holds the place of God and that the presbyters stand in place of the apostolic college.[18] So likewise in the universal Church, it would

---

[17]Cardinal Joseph Ratzinger, *Church, Ecumenism and Politics* (New York: Crossroad, 1988), 34.
[18]Ignatius of Antioch, *Magn.* 6:1; ANF 1:61.

seem, the Pope holds a monarchical position. In the words of Ratz-inger, the Petrine ministry "can only exist as a person and in personal responsibility tied to a particular man."[19]

The monarchical principle is not easy to defend in an age of democracy. But there are practical as well as dogmatic arguments for it. Cardinal Ratzinger points out that when bishops issue collective statements they usually fail to be bold and assertive. In Nazi Germany, he recalls, the conference of bishops failed to stand up against evil, whereas some individual bishops did so.[20]

6. Identity of the Bishop.

It is often imagined that the bishop is first of all the head of a particular church and only secondarily a member of the universal college. But Vatican II, as I read it, taught otherwise. It declared that episcopal ordination makes one a member of the order of bishops and thus a successor of the apostles. Ordination itself confers the of-fices (*munera*) of sanctifying, teaching, and governing. Unless there be some obstacle, every bishop becomes a member of the episcopal col-lege (LG 21). Only some bishops receive pastoral charge of a particular diocese, and this they do not simply by reason of being bishops but rather through canonical mission (LG 24). Bishops who are not pas-tors of particular dioceses are bishops in the full sense of the term and can exercise their threefold *munus* as members of the college. Thus the episcopal office is most fundamentally a relationship to the universal, not the particular, Church.

Pope John Paul II in the motu proprio *Apostolos suos* of 1998 taught that "the College of Bishops is not to be understood as the ag-gregate of the Bishops who govern the particular Churches, nor as the result of their communion; rather, as an essential element of the uni-versal Church, it is a reality which precedes the office of being the head of a particular Church."[21] The recent Apostolic Exhortation *Pastores gregis* draws the conclusion: "Precisely because the College of Bishops

---

[19]Ratzinger, *Church, Ecumenism and Politics*, 36
[20]Joseph Cardinal Ratzinger and Vittorio Messori, *The Ratzinger Report* (San Francisco: Ignatius, 1985), 61.
[21]John Paul II, Apostolic Letter *Apostolos suos* on the Theological and Juridical Nature of Episcopal Conferences, 12 (Vatican City: Libreria Editrice Vaticana, 1998), 20.

is a reality prior to the office of heading a particular Church, there are many bishops who, while carrying out tasks that are properly episcopal, are not heads of particular Churches."[22]

It would be possible at this point to include some discussion of the identity of the priest (presbyter), which has likewise been a subject of dispute. Some see the priest as simply the representative of the local community chosen to preside at certain functions, but Catholic doctrine makes it clear that priesthood is conferred by the sacrament of ordination, administered by the bishop. There can be no priesthood except from above. Those who neglect the sacral dimension of the priesthood frequently have difficulty in seeing the rationale for its reservation to men and for the rule of celibacy. In a democratic society that has a merely functional concept of priesthood these restrictions can easily be portrayed as offensive.

7. The Church and Salvation.

Seen from below, the Church appears as a congregation of believers who turn to Jesus Christ as Savior. In this view, Christ the Lord can act through the Church and its sacraments, but he is not bound to do so.[23] Yves Congar maintained that all grace orients people toward the Church as "final cause," but grace does not necessarily come through the Church as its efficient or instrumental cause.[24] Taking the argument a step further, Hans Küng holds that all salvation comes through Christ, but not necessarily through the Church.[25] Jacques Dupuis, in his *Toward a Christian Theology of Religious Pluralism*, wrote: "Divine grace is operative where the Church is not present, but the Church is the sacramental sign of the presence of divine grace in the world."[26]

---

[22]John Paul II, *Pastores gregis* 8, p. 24.

[23]The mediaeval maxim that "God is not bound by the sacraments" (*Deus non alligatur sacramentis*) is invoked as proof.

[24]Yves Congar, Sainte Église: *Études et approches ecclésiologiques* (Paris: Cerf, 1932), 431-32.

[25]Hans Küng, *The Church* (New York: Sheed & Ward, 1968), 313-19.

[26]Jacques Dupuis, *Toward a Christian Theology of Religious Pluralism* (Maryknoll, N.Y.: Orbis, 1998), 352. See also his *Christianity and the Religions* (Maryknoll, N.Y.: Orbis, 2002), 210. For an interesting discussion of the question whether the Church is merely a sign or also a mediator of saving grace see J. Peter Schineller, "Christ and Church: A Spectrum of Views," *Theological Studies* 37 (1976): 545-66.

These views, however, are contested by ecclesiologies from above, which begin with the idea of the Church as body and spouse of Christ, taken up by him into the economy of salvation history. Vatican II speaks of the Church not only as sign but as the "universal sacrament of salvation" (LG 48), which I take to mean both sign and instrument of all saving grace. Again in LG 9, the Council affirms that Christ uses the Church as his "instrument for the redemption of all" (LG 9). The Church does not reach everyone through her preaching and sacraments, but her prayers and intercession, especially in the sacrifice of the Mass, are taken up in union with the mediation of Christ to avail for the salvation of those who, through no fault of their own, are ignorant of the gospel.

This high ecclesiology is taken up by Pope John Paul II in *Redemptoris missio* (esp. §9) and by the CDF in *Dominus Iesus*. In a notification on the work of Dupuis cited above, the CDF stated: "It must be firmly believed that the Church is sign and instrument of salvation for all people. It is contrary to Catholic faith to consider the different religions of the world as ways of salvation complementary to the Church."[27]

8. The Church and the Churches.

From an empirical or sociological point of view, which is that of theology from below, Christianity appears as a collection of churches, no one of which enjoys a unique status. But many Catholic and Orthodox theologians, adhering to an ecclesiology from above, have regarded their own communion as coterminous with the one Church of Christ, the Mystical Body, the *una sancta*. Vatican II took a nuanced position based on a theology of communion. The fullness of communion, it taught, exists only within the Catholic Church, but other Christian communities have limited or imperfect communion. The Orthodox churches have sufficient ecclesial substance to be properly called "churches."

The Catholic Church alone, says the Council, is the "all-embracing means of salvation." The elements of grace in other churches

---

[27]CDF, "Notification on Jacques Dupuis, *Toward a Christian Theology of Religious Pluralism*," II,6; *Origins* 30 (March 8, 2001): 605-8, at 608.

and ecclesial communities belong by right to the Catholic Church and are in a certain sense derived from her (UR 3). According to *Lumen gentium* the Church of Christ "subsists" in the Roman Catholic Church. The implication is that because other churches are institutionally deficient, the Church of Christ does not subsist in them. The teaching of Vatican II has been misunderstood or misrepresented in some of the ecumenical literature. Various theologians have taught that the Church of Christ is in fragments, which together make up the one Church. Some contend that the Church today exists only partically in Roman Catholicism.[28] *Dominus Iesus* issued a corrective on this point, recalling the teaching of Vatican II and John Paul II, which I have summarized.[29]

9. Evangelization and Inculturation.

Although the term "evangelization" appears here and there in the documents of Vatican II, "inculturation" does not. The idea could however be said to be present in GS 44, which states: "The accommodated preaching of the revealed word ought to remain the law of all evangelization" with the result that "each nation develops the ability to express Christ's message in its own way." After Vatican II the term "inculturation" became a kind of slogan, especially among those who practiced an ecclesiology from below. Missionaries, afraid of imposing their own culture, encouraged the new Christians find their own ways of speaking about Christ and organizing their worship. In some cases they allowed the sacred literature of other religions to be substituted for liturgical readings from the Old Testament as their own kind of preparation for the gospel. This and similar experiments created the risk of syncretism. The regional churches might become so deeply immersed in the cultures that the one faith would no longer be recognized and experienced in them.

Taking note of this deviation, Paul VI in *Evangelii nuntiandi* called for an evangelization of cultures. Since every culture carries with

---

[28]Leonardo Boff, *Church: Charism and Power* (New York: Crossroad, 1985), 75, and the interpretation given to this text by the CDF in its "Notification" on this book, *Origins* 14 (April 4, 1985)" 683-87, at 685.
[29]See Congregation for the Doctrine of the Faith, Declaration *Dominus Iesus* (August 6, 2000), 16-17.

it a set of meanings, attitudes, and behavioral patterns, the Church cannot simply accept the cultures of native populations as they stand. Each culture, said Paul VI, has to be "regenerated by an encounter with the gospel" (EN 20).

John Paul II adopts a similar program. He calls for an "apostolic dialogue" between faith and cultures. Inculturation, he says, must be pursued with caution, guided by two principles: compatibility with the gospel and communion with the universal Church." Here, as in other areas, the magisterium uses a universalist ecclesiology from above as a corrective for the excesses of particularist ecclesiologies from below.

10. Church and Kingdom of God.

A final problem extensively discussed in the literature of the past forty years has to do with the relationship between the Church and the Kingdom of God. Those who espouse a high ecclesiology, constructed from above, tend to see Church and Kingdom as closely connected, even identical. For them, the realization of the Kingdom would mean, in the words of LG 17, that the entire world would "become the People of God, the Body of the Lord, and the Temple of the Holy Spirit."

In an ecclesiology from below, the Church is portrayed more modestly as an instrument for bringing about the Kingdom. Richard McBrien, some years back, declared that the Church must get out of the salvation business and "must offer itself as one of the principal agents whereby the human community is made to stand under the enduring values of the Gospel of Jesus Christ: freedom, justice, peace, charity, compassion, reconciliation."[30]

This merely instrumental view of the Church does not cohere with Vatican II or sound ecclesiology. The Church is, after all, the beloved Bride for whom Christ sacrificed himself (Eph 5:23-27). According to *Lumen gentium* the Church on earth is the "initial budding forth" of the Kingdom (LG 5), the place where "the Kingdom of God, now present in mystery, grows visibly in the world through the power of God" (LG 3)

---

[30]Richard P. McBrien, *Do We Need the Church?* (New York: Harper & Row, 1969), 229.

John Paul II, in *Redemptoris missio,* devoted a whole chapter (no. 2) to the theme of the Kingdom. He rejected views that translate into purely earthly understandings of the Kingdom, in terms of values such as peace, justice, freedom, and brotherhood. The Kingdom, he insisted, cannot be separated either from Christ or from the Church, even though "the inchoate reality of the kingdom can also be found beyond the confines of the Church among peoples everywhere" (RMis 20). The inchoate realizations of the Kingdom outside the visible boundaries of the Church are in some respects ecclesial, since all grace, as we have seen, is related to the Church of Christ. The Kingdom, to be sure, does not exist completely in the Church on earth, but the full realization of the Kingdom at the end of time will involve the glorious consummation of the Church herself.[31]

Conclusion

It would be gratifying to be able to report that the theology of the Church has been developing in healthy ways. But I do not find much progress in the past forty years. The renaissance that should have followed Vatican II has not yet occurred except here and there in isolated cases. Whatever development has occurred may be found most clearly in official teaching. The Roman magisterium and the Synod of Bishops have responsibly interpreted and in some ways advanced the teaching of Vatican II on the various questions treated in this survey.

I am aware that I have hardly scratched the surface in dealing with the ten areas of controversy, some of which are treated with greater depth in other essays in this volume. My intent has been not to solve individual disputes but to show that the issues are interconnected. Underlying them all is a difference of mentality. Those pursuing a theology of above must make sure that they do not remain hovering on high but that they reach the depth and breadth of humanity which God embraced in his incarnate life. Those practicing an ecclesiology from below must make sure that they are open not only to the human situation but to the action of God, which in the nature of the case is always from above.

---

[31]For a careful discussion see John Fuellenbach, *Church: Community for the Kingdom* (Maryknoll, N.Y.: Orbis, 2002).

CHAPTER 2

CHRIST,
THE LIGHT OF THE NATIONS;
THE CHURCH,
HIS SPOUSE AND HELPMATE

+Angelo Card. Scola, Patriarch of Venice
(Translated by Cyprian Blamires)

"Man goes infinitely beyond man."[32] Does the dynamic anthropological vision championed by Pascal really correspond to the outlook of individuals and the community as addressed by ecclesial reality today? Or has that vision in fact been supplanted by Nietzsche's violent assertion that *man is something that* must *be "overcome"* (or surpassed, we could say) — since, like '*the ape for human beings*', he is only '*a laughing stock*' or something that at most inspires '*a painful sense of shame*'?[33] If this conviction of 'the tragic prophet of our time', which culminates in talk of the 'death of the subject', were true, then strictly speaking the Church would no longer have an interlocutor, and her mission would consequently be meaningless. In the United States as elsewhere, many cultured elites are perhaps caught on the horns of this painful dilemma: Pascal or Nietzsche? And it would be difficult to resolve it by simply analysing the historical and cultural processes that have come to characterise the constitutive *mind* of western civilisation

---

[32] B. Pascal, *Pensées*, 131 (ed.) Brunschvicg, 434.
[33] F. Nietzsche, *Thus Spoke Zarathustra,* in *The Portable Nietzsche,* tr. Walter Kaufmann (New York: The Viking Press, 1968), 124-125. "When Zarathustra arrived at the nearest of the towns lying against the forest, he found in that very place many people assembled in the market square: for it had been announced that a tight-rope walker would be appearing. And Zarathustra spoke thus to the people: "I teach you the Superman. Man is something that should be overcome. What have you done to overcome him? All creatures hitherto have created something beyond themselves: and do you want to be the ebb of this great tide, and return to the animals rather than overcome man? What is the ape to men? A laughing-stock or a painful embarrassment. And just so shall man be to the Superman: a laughing-stock or a painful embarrassment."

in modern times. All the more so in that the societies which express it are convinced that we now have to replace the classic vision of the human person understood as a subject of rights and duties, a vision current throughout the modern era, with the relentlessly developing conviction that man is only *'his own experiment'*.[34]

Not wishing to resign ourselves to chasing down *dead ends*, and refusing *a priori* (since we are as Christians inspired by the sure and certain hope of the resurrection of the flesh) to abandon ourselves to maudlin lamentations about the danger of the abolition of the *humanum*,[35] we need to find a solid foundation that will enable us to show that Pascal's famous assertion has not lost its relevance and its force. Powerful expression has been given to this by Karol Wojtyla in an important passage in *The Acting Person*, a passage which the author deliberately begins with an adversative adverb: *"Even so there is something that [...] can be called the experience of man"*.[36] This brilliant book by the Cracow Cardinal turns around a fixed point: the elementary experience of the person, in *"its intrinsic simplicity,"* overcomes every kind of *"irreducibility"* and *"complexity."*[37] If the Church is to allow Jesus Christ, *Lumen gentium*, to shine out, she must tap into the experience common to all people of all times and places, rooted as they always are in community.[38] Now the Second Vatican Council (whose four Constitutions have to be read as a unit following the rules of all good conciliar hermeneutics)[39] undoubtedly opened the way for Christians to rediscover this elementary experience of the person, in the witness of following Jesus.

The Churches on all continents are now embarked on this road, in accordance with the criterion of pluriformity in unity[40]; this

---

[34]Cf. M. Jongen, *Der Mensch ist sein eigenes Experiment,* in 'Feuilleton. Die Zeit' 9 August 2001.

[35]Cf. C. S. Lewis, *The Abolition of Man* (London: Oxford University Press. 1943).

[36]K. Wojtyla, *The Acting Person*, tr. Andrzej Potocki, Dordrecht; Boston: D. Reidel Pub. Co. 1979. Here, Introduction, section 1, paragraph 5. [The complete text can be found on the internet, see http://personalism.net/jp2.]

[37]Ibid.

[38]John Paul II has reminded the Church of this requirement since the very beginning of his pontificate: "We are not dealing with the 'abstract' man, but the real, 'concrete', 'historical' man. We are dealing with 'each' man, for each one is included in the mystery of the Redemption and with each one Christ has united himself for ever through this mystery" *Redemptor Hominis* 13.

[39]Cf. SYNODUS EPISCOPORUM, *Relatio finalis Ecclesia sub verbo Dei mysteria Christi celebrans pro saluti mundi, in Enchiridion Vaticanum* 9, 1779-1818, here 1785.

[40]Cf. ibid. 1801.

is a reality that cannot be denied, notwithstanding the conflicts of opinion that still shake the ecclesial body, dividing the followers of Christ in so many ways.

As Pascal's dictum clearly indicates, if "man goes *infinitely* beyond man," elementary experience is dramatic, and the gift of faith (constantly on offer but never imposed on the liberty of the individual) heightens the drama of it. In fact, freedom of itself, in each of its acts, is always historically determined, and therefore cannot ultimately be grasped. And the Christian event, an unequalled interweaving of grace with freedom, is the surprising and always unforeseen encounter between Jesus Christ and the individual. The ecclesial community can mediate it, but not reduce it to the level of "something" that she possesses once and for all by treating it as an "object" to be granted to the individual once and for all. The believer is required not only to take the risk inherent in every act of freedom, but also the ultimately dramatic risk involved in the ratification of such acts by faith in Jesus Christ.

These introductory observations are perhaps sufficient to enable us to wake up to the fact that ecclesiological reflection and, before that, ecclesial life are headed down a *cul de sac* in our times. Among other things, they show how the work of the *reception* of Vatican II remains to a great extent a task as yet unfulfilled, even after the invitation issued by the Extraordinary Assembly of the Episcopal Synod of 1985.[41]

2. Con-centrating Ecclesiology

To make it easier to follow, I am putting forward the thesis I propose right at the start. Today, an adequate Ecclesiology calls more than ever for a dual con-*centration* on the *anthropological* and on the *sacramental*. Without these two *foci*, even the rediscovery of the *Ecclesia de Trinitate* through *Lumen gentium*[42] and the decisive opening of Ecclesiology to Christocentrism as desired by the Conciliar

---

[41]Cf. R. FISICHELLA (a cura di), *Il Concilio Vaticano II. Recezione e attualità alla luce del Giubileo.* Cinisello Balsamo: San Paolo, 2000.

[42]Cf. *Lumen gentium* 3-5. In this connection see: G. Philips, *L'Église Et Son Mystère Au IIe Concile Du Vatican: Histoire, Texte Et Commentaire De La Constitution Lumen Gentium.* Paris: Desclée, 1967, pp. 79-93; M. KEHL, *Die Kirche:eine katholische Ekklesiologie*, Würzburg: Echter, 1994, pp. 67-103.

Fathers[43] (and vigorously reproposed by the Extraordinary Assembly of the Episcopal Synod[44]) would remain ineffective. To avoid any possible misunderstanding, we also need to state immediately that the *Ecclesiology of communion* (an expression employed by many as a *reductio ad unum* of conciliar Ecclesiology[45]) would run into insuperable *aporias*[46] if it were not based on a dramatic anthropology, and on the *ratio sacramentalis* of the Christian revelation.[47]

As I have said, despite the fact that it was put forward by the Council,[48] this task remains for the most part still to be tackled forty years on from the promulgation of *Lumen gentium*. Even if the dominant mentality had opted for Nietzsche rather than Pascal, solid reasons based on Christian hope would continue to inspire a summons to the fulfilment of the task. The summons would be all the more vigorous in that it is only when she rediscovers her *pastoral* role[49] — which John XXIII had wanted to impress on the whole conciliar assembly through *Gaudet Mater Ecclesia*[50] — that the Church rediscovers her authentic care for the individual with his or her constitutive relationships and

---

[43]Cf. A. SCOLA, "Gaudium et spes: dialogo e discernimento nella testimonianza della verità," in R. FISICHELLA (a cura di), *Il Concilio Vaticano II...* pp. 82-114, where there is relevant bibliographical material.

[44]Cf. SYNODUS EPISCOPORUM, *Relatio..*, 1789.

[45]Cf. Ibid., 1800. We should also bear in mind the important clarifications provided by the Congregation for the Doctrine of the Faith, *'Letter to the Bishops of the Catholic Church on Some Aspects of the Church Understood as Communion'*, 28 May 1992.

[46]Some difficulties inherent in the employment of the notion of communio are noted in: L. SCHEFFCZYK, *Aspekte der Kirche in der Krise. Um die Entscheidung für das authentische Konzil*, Siegburg: Verlag Franz Schmitt, 1993, pp. 69-83; J. RATZINGER, *L'ecclesiologia della Costituzione "Lumen gentium"*, in R. FISICHELLA (a cura di), Il Concilio..., pp. 66-81, particularly 69-77.

[47]Cf. *Fides et ratio* 13.

[48]The validation of the concept of truth through the Constitution *Dei verbum* on the one hand (cf. H. DE LUBAC, *La Révélation Divine*, 3e éd. Revue et augmentée, Paris: Cerf, 1983, pp.58-9) and the affirmation of a Christocentric anthropology in the Constitution *Gaudium et spes* on the other (cf. A. SCOLA, *'Gaudium et spes'*, 92-102), might have led to the called-for deepening of Ecclesiology.

[49]The pastoral role of the Church was particularly emphasized in the Pastoral Constitution *Gaudium et spes*, and especially by the contents of the second part which are of their nature subject to evolution: "Undeniably this conciliar program is but a general one in several of its parts; and deliberately so, given the immense variety of situations and forms of human culture in the world. Indeed while it presents teaching already accepted in the Church, the program will have to be followed up and amplified since it sometimes deals with matters in a constant state of development. Still, we have relied on the word of God and the spirit of the Gospel. Hence we entertain the hope that many of our proposals will prove to be of substantial benefit to everyone, especially after they have been adapted to individual nations and mentalities by the faithful, under the guidance of their pastors." *Gaudium et spes* 91.

[50]Cf. G. RUGGIERI, *La lotta per la pastoralità della dottrina: la recezione della "Gaudet Mater Ecclesia" nel primo periodo del Concilio Vaticano II*, in W. WEIß (ed.), *Zeugnis und Dialog*. Würzburg: Echter, 1996, pp. 118-137, particularly 122-123.

interactions with the cosmos. It is only then that she becomes capable of facing such burning issues as participation, representation, and the nature of, and conditions for the exercise of the ordained ministry. An ecclesiology renewed in this way will also allow for full commitment to the urgent ecumenical task and to interreligious dialogue as *essential dimensions* and not merely contingent aspects of the act of faith.[51]

Thus, inviting theologians and their schools to tackle the task we have set out, on this occasion we can just put forward some inevitably brief and fragmentary hypotheses for reflection. For ease of understanding I will group them under the two headings I have already mentioned. In the first section, I will try to say what is involved in the anthropological con-*centration* of ecclesiology, and I will deal with the sacramental con-*centration* in the second.

PART ONE
THE ANTHROPOLOGICAL CON-CENTRATION OF THE CHURCH

1. The two foci of the ellipse

With his celebrated statement that the Church must *"be reborn from souls,"*[52] Romano Guardini had already intuited the pressing need to rethink ecclesiology in terms of anthropology. Profiting from the renewal inspired by the Roman school of Schrader and Passaglia[53] and independently deepened by the Tübingen School[54] (not only by the authoritative figure of Mohler) — while clearly present also in Newman and the Oxford Movement,[55] Guardini had understood that in her *actuational dynamism* the Church can never go beyond the freedom of

---

[51]Cf. A. SCOLA, 'Ecclesiologia in prospettiva ecumenica: qualche linea di metodo', in *Studi Ecumenici* 20 (2002) pp. 377-402

[52]R. GUARDINI, *The Church and the Catholic and the Spirit of the Liturgy*, tr. Ada Lane, New York: Sheed and Ward, 1953, p. 111.

[53]Cf A. ANTÓN, *El misterio de la Iglesia* 2, Madrid: BAC, 1987, pp. 428-447; W. KASPER, *Die Lehre von der Tradition in der römischen Schule*, Freiburg: Herder, 1962; H. SCHAUF, *Carl Passaglia und Clemens Schrader. Beitrag zur Theologiegeschichte des 19. Jahrhunderts*, Rome: PUG, 1938.

[54]Cfr. R. M. SCHMITZ, *Aufbruch zum Geheimnis der Kirche Jesu Christi*, St. Ottilien: Eos Verlag, 1991, pp. 140-152; J.R. GEISELMANN, *Die katholische Tübinger Schule. Ihre theologische Eigenart*, Freiburg: Herder, 1964; A. ANTÓN, *El misterio ...* pp. 218-257.

[55]L. BOUYER, *The Church of God, Body of Christ and Temple of the Spirit*, tr. Charles Underhill Quinn. Chicago, Ill.: Franciscan Herald Press, c1982, pp. 107-21.

the individual. By virtue of grace, the Church does indeed possess an autonomous nature, which exists prior to that of the baptised person, but ultimately she exists always and only in individual subjects, and she communicates her salvific power through their testimony.

Expounding this viewpoint, Hans Urs von Balthasar affirms that the appropriate ecclesiological question does not find expression in the formula, "*What* is the Church?," but in the anthropologically important inquiry "*Who* is the Church?."[56] Obviously this statement in no way means that the Church can "be produced" by human liberty. If this were the case, she would lose her innate character as *intrinsic salvific mediation* of the Trinitarian revelation operative in Jesus Christ.[57] It must be acknowledged that the Church lives by these two inseparable factors, and this is equivalent to affirming the insuperably polar character of ecclesiology. It always involves a beneficent tension between the divine pole of salvific representation and the pole of human testimonial freedom, which is called to ratify it.

This conclusion involves a methodological consequence of capital importance for ecclesiology: namely, that ecclesiology has the nature of an *ellipse* rather than that of a *circle*. The consequence of this is to exclude any possibility of finding a *center understood as a unique formal principle* for the development of ecclesiology — a mirage that has fascinated many a scholar since Vatican II. Neither the category of *mystery*, nor that of *sacrament*, nor the Scriptural themes of *the Body of Christ* and *the People of God* and not even the category of *communion* (just to limit ourselves to the chief elements of *Lumen gentium)* taken on their own are enough to define the essence of the Church fully. In this sense, the conciliar fathers were farsighted when, in composing the Dogmatic Constitution on the Church, they adopted all these categories, and did not make any one of them a formal unitary principle that could serve as the sole basis of ecclesiology.[58]

---

[56]Cf. H.U. VON BALTHASAR, *Explorations in Theology*. Vol. 2: Spouse of the Word. San Francisco: Ignatius Press, 1991, pp. 143-91.

[57]ID., "We will discuss the Church only in so far as she can be and intends to be a medium of God's form of the Revelation of God in Christ. This is probably to pose the decisive question beyond which there is theologically speaking probably nothing more that can be asked of the Church. [...] This is not necessarily immediately obvious..." *The Glory of the Lord. A Theological Aesthetics. Vol. 1*, tr. Erasmo Leiva-Merikakis, ed. Joseph Fessio S.J. and John Riches. San Francisco: Ignatius Press, 1982, p. 556.

[58]Cf. SYNODUS EPISCOPORUM, *Relatio...*, 1790; J. RATZINGER, *L'ecclesiologia della Costituzione "Lumen gentium"*, 66-81.

However, once we have adequately posed the ecclesiological question, *Who is the Church?*, we face the onerous task of clarifying it. Having affirmed the necessity for an anthropological con-*centration*, we need to identify the essential articulations of the *who* without its unity being lost. The result will be an ecclesiology that is dramatic in its genesis and in its nature. Nor must we forget that the *who*, bringing the question of the subject immediately to the fore, allows for a more attentive dialogue with the dominant culture, which, as we hinted at the start, has been turning on this same axis right from the start of the modern era.

To analyse this *who* we cannot but start from the mediational character that is constitutive of the Church, given that her *raison d'être* resides wholly in letting Christ, the Light of the nations, shine out.[59] She therefore has a nature that is essentially relative to Jesus Christ, the self-revelation of the *Deus Trinitas*. And yet, in her secondariness, the Church is the subject-means pre-established by the Trinity and ultimately willed by Jesus Christ himself to the end that salvation should be contemporaneous with the individual in every time and in every place. This condition is absolutely crucial, and is a real *articulus stantis vel cadentis* not only of ecclesiology, but of the very credibility of the entire Christian fact.[60] Indeed, as Kierkegaard put it so ingeniously, salvation can come only from someone who makes himself present to me here and now.[61] Either Christ lives today in his Church or He himself and His followers become completely irrelevant and superfluous.

---

[59] Cf. *Lumen gentium* 1; SYNODUS EPISCOPORUM, *Relatio*... 1790.

[60] This is the problem at the root of the question of the foundation of the Church in Jesus Christ. We can agree with Kehl: "There is an assumption prevalent in the thinking of the Church today — and it has in fact held almost exclusive sway since the Counter-Reformation — that Jesus 'founded' the (Catholic) Church. The Second Vatican Council took up and confirmed this theory in the third chapter of the Constitution on the Church ('The hierarchical structure of the Church, with special reference to the episcopate', see *Lumen gentium* III esp. sections 18-20); at the same time, however, the Council clearly relativised it, given that in the first chapter it places the theological origin of the Church in the Trinitarian self-lowering of God (*LG* I, 2-4) and her historical foundation in the proclamation of the Kingdom of God by Jesus (*LG* I, 5); there is no recourse here to the 'classic' proofs on the theory of the institution." M. KEHL, *Die Kirche*... pp. 267-319, here 269; L. BOUYER, *The Church of God*..., p. 551.

[61] "The only ethical relationship one can have with greatness (and in the same way also with Christ) is contemporaneity. To relate to a deceased person is an aesthetic relationship: the life of the deceased has lost its sting, it does not judge my life, it allows me to admire him... and it lets me live according to completely different categories of thought: it does not oblige me to judge in any crucial way." S. KIERKEGAARD, *Diario*, Milan: BUR, 1988, p. 348. [The selections from Kierkegaard's *Diary* as published in English (New York: Philosophical Library, 1960) do

2. Mary — the woman and the Church

A careful look at the *universale concretum* that is Jesus Christ brings an important anthropological insight to the Church as subject.[62] For our salvation — the *raison d'être* of the Church — the Word was made flesh, and in His *kenosis,* as a real man, He came to take on the nature of a man of the male sex. Therefore the datum of the incarnation immediately brings into play a crucial anthropological factor: the man-woman polarity. The man-woman polarity along with the body-soul and individual-community polarities is constitutive of elementary human experience, whose rediscovery is absolutely essential for us today, as we stated at the outset.[63]

Incidentally, it should be noted that through these constitutive polarities anthropology proves to be dramatic. This validates the classic anthropology of the concrete whole (*synolos*) by making explicit the fact that humans can reflect on their essence only from within their own existence.[64] They are placed on the stage of "the great theatre of the world" and have absolutely no say in which "part" or "role" they are to play before acting it out. Now the man-woman polarity, when fully investigated, reveals two significant elements. The woman, endowed with free and independent personal dignity, is simultaneously the answer to the question that is man (*Wort-Ant-Wort*), or the face that answers his look (*Litz-Ant-Litz*), and the principle that saves his fruitfulness from being wasted. In the first sense the woman is "relative" to the man, while in the second she is 'foundation' with respect to him with

not include this passage, which has been translated direct from the Italian version for purposes of this essay.] And similarly Kafka, when he writes: "… she … all the time experiences in her own person that one can save the other only by one's existence and by nothing else. And she has already saved me with her existence and now in addition she tries to do the same with other infinitely smaller remedies. If one person rescues another from drowning it is of course a very great deed, but if he afterwards gives the rescued a subscription for swimming lessons, what good will that do? Why does the Saviour want to make it so easy for himself? Why does he not want to continue forever to save the other by his existence, by his ever-ready existence? Why does he try to transfer the task to the swimming-teacher … ? " (Prague, 31st July, 1920) F. KAFKA, *Letters to Milena,* ed. Willi Haas, tr. T & J Stern, London: Secker & Warburg, 1953, p.126.
[62]On the light that Christology sheds on the human person as *imago Dei* cfr. D. SCHINDLER, 'Christology and the *Imago Dei*: interpreting *Gaudium et spes*' in *Communio* 23, n. 1 (1996) pp. 156-184.
[63]H.U. VON BALTHASAR, *Theo-Drama: Theological Dramatic Theory.* Vol.2: *The Dramatis Personae: Man in God,* tr. Graham Harrison, San Francisco: Ignatius Press, 1990.
[64]Cf. Ibid., "If we want to ask about man's essence, we can only do so in the midst of his dramatic performance of existence. There is no other anthropology but the dramatic." (p. 335)

regard to life. Over against the danger inherent in Greek thought of absolutizing the male man as *monad*, the Judaeo-Christian vision has always preserved the truth of things by taking note of the dyadic nature of the feminine. The woman is always simultaneously bride, helpmate, glory of man (and therefore relative to him), but at the same time, with respect to him she is wholly primary (principle) in terms of the generation of offspring. The communion dimension of the *imago Dei* — a crucial extension of the classic doctrine carried out by John Paul II — does not consist solely in the analogy of communion between the trinitarian relations and the man-woman relation.[65] It goes much further to include the *principium ordinis*[66] that describes the dynamism of their communion. Just as *communio* circulates in the Trinity from the Father (origin) to the Son, who by his dyadic nature (relative through the line of generation but co-original or "originary" in that of spiration) secures the *relationship* and the *fruit* of the relationship (the Holy Spirit), so in the human event the order of communion of the male, through the dyadic nature of the woman, culminates in the relationship-fruit of the child.

All this throws an important light on ecclesiology. If the Church is the *medium intrinsicum* of Jesus Christ, then the significance of the man-woman polarity, objectively involved in the incarnation of the Word of God, cannot be removed from ecclesiology, as has been the case for too long, perhaps right from the end of medieval theology. We can no longer prescind from her "feminine" nature when we are seeking to understand *who* the Church is.[67] But to speak of the Church in these terms would be impossible, and would be deservedly rejected as some kind of gnostic rhetoric, if humanity had not been placed by the mysterious will of the Father through the power of the Spirit before *the individual person of Mary of Nazareth, Mother of Jesus, Son of God*. Here we can immediately see a crucial methodological datum: the relationship

---

In this regard, one also needs to take careful account of Von Balthasar's clear remarks on the relationship between virginity, sexuality and over-sexuality also in reference to the Freudian approach to the Oedipus complex (vol. iii, 300-303; vol. ii, 344-350).

[65]Cf. JOHN PAUL II, *Mulieris dignitatem*, 7.

[66]Cfr. THOMAS AQUINAS, *In Sententiis. Liber primus*, d. 29, exp. Text; A. SCOLA - G. MARENGO - J. PRADES, *La persona umana. Antropologia teologica*, Milan: Jaca Book, 2000, pp. 84-85; G. MARENGO, *Trinità e creazione*. Rome: Città Nuova, 1990, pp. 27-83.

[67]Cfr. M.J. SCHEEBEN, *The Mysteries of Christianity*, tr. Cyril Vollert, S.J., New York: Herder, 1946, pp. 542-57; L. BOUYER, The Church of God, pp. 491-532; M. KEHL, Die Kirche... p. 89.

between Mariology and ecclesiology is not sufficiently illuminated just by the affirmation of a necessary and intrinsic connection between these two dogmas (resulting in a close connection between the two respective theological treatises). *Rather, we must strongly affirm that any kind of ecclesiological intellectus fidei without Mariology, or vice-versa, is simply impossible.* Theologically speaking, Mariology and ecclesiology must give birth to one single treatise.

Indeed, if it is true that the Church includes Mary from a certain point of view, since she is a member of the Church — and therefore if we must postulate some kind of priority of ecclesiology over Mariology — it is necessary to affirm at the same time that without the precedence of Mary over the Church, the mystery of the Church at her incandescent core would be completely incomprehensible. At most, the Church would be the most noble of the organisations more or less directly willed by Jesus Christ for the benefit of humanity. This makes it necessary for us to reflect for a moment on the dyadic character of the figure of Mary.

Mary, the woman (cf. *Gal.* 4,4), is not merely Mother of Jesus and Mother of the redeemed — by analogy with Eve, mother of the living (cf. *Gen.* 3,1) — she is also the Bride of the Lord. This is an audacious thesis, but one that is fully documented in the most genuine tradition, as Balthasar has shown.[68] It is linked to the theme of the bride peculiar to the Song of Songs and to numerous liturgical texts of praise in honour of Our Lady, and in particular to the Feast of the Assumption.[69] The dyadic nature of the woman who pre-eminently faces Christ is thus evident.

And yet Jesus Christ is not only a man of the male sex who encounters in Mary-the woman-the Bride-the Mother, but His humanity, by virtue of the hypostatic union, is the sacrament of His divine nature as the Word of God. It is no surprise therefore that

---

[68]H.U. VON BALTHASAR, *Theo-Drama: Theological Dramatic Theory.* Vol. 3, pp. 318-339.
[69]It is worth citing a fragment from a Christmas homily by an anonymous fifth century author: "To the Virgin was presented a son who was spouse; one generated who was himself generator. In this mystery it was faith that acted as matchmaker; the matchmaker however was the archangel. The mother was the spouse and Christ himself was spouse to whom she had given birth and whom the Holy Spirit had united. The Angel Gabriel had announced it; the angelic host had glorified him and the shining star had pointed him out. The Virgin was impregnated by the one who was to be born of the Virgin. At her delivery the Mother suddenly grew afraid: God spoke through the mouth of the angel and the Virgin felt herself to be impregnated in the ears. All ages heard an unheard-of announcement: the Virgin became spouse in her delivery; while she gave birth she redoubled her virginity; she adored the Son to whom

through the incarnation (*ratio sacramentalis*), the Church, the feminine helpmate who corresponds to him, possesses a kind of social dimension in which the universal salvific plan (*Lumen gentium* calls it "mystery") is manifested for the benefit of all of humanity.

At this point, it is clear how the transition comes about from Mary-the woman to the Church, redeemed humanity. The objective event of the incarnation tells us that the Word assumes human nature through the conception, pregnancy and parturition of Mary who, quite justifiably, must be called the *genitrix* (mother) of God (*Theotokos*). But, if Mary-the woman is also bride and helpmate (cf. *1 Cor* 11, 2; *Eph* 5, 36; *Apoc* 19, 7 and 21, 2.9), we must recognise that the definitive universal fulfilment of the event of the redemption of Jesus Christ passes through her.

The dyadic nature of Mary-the woman — that is, her being helpmate, spouse and mother — also adequately configures the genesis and nature of the Church. From Jesus Christ-male through Mary-Church (as woman, helpmate, spouse and mother) the family of the redeemed takes its form. In this way the Church happens in the person of every individual marked by communion with his brothers and sisters. And she happens so that the *Light of the nations* may shine resplendently before the eyes of all our fellow human beings.

---

she had given birth (...) ... Let us therefore consider who is this Virgin so holy, on whom the Holy Spirit deigned to descend; so beautiful that God chose her as spouse; so fruitful that she gave an offspring welcomed by the entire world; so chaste as to remain virgin even after her delivery. In the figure of Mary do we not perhaps see the type of Holy Church? On her too the Holy Spirit has descended; she has been overshadowed by the power of the Most High; from her too Christ, potent in virtue, was born. She too is immaculate in marriage, fruitful in birth, virgin in purity. She too conceives not through the work of man but by virtue of the Spirit; she too gives birth without labour pains, with joy even; she too nourishes not with the breast of the body, but with the milk of the master. So she is the spouse of Christ and the mother of the nations; she reveals herself to be pregnant and rejoices in birth." Anonymous fifth century author, *In natali Domini*, PL 39, 1987-1989. Other testimonies on the subject in: *Le Theotokie del Ciclo Ebdomadario*, in M. BROGI, (ed.), *La santa Salmodia annuale della Chiesa copta*, Cairo, 1962, 28; *Inni per la festa della santa Teofania e per diverse altre solennità*, in *Laudes et hymni ad Ss. Mariae Virginis honorem ex Armenorum Breviario excerpta*, (collected essays), Venice, 1877, VIII, 50-71; *Ufficio del Giovedì*, in *Ufficio semplice dei sette giorni della settimana secondo il rito siro-maronita*, Jounieh 1937, 364-369; PSEUDO-PROCLUS OF CONSTANTINOPLE, *Encomio della santa Madre di Dio Maria*, in F. J. LEROY, *L'homilétique de Proclus de Constantinople. Tradition manuscrite, inédits, études connexes*, Studi e Testi 247, Città del Vaticano, 1967, 298-324; GERMANUS OF CONSTANTINOPLE, *Omelia per l'Annunciazione della santissima Madre di Dio*, in V. FAZZO, *Germano de Constantinopoli. Omelie mariologiche*, Rome: Città Nuova, 1985, 73-102; PETER CHRYSOLOGUS, *Sermon* 140, 1-6, PL 52, 557; ALDHELM OF MALMESBURY, *The praise of virginity*, in PL 89, 141 C; THE VENERABLE BEDE, *Homily on the holy Virgin Mary*, in PL 39, 2129-2134; PAUL THE DEACON, Homily *2 on the Assumption of the Blessed Virgin Mary*, PL 95, 1490-1507; *Corpus Praefationum* n. 202, *Corpus Christianorum Series Latina* 161 A, 62.

The essential reference to Christ in thinking Mariology-ecclesiology demands respect for the Chalcedonian dogma. These two articulations of a single reality, Mariology and ecclesiology, can never be confused, but neither can they be separated. They stand in relation to each other as *inconfuse et indivise.*[70]

The *nuptial mystery* (as distinct from mere spousal vocabulary and simple nuptial language)[71] thus shows all its force in relation to the development of an adequate Mariological-ecclesiological *intellectus fidei.* Just as at the level of elementary experience, each individual of every time and in every place is called to *learn* the meaning of belonging according to flesh and blood in the man-woman, and in the mysterious relation of fruitful love, so in the integral experience of the Christian something analogous takes place. Believers learn what belonging to Christ is, that is, they learn the love of Christ, which induces them to love others, because they are conceived and generated to faith in the most pure bosom of the Church. The bridehood and motherhood of the Church is clearly visible and indeed inseparable from Mary-Spouse and Mother of the Redeemer. Mary-Church is mother of the redeemed not only because she is mother of the Redeemer, but also because she is that spouse and helpmate whom — analogously with the original couple Adam and Eve — Christ has "generated" in the radical abasement of His incarnation, passion and death.[72] And here the element of difference in the analogy emerges forcibly: Christ actually *generates* the woman-Spouse from His wounded side, while Adam just finds her before him created by God.

To give effective shape to the face of the Church — Spouse and Mother, that is to say, who the Church is, Mariology-ecclesiology should give space to the careful narration of the mysteries of the life of the Virgin, from which the Marian dogmas flow. There is not space here to pursue this, but it would clearly show the dramatic nature of Mariology-ecclesiology as corresponding to that of anthropology. This stems from the fact that Mary-the *woman* is inexorably suspended

---

[70]Cf. DS 302.
[71]Cf. A. SCOLA, *Il mistero nuziale: una prospettiva di teologia sistematica?.* Rome: Lateran University Press, 2003, pp. 14-17.
[72]On the Church as Mother, see G. ZIVIANI, *La Chiesa Madre nel Concilio Vaticano II,* Rome: PUG, 2001.

between terrestrial paradise and fall, between Old and New Covenant, between time and eternity.[73]

The classic problematics of ecclesiology, admirably set out in *Lumen gentium*, take on a more adequate focus within the horizon opened up by this anthropological con-*centration*. The "Who is the Church" takes shape. It is '*the unity of those who, gathered and formed by the immaculate and therefore limitless assent of Mary which through grace has the form of Christ, are prepared to let the saving will of God take place in themselves and for all their brothers.*'.[74] The mission of each individual Christian, starting with the mission of Mary, is illuminated by the mission of Christ. This generates the constellation of persons who, objectively included in Christ, make His face shine out through time and space. The Church therefore appears in Mary as the nuptial event in which the insuperable tension (polarity) between spousality and motherhood, communicating itself from person to person, from experience to experience, is destined to bring Christ to the world. Her nature as *intrinsic medium* of the event of Jesus Christ, to which we shall shortly be returning, allows us to affirm that the Church in Mary precedes the individual, but at the same time, the individual who enters the Church is never absorbed by the collectivity. His free individuality is exalted in an authentic *communio* whose archetype is in the Trinitarian mystery itself. In the Church the person can be 'free indeed' (cf. *John* 8,36).

From this point of view, talk of a co-essentiality of the Marian and the Petrine dimensions in the manner of conceiving the Church has an adequate foundation.[75]

New light on burning questions?

It would be useful now to show how the reflections presented so far enable us to look more carefully at numerous burning questions that trouble the ecclesial community today. I will limit myself to

---

[73]Cf. H. U. VON BALTHASAR, *Theo-Drama: Theological Dramatic Theory*. Vol. 3. pp. 306-12.
[74]ID., *My Work: In Retrospect.*(San Francisco: Communio Books and Ignatius Press, 1993) p. 63.
[75]Cf. JOHN PAUL II, *Mulieris dignitatem* 27; L. SCHEFFCZYK, *Aspekte der Kirche in der Krise...* pp. 103-105.

one area. Many ecclesiological problems, which involve the affective dimension of the *I*, can perhaps receive new light from this approach. I am thinking of the problems that involve the radical significance of sexual difference, such as those that relate to the delicate and complex relationship between spouses (from contraception to abortion and artificial procreation) or those that have to do with the question of the inadmissibility of women to the ordained ministry and with the celibacy of priests. Many men and women in the Church find it difficult to adhere to the pronouncements of the Magisterium on these questions, because they perceive them as outdated impositions *incapable of meeting the authentic desire for self-realisation of human freedom.* The Church — and here especially the Church as Institution — is no longer perceived as Mother, still less as Spouse and Helpmate. Even the Marian-ecclesiological reference to spousality and maternity is rejected by many Christian women because it is felt as a means for continuing to impose on them heavy burdens that perpetuate discrimination. Likewise, the fact that the Church does not have the power to admit women to the ordained ministry, and the law of ecclesiastical celibacy are perceived as an obstinate and arbitrary expression of the will to power of the hierarchy. The judgment of the Magisterium on the homosexual tendency looks like violence devoid of mercy. As for contraception, the position of the Magisterium is not only widely but even sarcastically disregarded. The Church's firm opposition to abortion and to artificial procreation is felt as anachronistic and contrary to the liberating forces of scientific and technological progress. In many cases, the difficulty felt in the face of the positions adopted by the constituted authority takes on the character of a rebellion, which develops in good faith from a conviction that the constitutive desire of the *I* is not taken into consideration or accompanied towards its realisation. The very frailties of men of the Church, above all the weaknesses of her ordained ministers, are often taken as confirmation of this incapacity of the constituted authority to promote authentic freedom. Its ultimate motivation is believed to be the cutting of the tree of liberty off from its vital roots, those of desire.[76]

---

[76]The term *desire* indicates in this context the first, elementary level of human freedom , which drives the action of the subject inevitably towards its fulfilment. St. Thomas calls it

At this point we want to limit ourselves to noting in purely general terms *the fair point that underlies this objectively mistaken judgement.* What is this fair point? It is the fact that this Jesus Christ gave his life for the fulfillment of the freedom of every individual, and this is one of the most important *raisons d'etre* of the Church. Therefore, the Church cannot but seek the full satisfaction of human desire. Obviously, this passes through the person's free will and yearning for the infinite.

Through its reference to the categories of *mystery, sacrament, body, people* and *communion, Lumen gentium* inaugurated a vision of the Church as living salvific reality.[77] The question *who is the Church?* and the answer to it made possible by the anthropological con-*centration* can perhaps represent an important step in understanding the exaltation of freedom in its personal and community dimension.. To say who the Church is, you have to say who Mary is, with the evident methodological advantage that the anthropological question *who is Mary* is — at the same time — a question about the individual (Mary of Nazareth) and about the collective (Mary the Church).[78] In her, the path opens up for the individual believer to take on the dual unity Christ-Church, by analogy with the way that in the individual woman (spouse and mother) the path opens for the individual to the necessary discovery of the dual unity man-woman. The woman, who is already of herself a complete person, is, at the same time, the *other* of each other human being. In this way, in a certain sense, she takes the part of God.

In Mary-Church through the power of the Spirit of the Risen Jesus, the definitive manifestation of the plan of the Father for the man-woman is given in concrete terms. This constitutive polarity is in

---

amor naturalis. Cf. A. SCOLA, *Questioni di Antropologia Teologica,* Rome: PUL-Mursia, 1997, pp. 89-94.

[77]The very inclusion of Mariology within the scheme of the Church encourages such an interpretation. Philips, commenting on the title of Chapter VIII of *Lumen gentium* remarks in this regard: "In fact, strictly speaking, there are not different mysteries but only one: Christ, born of Mary, who comes to us as our Saviour through the Church and in the Church. The reference to the mystery of Christ in relation to the Church is meant to demonstrate that we simply cannot reduce Mariology to ecclesiology. On the contrary, Mariological doctrine constitutes the link that connects Christology to the doctrine of the ecclesial community". G. Philips, *L'Église Et Son Mystère Au IIe Concile Du Vatican,* Tome II, Paris: Desclée et Cie, 1968, p. 215.

[78]From this point of view we can see the essential role of Mariology as bridge between anthropology and Ecclesiology.

fact thus stabilised here,[79] but not in the Hegelian-style of *Auf-Hebung* (overcoming), which would empty man and woman of their individual freedom by subsuming anthropology into Mariology-ecclesiology.

This stabilisation of the dramatic polarity takes place in two directions. The first has to do with the spousal dimension. We are talking about the manifestation of the new relationship in Jesus Christ that reveals the truth of the relationship of flesh and blood. Inaugurated in one sense, as John's Gospel tells us, under the cross, by Jesus' unprecedented initiative: *"Seeing his mother and the disciple he loved standing near her, Jesus said to his mother, 'Woman, this is your son'. Then to his disciple he said, 'This is your mother!' And from that moment the disciple made a place for her in his home"* (John 19, 26-7), the new relationship of Christian *communio* is made possible — as St Bernard observes - by the spiritual martyrdom of Our Lady of Sorrows, who accepts the "unequal exchange that gives her the son of Zebedee in place of the Son of God, the servant in place of the Lord."[80] The affective dynamic of the *I* thus encounters a real chance of fulfilment, since Mary actuates that possession in detachment (virginity,)[81] which shows all the realistic dizziness of desire. As depth psychology has in fact shown us, without the law of sacrifice (detachment) there is no possibility of total satisfaction for desire. The drama of the man-woman is not taken away in the Church but stabilised, so that it may encounter in the Marian principle the way that calls freedom to a constant involvement. Freedom, exposing itself, that is, paying in its own person, moves forward on the path to a sure fulfilment of the desire that feeds it.

Analogously, Mary-Church offers stability to the natural procreative dimension linked to the affective sphere. Breaking the implacable cycle of generation-death, she establishes the full meaning of fruitfulness.[82] On the strength of the virgin birth and the resurrection of her beloved Son, Mary-Church generates sons and

---

[79]Cfr. H. U. VON BALTHASAR, *Theo-Drama: Theological Dramatic Theory.* Vol.2... pp.405-10.

[80]Cf. ST BERNARD, *Sermons,* from the Divine Office, 15th September, Memoria of Our Lady of Sorrows.

[81]L. GIUSSANI, *Affezione e dimora,* Milan: Rizzoli, 2001, p. 250.

[82]Cf. A. SCOLA, *Il mistero nuziale 2. Matrimonio-famiglia,* Rome: PUL-Mursia, 2000, pp. 134-136; ID., H. U. VON BALTHASAR, *Uno stile teologico,* Milan: Jaca Book, 1991, pp. 115-116.

daughters according to an unprecedented modality no longer marked by the shadow of death. Sexuality itself, understood in its fullest sense, is rendered true. In this way the stabilisation of the man-woman polarity offered by Christ identifies in Mary-Church the meaning of radical virginity. This is not exhausted within one specific state of life, but describes the perfect plan of God the Father for each man and woman. At the same time, this virginity pre-established from all eternity by the Father in Mary is nuptial because it is fully spousal and fruitful. Virginity and nuptiality give life to a virtuous circle that is reflected in the circumincession of states of life.[83] There is no doubt that on this terrain, which could only be classed as abstract through inattentiveness, the freedom-desire relation is interpreted in a balanced manner. From this perspective, even the burning questions referred to could find a new theological-anthropological approach. This could show that the answer of the Magisterium that seems to be a "no," is in reality a "yes", directed towards the authentic promotion of the person and the community.

Like all the steps that for two thousand years have allowed a deepening of ecclesial self-awareness, this one cannot set the Spouse free from the law established by her Husband: the law of the total gift of self that calls for the sacrifice of authentic *metanoia* to which all believers are always called. In this spirit, I would suggest that theologians should study further the essential elements of the salvific event of Jesus Christ that are still neglected, even though they are closely connected with the elementary experience of each individual. Among these elements, in our anthropological con-*centration* of ecclesiology, we have referred to the theme of Jesus Christ male and to that of the dyadic nature of Mary — the woman, which are two crucial expressions of the insuperably dramatic character of Mariology-ecclesiology.

Everyone in the Church, authorities and simple faithful, are always invited to identify themselves intensely with the marvels of divine grace that open up in Mary, *Ecclesia immaculata*, man to woman and vice versa and both to the Church, exalting the freedom of each individual harmoniously embedded in the living communion. Perhaps

---

[83]Cf. *Christifideles laici* 55.

even the present-day wounds of freedom related to the affective sphere can be healed in the face to face encounter of the new Adam and the new Eve.

PART TWO:

THE SACRAMENTAL CONCENTRATION

Once we have introduced Mary-Church (fruit of the merciful love of the Father propitiated by the Holy Spirit in Jesus Christ dead and risen) as *co-agonista* in the Theo-drama, there arises the question of her mission. We have to understand how in concrete terms, as Mother of Christ and Spouse of the Lord, she can generate believers to be subject-means (intrinsic *medium*) of the salvific event of Jesus Christ for the person of all times, who is always rooted in community.[84] This question immediately opens up two orders of problems: the first consists in the crucial question of how it is possible to make ourselves followers through time and space of the One who has risen and set out on the new *aeon*. In other words, it means asking how the Church renders Jesus Christ effectively contemporaneous with the freedom of the individual, even when the latter is temporally moving further and further away from Him. The reply to this question must give an answer to the second problem. How it happens that the intrinsic *medium* gives life to the formation of the holy people of God as a people *sui generis*, as a "people of peoples".

To situate this dual ecclesiological problematic, we must refer once more to elementary human experience, in which not only the man-woman polarity mentioned earlier, but the person-community polarity too is manifest. And once again, we face the need for an adequate ecclesiology to respect its elliptical nature and therefore the insuperable polarity of the two *foci*. Hence the intrinsic *medium* (Mary-the Church) must on the one hand save the freedom of Jesus Christ, the living One, and on the other, the freedom of the individual man. She must moreover profoundly respect the individual-people (person-

[84]Cf. A. SCOLA, *La logica dell'Incarnazione come logica sacramentale: avvenimento ecclesiale e libertà*, in AA. VV., *Wer ist die Kirche? Symposion zum 10 Todesjahr von Hans Urs von Balthasar*, Johannes Verlag, Einsiedeln, 1999, pp. 99-135.

community) tension (polarity). It is not by accident that throughout the history of ecclesiology, there have been many attempts to resolve this constitutive polarity by sacrificing first one and then the other pole, and all such attempts have found themselves in an impasse. One approach that is inadequate in this sense is the way of subsuming the persons of individual believers in the category of one *mystica persona*:[85] likewise the approach that presents the Church as an organisation constituted prior to the freedom of the individual, thereby annulling even its quality as event.[86]

1. The contemporaneity of the event of Jesus Christ

The problem raised in a critical manner from the time of the Enlightenment-Romanticism[87] as to how the contemporaneity of the event of Jesus Christ with the freedom of the individual in all times is possible, continues to trouble the body of believers.

Lumen Gentium faced it head on by introducing the notion of Church-sacrament,[88] authoritatively confirmed as crucial by the Extraordinary Assembly of the Episcopal Synod in 1985.[89] Once the anthropological con-*centration* of Mariology-ecclesiology has been put into practice, it shows even more clearly the need for this sacramental con-*centration*. Obviously, the sacramentality of the Church, which can never be thought of as separate from the sevenfold sacraments in which it is concretely actualised, is not to be considered as a magic transposition of the Christian fact in its constitutive historicity: the Person, the life, the preaching and the works of Jesus Christ. To be salvific, it must in fact have the character of a present event. Only in this way can it address the freedom of the individual, which is always located in history. And in effect the sacrament — thought rigorously

---

[85]Cf. H. MÜHLEN, *Una mystica persona. Die Kirche als das Mysterium der Identität des Heiligen Geistes in Christus und den Christen: eine Person in vielen Personen*, 2nd ed. (enlarged), Munich, 1967.

[86]On the contrary, as Kehl affirms, we should understand the Church as "the community of those who believe in Christ, who hope in his promise and love while following him (cf. *LG, n. 8*)", M. KEHL, *Die Kirche...* , p. 43.

[87]How is it possible that *'contingent historical truths'* to cite Lessing, *'can become a proof of the truth of necessary reasons'*? Cf. G. E. LESSING, *Über den Beweis des Geistes und der Kraft*, in Lessing's Werke, ed. Richard Gosche, Berlin: G. Grote'sche Verlagsbuchhandlung, 1884, vol. 7, p. 273.

[88]Cf. *Lumen gentium* 1. 9. 48; G. PHILIPS, *L'Église Et Son Mystère* 1, pp. 71-76; L. SCHEFFCZYK, *Die Kirche...*, pp. 24-38.

[89]Cf. SYNODUS EPISCOPORUM, *Relatio....*, 1789.

beginning from the Eucharist — is the *symbol* in which the event of Truth-Good is offered to the believer, calling him to decision.[90] It is the effectual encounter in Jesus Christ of the infinite freedom of the Father with the finite freedom of man. It is the way of the concrete actuation of faith. Through the sacrament, each act of freedom through which the individual decides about his humanity constitutes the place of communication of the transcendent foundation (Truth-Good) itself.

Here we see how the anthropological and sacramental con-*centration* of ecclesiology culminates in the call for an ontological foundation.[91] Indeed, the act of faith of the Christian is a free decision for that event which concretely reveals through grace the evidence of the Foundation.[92] Truth did not choose the form (*Gestalt*) of an idea in order to reveal itself, but that of an historical figure that coincides with the unique person and history of Jesus Christ. This means that the relationship between man and truth is not the fruit of a mere conceptual operation that must then be put into practice by action, for in fact it possesses an irrepressible character as event. Just as everything that happens to me calls into question the individual decision proper to each act of freedom, so if it is true, as I am forcefully reaffirming, that truth is not the result of a decision by man, it is equally true that the very event of transcendent absolute Truth chose to lower itself to the point of passing through the act of such a decision, and to expose itself even to the cross, in order to make itself present in the history of men and save them.

If this physiognomy of the communication of Truth-Goodness to the individual is clearly visible,[93] we understand how the notion of Church-sacrament as introduced by *Lumen Gentium* can meet the objectively often-unsatisfied demands of modernity and contemporary thought, without falling into relativisms and subjectivisms. Concretely speaking, we shall see how the affirmation of Pascal noted above — and not that of Nietzsche — interprets the integral truth of man. In

---

[90]On the notion of *event* and its understanding within so-called *symbolic ontology*, A. SCOLA, *Questioni di Antropologia Teologica*, pp. 162-166.

[91]Cf. A. SCOLA, 'Ecclesiologia in prospettiva ecumenica: qualche linea di metodo', in *Studi Ecumenici* 20, (2002) pp. 377-402.

[92]Cf. ID., 'Which Foundation? Introductiory notes', in *Communio* 28 n. 3 (2001) pp. 549-567.

[93]Cf. H. U. VON BALTHASAR, *Theo-logic: Theological Logical Theory*. Translated by Adrian J. Walker. San Francisco: Ignatius Press, 2000, pp. 35-78; A. SCOLA, 'Human Freedom and Truth according to the Encyclical Fides et Ratio', in *Communio* n.3 (1999) pp. 486-509.

all the sevenfold sacraments — and in particular in Baptism and the Eucharist — the notion of Church-sacrament reveals that *sacramental logic*, closely bound up with the logic of the incarnation, to which John Paul II referred so insightfully in *Fides et ratio*.[94] Immersed in the maternal spousal bosom of Mary-the Church, the individual believer of every time and place is invited to take on this sacramental logic in every circumstance and in every relationship. St Paul defined this attitude as *existing in Christ (en Christoi)*.[95] From this point of view we can also say that the whole Christian life — an articulated thread of circumstances and relationships whose ultimate form is defined by the privileged circumstance of the sacrament in which the salvific relation with Jesus Christ is actuated — is conceived as vocation.

In the horizon of the Church as sacrament of Mystery - creatively established by *Lumen gentium* — the problem of the contemporaneity of the event of Jesus Christ with the individual of every period finds an objective answer. This is never reducible to something given once and for all, as is appropriate to every reality that touches intimately the foundation in itself and in its relationship with human freedom. This is confirmed by the character — proper to truth — of being event, but also by the dynamism with which freedom attests to itself. Both truth and freedom are only ever given in their actual happening.

This is the reason why Balthasar states very astutely that the event of Jesus Christ resolves the enigma of man, but does not decide the drama of man in advance.[96] Faith reveals the fulfilled meaning of man and thus stabilises the polar nature that permeates all his being in his concrete existence, but maintains it in all its dramatic intensity. Referring to the persistence of the consequences of original sin after baptism, the Council of Trent affirmed that these remain *'ad agonem'*.[97] And this struggle is the one set up by the encounter of the infinite freedom of God with the finite freedom of each individual man. The person who follows Christ follows the truth and *"will be free indeed"* (cf. *John* 8, 31-36 and *Gal* 5, 1); but this is impossible unless the individual

---

[94]Cf. *Fides et ratio* 12-13, 94.
[95]Cf. 1 *Cor* 1, 30.
[96]Cf. H. U. VON BALTHASAR, 1992, *Theo-Drama:Theological Dramatic Theory. Vol.3. The Dramatis Personae: The Person in Christ*, tr. Graham Harrison. San Francisco: Ignatius Press, 23-56.
[97]Cf. *DS* 1515.

risks his personal and irreplaceable response to the truth that calls to him in every act of freedom. Jesus Christ truth, living personal law,[98] thus urges the person of faith to bear witness. In this again we are preceded by Mary, *Ecclesia immaculata*.

2. People of peoples

The ontological key at the root of the sacramental con-*centration* of Mariology-ecclesiology also offers us the way to a solution to the second complex of problems: the one that is linked to the Church as *people of peoples*.

A crucial point that shows how *truth through freedom* is also the *truth of freedom* is linked again to the symbolical quality proper to the evidence of truth. By virtue of the latter, the foundation given to the act of freedom presses man to go *beyond* himself (*dif-ferre*: to carry the self elsewhere). The constitutive bond with this *beyond* is best expressed when this *beyond* is represented by a subject like me: when the *beyond* becomes the *other*. The *co-existing, co-belonging* of persons always immersed in community (person-community is the third constitutive polarity of anthropology) thus reveals a factor of primary importance. The truth in its absolute transcendence not only decides to manifest itself by passing through the act of freedom, but presents itself to such an act according to a communitarian form.[99] *Lumen gentium* had recourse to the Pauline notion of *body of Christ*[100] to express this datum, while nevertheless joining it to the equally crucial notion of *people of God*.[101]

Theological literature has carefully sounded the options of the conciliar fathers in this area, bringing to light (after an initially rather

---

[98]*Veritatis splendor,* 15.

[99]In this connection Zizioulas writes: "Christ Himself becomes revealed as truth not in a community, but as a community. So truth is not just something "expressed" or "heard," a propositional or a logical truth; but something which is, i.e., an ontological truth: the community itself becoming the truth. Because the Christ-truth is not only revealed but also realized, in our existence, as communion within a community, truth is not imposed upon us but springs up from our midst." J. ZIZIOULAS, *Being as Communion. Studies in Personhood and the Church.* Crestwood, New York: St. Valdimir's Seminary Press, 1985, p. 115.

[100]Cfr. S. ALBERTO, *"Corpus Suum mastice constituit"* (LG 7). *La Chiesa Corpo Mistico di Cristo nel primo capitolo della "Lumen Gentium",* Regensburg: Verlag Friedich Pustet, 1996.

[101]Cfr. P. RODRÍGUEZ, (Ed.) *L'ecclesiologia trent'anni dopo la Lumen gentium. Popolo di Dio, Corpo di Cristo, Tempio dello Spirito Santo, Sacramento, Comunione.* Rome: Armando Editore, 1995.

wild period) the appropriate weight of these two themes and their interrelation. It has not neglected the task of locating them in their Scriptural, patristic and — more generally — Magisterial context. At this point it will suffice to note the balance now attained by interpreters, which requires that we do not make unilateral use of the two notions.[102] This is possible if the Church is conceived as the people of God whose heart is constituted by its being the body of Christ.[103] Through the sacramental body, the body of Christ gives its origin to the ecclesial body. Properly understood, the notion of body, beyond all its analogical significance, encounters that of spouse through the theme of *one flesh*. And here the popular element rejoins the element spouse and origin (mother), while the dual unity of individual-community shows that it has its first and most elementary expression in that of man-woman. Anthropological con-*centration* and sacramental con-*centration* of Ecclesiology are intimately connected by the necessary ontological foundation, which is quite comprehensible if we simply bear in mind the quality of *intellectus fidei* that is proper to theology. In this sense we can well understand the adage confirmed by the whole tradition of Christian thought: that there can be no theology without philosophy.[104]

From a historical point of view, the Church — people of peoples — begins with the mystery of the chosen people of Israel. Not considered simply as an antecedent fact but, at least through the notion of *remnant*[105] as a co-essential expression of the Church herself, made up of Jews and pagans. From this point of view we can grasp how the anthropological-sacramental concentration allows the formation of the people of God from many peoples. Universality, which is not alien to Judaism at its points of maximum self-awareness, becomes effective catholicity. As diachrony does not represent an obstacle to the present encounter (contemporaneity) of Jesus Christ with the individual, so likewise synchrony is no objection to it. In Mary-Church '*there are no*

[102]Cfr. J.RATZINGER, *Church, Ecumenism and Politics, New Essays in Ecclesiology*, (Slough: St. Paul Publications and New York: Crossroad Publishing Co., 1988), pp. 3-28; G. PHILIPS, L'Église Et Son Mystère 1, pp. 94-113; 131-137. L. BOUYER, *The Church of God, Body of Christ and Temple of the Spirit*, pp. 175-305; M. KEHL, *Die Kirche*, pp. 89; 91-93.
[103]Cf. J. RATZINGER, *Church, Ecumenism and Politics...* pp. 14-20.
[104]Cf. *Fides et ratio* 64.
[105]Cf. H.U. VON BALTHASAR, *Theo-Drama: Theological Dramatic Theory*. Vol 3. pp. 371-401.

more distinctions between Jew and Greek, slave and free, male and female, but all of you are one in Christ Jesus' (*Gal* 3,28). Truly Jesus *"has made the two into one and broken down the barrier which used to keep them apart"* (*Eph* 2, 14). No more can ethnic grouping, tribe, culture, or religion block the encounter of infinite freedom with finite freedom.

Not only, as the Fathers put it, is the Church *ab Abel*, but the pagans themselves — to whichever people they belong — are called to become persons in Christ in the Church. As von Balthasar writes: "The whole mystery of Christianity, that which distinguishes it radically from every other religious project, is that the form does not stand in opposition to infinite light. And although, being finite and worldly, this form must die, nevertheless it does not go down into the realm of formlessness. The form must participate in the process of death and resurrection."[106]

The drama of Jesus Christ, which culminates in the slaughtering of His flesh and in the shedding of His blood, becomes universal sacrament at the centre of history and of the world. It is in a position to take up into itself all quasi-sacramental procedures from the dramas of the Old Covenant to those of the Greek theatre to those of every other culture.[107] And as it was in the past so it remains today.

3. Two practical consequences

Thus from the sacramental con-*centration* of Mariology-ecclesiology, certain present-day historical processes, which give rise to many burning questions, can be illuminated.

We shall limit ourselves at this point to mentioning two of them. I have in mind the question of interreligious dialogue and the question of the compatibility of any given political-economic system with the salvific invitation of the Church.

With regard to the question of interreligious dialogue in which — perhaps above all with reference to the civil order in the United States — we have to understand the periodical recurrence of a certain *return of the gods*.[108] the correct truth-freedom relationship permitted

[106]ID. *The Glory of the Lord.*, 216.
[107]Cf. ID. *Explorations in Theology.* Vol. 3. *Creator Spirit,* tr. Brian McNeil, (San Francisco: Ignatius Press, 1993), pp. 391-411.
[108]Cf. R. CALASSO, *La letteratura e gli dei* (Milan: Adelphi, 2001). In this connection

by sacramental logic and propitiated by Mary. The Church-sacrament reveals how a useful and necessary exchange between faith and religion is established. On the one hand, by virtue of the symbolic structure of the real, faith opens finite freedom up to absolute transcendent truth. On the other hand, precisely because this freedom is always historically and communitarianly located, faith itself cannot live outside a religion. It inevitably passes through the religious phenomenon. In a certain way, it always lives within religion as the fact of a people characterised by rites, customs, and traditions. But any kind of religion, precisely by the very fact of bearing faith at its heart, is constrained by faith to put the question of the transcendent foundation. Therefore faith claims to be entitled to examine all religion critically, because it inevitably presses each religion to pronounce on absolute truth. And this claim is not extrinsic to religion, but is required by its very nature. Consequently the comparison between religions, that is to say a theology of religions and interreligious dialogue, represents an essential requirement for the development of faith.[109]

Such a requirement is maximally acute for the Christian religion, because in it the claim to a *truth through freedom* and a truth *of freedom* has, from the beginning, had to come to terms with the Greek logos, while today it has to face up to the contradictory conclusions of Western thought. This approach seems to me to overcome the limits of the widespread models of interreligious dialogue normally put forward by the theological literature — inclusivism, exclusivism, pluralism — laying the stress on the testimonial character of interreligious dialogue.

---

there is much to be learned from the extraordinary analysis of the phenomenon in a dense passage from an anecdote related in Baudelaire's *L'école païenne:* "One morning in 1851 in Paris an extraordinary event occurred. One word was buzzing around in everyone's mind: revolution. This is not itself the extraordinary event, but rather something else that occurred right in the middle of a banquet commemorating those killed in '48; a young man proposed a toast to the God Pan. "But what has Pan got to do with the Revolution?" – said Baudelaire to this young intellectual. He answered:"What do you mean? It's him! The God Pan is the Revolution!". And Baudelaire asked him: "Isn't it a fact that he died a long time ago! I thought a great voice had been heard abroad ...saying to the old world: 'The God Pan is dead' ...Surely you are not pagan?". Here came the haughty reply: "But of course; perhaps you don't know that only paganism can save the world? We have to go back to the true doctrine hidden from view for a moment by the infamous Galilean". [Translator's note: the author here paraphrases a story told in L'école païenne : see CH. BAUDELAIRE, *Curiosités esthétiques, l'Art romantique et autres œuvres critiques,* Paris : Editions Garnier Frères, 1962, pp. 575-6.]
[109]Ratzinger spoke perspicaciously about this more than thirty years ago: *The Church...* pp. 14-20. See also *Redemptoris missio* 55.

This removes it from any danger of intellectualism by preventing it from limiting itself to meetings between specialists and bringing it back to its natural place, which is that of the everyday existence of the people. Without wishing to undervalue the importance of philosophical-theological dialogues and, above all, without wishing to put any kind of parentheses around magisterial pronouncements,[110] I would suggest that this alone can be the highroad of interreligious dialogue.

This highlights the unavoidable urgency of ecumenism. Indeed, the absence of full unity between Christians damages the truth-freedom relationship, and inevitably humiliates the testimony required of an authentic Christian mission that alone can offer an adequate context for interreligious dialogue. It is important that the Christian communities never abandon the methodological criterion that there cannot be interreligious dialogue without sincere ecumenical practice.

The symbolic nature of truth might also allow us to examine with greater realism another question that is more crucial than ever since the fall of the Berlin Wall and the tragic facts of 11 September 2001. I am referring to the problem of the modality of the presence of Christians in social life. In this area too, analogously with that of ecumenical-interreligious dialogue, the Church must allow to emerge the foundation (Trinity) of the freedom of the individual who is always situated in a people. On this level too, we need to refer to the fact that we cannot abstract from the ontologically and not just ethically testimonial quality of the mission of the Christian community. So any theoretical discussion about the compatibility or otherwise of a political-economic system with the Christian *Weltanschauung* — I am thinking for example of the importance in American Catholicism of the debate about the relationship between liberalism and Christianity, especially since *Centesimus annus,* or of the way that the problem of Christianity and Marxism weighed heavily on all of European Christianity before the fall of the Berlin Wall — must be coordinated with and in a sense subordinated to the concrete testimonial action of the ecclesial subject, at once personal and communitarian.

[110]CONGREGATION FOR THE DOCTRINE OF THE FAITH, *Declaration "Dominus Iesus" On The Unicity And Salvific Universality Of Jesus Christ And The Church,* 6 August 2000.

From this point of view, the *pro-life* task, or action on behalf of immigrants, or the confrontation with the economic-financial world, or the debate on the task and the role of Catholic educational and university institutions — to restrict myself to citing a few *contentious issues* present in the ecclesial body of the United States too — find their appropriate context: that of an ecclesial subject deeply rooted in the culture and civilization of the American people and called to take the risk of bearing testimony. In particular the conception of the Church which we have put forward synthetically prevents the illusion that a correct reference to natural law and to certain objective elementary economic laws can take place through the creation of a neutral terrain on which the identity of the ecclesial subject must be put in brackets. Absolute respect for all is possible only when we respect the clear public identity of each.

CONCLUSION:

COMMUNIO

As a concluding element of the dual con-*centration* proposed, which starts from the four central categories of the ecclesiology of Vatican II — mystery, sacrament, body of Christ and people of God — it is useful to take a synthetic view of the concept of *communio*. The significance taken on by this important notion on the basis of the conciliar texts is well known.

The notion of *communio*, Biblical[111] and patristic[112] in derivation, indicates on the level of the life of the Church in each of its forms, universal and particular, the scope of the newness to which the People of God is called (cf. *LG* 4). In the texts of Vatican II, *Communion* already possesses several meanings. In fact, *Communion* is the meeting and the relationship with Christ that is revealed and that introduces us to the Mystery. *Communion* is the lifeblood that circulates among the various members and binds them to the Head of the Body, the

---

[111]Cf. F. HAUCK, *Koinonos,* in G. KITTEL, G. FRIEDRICH, G. W. BROMILEY (eds.) *Theological Dictionary of the New Testament,* 10 vols., (Grand Rapids: Eerdmans, 1965-).
[112]In this connection I have to make obligatory reference to two 'classic' works: L. HERTLING, *Communio und Primat,* Rome: Verlag der Herderschen Buchhandlung, 1943; W. ELERT, *Abendmahl und Kirchengemeinschaft in der alten Kirchen hauptsätlich des Ostens,* (Berlin: Lutherisches Verlaghaus, 1954).

44 CALLED TO HOLINESS AND COMMUNION

Church. *Communion* is the summit of the sacrament. *Communion* is the factor that melds into a new People the babel of nations coming from incredibly different peoples. Moreover, *Communion* represents a bond of unity, in the Spirit and through the work of the Spirit, which is realised at different levels in the Church: between its members; between those who exercise the various functions within the Church; between the Church universal and the individual Churches, in particular between the Successor of Peter and the College of Bishops of which he is the head. All these levels add richness to the great original significance of ecclesial communion.[113] This Christian communion is a people whose members have in common Christ, dead and risen, and who are called to a profound unity. This generates a free tendency to share every material and spiritual resource with a view to the growth of faith in the world, according to Christ's invitation *"so that the world may believe"* (*John* 17).[114]

The Ecclesiology of communion has been put forward with increasing insistence as appropriate to describe the phenomenon of the Church, especially since the Extraordinary Assembly of the Episcopal Synod of 1985. For a long time, even before the Council, this was considered to be the favoured road for ecumenical dialogue,[115] and today it is judged to be capable of giving an account of the nuptial and personal character of the Church herself.

Even if the conciliar texts have not given us a complete organic development of *communio*,[116] postconciliar theology has

---

[113]This plurality of meanings has been emphasized in contemporary theological literature, cf.: B.-D. DE LA SOUJEOLE, *Le sacrement de la communion*, Paris-Fribourg: Editions universitaires, 1998. Moreover one cannot avoid citing the contributions of Father Tillard, even though we cannot always share his conclusions, cf. J.-M.-R. TILLARD, 'L'église de Dieu est une communion', in *Irenikon* 53, (1980) pp. 451-68; ID. 'Ecclésiologie de communion et exigence oecuménique', in *Irenikon,* 59, (1986) pp. 201-230; ID. *L'Eglise locale. Ecclésiologie de communion et catholicité* (Paris: Cerf, 1995).

[114]In this connection cf. H. SCHLIER, *Der Brief an der Epheser. Ein Kommentar,* Düsseldorf: Patmos-Verlag, 1957; L. CERFAUX, *The Christian in the theology of St Paul,* tr. Lilian Soiron (New York: Herder and Herder, 1967), chs. 11 and 12.

[115]I need only cite here certain specialists in ecclesiology from the ecumenical viewpoint in the Francophone ambit: Congar, Hamer, Dumont, Le Guillou. In this connection cf. G. RICHI-ALBERTI, *Teologia del misterio. El pensamiento teologico de Marie-Joseph Le Guillou* (Madrid: Encuentro, 2000) p. 142. The perspectives that the Ecclesiology of communion opens up to ecumenical dialogue have been noted in various quarters cf. J. RIGAL, *L'ecclésiologie de communion,* (Paris: Cerf, 1997). pp. 345-374; B. FORTE, 'Il trattato di ecclesiologia: una impostazione ecumenica', in *Studi Ecumenici* 6 (1988) pp. 153-165, esp. 158-162.

[116]In this respect it is worth remembering Colombo's warning: *"The connotation of the Ecclesiology of Vatican II in terms of 'communion' is perhaps over-hasty, in the sense that it*

produced a definite deepening of it[117] which, above all if (as has been authoritatively stated) it preserves this central notion in close relation with those of mystery, sacrament, people of God and body of Christ,[118] can continue to bear good fruit. However, it would be a mistake to look to this notion for a formal unitary principle of ecclesiology. As we noted at the start, that would imply a claim to be able to overcome the structurally polar nature of the Church by nullifying her elliptical quality. As the essential *medium* of the salvific self-revelation of Jesus Christ, the Church turns inexorably around two *foci*:   that of the Pauline *mysterion* (cf. *Rom* 16, 25-27); *Col* 1, 25-27 and *Eph* 1, 1-21)[119] and that of the world, understood in Matthean terms as the field of the constitutive ecclesial mission (*"the field is the world," Matt* 13, 38).

However, the quality of the Church as communion, looked at from the point of view of the dual con-*centration* proposed, which gives a better account of her nature as subject (*who is the Church?*) and as spouse-mother (*Mary the Church*), suggests important elements for a better grasp of her mission. First of all, we have to remind ourselves of the fact that this mission does not get appended to the ecclesial subject as some kind of external addition. Analogously with the central Christological axiom that proposes an identity of person and mission in Christ,[120] the mission of the Church is all one with her essence. Here we come to one of the huge innovations brought in by the Second Vatican Council, above all with reference to *Gaudium et spes*. I am referring to the pastoral nature of the Christian message. With this the Council wanted to show the salvific nature of the Church. As the theological literature has abundantly demonstrated, in the delicate

---

overlooks crucial passages. It needs to be noted in fact that the term emerged only subordinately and almost unnoticed, as a happy surprise in the texts of the Council, where moreover it does not preserve conceptual univocity in the Council texts, nor even terminological clarity in the text of Lumen gentium," G. COLOMBO, 'Tesi per la revisione dell'esercizio del ministero petrino' in *Teologia* 21, (1996) pp. 322-339; here, p. 327.

[117]Cf. E. SCOGNAMIGLIO, 'L'ecclesiologia di comunione nella teologia post-conciliare', in *Miscellanea Francescana* 98, (1998) pp. 719-790.

[118]Cf. CONGREGATION FOR THE DOCTRINE OF THE FAITH, *Communionis notio* (28 May 1992), n.1.

[119]Scholars are aware that the term "mystery" in Pauline vocabulary has different dimensions: the ecumenical, the cosmic (which includes the reference to the Church) and the one that relates to the primacy of Christ. Cf. L. CERFAUX, *Christ in the theology of St Paul*, tr. Geoffrey Webb and Adrian Walker (New York/Edinburgh/London: 1959), pp. 419-432; R. PENNA, *Il 'mysterion' paolino*, (Brescia: Paideia, 1978), pp. 53-85; ID., *I ritratti originali di Gesù il Cristo. II* (San Paolo, Cinisello Balsamo 1996) pp. 240-242.

[120]Cf. H.U. VON BALTHASAR, *Theo-Drama. Theological Dramatic Theory.* Vol. 3, pp. 149-163.

debate consequent on the conciliar assembly and centering on the theme of the pastoral character of the Council, there were undertones of some crucial ecclesiological knotty points, which are still to some extent waiting to be resolved.[121]

We shall limit ourselves at this point to mentioning which they are. I have in mind first of all the question of a language that can adequately express the dialogical (pastoral) character of the Church. Secondly, there is the problem of the pastoral nature of doctrine and the overcoming of any opposition between the pastoral and the doctrinal. Finally we should mention the delicate question of the relation between Jesus Christ as the event of absolute truth and the insuperable freedom of each person.[122]

The mission of the Church as expressed by the communion that lives in her, demonstrating its salvific-pastoral nature, shows how the Church-communion theme is crucial on the methodological level more than it is on the direct level of content.

In concrete terms, it allows us to grasp the dynamism by which each individual ecclesial community must live. I am not referring solely to the particular Church and to the dioceses, but also to the parishes and to all the various forms of aggregations of the faithful, including the family. In fact, *communio* represents the principle of material organisation of Christian existence.

We shall limit ourselves to referring to two elements that demonstrate its importance. The first relates to the theme of ecclesial belonging. There is no doubt that the grave difficulties faced by Christianity and the smallness of the numbers of Christians, at least in Europe, depend on the well-known fact that their participation in visibly expressed community has become weakened. It is enough to quote the datum common to many European nations where the great majority of the people is composed of baptised persons, that only a

---

[121]Cfr. A. SCOLA, *«Gaudium et spes»*, pp. 103-113.

[122]The Conciliar Fathers faced up to this delicate issue also through their reflection on the signs of the times. In this connection it is worth recalling with Valadier: "Let us not look for signs of God in history, but rather try to discern in the events of our day that which the divine freedom is calling our own freedom to (...) That is why we shall say that these signs of the times are only signs of God because, through them, the divine freedom solicits our human freedoms (...) here, and as always, 'the action' of God consists in stirring up man's freedom and inviting him to want to be creative", P. VALADIER, *Signes des temps, signes de Dieu, in Etudes* 335, (1971) pp. 276-277. Translated here by C. Blamires.

fairly small minority bothers with Sunday practice, and only a derisory percentage of practising Christians is actively involved in the life of the community. It is clear that having Jesus Christ in common does not for the great mass of Christians become a liberating modality able to transfigure everyday experience of affections and work. In this context *communio* as a tendency to hold in common all material and spiritual goods is no longer held to be a factor of existential innovation. Thus the absence of a solid belongingness to a clearly identified community prevents the Church from being a credible interlocutor, capable of responding to those deep questions, which, though buried perhaps under the mass of detritus thrown up by the crisis of the subject, remain indistinguishable in his heart.

To the lack of a practice of communion that invests all of life we can attribute another grave weakness of our Christian communities, at least in Europe. I am referring to the loss of the awareness and practice of the event-aspect of the Christian fact. As can be deduced from what we have said about the ontological foundation of ecclesiology, this limitation results from the loss of the symbolic character of Christian truth and of the evidence of the faith. On the one hand this leads to an intellectualistic reification of faith itself, the doctrinalistic faith of the Magisterium, the conceptualistic faith of theology. On the other, it generates an inability to get freely involved with truth: for since the essential event-aspect of the Christian fact is not perceived, the ontologically testimonial nature of the freedom that is actualised in faith is lost.

However, as we have noted above, experience is communicated only by experience, life is communicated only by life. An event is communicated only through another event. Of themselves alone, no doctrine, no morality, no ascesis can mobilise freedom. And even truer is the fact that no organisation can produce life. "*Prius vita quam doctrinam, vita enim ad scientiam veritatis perducit*" says the great Thomist tradition.

As the Holy Gospel tells us repeatedly, as is evidenced in the life of the saints and their works, it is only the free encounter with Jesus Christ, the salvific event which takes place inexorably through sacramental *communio*, that shows the Holy Church as the holy people

CHRIST, THE MEASURE FOR THE INCULTURATION OF THE GOSPEL: HIS CHURCH, THE UNIVERSAL SACRAMENT OF SALVATION

Francis Cardinal George, O.M.I. S.T.D., Ph.D.,
Archbishop of Chicago

IN 2003, WE CELEBRATED THE 25TH ANNIVERSARY of Pope John Paul II's accession to the See of Peter. In those celebrations, with the aid of television, what the world saw was a man, now feeble and weak, in the same settings, the Basilica of St. Peter's and the Paul VI Audience Hall, where twenty-five years ago he had been so strong and vigorous. It was a poignant moment. But, what John Paul II wanted us to see was not himself but Mother Teresa. Her beatification on October 19, rather than the October 16 Mass and Papal anniversary, was deliberately intended to be the centerpiece of the celebrations of his own pontificate.

Pope John Paul saw his pontificate as an interpretation of the Second Vatican Council, and I wish to reflect on *Gaudium et spes* as the interpretative tool for understanding the Second Vatican Council. John Paul felt that Mother Teresa's life and work, her mission in the world, captured what Vatican II was essentially about. While the Pope's reading is disputed by some, I think it is clearly evident in *Humanae salutis*, Pope John XXIII's explanation for his calling the Council, that the purpose of the Council was to address a world divided by nationalism, divided by race in fascist ideologies culminating in the Holocaust, divided by class in Communist theory and divided by ideologies of all sorts. John XXIII asked, "Who will bind up the wounds of the world? Who will tell the world's people that they are brothers and sisters? Who except the Catholic Church?" The answer to that question defines the mission of the Church in the world. John XXIII felt that the Church was in fairly good shape, united in her doctrinal teaching, without great internal conflict and, therefore, from the strength of that internal unity, she could reach out in ecumenical endeavors to bind up into one visible unity all those who called Christ Lord; she could engage in interfaith dialogue so that we can have a common approach with Jews and Muslims and other major faiths to address the wounds and sufferings of the world; she should reach out in a mission of justice and universal charity, reaching out to be, as *Lumen gentium* says "the sacrament of the unity of the human race." That is the Church.

Pope John's conviction that we didn't need a doctrinal council because we're doctrinally in fundamentally good shape, but that we needed a pastoral council because the world was lethally devided and the Church unable to engage the world effectively, was the intuition guiding the calling of Vatican II. At the Council's end, in the homily for the mass concluding the Council, Pope Paul VI said, "The spirituality of the Second Vatican Council is that of the Good Samaritan who, going from Jericho up to Jerusalem to worship God, sees a wounded man by the wayside and stops to bind up the wounds of that man before going on to worship God." That missionary impetus has been, unfortunately, domesticated; and the Council is sometimes interpreted in ways that weaken the unity of the Church so that we are impeded from being the sign, the sacrament of the unity of the human race.

Mother Teresa's mission to stop to bind up the wounded people on the streets of Calcutta, of Chicago and in so many other places where her Missionaries of Charity are at work is clearly a sign, for Pope John Paul II, that the Council is bearing fruit. But if the world saw the Pope old and frail and if he wanted us to see Mother Teresa, what did Mother Teresa see? She saw Jesus Christ in the distressing disguise of the poor, distressing to us, very often, and distressing in itself, but nonetheless, a disguise for Jesus Christ himself.

I would therefore like to argue here that attention to the poor, in a very concrete and self-sacrificing manner, is the correct place to stand for interpreting *Gaudium et spes*, for properly relating the Church and world. When we see the poor, we see Christ as Savior of all, especially those otherwise neglected. In other words, we see Christ as *Lumen gentium*, as Savior of the world.

Why is it that the Council has been so often interpreted as the impetus for the Church's catching up with the Enlightenment or adapting itself to the world, rather than being Christ's instrument for saving the world? It's a question with many answers, but one reason for this misinterpretation is a misguided use of the theological method of correlation.

Over the past forty years, many interpreters of the documents of the Council have used the Pastoral Constitution *Gaudium et spes* as a canon within the canon, an interpretative tool by which the Council as a whole is best understood. The more liberally minded of *Gaudium et spes* devotees have tended to isolate an even more precise interpretative lens within the document itself, namely the reading of the "signs of the times." Under that rubric, they sometimes saw the Council as the entire Church, long overdue, turning to the modern world for inspiration. In the Council Fathers' renewed understanding of liturgy, ministry, politics, and the nature of the Church herself, the categories and assumptions of modernity were adopted, thus making Catholicism amenable to contemporary historical consciousness.

The problem of course is that such a construal of the Council relies on a very selective reading of *Gaudium et spes* as a whole and a too narrow understanding of the inspiring line about reading the signs of the times. *Gaudium et spes* specified that those signs are to be read always in light of the Gospel of Jesus Christ. The point is not that the Church should determine her teaching and practice on the basis of what the times are saying (and not in the light of timeless revelation) but, rather, that the Church should "read" the modern world and discern in it what is of the Holy Spirit and what runs contrary to that

Spirit, recognizing that the Spirit does indeed work in the world as well as in the Church. In the document on the mission of the Church we are told to look for the *semina Verbi* in every culture and in every religious manifestation of the human spirit, so that we can see the ways in which the Holy Spirit began to prepare peoples through the various "seeds" that run through all cultures and all societies for what would come to fruition in the Person and Gospel of Jesus Christ. Similarly, the same methodology is espoused for ecumenism, where we are to read the *vestigiae Ecclesiae* in all those ecclesial communities that, while separate from Catholic communion, nonetheless have genuine and true elements of Christian faith and enjoy many of the gifts of Jesus Christ, but not in their complete fullness.

Pope John and the Council Fathers wanted to establish contact with the modern world, to engage the contemporary world, because the Church's perennial mission is the transformation, the conversion, the evangelization of whatever culture surrounds it. This conversation is very forcefully presented in *Gaudium et spes*, where, for the first time in a Church document, an anthropological signification of culture is presented and the dynamics of conversion are applied to whole societies and whole cultures and not just to individuals.

The Council Fathers certainly knew that Christ is never measured by the culture but was himself the standard by which any culture is measured and assessed. It's not however, a simple this to that equation, because Christ himself is always "read," is always understood, is always seen in some cultural context, his own first of all, and then that of Rome and the other apostolic churches and then that of all the various cultures which have received missionaries throughout the twenty centuries of the Church's existence. The dialogue between faith and culture is a true conversation. The Church proclaims her faith in categories evolved in a particular culture, which, in turn, is purified and transformed into a home for the faith.

That doubling back, that constant dialogue between faith and culture, has been called inculturation of the faith and, simultaneously, evangelization of culture. Today, recognizing that cultures are not isolated in a global society, some speak of "inter-culturalism." What I want to do now, however, is to look, from within theological method itself, at the reason for a common misinterpretation of the Council. It's a tragic misinterpretation because we can't have the new Pentecost, we can't have the promised new springtime of the Gospel, unless we understand the Council — that great gift of the Holy Spirit to the Church in the last century — correctly.

What was it that made the misunderstanding of the Council so prevalent in the immediate post-Conciliar period? Some have suggested that, in this country at least, it was the influence of Francis X. Murphy's popular accounts of the Council proceedings, which appeared in serialized form in the pages of the *New Yorker* magazine. They presented the Council as a battle between reactionary anti-modern conservatives and forward-looking pro-modern progressives. For many that's still the predominant framework, even for good Catholics. Recently, I went to an anniversary of a fine Catholic high school in Chicago. One alumnus came up to me afterwards and, talking about the state of the Church and the papacy, he said "Well, you are conservative, so there are certain things that you can't do or think." I responded, "Well, really, I like to think of myself as Catholic." He said, "Well, you're a conservative Catholic," and I said, "No, I'm a Catholic Catholic." Once one tries to move out of those categories of conservative and liberal, the discussion often stops; so attuned are people to think only in those terms. There's always something to learn from any interpretation, even if it's a misinterpretation. But it's a great tragedy that a misinterpretation has become the sole theoretic device for interpreting the Council.

Others might claim that misinterpretation was the result of a lack of intellectual leadership among the bishops, particularly in this country, as they sought to implement the directives of the Council. Because they did not fully grasp the complexities of the theological issues involved, they allowed the implementation process to be dominated by trends in the secular culture, which had, by the late 60's, become fairly radicalized.

Still others maintain that this inadequate interpretation was made possible by the very length of the Conciliar documents which constitute, by far, the longest statement of official teaching in the history of the Church. The documents are lengthier than those of all the other Councils together. Historically, Conciliar statements were creeds, canons and anathemas, all of which are shorter than long reflective statements.

Since they were so hard to grasp in their entirety, the documents were easily co-opted by those who, in the service of particular agendas, could use them selectively. Nor are the documents of one piece, either stylistically or in emphasis. Even the effort to establish the fact that *communio* is the dominant ecclesiological *leitmotif* of Vatican II was hard fought. Only when one goes behind the various English translations does one discover how often the word *communio* occurs in the Latin texts. Then one can begin to make the theological argument, going back to the sources themselves, that *communio* ecclesiology is the dominant theology of the Council.

Without denying that these and other explanations for inadequate interpretations of the Council's teaching on the relations between Church and world are illuminating, I'm going to argue in this essay that the tension over the interpretation of the texts of Vatican II is really part of a much wider theological and hermeneutical struggle that stretches back well before the Council and that continues to the present day. The heart of the tension over correct understanding is the relationship between Christ and culture, or, to state it in more focused and classical theological language, between grace and nature. To grasp this relationship is a pre-requisite for comprehending not only the texts of Vatican II but also the structure of the Christian life itself, the life of discipleship.

The "signs of the times" reading of Vatican II, understood as the Church today taking direction from the culture in order to understand God's self-revelation, has it roots in the theological method developed by the Protestant theologian Friedrich Schleiermacher at the turn of the 19th century. Eager to make Christianity intelligible to its cultured despisers, Schleiermacher argued that Christian doctrine is rooted not in objective divine self-revelation in history but, rather, in subjective human experience. To substitute experience for history is, of course, a very modern turn. More precisely in the reputedly universal feeling of absolute dependency, Schleiermacher found the heart of religion. In the living nexus of conditioned relations, we feel proximately dependent upon any number of things. We sense however, amidst these partially determined relationships, a relationship that is undetermined or absolute. The source of this feeling of total dependency is what Christians mean by God. The task of this typically modern theology is to show the grounded-ness of doctrine in this experience, just as the task of the typically modern philosophy of Descartes was to show the rooted-ness of all truth claims in the primordial experience of the *cogito*. Schleiermacher argued that God's attributes of eternity, omnipotence and omniscience can be "read" from our feeling of total dependency and are religiously legitimate; by contrast, the Trinitarian structure of the Divine Being, having no reference to our grounding experience of absolute dependency, cannot be validated; it's a Greek aberration. Schleiermacher held that all doctrinal statements ought to change and evolve as our experiential substrate shifts. In a very real sense the "feeling" of the Church, mediated through a given culture and language, determines the style and content of the Church's proclamation of the Gospel. Once again, Schleiermacher's wager was that this subjectivist approach to Christianity would make religion palatable to those who considered its metaphysical claims to be unwarranted.

Schleiermacher's most faithful 20th century disciple was the Lutheran theologian, Paul Tillich, who gave formal expression to theological experientialism in his method of correlation. A professor of theology at the University of Chicago and at Union Theological Seminary in New York, Tillich had enormous influence among Protestant theologians and among some Catholic theologians as well. Tillich argued that the work of the theologian was to establish a correlation between the answers that emerged from biblical revelation and the questions that spring up from general human experience. Influenced by both St. Augustine and contemporary existentialism, Tillich maintained that human life is open-ended, unresolved, a question unto itself. Thus, to be "in time" is to be threatened by the inevitability of death. To be "in space" is to be afraid of losing one's place to stand. To be "finite" is to be caught in the conflict between freedom and destiny, dynamics and form. These tensions or ontological questions cannot be resolved by anything in this world, and thus they orient us toward the revelation of a properly transcendent God. Tillich fully accepts Augustine's dictum that only in God is the soul at rest. As for Schleiermacher, so for Tillich: experience is the final arbiter of the correlation, for it is in the feeling of ultimate concern that question and answer come together. Neither theologian was a secularist in the closed sense. The biblical revelation is interpreted and validated, however, in the measure that it corresponds to this primordial subjective but universal sensibility.

The 20th century Catholic thinker most associated with the Schleiermachian experiential method is the German Jesuit, Karl Rahner. In book after book, article after article, Rahner lays out what he terms a transcendental anthropology, an account that emphasizes the push of the human spirit outward toward a finally ungraspable horizon of truth and goodness, the famous *Vorgriff*. It is consistently on the basis of this fundamental anthropology that Rahner seeks to understand the positive doctrines of Catholic faith. Thus, Trinity, sacraments, Jesus Christ, grace and the Church are articulated in terms of their relationship to our own transcendent orientation, understood first through transcendental philosophy, not simply or even first of all in terms of their historical roots in God's self-revelation. A more contemporary proponent of the correlational method is Professor David Tracy, of the University of Chicago Divinity School. He has criticized classical correlationism on the grounds that it too neatly assumed experiential questions and biblical answers, overlooking the fact that the culture readily provides both questions and answers of its own. Nevertheless, Tracy accepted the basic Tillichean form, postulating that the theologian needs to find points of contact, of similarity, between the situation in general experience and the message of the Bible and tradition.

By the time of the final reception of the texts of Vatican II, the late 60s and 70s of the last century, Schleiermacher's form of religious liberalism had become widely accepted by the theology faculties of many of the leading universities, colleges and seminaries in Europe and the United States. From this powerfully influential base, it crept into schools, pulpits, dioceses, programs of religious education, and religious formation projects. During the years immediately after the

Council, in many Catholic circles, Karl Rahner's writings enjoyed nearly canonical authority. It was in this intellectual milieu that the conciliar documents were received. Culture and general subjective human experience, the "signs of the times," were the interpretative lens for the Gospel, and not vice-versa.

What are the critiques, within theological discussions, of correlational methodology? The basic critique of Schleiermacher was that by Karl Barth, the Reformed Church theologian from Switzerland. In his epoch-making *Commentary on Paul's Letter to the Romans*, in his studies of the theology of the 19th century and, especially, in his massive *Church Dogmatics*, Barth consistently maintained that the experiential method in theology depended on a dangerous over-estimation of the human subject, which in turn lead to a domesticating of biblical revelation. Instead of justifying the Bible through appeal to experience, Barth felt the theologian should take his reader on a tour of the specifically biblical world, the world of revelation, showing its peculiar logic and intelligibility, and then let that interpret the world. He characterized the theology of Schleiermacher as "anthropology shouted in a loud voice." He showed that there is, in point of fact, a very short road from this theological subjectivism to Feuerbach's atheistic assertion that theology is nothing but a projection of human consciousness.

When, late in his career, he was asked how he assessed the correlationism of Tillich, Barth replied, "that such a method would work splendidly in a different culture, in paradise or in heaven, because in both those states one would know the right questions to ask. But the problem is that in our fallen condition we don't even know how to formulate the questions that would adequately correspond or correlate to the answers that God gives us in divine revelation. When we try to make such connections on our terms we inevitably skew the contents of revelation."

Barth's closest Catholic collaborator was his fellow Swiss, Hans Urs von Balthasar who, though he maintained a life-long respect for the speculative range of Rahner's theology, remained suspicious of Rahner's transcendental or anthropological method. By focusing so exclusively in a quasi-Kantian manner on the conditions for the possibility of hearing a word of revelation, Rahner insufficiently attended to the complex content of that divine revelation. Balthasar compared the Rahnerian theologian to "someone who confidently places turbines at the foot of a mountain, in the hopes of channeling the spring waters and using them for his purposes. The problem is that the rushing waters of biblical revelation don't go through the turbines of our transcendental subjectivity; they swamp and overpower any receptive capacities that would try to contain them." "Better", Balthasar thought, "to attend to how thoroughly the hearer is overwhelmed and surprised by the Word that he actually hears." When he was asked to state the difference between his theological method and that of Karl Rahner, von Balthasar said, "Rahner went with Kant (and with Heidegger, whose philosophy is an interpretation of Kant); I went with Goethe." Von Balthasar signaled that Rahner opted for the rationalizing subjectivism so characteristic of modernity, while he himself chose a kind of iconic and contemplative objectivism. The Goethian subtitle to the first volume of Balthasar's *Herrlichkeit* gives away the game: *Schau der Gestalt*, seeing the form. Von Balthasar was far more interested in what is seen than in the one who is doing the seeing, or the reading.

In accord with these methodological assumptions and convinced that the quest for certitude, the modern quest which ended in epistemological bankruptcy, should not be allowed to destroy the theological enterprise, von Balthasar appreciated Jesus Christ as the *norma normans sed non normata* of theology. In the prologue to the Gospel according to St. John, Jesus is presented as the Divine Logos, in whom all things subsist and find their intelligibility. In St. Paul's letter to the Colossians, Jesus is described as the one through whom all things exist and in whom they hold together. For von Balthasar, these maximalist claims are incompatible with any theology that would propose a rationalistic framework, anthropological or otherwise, into which Jesus is then fitted. Nothing can norm or measure the One who is himself the norm and measure of all that exists. Balthasar characterized pejoratively as "epic" those theologies that would attempt to situate Jesus Christ in an overarching system, whereas he praised as "lyrical" a theology that would acknowledge Christ as constituting theology's own interior logic.

The Lutheran theologian George Lindbeck, who, like Barth, was an observer at the Second Vatican Council, summed up succinctly the difference between the two approaches that I've been outlining. He spoke of the Schleiermachian strain as "experiential expressivist" and the Barthian, von Balthasarian style as "cultural linguistic." In experiential expressivist method, doctrines are expressions of underlying experiential states, of a feeling of absolute dependency, of Tillich's ultimate concern, of a sense of absolute mystery; in cultural linguistic method, doctrines are the deep syntax or grammar by which a particular game of religious language in this accompanying world is structured. Though the liberal style of theological method has been regnant in the years since the Council, the cultural linguistic school has come increasingly to the fore because of Professor Lindbeck and his courage as a Lutheran in taking on the dominant understanding of doctrinal development in the Lutheran communion.

My contention is that *Gaudium et spes*, and the Council as a whole, are more adequately interpreted in these latter terms. The "signs of the times" are to be consulted, of course, for we live where we are; but they are to be read from the standpoint of an interpretative system that positions them. The world is to be engaged, but from a wider frame of reference that contextualizes the world and doesn't allow the world to simply be the context for interpreting the Gospel. This hermeneutical grid is the Gospel of Jesus Christ as received by the Church. Because Protestants relativized the Church as an article of faith and relate directly to the Gospel and Christ, there's no proper hermeneutical context or society of faith itself, no normative faith community to provide determinative interpretation of the mysteries of faith. Revelation is wide open to an interpretation based upon subjective and, in this country, individualistic experience. The Gospel of Jesus Christ, as received by the Church, must create the context for the hermeneutical grid, particularly for us as Catholics in a Protestant culture. Conversation in this context is complicated because these realities of faith (Gospel, Christ, Church) are not just hermeneutical instruments for interpreting the world; they are themselves part of what has to be interpreted in every conversation between faith and culture. If they are objects of faith, if they are part of the realm of belief and its proper syntax, then they and it will both be interpreted. The major and constant question is which, finally, is the determining voice in the ongoing conversation.

The Savior, Jesus Christ, recognized truly only in faith, the Gospel as message or vision of the faith, and the Church as the community of faith, are each received in faith in the cultural contexts lived and created by the disciples of Jesus Christ in different ages. The lived tension in the dialogue is present in the believer himself, who is both faith-filled and a person shaped by his own culture and who keeps shifting perspective as the faith is newly interpreted and the culture is transformed or converted by the proclamation of the Gospel. If the culture must finally be measured and judged by Christ, Gospel and Church, so must all three be culturally interpreted in order to be effective in a given culture. That point makes clear how the correlationist insight is of importance, if the dominant voice in this dialogue remains divine self-revelation in history.

From Vincent of Lerins to John Henry Newman and his "registers" for judging doctrinal development, theologians have given themselves to elaborating the particular signals for interpreting Christ, Gospel and Church in a way that isn't inconsistent with their origins in divine revelation itself in its original historical context. Since, however, the one doing the interpretation, the interpreter, the human subject, is the centerpiece for modernity, with its emphasis on self-conscious reflection, a final word has to speak of the actor in the faith-culture conversation, whose own self-understanding is a key part of the conversation. Here I return to what I said at the beginning: the mystery of man should be read not so much from the viewpoint of philosophical or cultural anthropology but from the viewpoint of the poor and those distanced from the main trends of the dominant culture. There's a fundamental biblical reason for this. Modern man's great temptation, the Promethean temptation, is to hubris, to control, through submitting nature itself to torture in a laboratory in order to control nature, through submitting himself to analysis in order to understand and control his own behavior. Lack of hubris is to be found among the poor. Therefore, if we are going to consider man as the interpreter and move to understanding man as the subject of interpretation, as part of the mysteries of faith, we must go back to the poor. This corrective was clearly said at the time of the Council; it has been ignored in this country to our detriment and it is time to return to that biblical context of interpretation to understand ourselves in God's eyes.

Gaudium et spes has rightly been read as a celebration of the human being and his incomparable dignity and destiny. But this valorization of the human is susceptible to a misinterpretation if its Christological context is overlooked. Pope John Paul II's first encyclical, *Redemptor hominis*, was written to respond to this challenge. Like the historical signs of the times, the human being has himself, in the wake of the Council, too often been read as the norm and measure of revelation. In point of fact, the dignity and glory, which the Council ascribes to man, are a gift of the creating and redeeming God. Human dignity is appreciated in its fullness only through the gift of God's own self-giving and divine revelation. But it matters where we stand as well as how we think when we see, and read, man in the signs of the times.

Let us develop this biblical contrast to contemporary thought by glancing at some typically modern construals of the human being, setting them in contrast to the Council's understanding of the mystery of man understood in the mystery of the God-man, who emptied himself, becoming poor for our salvation. The young René Descartes found himself, at the beginning of the 17th century, dissatisfied with the intellectual tradition he had received from the Jesuit Fathers at La Fléche in Paris. Wherever he looked at philosophy, poetry, religion, science or art, he discovered a hodge-podge of conflicting viewpoints, contradictory claims and irreconcilable perspectives. When he traveled through Europe, sampling the practices and beliefs of a variety of cultures, he encountered a similarly disconcerting pluralism. The restless philosopher, on a cold day in the German city of Ulm, finally decided to turn inward. In the indubitable certitude of the *cogito*, he found the epistemological *terra firma* that he had been seeking.

On the basis of that subjective and experiential foundation, Descartes then proceeded to reconstruct the whole of philosophy and science. In his revolutionary move, Descartes effectively invented the modern sense of the self as the ground of value and the source of meaning.

Prior to Descartes, there were plenty of philosophies that had subjectivist tendencies. Plato's, Plotinus', and Augustine's philosophies are obvious examples; but all these held that the subject recognized truth and goodness exterior to itself. As Professor Louis Dupré has insisted, "the modern Cartesian self plays a much more aggressive and determining role, proclaims that truth and value are brought to the subject for adjudication, and the ego itself functioning as the *norma normans sed non normata.*" The influence of this Cartesian interpretation of the self can be seen in Immanuel Kant's grounding of the moral life in the demand of the categorical imperative. And it is brought to culmination most dramatically in Nietzsche's celebration of the will to power as a force that stands beyond good and evil as received in any teaching.

That a casual Cartesianism holds sway in the popular culture today can be seen in an almost unquestioned sense that the only inviolable value is choice itself and the only real sin is the imposition of one's point of view on someone else. In its decision in the matter of Casey vs. Planned Parenthood, (1992) the United States Supreme Court gave legal sanction to this paradigmatically modern philosophical attitude. The famous "mystery passage" comes back in discussions again and again, because it is so blatantly clear and so obviously an embarrassment: "it belongs to the heart of liberty to determine the meaning of one's own life and the mystery of the universe on one's own terms." This is the total inversion of the classical self that stood in wonder before the mystery of the Real and sought to know it. What our Supreme Court defended was the Nietzschean self whose will to power determines everything. That is, of course, the fault line that runs through our culture.

The political correlate of the meaning-grounding Cartesian self is the civil society — creating Hobbesian-self. In accord with his materialist assumptions, Hobbes held that the human being is nothing but a bundle of often conflicting desires, the most elemental of which are the desires to live and to avoid violent death. Hobbes is one of the first in English-speaking cultures, (which generally ignore the thought of the Dominican theologians of Salamanca, reflecting on the rights of the indigenous peoples of this continent in the 15th and 16th centuries) to use this term: human rights. For Hobbes, these rights are rooted in unavoidable and irrepressible desires, in feelings. Whatever we cannot not desire, for example, life and its necessary conditions, is that to which we have a right. When a person's desires bring him into conflict with others and hence threaten public safety, because one person's desires are not another's, then we band together and form a social contract which grounds and sanctions civil society. Society's principal purpose is not to promote the common good but to prevent the individual members of the society from killing one another. This sharply reductionist political philosophy, which explicitly denies the objective and transcendent reference that marks most classical political thought, is rooted in the prerogatives and rights of the sovereign self.

John Locke, though he nuanced and softened the Hobbesian account, retained in his political philosophy the essential features of Hobbes' theory. In fact, the U.S. Constitution is more a Hobbesian document than it is a Lockean document, although one can argue that the Declaration of Independence is a Lockean document. The Lockean rights to life, liberty and property are rooted, as for Hobbes, in irreducibly basic desires. In the Lockean civil society, it is fundamentally for the protection of those rights that we enter into the civil contract and not for the inculcation of virtue. Political society flows from and centers on the demands and needs of the individual. The inculcation of virtue is not ignored; Washington talked about it in his farewell address and said that it was religion, not the state, that was to be concerned with virtue. That is a good Lockean response, but it reduces religion to personal, individual subjectivism.

The bracketing of objective moral reference can be seen perhaps most clearly in the best-known text of Locke's American disciple, Thomas Jefferson. The American Declaration of Independence argues that legitimate government is founded to protect the rights to life, liberty, and, in an interesting departure from Locke, the pursuit of happiness rather than the protection of property. The goal of that pursuit is left entirely unspecified and, for many Americans, property is integral to the pursuit of happiness. But the true nature of happiness remains always the product of the value-creating self.

Gaudium et spes comments explicitly and critically on this modern construal of the self in the document's chapter about human dignity. It says: "Our contemporaries are right in their evaluation and assiduous pursuit of freedom, although often they cultivate it in wrong ways, as a license to do anything they please, even evil" (*Gaudium et spes*, 17). Freedom is to be celebrated, but the Council's sense of freedom is not the liberty of the apotheosized subject; it is rather the authentic freedom that Christians receive as part of their dignity as creatures, made in the image and likeness of God. We receive our being; we also receive our freedom. God is supremely free, because he is utterly connected in thought and will to the goodness of his own being. Nothing constrains God or prevents him from expressing his own "to be," his own *esse*. In a similar way, we human beings are properly free in as much as we are unfettered in our attempt to find union with the good of God himself, which is nothing but our own deepest good. Because we are finite and creatures, we exist with a God-shaped hole that can be filled only by God.

Real liberty, therefore, has nothing to do with blind self-assertion, radical spontaneity, the will to power or the creation of value *ex nihilo* on the basis of one's own subjective desires. Rather, it is the freedom, as St. Anselm put it, "to say only yes to the invitation of the Holy Spirit." Paul the Apostle knew this paradox, and that is why he could declare both that he was a slave of Jesus Christ and that it was for freedom that Christ had set us free. That is the basic dynamic of the spiritual life and for the life of discipleship itself. *Gaudium et spes* further specifies the true nature of human liberty when it comments, "human dignity requires then to act through conscious and free choice, as motivated and prompted personally from within and not through blind internal impulse or merely external pressure"(no.17). There is free personal choice, but genuine freedom is found only in choices that ratify the ontological sub-structure that relates us to God.

Central to the philosophical work of Pope John Paul II, who had a substantive hand in the drafting of *Gaudium et spes*, is the development of a coherent anthropology that would integrate insights from both classical Catholic thought and modern phenomenology, a descriptive terminology used to address experience on its own terms but not to make experience the only set of terms that we have, nor the determining factor for judging everything else. With the help of both Thomas Aquinas and Max Scheler, Karol Wojtyla worked out a philosophical anthropology that hinged on the understanding of the relationship between self-creation and the objectivity of the good. Through a series of disciplined ethical acts, directing the person toward the truly and objectively good, the moral subject effectively forms his moral character, the kind of person that he would be. Every choice has a direct object, the good aimed at, and an indirect object, the good person that one is striving to become. Through careful, responsible, self-creation in relation to the objective good, the moral person becomes truly free, that is to say, liberated from all of those impulses, tendencies, temptations, and proclivities that militate against the self that he would and should be. In this way, Wojtyla honored the typically modern concern for freedom but without coming to the distorted idea of freedom as radical spontaneity based upon pure will. This is the peculiarly Christian idea of liberty that *Gaudium et spes* consistently assumes and promotes, the idea of liberty that often leaves one the recipient of blank stares when brought into a conversation on faith and culture.

The key for this discussion on human freedom is the text of *Gaudium et spes*. The text that John Paul himself has so often used as a sort of *leitmotif*, a canon within the canon of *Gaudium et spes*, is paragraph 22. "In fact, it is only in the mystery of the Word Incarnate that light is shed on the mystery of mankind. It is Christ, the last Adam, who fully discloses mankind to itself and enfolds its noble calling by revealing the mystery of the Father and the Father's love." One could argue that most of Pope John Paul II's encyclicals are commentaries on *Gaudium et spes*, paragraph 22, but they are so from the standpoint of the poor, especially in his major social encyclicals.

In modern construal, man in his self-bestowed freedom, is the measure of revelation, as he is of everything else; but in a Christian anthropology, it is revelation that measures us and serves as the mirror in which we properly view ourselves. The Word made flesh shows us simultaneously who God is and who we are in relation to God. The Word made flesh illumines the mystery of man. Jesus' humanity is not threatened or overwhelmed by his divinity, and God is not a competitor for our freedom. On the contrary, our freedom is enhanced, brought to perfection through union with God's grace. More specifically, Jesus' human freedom is not suppressed or rendered irrelevant by his divine will; rather, the former finds itself through active, loving and free cooperation with the latter. God is not, as both classical antiquity and early modernity imagined, in competition with the human race. Humanity is neither a plaything of God, nor a rival to divinity. All of this is expressed admirably in the laconic doctrinal language of the Council of Chalcedon: in Jesus, two natures, divine and human, come together in the unity of one divine *hypostasis* but without mixing, mingling or confusion. God's Godliness is revealed most fully in the act of giving himself away in love for his human creatures; and man's true humanity is most fully expressed in the act of surrendering to the will of God. Neither Descartes, nor Hobbes, nor Kant nor Nietzsche got it right. It is in the mystery of the Word made flesh that the mystery of human creatures is finally disclosed. What man comes to this self-discovery in the Word made flesh? What safeguards the proper reading of man by man himself? We must start with those who are last in this world but first in the kingdom: the poor. How do the poor, and we with them, interpret the culture and the Church's relationship to it? We do not elevate the "signs of the times" or man in his freedom to the status of interpretative grids by which revelation is read and according to which the Church is measured. Nor do we even give them co-equal status with the contents of revelation and seek to affect a dynamic co-relation. Rather, we clearly affirm the metaphysical and epistemological primacy of God's self-revelation and then, with confidence and joy, we read politics, economics, literature, art, architecture and the free human being himself, who gave rise to all of these, from the perspective of God's self-revelation. We meet Jesus, who always comes in history with the poor; and our obligations flow from that communal encounter. This it seems to me is the clear, though often misconstrued message of *Gaudium et spes*. The recovery of this vision is vital to the flourishing of the Church in this still unsettled time.

In every age and every culture, Jesus Christ, who is the same yesterday, today, and forever, is the norm or the measure for the inculturation of Church and Gospel and Christ himself, even as the Church strives to re-express the mystery of the Incarnation, using the resources of different cultures in various ages. The adequacy of each such attempt, however, is to be judged by the living Tradition itself, and not by the spirit of any particular age, nor any particular transcendentalist or subjectivist philosophy. Each attempt, moreover, is to be worked out in the company of the poor. This project, which shapes the Church's mission in every age, is possible because the grace won by Christ and mediated by the Church has unconditional validity and gives us strength and perseverance to the end.

OFFICIUM SIGNA TEMPORUM PERSCRUTANDI: NEW ENCOUNTERS OF GOSPEL AND CULTURE IN THE CONTEXT OF THE NEW EVANGELIZATION

Richard Schenk OP

> During the Council we walked through a vast desert, and we came closer to God's holy mountain. But were we now to settle down to rest under the broom-tree of a Conciliar triumphalism, tired, sleepy, and fed up, then would — then please may, then surely must — an angel of God wake us up from our sleep by persecutions, apostasy, and suffering of heart: "Get up, you have a great journey before you."[123]

I Today's Task of Interpreting the Council

Among the abiding lessons of the Second Vatican Council is the call to pay close attention to the strengths and the needs of the day. It is self-understood that the concrete duties of *aggiornamento* will change with the *"giorno"* from age to age. Alongside a core of perennial truths, the temporally conditioned emphases apparent in interpreting the documents of the Council in the 21st century cannot be expected to remain the same as those prominent in the early or even the late 1960s. A "Conciliar triumphalism," about which Karl Rahner warned emphatically just four days after the Council closed, might attempt to freeze the development of theology with the letter of

---

[123]Karl Rahner, *Das Konzil – ein neuer Beginn* (Freiburg et al., Herder, 1966) 22. The printed and vocally recorded text of Rahner's Munich lecture of 12 December 1965, four days after the close of the Council, reveals the dramatic sense of high purpose associated with the Council already in its own day.

select conciliar texts or the spirit of their immediately post-conciliar interpretations, but it would thereby violate a key formal principle of the Council itself, compounding post-conciliar experiences of "persecutions, apostasy, and suffering of heart." Forty years after the Council, the question that the Church must face is: What about the times has changed and, correspondingly, what needs to change in today's reading of the Conciliar texts? What do "the signs of the times" tell us about the vocation of the Church in the world of *today*? Forty years after the Council, identifying the altered hermeneutical situation for understanding what was meant by the task to scrutinize the signs of our times can provide us with a first step towards fulfilling that duty today.

Two recent publications, both describing themselves as postmodern, can provide us with a sense of how the Council tends to be read today. Together they define what the options are for understanding the task of theology in our time, if we accept their not uncommon interpretation of the Council.

The first is an essay by Lieven Boeve, entitled, "*Gaudium et Spes* and the Crisis of Modernity: The End of the Dialogue with the World?"[124] The essay develops its thought in three steps, first portraying the Pastoral Constitution as a prime example of the Council's share in the modern technological self-confidence prominent in the first half of the 1960s:

> The dialogue partner of the church in this Constitution was the modern world: a world finding itself in the dynamics of modernity, responding to the key-words of modernity such as emancipation, progress, technological development, economic growth, worldwide unity: humankind on its way to freedom, equal rights and happiness for all — in short, modernity as the project of the progressive realization of full humanity.[125]

---

[124]Lieven Boeve, "*Gaudium et Spes*" and the Crisis of Modernity: The End of Dialogue with the World? in: M. Lamberigts and L. Kenis (ed.), *Vatican II and its Legacy* (Leuven, University Press and Peeters 2002, 82-94.

[125]Op. cit., 83 sq. The text continues: "Considering the dialogue, the Council saw three major tasks for the church, which are reflected in the Pastoral Constitution. First of all, the church wanted to acknowledge the fruits of modernity and critically evaluate the strong and weak points of the modern dynamics (*GS* 4-10, 41-42). Secondly, the church sought to link the modern project to the Christian story: well-understood modern progress was part of the fulfillment of God's plan... Thirdly, the church had proposed concrete solutions to some urgent problems accompanying the realization of the modern projects (GS part II)."

In a second step, Boeve, Coordinator of the Research Group, Theology in a Postmodern Context, at the Katholieke Universiteit Leuven, details the way in which the world of our day has passed from its modern confidence to a postmodern situation: "Today, in our so-called post-modern world, modernity's projects of progress and emancipation have lost their plausibility."[126] He cites Jean-François Lyotard's references to Auschwitz and a fundamental crisis of the belief in the rationality of reality, followed by the loss of belief in the doctrine of historical materialism (Berlin 1953, Budapest 1956, Czechoslovakia 1968, Poland 1980) as well as by the loss of belief in parliamentary liberalism (May 1968).[127] Boeve might easily have expanded on his oblique reference to the oil embargo of 1974, which did in fact make clear the sheer physical limits of extending Western-style consumerism to the entire world and led even non-theological discourse to the paradigmatic shift from Ernst Bloch's *Das Prinzip Hoffnung* (1959) to Hans Jonas' *Das Prinzip Verantwortung* (1979). Among the other important dates that Boeve's narrative merely brushes is the year 1989, although it is, admittedly, still too early to say where we will be led by those centripetal and centrifugal forces that have replaced the polarity of the cold war with the new twin phenomena of American dominated globalization and America-fixated fragmentation. But whatever dates might have deserved a more sustained analysis in this narrative, it certainly must be admitted in line with Boeve that the days have passed when we would proclaim with *Gaudium et spes* that "... we are witnesses of the birth of a new humanism, one in which man is defined first of all by this responsibility to his brothers and to history."[128]

Far less certain is the advisability of that concrete alternative to the ideal of modern humanism which Boeve recommends in a third step: "the specific postmodern mode of 'open story'-telling."[129] The author

---

[126]Op. cit. 84.
[127]Op. cit. 84.
[128]*GS* 55. The words cited are prefaced by the following text: "From day to day, in every group or nation, there is an increase in the number of men and women who are conscious that they themselves are the authors and the artisans of the culture of their community. Throughout the whole world there is a mounting increase in the sense of autonomy as well as of responsibility. This is of paramount importance for the spiritual and moral maturity of the human race. This becomes more clear if we consider the unification of the world and the duty which is imposed upon us, that we build a better world based upon truth and justice."
[129]Op. cit. 92; cf. also Lieven Boeve, *Interrupting Tradition. An Essay on Christian Faith in a*

develops the suggestion out of his concern that a certain direction of theology that he terms neo-conservative might well seem to share with genuinely postmodern theologians like himself the common conviction that the ideals of modern progress have become untenable. Given his view of the Council as a monolithic affirmation of the precisely "modern" ideals of its day, a day since past, Boeve sees as possible only three interpretative strategies: (1) either to renounce the ideal of fitting into the world of our day, reverting to premodern models (which he dismisses with a not so postmodern univocity as neo-conservativism); or (2) to renounce the ideal of continuous accommodation, in order to use the Church to attempt a restoration of the otherwise abandoned, modernist culture of the 1960s (which he dismisses as outmoded post-conciliarism); or (3) to accept the alleged formal principle of the Council to conform the Church to the culture of the day, now a postmodern world. It is this final option that Boeve advocates.[130] And yet this postmodern author does not provide any reasons for assuming that, following the strategy suggested, the Christian faith could, would, or even should survive its incarnation into postmodernity. As J.H. Newman once argued, there are limits to the degree of assimilation that a genuine development can allow itself, before it starts to lose its unifying focal point to "disarrangement or dissolution;"[131] and certainly, there is nothing in the postmodern narrative itself to suggest that Christian faith should survive the test of time as anything more than one more faint and average memory among so many.

The second "postmodern" reading of the Council is that offered by Tracey Rowland[132] in the programmatic spirit of "Radical

---

Postmodern Context (Louvain, Peeters 2003) especially 65-111.

[130]Op. cit.: "Neo-conservative theologians are convinced that the only way out of this crisis is a retreat, as if our time could not have its own critical consciousness, which, in our opinion, should be located in the specific postmodern mode of 'open story'-telling. When Christian faith confronts itself with postmodern critical consciousness, it will have to lay down the specific(ally) modern features it incorporated from the dialogue with modernity, but it will also find a challenging dialogue partner providing an excellent opportunity for Christian faith to incarnate itself another time – an incarnation which will be valid as long as the present critical consciousness remains plausible."

[131]J.H. Newman, *An Essay on the Development of Christian Doctrine*, II, v, 3 (Garden City, New York, Image/Doubleday 1960, 190).

[132]Tracey Rowland, *Culture and the Thomist Tradition. After Vatican II* (London/New York, Routledge 2003).

[133]Cf. Aiden Nichols' sympathetic Foreward to Rowland's work, xiv: "And, how, finally, is

Orthodoxy," envisioning an ideal postmodern future for the Church, but one seemingly quite different from Boeve's. In her promotion of the retrieval of premodern elements for the core of a future renewal, Rowland might seem at first more genuinely postmodern than her colleague at Louvain, although her programmatic (Boeve might say "absolute") insistence on a uniform culture claiming to spring whole-cloth from one highly specific tradition within the Christian faith identifies her in the end as less typically postmodern; arguably, her vision of the postmodern might do better to name its goal antimodern.[133] It is hard to see what Rowland desires of postmodernity beyond the affirmation of narrative methods and the ideal of cultural contextualization on the one hand coupled with the rejection of modern cultural values on the other. Where Boeve seems to push the power of assimilation to its excess, Rowland seems to deny to the Christian tradition any significant use of that power. In her narrative of theology since *Gaudium et spes*, even the language of human rights needs to be rejected, since it did not originate in Catholic culture and the assimilation of this language by the faith has only forced the latter's self-alienation.[134]

In describing themselves as postmodern, both authors do, however, agree in their analysis that the concrete proposals of the Council were thoroughly "modern" and so deserve our rejection today. Showing little concern for what Newman termed the "Church's consistency and thoroughness in teaching,"[135] both authors see moving

---

this 'postmodern'? Chiefly by an unflinching rejection of the characteristic languages of modernity, even at their most seductive (such as the language of human rights)." While Rowland repeatedly criticizes "…Jacques Maritain's efforts to reconcile Thomistic natural law with the Liberal natural right doctrine and his endorsement of the natural rights doctrine of the United Nations' *Declaration on Human Rights* in 1948" (16; cf. 222), she might find his title *Antimoderne* more acceptable, as it preceded by some four years that papal condemnation of "Action française" (1926), which marked one of the key turning points in Maritain's Catholic thought.

[134]In rare cases, Rowland seems to suggest exceptions to her rule, such as A. MacIntyre's development of Thomism out of the experience of failed Marxism, and the addition of Balthasarian theology atop the independent basis of MacIntyre's philosophy. Admittedly, it is not easy to see how her theological principles could allow for that kind of *Überbau*; cf. op. cit. 68: "MacIntyre may be viewed as having travelled along the Marxist 'Romantic line' (in contrast to the 'Enlightenment line') and crossed to the Thomist at these various junctions."

[135]Cf. Newman, op. cit. II, vii, 5 (ed. cit. 334). While both of these contemporary authors reject the need to conserve the substance of what the Conciliar Church intended, associating its goals monolithically with the modern project, they employ contradictory strategies

forward theologically as still possible today only by a rupture with the major magisterial thrust of an incorrigibly modernistic Council. A Church that would no longer claim what Newman called "the power to assimilate" values and truths which had originated outside her visible boundaries, at least not without forfeiting willingly (Boeve) or unwillingly (Rowland) her previous identity, arguably would also fail "to preserve the type" of the ancient Church: Newman's first note of genuine development.[136] Unlike Rowland, Boeve does seek to acknowledge logical sequence[137] as a note of genuine development, although, like Rowland, he reads the innovations of the Council as a single-minded shift towards a program of accommodating the faith to the spirit of the day.

The view of the Council's past and future that will be developed in what follows here is seeking an alternative to both of these readings. That is not to say that there would be nothing in postmodern discourse worthy of assimilation by the faith of today; in particular, there is a need to admit as much of the limitations of concrete human existence as necessary, in order to affirm credibly in the human person as much dignity as possible.[138] But there is no obvious reason in principle, even on postmodernist grounds, why there could no longer be a resolute retrieval of certain premodern *and* modern elements of thought and culture as well. There is much historical evidence to suggest that the Council was not, in fact, marked by a monolithic rush to conform the Church to the visions of political, economic, and technological

---

to abandon Newman's positions on the power of assimilation as a note of genuine develop-ment: the one strategy would extend assimilation into self-alienation, while the other would restrict the power of assimilation by a form of sectarian isolation. In neither case would the Church be granted the resources to critically engage the world of its day.

[136]Op. cit. II, v, 1; and II, vi (ed. cit. 177-183; 209-308). Recalling repeatedly a character-istic quip by Balthasar, Rowland argues, or rather asserts, that the attempt to view as a new form of *spoliatio Aegyptorum* the various Christian appropriations from modern culture and its "human rights rhetoric" has only masked the more basic *spoliatio Christianorum* evident in the Council, "...where the 'Chosen People' start to believe that they *are Egyptians* because all traces of their specific differences have been suppressed" (op. cit., 165, with reference to *GS* 54; cf. op. cit. 154-157).

[137]Cf. Newman, op. cit. II, ix (ed. cit. 192-197).

[138]Cf. R. Schenk, *Die Gnade vollendeter Endlichkeit. Zur transzendentaltheologischen Ausle-gung der thomanischen Anthropologie* (FThSt 135) Herder, Freiburg 1989.

[139]Initially (18), Rowland mentions the dialectical character of GS, but then, failing to see any systematic significance in that dialectic, abstracts from it even in her lengthier historical presentation of the Council's views on culture.

progress common through the mid-1960s.[139] Rather, as a careful review of the Conciliar debate around "the signs of the times" can show, the Council, taken as a whole, was as divided as the world it saw around it, "buffeted between hope and anxiety." The more optimistic and culturally conformistic voices dominated much of the first twenty years of the reception of the Council and the attempts during those years to become involved in the wider culture of the day, as the Church sought to engage movements and issues outside of what had seemed to be her customary borders. Only in the last twenty years have the more dialectical and critical contributions to the Council begun to color in like measure the Church's unrelinquished resolve to participate in the cultural and political life of our time. In today's Church, the less and the more nuanced views concerning the relationship between Christianity and contemporary culture are still often set against one another. The goal of this essay is to show that a historically adequate retrieval of the Council and of the two waves of its post-Conciliar reception points towards a more highly differentiated theology, one that can well be described in the dual call to holiness *and* communion.

I The Conciliar Debate on "the Signs of the Times"

On Christmas day, 1961, Pope John XXIII issued the official call to the Council with the Apostolic Constitution, *Humanae salutis*. John first names a number of "*doloris anxitudinisque causae*". Then, wishing to confirm nonetheless his own continued trust in the divine "preserver" of the human race, John goes on to refer to *Mt* 16: 3 and certain "signs of the times" indicative of the advent of a better age. Despite the arms race, and made more urgent and more evident by it, the signs of the times point towards a growing interest in peace.

The pattern set by *Humanae salutis* was followed closely in its meaning and use of the phrase, "signs of the times," just over a year later in the vernacular versions of the encyclical, *Pacem in terris*, published in April of 1963. While lacking an equivalent in the official Latin text, the phrase "*segni dei tempi*" is used four times in the Italian version,

---

[140]Cf. *L'Osservatore romano*, 11 April 1963, the version that first made itself known at the Council; and *La Civiltà cattolica*, 114 (1963), II, 105 sqq.

[141]There seems to be a lack of uniformity among the official translations of the encyclical.

each time as a heading over indications of positive developments.[140]
The first sign already encompasses several positive trends at once,
which taken together are said to characterize the present day: the
"progressive improvement in the economic and social condition of
working men;" "the part that women are now playing in political life;"
and the following fact: "Since all peoples have either attained political
independence or are on the way to attaining it, soon no nation will
rule over another and none will be subject to an alien power."[141] The
subsequent headings naming signs of the times single out state charters
of fundamental human rights, the United Nations, and a perceptible
trend towards the universal rejection of war.[142] If mentioned at all, the
darker background of these signs is merely "acknowledged," but not
counted among the signs of the times themselves.

The Council, which had been in session for only half a year
when *Pacem in terris* appeared, gained momentum, focus, and purpose
from the encyclical; it also adopted that specific sense of reading the
signs of the times found in *Humanae salutis* and in the vernacular
versions of the encyclical. This is most evident in the *Declaration on
Religious Freedom*, which first identifies two facts for consideration, the
fact of contemporary widespread interest in religion and the second
fact that many states still try to impede its practice. Only the first fact
will count as a sign of the times: "This Council greets with joy the
first of these two facts as among the signs of the times. With sorrow,
however, it denounces the other fact, as only to be deplored."[143] Other
conciliar texts reflect much the same semiotic sense, notably the *Decree
on the Ministry and Life of Priests*;[144] the *Decree on the Apostolate of the*

While the Latin version omits headings and thus the phrase altogether (*AAS*, LV 20 IV
1963, 257-304; cf. M.-D. Chenu, "Les signes des temps," in: *Nouvelle Revue théologique*, a.
97, t. 87, 1965, 29-40, here 30, n. 2), the Italian version brings the phrase, *"segni dei tempi"*,
four times as section headings, underlining the programmatic character of the phrase. The
numeration of the sections also differs. The heading referred to below precedes number 67 of
the Italian text.

[142]It was this last event that the English version, too, would identify in the heading of
paragraph 126 as a "sign of the times".

[143]Ibid.

[144]Cf. *Presbyterorum ordinis* (December 7, 1965) Nr. 9., which ties the "signs of the times" to
the ability of priests to "acknowledge with joy and foster with diligence the various humble
and exalted charisms of the laity;" this is "...so that together with them they will be able to
recognize the signs of the times."

[145]*Apostolicam actuositatem* (November 18, 1965) Nr. 14, where the text restricts its use of
the phrase to indications of positive developments: "... Among the signs of our times, the

Laity;[145] and the *Decree on Ecumenism*.[146] Both the positive meaning and the programmatic position attached to "the signs of the times" as a watchword would be affirmed again during the Council by Pope Paul VI in the encyclical, *Ecclesiam suam* (6 August 1964).[147]

Given its thematic, what came to be entitled *The Pastoral Constitution on the Church in the World of this Time*[148] might be expected to contain the most numerous and the most significant references to the task of reading "the signs of the times." "The schema, which Henri Fesquet described as the "star of the show" and which Father Yves Congar called "the promised land" of the Council, went through a dozen versions."[149] What in the end is its cautious use of the programmatic term will be telling for the dynamic of the Council as a whole. The discussion of "the signs of the times" in the preparatory commissions of *GS* showed where the fault-lines ran through the Council regarding the mode and degree with which it could assimilate aspects of the culture of its day. Like the deeper soul of the times, the Council would show itself to be "buffeted between hope and anxiety" (*GS* 4).

---

irresistibly increasing sense of the solidarity of all peoples is especially noteworthy. It is a function of the lay apostolate sedulously to promote this awareness and to transform it into a sincere and genuine love of brotherhood."

[146]*Unitatis redintegratio* (November 21, 1964) Nr. 4: "Today, in many parts of the world, under the inspiring grace of the Holy Spirit, many efforts are being made in prayer, word and action to attain that fullness of unity which Jesus Christ desires. The Sacred Council exhorts all the Catholic faithful to recognize the signs of the times and to take an active and intelligent part in the work of ecumenism."

[147]"50. … We cannot forget Pope John XXIII's word *aggiornamento* which We have adopted as expressing the aim and object of Our own pontificate. Besides ratifying it and confirming it as the guiding principle of the Ecumenical Council, We want to bring it to the notice of the whole Church. It should prove a stimulus to the Church to increase its ever growing vitality and its ability to take stock of itself and give careful consideration to the signs (*indicia*) of our times, always and everywhere 'proving all things and holding fast that which is good' (cf. *1 Thess* 5. 21) with the enthusiasm of youth."

[148]Presumably to avoid confusion of the present day with 17th and 18th century Europe, the *Constitutio pastoralis de ecclesia in mundo huius temporis* (7 December 1965) studiously avoided the term, "modern", restricting its use to four scattered passages: Nr. 8, "modernum intellectum practicum"; Nr. 20, "Atheismus modernus"; Nr. 54, "Condiciones vitae hominis moderni; and Nr. 69, Note 11, "praeter modernos probates auctores". The standard English translations of the document did not manage to save the point.

[149]Evangelista Vilanova, "V. The Intercession (1963-1964)", in: Giuseppe Alberigo and Joseph A. Komonchak (ed.), *The History of Vatican II. Vol. III: The Mature Council. Second Period and Intercession. September 1963-September 1964* (Maryknoll, Orbis, and Peeters, Leuven 2000) 347 sqq., esp. 401-415, here 402. Vilanova refers here in general to G. Turbanti, *La redazione della constituzione pastorale "Gaudium et spes"* (doctoral dissertation, University of Bologna 1996). This same view of *Gaudium et spes* as the key to the Council as a whole is

The preparatory commissions were in fact quick to notice the importance of the notion as it was used in the vernacular versions of *Pacem in terris*.[150] There had already been widespread agreement in 1963 to focus not only on questions *ad intra* of the self-understanding of the Church, but to ask as well about the situation and effective presence of today's Church *ad extra* in the cultural, political, economic, and scientific "worlds" in which it is set.[151] World and unity, roughly equivalent to horizons *ad extra* and *ad intra*, had constituted Pope John's two original *foci* for the parabolic thematic of the Council.[152] These were to be strengthened now. *Ad extra*, the ideal Christian involvement was to be sought in the wider cultural, political, and economic worlds of the day, especially those seeming to embrace the vocation of the human being to the *dominium terrae*. To this came the varied tasks of promoting ecclesial, religious, and international unity.

As the Council took stock of how to proceed after the death of Pope John (3 June 1963), the phrase "signs of the times" grew in symbolic significance.[153] But the phrase would also meet what one participant has called "a strange fate,"[154] and it shows the strange outcome of the Council as a whole. The debate about this phrase became the shorthand for a far-reaching issue of the Church's mission in the world of her time. The fundamentally new text of *GS* composed in January of 1964 as the third major draft was deeply marked by the influence of *Pacem in terris*. The culturally more optimistic

---

shared, although under a largely negative judgement, by Tracey Rowland,

[150]The following notes on the genesis of *GS* rely above all on the facts related soon after the Council by one of the participants in the commission that drafted *GS*, Charles Moeller, "Die Geschichte der Pastoralkonstitution," in *Lexikon für Theologie und Kirche* (2nd ed., Freiburg – Basel – Wien, Herder 1968) Vol. 14, 242-279. The text of this entire commentary on *GS* is available in English: Herbert Vorgrimler et al. (ed.), *Commentary on the Documents of Vatican II. Vol. V: Pastoral Constitution on the Church in the Modern World* (New York, Herder and Herder 1969). The following citations refer to the original publication; English translations of the *LThK* are from the author of the present essay.

[151]Moeller, op. cit., 247 AB.

[152]Moeller, op. cit., 242 AB.

[153]Cf. Evangelista Vilanova, op. cit. 405; and Moeller, op. cit., 255, n. 28. M.-D. Chenu, Les signes des temps, op. cit., 38, n. 7, wished to exclude atheism as an unnecessary ideology from the "signs of the times", which should be reserved in Pope John's sense for healthier forms of new, cultural desacralization, such as science, the domination of nature, and the common organization of economy and culture.

[154]Moeller, op. cit., 260 A: "Er hatte ein seltsames Schicksal."

[155]Vilanova, op. cit. 406.

party proposed reading the signs of the times in the sense of the ancient Roman axiom, *vox temporis, vox Dei*. A "signs of the times subcommittee" of the *GS* preparatory group was formed especially to respond to the worry that the attitude behind the previous drafts had been too "Eurocentric," more concerned with theological principles than with their practical application. The assumption appears to have been widespread that the readiness of industrialized nations to export technological developments also implied their readiness to overcome Eurocentrism. Concern for "development" was equated frequently with a genuine concern for the comprehensive flourishing of the non-industrialized parts of the world. From September of 1964 on, the signs of the times subcommittee met regularly during the Council's third session to learn from invited experts the political and economic challenges of different regions of the globe. The more optimistic passages of the final document, the ones seen today by Boeve and Rowland as hopelessly out of date, were the work of those who saw themselves as champions of reading "the signs of the times." The articles in the second half of the evolving text were reworked to reflect the style and method of *Pacem in terris*. "Every section ought to begin with a description of the signs of the times, move on to a description of the signs of God's presence, and finally take up those signs of the times that rouse concern, always in the spirit of availability to people and the optimism of John XXIII."[55] While in 1964 the working text still had proposed to let the document begin with the words, *Gaudium et luctus*, "The joy and the sorrows...", the words would be reordered in spring of the next year, in order to present a more obviously positive spin: *Gaudium et spes*.[56] After its promulgation, only a select few would be able to name the second set of three words in the Pastoral Constitution: "...*luctus et angor*". As the document, so, too, its reception began programmatically with an optimistic reading of contemporary culture.

But the momentum of the more optimistic potential for reading

---

[56]Moeller, op. cit., 271 A; and Xavier Quinzá Lleó, "Signa temporum. La semiótica de lo temporal en el proceso de redacción de la *Gaudium et spes*", in: *"Miscelanea Comillas. Revista de teología y Ciencias humanas"* (Vol. 48, 1990, 323-369), 330 sq.

[57]Making its own suggestions authored in Cracow by C. Wotyla, the Polish episcopate

the signs of the times, one that would be strengthened in the fourth major draft,[157] did not find universal acceptance at the Council. From January of 1964 on, criticism had been growing about the program of reading of the signs of the times so exclusively as indications of progress. By spring of 1964, these and similar worries had come to be shared by many of those responsible for revising first versions of the third draft.

> ...There was criticism of the excessively optimistic spirit of the schema, which ended up obscuring the reality of evil in the contemporary world, as well as the reality of suffering and injustices, and in particular the problems of poverty, concerning which the Church could not remain silent because the Church's credibility was at stake.[158]

The critique of these first attempts to integrate the program of reading the signs of the times was strengthened by the advice and comments of the Reformed theologian, Lukas Vischer. Representing the World Council of Churches, Vischer had been involved in the discussions around *GS* since the spring of the 1963.[159] He was one of the first to comment on the new draft of 1964.[160] By the summer of that year, Vischer had articulated verbally and in writing his criticisms

had a marked influence on the Ariccia text; cf. Moeller, op. cit., 261 B.

[158]Vilanova, op. cit., 410 sq. As even one of the early proponents of the signs of the times programmatic, B. Häring, put it: "Optimism toward the 'world' is false and dangerous if not balanced by another focus, that is, without the spirit of poverty and self-denial" (*De historia, stilo, methodo et spiritualitate schematis XVII:* Häring Archive, 1857-2446, as cited and translated by Vilanova, op. cit., 410).

[159]Moeller points both to the letter of 18 April 1963 by L. Vischer to Bishop Guano, distributed widely that spring within the commission, and to Vischer's participation in the conversations at Glion at the beginning of 1964 as influential for reformulating the first version of the Zurich text. Cf. also Moeller, op. cit., 260 A. This criticism was directed to the manner in which the phrase was employed in the early versions of the Zurich draft, "...because in the biblical text the phrase had a special, eschatological sense that in the context of this new paragraph had almost disappeared entirely. Its use here threatened first 'to read history in merely human fashion', in order then to push a 'prophetic exegesis' of the events".

[160]Cf. Moeller, op. cit., 258 AB: "From the perspective of Reformed theology, the draft had appeared 'too unproblematic', too lacking in eschatological depth and eschatological reserve over and against earthly kingdoms, especially with regards to expressions such as *vox temporis, vox Dei.* ... It puts forth a rather shallow belief in progress, such as one could just as easily find in non-Christian documents." Cf. Moeller, op. cit., 260 B, with reference to his own notes, to unpublished documents, and to Roberto Tucci, *Introduzione storico-dottrinale alla Constituzione pastorale "Gaudium et spes": La Chiesa e il mondo contemporaneo nel Vaticano II* (Turino 1966) 17-143, here 39, § 2

[161]Cf. Marcos McGrath Papers (MCG), University of Notre Dame Archives (UNDA),

of the way in which the phrase "signs of the times" was used in the newest drafts.

Lukas Vischer began his written comments on the "signs of the times" with the remark that, "...the concept of the *'signa temporum'* belongs to the most important concepts" of the draft.[161] The notion that "...time is a sign and a voice... introduces a thought that is decisive for understanding the whole text."[162] The problems that Vischer saw in the use of the phrase suggested to him deeper problems of the entire text. In hindsight, they appear also as problems that would characterize the initial phase of the reception of the Council as a whole.

> The text does not state in what fashion God speaks to us. It never names a criterion that would allow us to distinguish God's voice from any deceptive voices. It doesn't even mention that the phenomena of the times have a polyvalent character and thus are not easy to interpret. It settles for the simple statement of fact that God's voice *is* to be heard in our times.[163]
> ... The draft shows few traces of this epistemological problem. It speaks of God's voice as if it were easy to recognize. It opens the way for interpretations of history that are not grounded in the word of God. And the history of the Church is full of such interpretations...[164]

Vischer reviewed briefly but pointedly the use of the phrase, *"signa temporum"*, and closely related notions as found in the Gospels and other New Testament sources.[165] He underlined the inability of Jesus' contemporaries to see in him the sign of the final time of

---

Notre Dame, IN 46556, CMCG 1/03 Document : "Remarks on Signa Temporum by Lukas Vischer", here pg. 1. The typed, undated memorandum, entitled "signa temporum" and extending over five and a half pages, is hand-signed by Lukas Vischer on page 6 together with his Roman address and telephone number during the Council. In the following this text is cited as Vischer, Memorandum; the translations are by the author of this essay. On Vischer's various reactions to the Zurich text, especially in the letter of 29 May, 1964, cf. Moeller, op. cit., 251-260.

[162]Vischer, ibid. Vischer pointed out just how problematic this feature was, a point recalled shortly thereafter by Joseph Ratzinger, Erstes Kapitel des ersten Teiles. Kommentar, in: *Lexikon für Theologie und Kirche* (2nd ed., Freiburg – Basel – Wien, Herder 1968) Vol. 14, 313-354, here 313 sq. The hermeneutical problems involved in combining the ancient Roman description of time as the voice of God with an exegetically responsible interpretation of Jesus' eschatological warning about not recognizing him the sign of the decisive moment of history (*ta de semeia ton kairon*) were viewed as a further argument against adopting the phrase.

[163]Ibid.

[164]Ibid.

[165]Vischer, Memorandum, 3-5.

[166]Vischer, Memorandum, 5 sq.; cf. also on page 5: "The Church that recognizes the sign

history. Offering them rather the "sign of Jonah," Jesus refused an easy read of God's providence in the events of history. Vischer noted how completely he missed in the draft that eschatological meaning of the decisive sign referred to by the New Testament. He made clear that he was not suggesting that the phrase be removed, but rather improved upon and expanded.[166] Vischer concluded his comments by arguing that, precisely because the draft "…gives too innocent a picture of the world, it cannot mediate any real hope" to the world.[167] On the basis of these and similar objections in 1964, a compromise was sought. When no consensus could be reached on expanding and deepening the notion of the "*signa temporum*", "…the term was largely eliminated from the draft, surfacing in the final text (of *GS*) just this one time, in the first paragraph of article 4, where it is further qualified by the remark that these signs need to be read in the light of the Gospel."[168] The verb "*perscrutandi*" was restored to the draft, suggesting the need to sort through and test the signs of the times.

Despite this added reference in *GS* 4 to our need to read such signs "in light of the Gospel,"[169] the paragraph on signs that had been developed following Vischer's suggestions would be pared back to a single sentence. In a spirit more of compromise than of consensus, both the axiom of "*vox temporis, vox Dei*" *and* the characterization of this voice of the times as multivalent were removed from the evolving text. Where *Humanae salutis* had chosen the verb, "*dignoscamus*", to say that we should identify the signs of progress in the midst of gloom,[170] the final text returned to the verb suggested by the third draft to speak

---

given to her by God in Christ is indeed called to hope. But she also needs to acknowledge in penance how little of this hope she has lived from and how little she has projected it out. She will live in hope only if she lives at the same time in penance. She can proclaim hope for humankind only if she is willing to do penance. To have open eyes for the times leads her to the affirmation both of her hope and her penance."

[167]Vischer, Memorandum, 6.

[168]Moeller, op. cit., 260 A: "Der Terminus verschwand schliesslich völlig, um im endgültigen Text ein einziges Mal wieder aufzutauchen (Artikel 4, § 1) – wobei allerdings festgestellt wurde, daß diese Zeichen im Lichte des Evangeliums zu lesen seien."

[169]In addition, a more programmatic attempt was made to complement this sentence by explicit reference to both the progress and the failures of humanity; cf. Moeller, op. cit., 255 B.

[170]Moeller, op. cit., 294 B, speaks of an interim suggestion to coin the term "diagnoscendi" to suggest our need to analyze the signs of the times for their deeper problematic.

[171]The words cited are prefaced by the following text: "From day to day, in every group or

of the "*officium signa temporum perscrutandi*", suggesting our vocation "to sort through" the signs of the times and to distinguish their very mixed messages.

Despite the reservations, which led to a more critical sense of the phrase about the signs of the times, the more simply optimistic view of contemporary developments also held its ground. The final version of *GS* would retain much of this perspective, e.g., in article 55 of the final document: "...Thus we are witnesses of the birth of a new humanism, one in which man is defined first of all by this responsibility to his brothers and to history."[171] The *Relatio* of November 12th, 1965, with which Bishop M. McGrath would present the nearly final text to the Council, stressed that the sentence calling upon the Church to scrutinize the signs of the times intended to take these signs not in the apocalyptical context of exegetical commentaries on *Mt* 16, but in the more general and more positive sense suggested by Pope John.[172] Far from apocalyptic, the signs were to serve as means of building confidence in the world's own dynamic of continuous self-improvement and in the potential participation of the Church in this process.

The list of such textual witnesses to a widespread confidence in the developments of the times could easily be expanded; notably, it colored the presentation of *de facto* consciences as the voice of God.[173] But as this wave of optimism from 1964 and 1965 continued to shape the growing text of *GS*, so, too, did the frustrations and objections grow. The suggested addition of a note stating that the "world" stands "*sub signo Maligni*" was first inserted in early 1965 to amend the fourth (the Ariccia) draft, but, then, upon further reflection, the phrase was removed again as infelicitous.[174] To the contrary, the final text of article

---

nation, there is an increase in the number of men and women who are conscious that they themselves are the authors and the artisans of the culture of their community. Throughout the whole world there is a mounting increase in the sense of autonomy as well as of responsibility. This is of paramount importance for the spiritual and moral maturity of the human race. This becomes more clear if we consider the unification of the world and the duty which is imposed upon us, that we build a better world based upon truth and justice."

[172]Excerpted by Moeller from the Relatio to 5, 9, op. cit., 291 B.

[173]Cf. R. Schenk, Evangelisierung und Religionstoleranz: Thomas von Aquin und die Gewissenslehre des II. Vatikanums, in: *Forum Katholische Theologie* 8 (1992) pg. 1 - 17.

[174]Moeller 287 B; even in the late addition of an article (13) on sin, the reference "suadente Maligno" is historicized.

[175]For Vischer's final evaluations, cf. his *Überlegungen nach dem Vatikanischen Konzil* (Zur-

2 will characterize the world after the resurrection of Christ as *fracta potestate Maligni*. And yet, as this failed attempt at overreaction to the perceived self-confidence of the developing document suggests, the fourth draft of the text also failed to find the necessary *consensus*. In particular, the German bishops, who first had gathered among themselves at Fulda to review the Ariccia text, found this text of 1965 too "optimistic". Memories were still fresh of the social and political developments that had ended less than twenty years before, when many idealistic souls had followed their fatally flawed consciences. These criticisms notably of the German participants recalled many of Lukas Vischer's remarks on earlier versions.[175] They noted that the lack of an adequate sense of historicality leads to a loss of insight into the mystery of sin, together with the mysteries of the Cross and eschatology.

> They complained of the draft's *naturalism*, its *optimism*, and its *simplification* of too many problems. It had failed to recognize what could be gained by faith or what the task of the Church in her hierarchy and her faithful could possibly be. It had distinguished too little between *norms* and mere *counsels*. In the very way it posed its problems, it had taken too little notice of the ecumenical perspective.[176]

The ambivalence of the *de facto* developments of human history is at least indicated in the opening sentence of the final document, where not just the *gaudium et spes*, but also the *luctus et angor* of the times are said to be shared by the Church. Article two spells out this ambivalence, characterizing the world as a "theater of humanity's history, marked (*signatum*) by its energies, its tragedies and its triumphs".[177] The need for a discernment aided by the Spirit is referred to again in article 11: "The People of God believes that it is led by the Lord's Spirit, Who fills the earth. Motivated by this faith, it labors to decipher (*discernere*) authentic signs (*vera signa*) of God's presence and purpose in the happenings, needs and desires in which this People has a part along

---

ich, EVZ 1966) Polis. Evangelische Zeitbuchreihe 26, esp. 58-73.

[176]Moeller, op. cit., 271 B. The italicized emphases are his.

[177]*GS* 2: "...theatrum historiae generis humani, eiusque industria, cladibus ac victoriis signatum..." The introduction in the standard English translation of "heirs" to convey "sig-natum" veils the connection to the discussion of the *signa temporum*.

[178]Cf. J. Ratzinger, op. cit., 318 A sqq.; cf. already Nr. 9 of the final text's introduction:

with other men of our age." While interested here more in signs of God's presence and purpose in world affairs than in signs of what mitigates against them, the text acknowledges that it is no easy task to discern true from false signs of divine benevolence. Article 13 of the final text will add references to the historical presence of sin, a topic which had been neglected in the Ariccia draft. Finally, the profound ambivalence of human history is named directly, even bluntly: "*Ideo in seipso divisus est homo.*"[178] Naming many of the divided dynamics of today's world, the final version of article 4 would conclude much the same: all human beings of this age are "buffeted between hope and anxiety" (*inter spem et angorem agitati*).

The final text, when quoted in full, begins with a profoundly moving and memorable truth:

> The joys and the hopes, the griefs and the anxieties of the men of this age, especially those who are poor or in any way afflicted, these are the joys and hopes, the griefs and anxieties of the followers of Christ. Indeed, nothing genuinely human fails to raise an echo in their hearts. For theirs is a community composed of men.

The genesis of the document and its final text show that the Church not only shares in all of this, but that she also shares in being "buffeted between hope and anxiety." Charles Moeller recalled the opposed reactions to the fourth draft of *GS*:

> The future consensus would be one between two dominant tendencies, which had stood in opposition to each other from the very beginning of work on this Schema 13: on the one hand, the tendency to consider very concrete developments under the aspect of a certain fundamental optimism taken as a matter of principle; and, on the other hand, the tendency to stress a dialectical, even paradoxical aspect, marked by insisting upon the polyvalence of the universe in which the Church lives.[179]

"Since all these things are so, today's world shows itself at once powerful and weak, capable of the noblest deeds or the foulest; before it lies the path to freedom or to slavery, to progress or retreat, to brotherhood or hatred. Moreover, man is becoming aware that it is his responsibility to guide aright the forces which he has unleashed and which can enslave him or minister to him. That is why he is putting questions to himself."

[179]Moeller, op. cit., 272 B.

Parallel to this tension between a dominant optimism and a programmatic dialectic, the genesis of the text had been marked from early on by pendulum swings between theological and sociological emphases. The final draft would be characterized "by a juxtaposition rather than an integration of the two perspectives."[180] Right alongside passages that point to very mixed realities, there are passages in *GS* that are obvious children of their day. The hopes were widespread in the industrial nations of the early 1960's that common decency and normal good will, the unlimited plenitude of natural resources, and the technological ingenuity of the 20th century, taken together with the lack of viable alternatives, would together lead to a shared progress, prosperity, and peace for the whole world. Such great expectations were fostered by many in the Church, with the added hope that the Church would become an influential player in the likely forward march of progress. Not even the sky was the limit: "Technology is now transforming the face of the earth and is already trying to master outer space."[181] In 1965, those words could still be spoken without self-irony or derision.

III. The Reception of the Office of "Reading the Signs" in the Immediately Post-Conciliar Period

It would be exaggerated to claim that the diversity of opposed views that had enriched *GS* during the time of its composition was fully appreciated in the period of its initial reception by the most dominant theologies of the immediately post-Conciliar Church. From today's perspective, it appears rather that the post-Conciliar reception of the document developed in two waves, beginning with a period of roughly two decades in which the more optimistic reading dominated its interpretation, before a further two decades that, without dismissing the vocation of the Church to be present to the political and cultural world of its time, would add to the understanding of this call that more "...dialectical, even paradoxical aspect, marked by insisting upon the polyvalence of the universe in which the Church lives."[182]

The initial wave of reception was dominated by a decidedly

---

[180]Evangelista Vilanova, op. cit., 403.

[181]Art. 5, a testimony throughout of the hopes placed in the technology of the day.

[182]Moeller, op. cit., 272 B.

non-apocalyptic reading the *signa temporum*, by the more singularly optimistic understanding of the axiom, *vox temporis, vox Dei*, and by what Moeller had called "the tendency to consider very concrete developments under the aspect of a certain fundamental optimism taken as a matter of principle". The most widespread interpretation of *GS* stressed more obviously the Church's share in "the joys and the hopes" of the world than it did her share in "the griefs and the anxieties of the men of this age". However, those very "griefs and anxieties", which had already dominated so much of the 20th century, were making themselves felt again in its final decades, and theologians especially from the 1980s on would come to hear them more clearly again. Only then, as a second wave of reception intersected the first, would it become apparent how deeply the Church shares in the ambivalence of the age, "buffeted between hope and anxiety."

The ascendancy in the ecclesial and the secular cultures of the early 1960's of this "tendency to consider very concrete developments under the aspect of a certain fundamental optimism taken as a matter of principle" makes understandable in large part the attraction and dominance of the remarkable theological system developed by Karl Rahner († 1984). From 1965–1985, K. Rahner's system was arguably the *sententia communis* among the majority of Roman Catholic theologians across Europe and the United States and often well beyond. The core of the central column (the grace-nature theses) supporting the Rahnerian system consisted in the interconnected assertions woven into the much-discussed theory of the "supernatural existential": the theory of an experientially accessible, dynamic transcendence that God has always and everywhere freely infused into human nature. It was around this *Leitmotiv* that Rahner grouped the theses most characteristic of his system: As what marks human existence always and most centrally, the supernatural existential is the decisive beginning of God's giving his very self to humanity, becoming himself fully in this other than himself (theology of the Triune God},[183] the trajectory

---

[183]For the implications of this axiom of the changing God for the question of human suffering cf. R. Schenk, Ist die Rede vom leidenden Gott theologisch zu vermeiden? Reflexionen über den Streit von K. Rahner und H.U. von Balthasar, in: Friedrich Hermanni and Peter Koslowski (ed.), *Der leidende Gott. Eine philosophische und theologische Kritik* (Wilhelm Fink, Munich 2001) 225-239.

of an irreversible, infinite, if asymptotic, approximation to the *unio hypostatica* (Christology), where God, too, is known by each human being not merely as the other but also somehow as itself: a *de facto*-natural subjectivity, whose intrinsic quasi-formal cause is always and in each case unfolding as God himself. In the view of the Rahnerian system, this dynamic was already at work in the pre-human phases of evolution. Understandable only as frozen spirit, matter had always been tending to heat up and thaw into spirit — not just finite, but absolute Spirit.[184] Characteristic of this particular theological reading of evolution is the lack of any serious development of the principle of entropy: "becoming" is, of its essence, "becoming more".[185] Without thematizing *creatio ex nihilo*, the evolutionary vision that Rahner had claimed was *the* alternative to mythology was portrayed here as the fundamental truth of all present experience, the "experience" of the irreversible and "victorious" (*siegreich*) march from matter to supernaturally elevated spirit, to grace, glory, and a Godhead shared with infinitely diminishing mediation or alterity: a story which by today's standards sounds anything but myth-free.

To return to the terms of Moeller's description of the conflicting parties to *GS*, Rahner's system was marked both by a "dialectical aspect" *and* by "a certain fundamental optimism taken as a matter of principle". The programmatic dialectic was structured largely in terms of the tension between the transcendental and the categorical dimensions of human subjectivity, and between what P. Eicher has called the theological mediation of philosophy on the one hand and the reabsorption of theology into common thought on the other.[186] Rahner can even speak of a dialectic between transcendental "optimism" and categorical "pessimism", but the latter is rendered harmless and merely hypothetical by the more "fundamental optimism taken as a matter of principle", ensuring salvation through historical events, not despite them.[187] The transcendental or the categorical side

---

[184]Among the many times Rahner returns to this theme cf. especially K. Rahner, Die Hominsation as theologisches Problem, in: id. and Paul Overhage, *Das Problem der Hominisation* (QD 12/13) Freiburg et al., Herder 1961, 13-90, especially 44-55.

[185]Op. cit., 55-78.

[186]Peter Eicher, *Offenbarung. Prinzip neuzeitlicher Theologie* (Munich, Kösel 1977) 356-368.

of the dialectic, which comes to be stressed here, will vary from issue to issue, but the decision about which side would be stressed in any given context is made consistently on the basis of what better served "fundamental optimism taken as a matter of principle". The optimistic and intrinsic dynamic of the evolutionary march through time first makes itself felt from within in answer to the three key questions about human identity: (1) What can I know? (2) What should I do? (3) What may I hope for?[188] If Rahner's theology is based on an anthropocentric turn, the answers to these three interrelated questions, taken together, "define" what the human being is.

(1) *What can I know?*

Human knowledge is made possible by a transcendental affirmation of God more fundamental, universal and infallible than any known atheistic denial, which *de facto* seems to affirm God even as it denies him. Given the seeming unlikelihood of final loss,[189] all human beings likely are and have been from the beginning of humankind either explicitly Christian or at least anonymously Christian; while hypothetically it could have been otherwise, *de facto*, the *ecclesia ab Abel* is likely coterminous with the entire human race, not just with certain especially graced individuals throughout its history. What is more, human beings experience this supernatural elevation as part of their *de facto* nature and dynamic, not as a gift that they had ever been lacking. Demonstrating the type of "resigned optimism" typical of this arm of the sapiential tradition in theology, the stress here on the primacy and universality of transcendental knowledge also insisted dialectically upon the inadequacy in principle of concrete, categorical knowledge, including the *fides quae* affirmed in biblical, creedal or doctrinal formulations of Christian belief. This relativizing dimension of negative theology could easily be borne, however, given the transcendental dynamic and a closely related confidence that the

[187]Cf. K. Rahner, *Grundkurs des Glaubens* (Sämtliche Werke 26) Zürich et al./ Freiburg, Benziger/Herder 1999) 109 sq.
[188]For a more extensive consideration of the anthropology of the Rahnerian system, cf. R. Schenk, *Die Gnade,* op. cit.

scriptural and dogmatic statements about the incarnation of Christ and about the beatific vision came closest to the best possible categorical grasp of the universal and to the transcendental self-sharing of God. The strongly Catholic identity that had been developed in the decades prior to the Council was still able to bear the weight of those elements of a *theologia negativa* demanded by the dialectic of the Rahnerian system as the price of its identification with an anonymously Christian world. The system was built on the conviction that the intrinsic dynamic of a world always already justified and transformed would continue to carry humankind onward and upward, even while relativizing the concrete senses of the *fides quae,* which previously had been thought to sustain the Christian faith. Whether non-Christians came to an acceptance of the Christian creeds, or whether divided Christians agreed upon the proper formulation of the same, or finally whether Catholics developed and maintained a firm grasp of the content of their faith were matters neither of complete indifference nor of special urgency. Designed more to address the problem of Western atheism than that of non-Christian religions, the primacy of transcendental experience over categorical knowledge in the theory of anonymous Christianity served the cause of a greater *Gelassenheit* toward the modern world.

(2) *What should I do?*

Founded in that dynamic to perfection which God freely made an intrinsic and self-sustaining feature of human existence from the start, salvation-from-without and self-salvation have according to the Rahnerian system always formed a strict unity with one another.[190] Ever enabled to do so by God, human beings make their own perfection by acts of freedom, if at all.[191] With reference to the unbinding character of the Fifth Lateran Synod, Rahner repeatedly calls into doubt the possibility of afterlife for those who die before the use of reason and moral freedom.[192] The primacy here of free, categorical

---

[189]Cf. R. Schenk, The Epoché of Factical Damnation? On the Costs of Bracketing Out the Likelihood of Final Loss, in: *Logos,* Vol.1, No. 3, St. Paul (Minnesota) 1997, 122 - 154.

[190]Cf. Karl Rahner, Das christliche Verständnis der Erlösung, in: id. *Schriften zur Theologie* XV (Einsiedeln, et al., Benziger 1983) 236-250, especially 237 and 244.

[191]E.g. op. cit., 238: "Wenn man sagen würde, der Mensch ist derjenige, der seine absolute Transzendenz in Glaube, Hoffnung, und Liebe als Tat seiner Freiheit vollzieht und dadurch sich selber erlöst, dann hat man noch nichts Unchristliches gesagt."

acts over transcendental grace stands in the service of the greater affirmation of our own free activity in the world.[193] Even where Rahner — without much show of commitment — leaves open the possibility of some unknown, postmortal exercise of freedom, on the basis of which those who died before the use of reason might attain eternal life,[194] the point is the same: to portray eternal life as the merit and fruit of our historical freedom. Likewise, in speaking about the unity between love of neighbor and love of God, the categorical act becomes the preferable mode of approaching the transcendent and the real symbol effective of it. Freed by the widespread caricature of Thomistic notions of grace as neoscholastic "*Stockwerktheorie*" from any need to search for a grace beyond *de facto* human nature, for any goal unmerited by historical deeds, or for a God outside of evolutionary self-progression, what begins as an improbable transcendentalism ends with a novel horizontalism, quite at peace with a world that has always already answered in principle the

---

[192]Cf. Karl Rahner, Fegfeuer, first in Johannes Brantschen and Pietro Selvatico (ed.), *Unterwegs zur Einheit: Festschrift für Heinrich Stirnimann* (Fribourg, Universitätsverlag; and Freiburg, Herder 1980), here from *Schriften zur Theologie* XIV (Einsiedeln, et al., Benziger 1980) 435-449, here 445 sq.: "Sind die eschatologischen Aussagen des Christentums wirklich und glaubensmäßig verpflichtend auf schlechthin alle Menschen zu beziehen, die biologisch und in geistiger Potentialität Menschen waren, oder sind diese Aussagen Glaubensaussagen nur über solche Menschen, die in freier Entscheidung sich selbst in Endgültigkeit hinein vollzogen haben? Die traditionelle Lehre nimmt den ersten Teil dieser Alternative als selbstverständlich richtig an, betrachtet z.B. die Lehre des V. Laterankonzils von der Unsterblichkeit der Seele als von jedweder Seele geltend, die einmal existiert hat, gleichgültig in welcher sonstigen Fassung die eine dem Tod gewesen sein mag. Ist das aber sicher richtig? ..."; the 1981 essay, id., Das christliche Verständnis der Erlösung, op. cit., 236 sq., dealing with "the complicated and difficult reflexions" on the question of the salvation of those who die before the age of reason: "...Über diese Frage, meine ich, wissen wir nichts zu sagen,... zumal es nach meiner unmaßgeblichen Meinung doch eine offene Frage sein darf, ob wirklich, wie man traditionell denkt, der Glaubenssatz des 5. Lateranischen Konzils über die Unsterblichkeit der Seele notwendig auch als für die geistigen Personen gültig zu denken ist, die nie durch eine Freiheitsgeschichte hindurchgegangen sind"; and id., Das Sterben vom Tod gesehen, in: Johannes Feiner et al. (ed.), *Mysterium salutis. Grundriss heilsgeschichtlicher Dogmatik*, Vol. V (Einsiedeln, et al., Benziger 1976) 466-493, here 475: "Man wird aber trotz der Erklärung des 5. Laterankonzils (DS 1440, vgl. 2766, 3771, 3998) und des durchschnittlichen Glaubensverständnisses sagen dürfen, daß wir letztlich nicht wissen, ob und wie diese Lehre von einer je einmaligen und durch den Tod in Endgültigkeit übergehenden Freiheitsgeschichte anzuwenden sei auf jene, die vor dem Augenblick sterben, in dem man ihnen nach einer durchschnittlichen Empirie eine aktuelle Freiheitsentscheidung im radikalen Sinn zuzubilligen geneigt ist und ob tatsächlich jeder Mensch, der in einem bürgerlichen Sinne 'mündig' ist, zu der Freiheitsentscheidung kommt, von der diese kirchenamtliche Lehre sagt, daß sie sich durch den Tod in Endgültigkeit aufhebt."

[193]That is especially clear in the text of the contribution to the Stirnimann Fesrtschrift as it continues at the place cited.

[194]Fegfeuer, op. cit., 446 sq.

most serious challenges that the faith might present it. The perceived danger of a spiritualism that would withdraw from commitment to the world was replaced by the largely repressed danger of a loss of spiritual resources by which to help that world.

But if perfection is restricted here to those human beings who can construct it in freedom, this, dialectically, is in all likelihood the achievement of each and every person who happens to reach the age of reason and freedom. Final loss, though a "real possibility", appears highly unlikely, given what is now the primacy of the transcendental affirmation of one's future perfection hidden beneath every categorical denial.[195] Not conversion from self, but the acceptance of self is the basis for perfection, and it is hard to imagine that it ever fails; for to do so, it would need to call upon the very self-affirmative, transcendental dynamic that leads to fulfillment. The unity of the love of the transcendent God with the categorical love of neighbor no longer needs to liberate neighbor and fellow-creatures by first letting God be God; it is no longer by their very tension that these two commandments are one.[196] The primacy accorded here both to the transcendental dynamic of universal justification as the mark of every human existence and to the divine formal object behind, not just some, but likely every categorical deed has already eliminated the need to first overcome idolatry as the "form, goal, and source" of every sin, before ever meriting eternal life. Universal justification, once it has become a structural existential, removes from the conscience the danger and the possibility of perplexity.[197] Again, the choice of emphasis between transcendental and categorical structures in the questions of freedom always serves "a certain fundamental optimism taken as a matter of principle".

---

[195]Cf. R. Schenk, The Epoché of Final Damnation? On the Costs of Bracketing Out the Likelihood of Final Loss, in: *Logos* (Fall 1997) 122-154.

[196]Cf. e.g. Rahner's mid-1965 reflection, Ueber die Einheit von Naechsten- und Gottesliebe, in: K. Rahner, *Schriften zur Theologie* VI (2nd edition, Zuerich, Benziger et al., 1968) 277-298.

[197]Cf. R. Schenk, *Perplexus supposito quodam*. Notizen zu einem vergessenen Schluesselbegriff thomanischer Gewissenslehre, in: *Recherches de Théologie Ancienne et Médiévale* LVII (Loewen 1990) pg. 62 - 95.

(3) *What may I hope for?*

The intrinsic dynamic of our God-enabled self-perfection showed itself in K. Rahner's system above all in the life-long process of dying. Even in his earliest attempts at a theology of death, Rahner had stressed the unity of one actively salvific dynamic linking Christ's death and the death of every human, exemplified in the death of the martyr.[198] In each of these cases, death can become self-transcending and redemptive by the affirmation of hope in the midst of darkness. The negativity of death is reduced to what is *not* known about death, rather than to a destructiveness needing to be countered as such, to those secondary aspects of death that we necessarily endure and cannot make our own: the natural as opposed to the personal face of death. But, as personalized, death is perfective of the self.[199] This aspect of Rahner's interpretation of death would develop notably but consistently as Rahner's system matured. Far from being opposed to life, death is viewed as the paradigmatic act of freedom, the "basic pattern of freedom", with "the comprehensive structures of all the other acts of life."[200] Rahner's theology of death becomes increasingly positive in its emphasis, shifting from the early theory of personalized death's gaining a closer relationship to the entire cosmos to a later theory of resurrection-in-death, or better, death-as-resurrection,[201] as self-perfecting act (*"Selbstvollendung"*), maturation (*"Reife"*), fruition (*"Frucht"*, *"Zeitigung"*) and the harvest of time (*"Ernte"*).[202] Resurrection is not expected chiefly as a grace from without, creating life anew against the forces of death, but rather as the immediate product of personalized dying and from the beginning the focal point of its intrinsic dynamic. In language reminiscent of Plato's, death is

---

[198]Cf. K. Rahner, *Zur Theologie des Todes. Mit einem Exkurs ueber das Martyrium* (QD 2) Freiburg, Herder, et al. 1958

[199]Cf. R. Schenk, Tod und Theodizee. Ansaetze zu einer Theologie der Trauer bei Thomas von Aquin, *Forum Katholische Theologie*, 10 (1994), 161 - 178.

[200]Kl. Baake, *Praxis und Heil. Versuch eines konstruktiven Dialogs zwischen der lateinameri-kanischen Theologie der Befreiung und der Theologie Karl Rahners* (BthSt 6) Wuerzburg, Echter 1990, 227, note 97.

[201]On the internal development of Rahner's theology of death cf. R. Schenk, *Die Gnade,* op. cit., 458-477.

[202]K. Rahner, *Grundkurs des Glaubens. Einführung in den Begriff des Christentums* (Freiburg et al. 1976) 267 f., 419 ff.

described as liberation from the prison of time (*"Befreiung aus dem Kerker der Zeit"*).[203] Emphatically non-apocalyptic in its eschatology of organically progressive self-development, this spiritual reading of the supposedly "good death" was offered by the Rahnerian system as the key to understanding death in the world of our time. The transcendental dynamic within categorical deeds was intended here presumably as a help against despair during the century of the holocaust. While helping us to relativize the categorical evil that is suffered, it sought to provide absolute efficacy to the categorical good that is done. In both cases, the choices made within the options of the system serve "a certain fundamental optimism taken as a matter of principle".

IV. The Second Wave of "Reading the Signs" in the Later Post-Conciliar Period

Rahner's system employed loosely Hegelian strategies for restoring the confidence of modern subjectivity after the rise of doubts articulated by Kant's (and now Heidegger's) dialectic.[204] Not unlike the collapse of Hegelian optimism in the disappointments surrounding the revolutions of 1848, the end to the Rahnerian era of Post-Conciliar theology was ushered in less by the rebuttal of select tenets of the system than by a general realization that such self-immunization against the sufferings of the world was ill-advised and even untimely. Certainly from the mid-1980s on, there was an attempt in each of the key areas of theological anthropology to hear more acutely the *luctus et angor* of the world of this time. These attempts would not always leave theology a "safer" or more predictable space than it had been during the Rahnerian era. But the three key anthropological themes, discussed here in reverse order, display well the shift to a post-Rahnerian era.

---

[203]K. Rahner, *Schriften zur Theologie* VII 165.

[204]Regrettably for the reception of Rahner's own development, the second edition of *Hoerer des Wortes* expurgated the helpful references to Kant and Heidegger that had been contained in Rahner's own edition and fortunately have recently been made available again by A. Raffelt in K. Rahner, *Saemtliche Werke*, Band 4 (Duesseldorf, Benziger / Freiburg , Herder 1997); cf. also now the re-translation of the 1940 publication by K. Rahner, Einfuehrung in den Begriff der Existentialphilosophie bei Heidegger (*Saemtliche Werke*, Band 2, Duesseldorf, Benziger / Freiburg , Herder 1997) 317-346.

Ad 3: *What may I hope for? The Contribution of Political Theology*

The growing dissatisfaction with the approach of transcendental theology towards death, suffering, and the questions of
theodicy strengthened even among many of K. Rahner's most loyal
disciples the call for an alternative, political theology. In his influential
reflections on *Glaube in Geschichte und Gesellschaft*,[205] J.B. Metz had
compared already in 1977 the notion of "transcendental Christianity"
to the tale of the hare and the tortoise: to a transcendentality of *a
priori* triumphant structures of existence, all historical events come to
look pretty much alike, whether they are the cause of categorical joys
or of sorrows, of concrete hopes or of fears.[206] For the self-identity of
absolute transcendental reason, historical events are, all alike, signs of
the inevitable victory of that self-perfective dynamic of spirit which
is always already the positive condition of any negative events. The
increasing sense of the need in the course of the 1980s for a more
critical theology of political and cultural engagement was one of the
factors ushering in a post-Rahnerian era.

This sense of the need to take the signs against hope more
seriously was underlined by the development of political theology in
Latin America and by its reception by the wider church. The general
conferences of the Latin American episcopate held at Medellín (1968),
Puebla (1979), and Santo Domingo (1992) showed in their developing
use of the phrase, "signs of the times," the very shift in the reception
of *GS* that they would help to effect. Dedicated to promoting "The
Church in the Present-Day Transformation of Latin America in the
Light of the Council", the conference at Medellín published several
official position papers, including an address by the then bishop of

---

[205]Mainz, Matthias-Gruenewald 1977, especially 144 sq. The observation, "The transcendental magic circle is complete, and it is, like the two tortoises, invincible", is followed by an
apology for K. Rahner's own theological – and non-tautological – spirituality, 195 sqq.

[206]The consequences of this form of political theology for ending the dominance of
Rahnerian theology were explicated i.a. by Gerd Neuhaus, *Transzendentale Erfahrung als
Geschichtsverlust?* (Düsseldorf, Patmos 1982). The neglect of the German discussion of Metz'
developing criticism of transcendental theology is telling in much of the American literature,
notably James Matthew Ashley, *Interruptions. Mysticism, Politics, and Theology in the Work of
Johann Baptist Metz* (Notre Dame, University Press 1998).

Santiago de Veraguas, Panama, Marcos McGrath, on "The Signs of
the Times in Latin America Today". Marcos, who would be named
archbishop of Panama City the following year, recalled the work he
had witnessed during the composition of *GS*. The former head of the
subcommision on the "Signs of the Times" urged the conference
to adopt the decidedly non-eschatological understanding of "*signa
temporum*" suggested by *Pacem in terries*.[207] McGrath called attention
to three "great signs of the times" in Latin America: the rapid pace of
change in Church and society;[208] the greater stress on the temporal
and the personal in the context of secularization;[209] and the worldly
focus ("*el enfoque mundial*") of recent magisterial teaching.[210]

But other voices were heard as well. An alternative position
paper was presented by, the Secretary General of the Conference and
the Latin American Episcopal Counsel at the time, Eduardo Francisco
Pironio. Especially in the third part of his paper, "*Interpretación
Cristiana de los Signos de los Tiempos hoy en América Latina*,"[211] the
former *peritus* of the Council would anticipate several aspects of the
notion of *communio*,[212] though still without the clear tie to the notion
of solidarity which some thirty years later the World Synod of Bishops
would insist upon at the Special Assembly for America in 1997, the
year prior to Cardinal Pironio's death. With his position paper on *La
Evangelización en América Latina*,[213] the bishop of Chiapas, Samuel
Ruiz, in supporting the call for the Church to engage the political
and cultural issues of the day, called the neglect of efforts to support
the indigenous cultures of Latin America an "*anti-signo*".[214] The final
documents of Medellín reflect much of this initial discussion. On the
one hand, the signs of the times, "...expressed above all in the social

[207]"Los signos de los tiempos en América Latina hoy", in: Segunda Conferencia General
del Episcopada Latinoamericano (ed.), *La Iglesia en la actual transformación de América Latina
a la luz del Concilio Vaticano II. I. Ponencias* (Bogotá, CELAM 1968/Buenos Aires, Bonum
1969) 73-100, here 75.
[208]Op. cit., 78-86.
[209]Op. cit., 86-93.
[210]Op. cit., 93-96.
[211]Op. cit, 101-122.
[212]Op. cit., 117-121.
[213]145-172
[214]Op. cit., 170 sq. The references to the term at 10, 13, and 13, 26, are neutral.

order, constitute a 'theological situation' and a mandate from God."²¹⁵ On the other hand, the globalizing effects of visual media on Latin America, seen as at best a very mixed development, are also included among the signs of the times.²¹⁶

A good ten years after Medellín, the conference at Puebla would reflect the maturing of this combination of commitment to engage the political and cultural realities and an awareness of the limitations of such engagement, reflected in the more critical sense of the "*signa temporum*". Archbishop McGrath summarized this theological development as follows:

> Puebla avoids a superficial reading of the conciliar dynamic that would pretend to such an "objective" presentation of the 'signs of the times' as to preclude even the vision or interpretation of faith. On the other hand, it also carefully avoids the further analyses, economic, social, or political, that would, by the mediation of particular interpretations, lead to options beyond the area that is the proper and original contribution of the Gospel and the Church.²¹⁷

The signs of the times underlined by the Puebla document point to still unrealized hopes for a just society, "a crying need of our people."²¹⁸ They reveal a mixed reality that calls at times for affirmation, especially where there is a correspondence to the "evangelical values of communion and participation," but calling at other times for denunciation of *de facto* developments.²¹⁹ The Church is no longer simply to follow the signs of the times. "The problems are manifestations of the signs of the times, pointing toward the future where culture is now heading. The Church must be able to consolidate the values and overthrow the idols that are feeding this historical process."²²⁰ This

---

²¹⁵7, 13; cited here from Second General Conference of Latin American Bishops (ed.), The Church in the Present-day Transformation of Latin America in the Light of the Council. II. Conclusions (2ⁿᵈ ed., USCC, Washington, D.C. 1968), 113.

²¹⁶8, 12 (ed. cit., 124).

²¹⁷M. McGrath, The Puebla Final Document: Introduction and Commentary, in: John Eagleson and Philip Scharper (ed.), *Puebla and Beyond* (Maryknoll, Orbis 1979): 87-110, here 89.

²¹⁸Nr. 12 (ed. cit., 125 sq.).

²¹⁹Nr. 15 (ed. cit., 126); for the stress on "communion" as the basis or reading the signs, cf. also Nr. 653 (ed. cit., 214).

²²⁰Nr. 420 (ed. cit., 181).

critical potential is to be developed by interpreting the signs in the context of Catholic social tradition, "...the light of the Gospel, and the Church's Magisterium."[221] Signs of more authentic developments, such as "the human advancement of the woman" or the ecumenical movement outside the Catholic community, can also call the Catholic Church to reflect more clearly on her own biblical heritage.[222]

Puebla had demonstrated an increasing conviction about the need and the ability of the Church to engage political and cultural developments, coupled with an increasingly critical sense that no set of cultural developments and no single method for their analysis would be sufficient for the Church to assimilate without also drawing on her own unique resources. This dynamic widened[223] and continued into the 1992 meeting at Santo Domingo. There the final document devotes the major part of its Chapter II to "2.2 The New Signs of the Times in the Area of the Promotion of the Human Being." Nine signs are singled out here for detailed consideration, but none is presented as an area of simple progress. From merely partial progress on human rights issues, from the tensions between economic development and environmental concerns, and from a relative preference for democratization to uneven trends in economy, labor, and migration, the temporal signs are presented as very mixed developments calling the Church to differentiated reactions. The chapter preceding this one begins its reflections on "The New Evangelization" by recalling the vocation of the Church to holiness (1.1).

---

[221]Nr. 473 (ed. cit., 189).

[222]Nr. 847 (ed. cit., 234); and Nr. 1100-1127, especially 1115 (ed. cit., 259-262): the ecumenical movement, in particular, is seen as needing to respond to a very mixed situation.

[223]Juan Luis Segundo's 1988 essay, "Revelación, fe, signos de los tiempos", would be included in the 1990 compendium edited by J. Sobrino and, posthumously, I. Ellacuria, *Mysterium Liberationis. Conceptos Fudamentales de la Teología de la Liberación* (Madrid, Trotta 1990), cited below in the English translation (Maryknoll, Orbis, and Victoria, Australia, Collins Dove 1993, 328-349). The essay would also lend its title to a collection of Segundo's essays in 1992. Segundo uses the phrase *"signa temporum"* in both of its received senses. At times seeming to assume only good aspirations in humanity, such temporal indications are said to aid us in the "...interpretation and discernment of all human aspirations, which, like the aspiration for liberation, arise in history as signs of the times" op. cit. 346, with reference to the 1984 CDF document on liberation theology. But Segundo also knows a more ambivalent and problem-conscious sense of reading the temporal signs: "Finally, a theology like liberation theology ... cannot, in its work of 'understanding' that faith, prescind from the signs that the history of that practice and its crisis throw up to it as so many interrogations: 'the signs of the times', as Jesus calls them in Matthew's Gospel (16:3)" (328 sq.). The major

Ad 2: *What should I do? The Contribution of Ecumenical Theology*

Besides this fundamental shift of paradigm in answering the question, "What may I hope for?" there was remarkable movement in the last two decades of the 20th century on the second anthropological question, as well. The Rahnerian system that had formulated so well the side of the Council which had promoted a "certain fundamental optimism taken as a matter of principle" had also viewed the ecumenical discussion in this light, suggesting a largely inclusivist model of convergent dialogue aided by a general caution about the adequacy of creedal and doctrinal formulations in either Christian community. Following the 1980 visit of Pope John Paul II to Germany, the "*Ökumenische Arbeitsgruppe*" that had been founded in 1946 was asked to take up anew the questions raised during that visit as to the present relationship between the Roman Catholic and the Lutheran communities. By 1990, this discussion of Catholic-Lutheran agreement on justification summed up what was seen as the already existing state of widespread agreement on seven points[224] that, if accurate, show how distant Catholic theology had grown during the 1980's from the supernatural existential of the two preceding decades. The Catholic partners to the discussion, including several of the most acknowledged students of K. Rahner, argued that there was a Catholic consensus on the following issues:

1.   Regarding the depravity of human nature,[225] it is commonly accepted by Roman Catholics that justification is "nothing self-understood," but needs to be given by grace to a human nature not always already justified *de facto*.

2. Regarding concupiscence,[226] it is the common view of Roman Catholics theologians of our day that the mystery of sin remains so strong, even after justification, that the effective dynamic of human deeds toward God cannot be assumed.

3. and 4. On the complete passivity of human beings[227] and on the

---

question investigated in Segundo's essay regards the transformation of ambivalent events or even the lack of awaited events into signs by faith. The providential meaning of history is anything but evident.

[224]Karl Lehmann and Wolfhart Pannenberg (ed.), *The condemnations of the Reformation era: do they still divide?* (Minneapolis: Fortress Press 1990).

[225]Op. cit., 1-31, 36-43.

[226]Op. cit., 30-31, 44-46.

[227]Op. cit., 32-33, 46-47.

issue of merit,[228] it is held by the majority of today's Roman Catholic theologians that salvation cannot be expected as the maturation of the intrinsic dynamic of human actions.

5. Concerning the question of justifying grace as merely a divine or also a human reality,[229] Catholic theology is concerned today not only with seeing grace as uncreated, i.e., God's own reality, but as insisting that this reality remain "extrinsic" enough to the human recipients to be viewed by them consistently as a gift tied to the revelatory word of the Other (*"personal und worthaft"*).

6. Regarding the controversies around the grace of justification *sola fide*[230] the *"Ökumenische Arbeitsgruppe"* saw only a partial consensus, with neither side wanting the grace of justification and faith to follow automatically from the universal renewal of human being.

7. On the controversies around the certainty of salvation that Cajetan had first underscored as divisive,[231] the Catholic side agrees that the kind of certainty that would be based on the dynamic of human actions would be self-delusional.

Not all of the points said here to constitute the *sententia communis* of Roman Catholic theologians around 1990 contradict in equal measure the letter of the system built up around the supernatural existential. Nor does the irenic context of predominantly convergent ecumenism invite us to suspect that either side had expressed all that is important to it; the interconfessional consensus is overstated, the intraconfessional *dissensus* is understated (notably that within 16th century Lutheranism and 17th century Catholicism); and both excesses, regarding agreements and differences, would prove unkind to the dialogue, as it developed towards the Common Declaration and beyond. But the reflections do indicate the very different existential stance that had developed in Roman Catholic circles during the 1980s: one with a keener sense of human impotence, of the limits of both secular and theological wisdom, and of the abidingly acute need for novel divine intervention. It was a changed spirit, now, one more likely to appreciate the

---

[228]Op. cit., 35-36, 66-69. On the question itself, cf. now Joseph Wawrykow, *God's grace and human action : 'Merit' in the theology of Thomas Aquinas* (Notre Dame, University Press 1995).
[229]Op. cit., 33, 47-49.
[230]Op. cit., 33-34, 49-53.
[231]Op. cit., 34-35, 53-56.

objections that Lukas Vischer had raised twenty-five years earlier about answering the key anthropological question, "What should I do?" by simply pointing to the signs of assumed progress visible in the culture of the day. The shift in perspective puts into sharper relief the Counter-Reformational headwaters of the optimism gushing into Roman Catholic circles of the 1960s. For all of that, the ecumenical texts admittedly fail to make clear where a genuinely Roman Catholic theology would need to "patiently struggle" for its own legitimate sense of graced participation in God's providence, to borrow a phrase from two leading Catholic participants in these discussions.[232] There is undoubtedly a necessity here, too, for *"geduldiges Streiten,"* but the perspectives on human freedom set forth 25 years after the Council show that the genuinely Catholic sense of the *grandeur* and *misère* of human initiatives had begun to allow itself to be more "buffeted between hope and anxiety" than at any time since the end of the Council. The two waves of the Council's reception had finally met.

Ad 1: What can I know? The Contribution of the Theology of Religions
    Perhaps the most apparent symptom of the transition into a post-Rahnerian era of Catholic theology was the demise of the universal, anonymous Christian and of the radical inclusivism of the theology of religions associated with it. The popularity of the theory so closely associated with the supernatural existential fell in the late 1980's with the same speed with which it had risen in the 1960s and 70s.[233] Had it once exemplified Catholic willingness to acknowledge other religions (and even, prior to them, humanistic atheism) as high goods, it came to be seen widely as an obstacle to such acknowledgement. As

---

[232]Theodor Schneider and Dorothea Sattler, Hermeneutische Erwaegungen zur Allgemeinen Sakramentenlehre, in: W. Pannenberg, *Lehrverurteilungen – kirchentrennend? III. Materialien zur Lehre von den Sakramenten und vom kirchlichen Amt* (Freiburg, Herder / Goettingen , Vandenhoeck & Ruprecht 1990) 15-32, here 30. The authors are referring here directly to the lack of consensus within sacramental theology on the closely related idea of the analogical sense of sacrament.
[233]For the reception contemporary with the Catholic enthusiasm for this strictly inclusivist model, cf. Albert Raffelt, Karl Rahner im Gespräch. Eine bibliographische Übersicht, in: Elmar Klinger (ed.), *Christentum innerhalb und außerhalb der Kirche* (QD 73), Freiburg et al., Herder1976, 275-294; for a critically retrospective view within the confines of enthusiasm for the then still self-confident program of pluralism in the style of John Hick cf. Perry Schmidt-Leukel, Theologie der Religionen. Probleme, Optionen, Argumente (Neuried, Ars una 1997).

with the issues of political theology and ecumenism, what immediately followed the predominance of the universal, anonymous Christian was by no means "safer" and easier for Roman Catholic theology. In the meantime, the pluralistic theories of religion that in the 1980s first supplanted the Rahnerian model of pure inclusivism have matured to the point where they, too, have begun in our own day to see their own inadequacies and internal contradictions.[234] At the present time it is unclear where the Catholic theology of religions is headed, but presumably away from pure forms of the four argumentative options: inclusivism, pluralism, exclusivism, and negative theology; the truth should likely be sought somewhere in the mix.[235] A widespread consensus seems to have developed since the late 1990s regarding that first anthropological question, What can I know? It is that for the sake of both openness towards other religions and the identity of the Christian community the value attached to concrete doctrinal understandings of belief has risen again. The Christians of tomorrow will need to be not only mystics (although that, too), but also genuine *confessors* of the creed, or they will not be Christians at all. The new evangelization must make the Gospel message accessible to new believers of new generations, which is not possible without a sharing (*communicatio*) of the *fides quae*. It is the hope of the Pope John Paul II Cultural Center with its Intercultural Forum for Studies in Faith and Culture that it might be able to serve that mission in this new and uncharted era of Church and society.

V. Conclusion

As even this abbreviated view of the debate around "the signs of the times" has shown, the Council, taken as a whole, was as divided

---

[234]For the growing Catholic dissatisfaction with pluralistic theories among pluralistically oriented theologies cf. James L. Fredericks, *Faith Among Faiths. Christian Theology and Non-Christian Religions* (New York/Mahwah N.J. 1999); and Paul F. Knitter, *Introducing Theologies of Religions* (Maryknoll, Orbis 2002); but already the ecumenically motivated work by George Lindbeck, *The Nature of Doctrine. Religion and Theology in a Postliberal Age* (Philadelphia 1984). For its impact on Catholic theology cf. J. Augustine Di Noia, The Diversity of Religions: A Christian Perspective (Washington, D.C., The Catholic University of America Press, 1992).

[235]Cf. R. Schenk, Debatable Ambiguity: Paradigms of Truth as a Measure of the Differences among Christian Theologies of Religion, in: R. Schenk, Vittorio Hoesle and Peter Koslowski (ed.), *Jahrbuch fuer Philosophie des Forschungsinstituts fuer Philosophie Hannover, Vol. 11, 2000* (Vienna, Passagen 2000) 121-161.

as the world it saw around it, "buffeted between hope and anxiety." An adequate hermeneutic of the Council needs to understand and make its own both sets of voices as it seeks a Catholicism for today and tomorrow in continuity with the principle emphases of the Council, which represent a moment too intimate in the history of the Church and her *magisterium* for us to renounce as part of her genuine development. Taken as a community, the voices at the Council joined with each other to say that the Church must engage the political and cultural world outside its immediate boundaries (*pace* Boeve), but that it should do so with a sense of "eschatological reserve", with a sense of the inadequacies of any secular, any temporal, technique, institution or state (*pace* Rowland), aware, too, of the limits of ecclesial wisdom, interweaving hermeneutical strategies of suspicion and retrieval towards itself and the world around it. "But test everything; hold fast what is good" (*I Thes* 5, 21). The Church must encounter the world of its day with the dual program of affirmation and admonition.[236] In the interests of entering the wider forum of cultural discourse, the initial reception of the Council tended to separate these two collaborative voices for a time, making it harder even until today to hear them synchronically, much less as a harmony. Yet a qualified participation in the wider forum demands their mutual presence. The call to holiness *and* communion is, as the post-synodal document on the Church in America put it, the call to the three necessities of conversion, community, *and* solidarity.[237] The pre-established trajectory of humanity's dynamic must be corrected (conversion) in

---

[236]Cf. the use of these twin approaches in Gabriel Fackre and Michael Root, *Affirmations and Admonitions: Lutheran Decisions and Dialogue with Reformed, Episcopal, and Roman Catholic Churches* (Grand Rapids, Eerdmans, 1998).

[237]Cf. Peter Casarella, Solidarity as the Fruit of Communion: Ecclesia in America, "Post-Liberation Theology," and the Earth, in: *Communio* 27 (Spring 2000) 98-123. While Casarella underlines the relative ease with which societies of Catholic provenance can (but by no means always do) foster communion and solidarity, he does not address with the same resoluteness as Rowland the issue of denying the Church's ability to develop in genuine fashion by assimilating liberal traditions such as the acknowledgement of human rights. In seeming to question the ability of Calvinist traditions to foster similar values, however, while at the same time appealing to the theology of H.U. von Balthasar for his theology of culture, Casarella faces – albeit in a weaker form – one of the many difficulties that the reader is left with by Rowland's book. Stressing over and over again the need for a congenial "pedigree" for cultural values, Rowland doubts "...whether Christianity has anything to learn from Enlightenment secularism, whether the Thomist tradition has anything to learn from the Calvinist tradition..." (op. cit. 165). Even without associating Balthasar more closely with the

order for our graced community in Christ with the triune God and his creation to be the sort that deepens our communion and solidarity with one another. Conscious of the eternal vocation of every person, this three-dimensional vocation of conversion, community, *and* solidarity will seek for humankind "a future from the memory of suffering,"[238] a future that has learned from the painful spiritualistic and materialistic reductionisms common in our times. A profound communion with God *and* one another will link conversion from what we are (but should not be) to solidarity with those who are kept by what we are from what they could and should be. Avoiding every assimilation to the poltical and cultural relativism of postmodern neo-paganism and every retreat into the enclaves and spiritually gated communities of postmodern neo-tribalism, but avoiding, too, the naïve absolutizing of political, technical or economic strategies and long outmoded attempts at the restoration of what was ever at best a dialectical Enlightenment, this vocation to holiness *and* communion, as rightly ambivalent as it might be, is a timely reformulation of the age-old task to be in this world but not — at least not merely — of it. The selfhood of the Church and her critical relationality to the non-Christian world will grow hand-in-hand, or not at all.[239] If the Church "...gives too innocent a picture of the world, it cannot mediate (to the world) any real hope."[240] The Church can share in the aspirations

Thomistic tradition than he might have desired (another problem raised but left unaddressed by Rowland's work), the interpretation hardly seems likely to succeed that would understand Balthasar apart from what he had learned through the later K. Barth from the Reformed tradition. That includes the very skepticism expressed by Rowland and possibly implied by Casarella about values given prior to explicit revelation and first articulated outside – much less, against – a genuinely Christian culture; cf. Joseph Capizzi, Solidarity as a Basis for Conversion and Communion: A Response to Peter Casarella, in: *Communio* 27 (Spring 2000) 124-133. Rowland's chief interest in denying those aspects of culture that originate outside the faith tradition exhibits more obviously its Calvinist than its Catholic "pedigree".

[238]The phrase that J.B. Metz appropriated well from the Frankfurt School of Social Research and inscribed into his theology, in order to correct much of the one-sided optimism of the early post-Conciliar years, is arguably an example of the power of successful assimilation; cf. Gerd Neuhaus, op. cit.

[239]For the underlying model of the necessary interconnection between developed selfhood and developed relationalty cf. the 1990 monograph of Paul Ricoeur, *Oneself as Another* (University of Chicago Press 1992).

[240]So the closing words of Vischer, Memorandum, 6.Vischer could easily have mustered other Protestant voices to support his insights, e.g. Reinhold Niebuhr, *Discerning the Signs of the Times. Sermons for Today and Tomorrow* (New York, C. Scribner's Sons 1946, esp. 1-20): "There is thus a reliability in our knowledge of the 'face of the sky' which is practically

of the world only by participating in its spoken and its anonymous tears and fears, recognizing, alongside obvious signs of its progress, the symptoms of its fatal traps and hopeless dead-ends. If the Church of today cannot share in the spiritual and physical *luctus et angor* of the men and women of our day, it will soon cease to share in their *gaudium et spes*.

unattainable in our discernment of the 'signs of the times.' 'Signs of the times' include all forms of historical, in contrast to, natural knowledge. To discern signs of the times means to interpret historical events and values. The interpretation of history includes all judgments we make of the purpose of our own actions and those of others; it includes the assessment of the virtue of our own and other interests, both individual and collective; and finally it includes our interpretation of the meaning of history itself... Jesus' answer implied that the 'signs' were already manifest, but that those who desired them could not discern them because of their hypocrisy. The hypocritical element which entered into all Messianic calculations was the egotistical hope that the end of history would give Israel as the chosen nation, or the righteous of Israel, victory over their enemies and final justification in the sight of God and man" (2 sq.). One point of ecumenical consensus is that the Church, too, must resist her own temptation to hypocrisy by admitting that the *ecclesia huius temporis* remains necessarily a struggling church, in the ancient sense an *ecclesia militans*.

CHAPTER 5

Eucharist: Source and Summit of the Church's Communion

Rev. Jeremy Driscoll, OSB

Introduction

ANYONE VAGUELY FAMILIAR with the practice of Catholic theology in the time since Vatican II will recognize in the title of this presentation an expression that occurs in several places throughout the Council documents and frequently cited ever since; namely, "eucharist as source and summit." The phrase is completed in various ways according to the document in which it occurs, but all occurrences amount to saying the same thing: source and summit of the Church's life.[241] I do not think there is an instance where the Eucharist is described precisely as source and summit of the Church's communion. It was for this reason that I accepted with some interest the particular title offered to me for my contribution in this volume. I think it is representative of a certain interpretation that has been given both to the liturgical theology and the ecclesiology of the Council, and it is as an interpretation of the Council that I wish to explore: namely, the Eucharist as the source and summit of the Church's communion.

This volume is a celebration of the Second Vatican Council. As such, it lays a particular set of requirements on a contributor, in this case, on me as I attempt to reflect on the theme of this essay I gladly yield to the requirement of shaping my reflections under the influence of conciliar documents and under what might be called the conciliar era. I hope to show in this way how fruitful the Council has been and to indicate as well how much remains to be explored. By way of establishing the context, I want first to say something about Eucharist

---

[241]SC 10; PO 2, 5; LG 11; UR 15; PC 6.

and communion as these themes occur in Council documents and in post-conciliar documents of the magisterium. Then, in the major part of my essay, I want to discuss Eucharist and communion around a particular theme; namely, our communion in the sacrifice of Christ.

I. Communion and Eucharist in the Council Documents and in Post-conciliar Magisterial Teaching

Communion and related words are used frequently throughout the Council documents. Certainly the most significant use of the word communion is in the documents, which develop the ecclesiology envisioned by the Council, most notably but not exclusively in *Lumen gentium*.[242] In addition, the Eucharist is not infrequently discussed in key passages that bear on the Council's ecclesiology, often combined with the word communion in this context.[243] Yet if we think of the years immediately following the Council, the themes and images which most dominated the work of absorbing its ecclesiology tended to be the Church as Mystery or Sacrament (the name of LG's first chapter), the People of God (chapter two), and the Church's relation to the world, the theme of *Gaudium et spes*. All of these themes are closely related to what could be called a communion ecclesiology or a Eucharistic ecclesiology, but such terms were not very much used in the first decades after the Council.

By 1985, twenty years after the Council, the situation had changed. The Final Report of the Synod of 1985 states bluntly, "The ecclesiology of communion is the central and fundamental idea of the Council's documents."[244] This is certainly correct, but it must be admitted that it was seldom put that way in 1965. This is why, as I suggested at the beginning, the theme of communion ecclesiology should be considered as an interpretation of the Council. It is the fruit of sifting the abundant themes and images provided by the documents. This sifting process settles more and more explicitly around communion ecclesiology.[245]

---

[242]The following are representative of communion in the ecclesiology of the Council: LG 4, 8, 11, 13-15, 18, 21, 24-26, 50; DV 10; GS 32; UR 2-4, 14-15, 17-19, 22.
[243]LG 3, 7, 11, 26, 48; CD 11, 15; AG 39; GS 38; SC 41; PO 5, 6.
[244]*The Final Report of the Extraordinary Synod of Bishops, Rome,* 1985. Washington, D.C.: US Catholic Conference, Inc. C, 1
[245]This seems especially influenced by LG, 26, which speaks of the bishop's Eucharist as the manifestation of the Church in a particular locality. This whole paragraph is a clear

This interpretation appears in other major post-conciliar documents as well. Its prominence in the *Catechism of the Catholic Church* is symptomatic. There is no question that this catechism is a Vatican II catechism. By this time also the word communion begins to be used more often as well in connection with the Eucharist, and in this and other contexts communion is a word used to express our share in the life of the Holy Trinity. This stress on Trinity comes more and more to the fore, and I think it is a result of absorbing at depth the first chapter of *Lumen gentium*, where the Mystery of the Church is treated together with the Mystery of the Trinity. The words of St. Cyprian cited in this chapter have been very influential: the Church is seen as "a people brought into unity from the unity of the Father, the Son and the Holy Spirit."[246] The *Catechism* says, "The mystery of the Most Holy Trinity is the central mystery of Christian faith and life."[247] The magisterial teaching of John Paul II has again and again driven home the theme of ecclesiology of communion, Eucharist, and communion in the life of the Trinity.[248]

Communion also became a word around which controversy began to swirl. It became suspect of surreptitiously promoting an ecclesiology that was Orthodox as opposed to Roman Catholic. In 1992 the Congregation for Doctrine and Faith issued a document that weighed into this controversy in a balanced way. It was titled "Some Aspects of the Church Understood as Communion."[249] In the balanced view, communion remains in fact a term for describing ecclesiology and Eucharistic theology in a way that is full of promise not only

---

example of the Eucharistic and communion ecclesiology of the Council. See also SC, 41: "Bishops must be convinced that the principal manifestation of the Church consists in the full, active participation of all God's holy people in the same liturgical celebrations, especially in the same Eucharist, in one prayer, at one altar, at which the bishop resides, surrounded by his college of priests and by his ministers." See AG, 3: "In order to establish a relationship of peace and communion with himself, and in order to bring about brotherly union among men, and they sinners, God decided to enter into the history of mankind in a new and definitive manner, by sending his own Son in human flesh..." See also AG 19-22, 38, 39; CD 11.

[246]LG, 4. See LG 1-8 for the trinitarian shape of the Church.

[247]CCC, 234.

[248]A representative example would be in *Christifideles laici*, Chapter 2, nn. 18ff. In these paragraphs the participation of the laity in the life of the Church is developed around the notion of communion. The Trinity is called the prototype of communion. In n. 19 he says that the Church as communion is the central content of the mystery or design of God. The most recent example, and a very clear one, would be the encyclical *Ecclesia de Eucharistia* (2003) especially chapter 4, "The Eucharist and Ecclesial Communion."

[249]AAS 85 (1993) 835-850. Origins 22, June 15, 1992, 108-111.

for ecumenical dialogue, especially with the Orthodox, but also for understanding Church and Eucharist within Roman Catholicism itself. Critics of the term call it a sellout on the part of the Latin tradition to the theological traditions of the East. But this betrays an ignorance of the patristic sources, East and West. There is no question that the ecclesiology of Vatican II represents a shift from the ecclesiology that held sway in the Latin Church in the immediately preceding centuries. But the Council recovers an ecclesiology rooted in the best traditions of the undivided Church, and it was precisely for this reason that the Council adopted it.[250]

In the midst of all this there are conciliar texts that speak of the Eucharist, and more generally, the entire liturgy, as the source and summit of the Church's life. These are the texts that inform the title to this volume. Probably most well known is this statement from *Sacrosanctum concilium*: "The liturgy is the summit toward which the activity of the Church is directed; it is also the fount from which all her power flows."[251] But I find just as powerful and suggestive the following from *Presbyterorum ordinis*, and this text gets us closer to our topic, the Eucharist: "In the most blessed Eucharist is contained the whole spiritual good of the Church, namely, Christ himself our Pasch... Thus men are invited and led to offer themselves, their works, and all creation with Christ. For this reason the Eucharist appears as the source and the summit of all preaching of the Gospel."[252]

I am summarizing here what is well known and widely discussed in an extensive bibliography on the question. I do not imagine the contribution of my own essay to be primarily in the continuation of such a discussion on this level of what the Council may or may not have said about communion ecclesiology or whether or not this should be considered a sad or happy time in the history of the Church.[253] I prefer, rather, to reflect on Eucharist and communion in a way that I think represents the new situation in the practice of

---

[250]See J. –M.-R. Tillard *Flesh of the Church, Flesh of Christ, At the Source of the Ecclesiology of Communion*. Collegeville: The Liturgical Press, 2001. This entire study is dedicated to seeing how deep the roots of communion ecclesiology lie in the New Testament and in the Eucharistic ecclesiology of Latin and Greek fathers alike.
[251]SC, 10.
[252]PO 5.
[253]This has been amply studied. For good summaries, see the following: J. –M.-R. Til-lard, *Church of Churches, The Ecclesiology of Communion*. Collegeville: The Liturgical Press,

theology and in a way that I think consistent with major theological themes represented in the Council.

To introduce the particular theme I hope to develop, a paragraph from *Presbyterorum ordinis* deserves special consideration:

> ... priests are given the grace by God to be the ministers of Jesus Christ among the nations, fulfilling the sacred task of the Gospel, that the oblation of the gentiles may be made acceptable and sanctified in the Holy Spirit. For it is by the apostolic herald of the Gospel that the People of God is called together and gathered so that all who belong to this people, sanctified as they are by the Holy Spirit, may offer themselves 'a living sacrifice, holy and acceptable to God' (Rom 12: 1). Through the ministry of priests the spiritual sacrifice of the faithful is completed in union with the sacrifice of Christ the only mediator, which in the Eucharist is offered through the priests' hands in the name of the whole Church in an unbloody and sacramental manner until the Lord himself come. The ministry of priests is directed to this and finds its consummation in it. For their ministration, which begins with the announcement of the Gospel, draws its force and power from the sacrifice of Christ and tends to this... (no. 2).[254]

This is a lofty text. Let us see if we can unfold its meaning more concretely as to how the actual rite of the Eucharistic celebration accomplishes all this. I want to center my remarks around the word sacrifice, which this text uses several times, as well as around communion which this text suggests.

II. Communion in the Sacrifice of Christ

Among a number of ways that the word communion can be used to deepen our theological understanding of the Eucharistic celebration, the idea of communion in the sacrifice of Christ is certainly one worth pursuing.[255] Both the word sacrifice and the word

---

1992. D. Doyle, *Communion Ecclesiology: Vision and Versions.*(New York: Orbis, 2000). J. Markey, *Creating Communion, The Theology of the Constitutions of the Church.* (Hyde Park: New City Press, 2003).

[254]See also LG, 28: "It is in the eucharistic cult or in the eucharistic assembly of the faithful (synaxis) that they [priests] exercise in a supreme degree their sacred functions; there, acting in the person of Christ and proclaiming his mystery, they unite the votive offerings of the faithful to the sacrifice of Christ their head, and in the sacrifice of the Mass they make present again and apply, until the coming of the Lord (cf. 1 Cor 11: 26), the unique sacrifice of the New Testament, that namely of Christ offering himself once for all a spotless victim to the Father (cf. Heb 9: 11-28)."

[255]For the biblical and patristic sources, see J. –M. –R. Tillard, *Flesh of Christ*, chapter 3,

communion have been associated with the Eucharist virtually from the beginning, but in different ways and with different histories.

In the first letter to the Corinthians St. Paul says, "The cup of blessing that we bless, is it not communion in the blood of Christ? The bread that we break, is it not communion in the body of Christ." (1 Cor 10: 16) What this communion accomplishes is explained in the next verse: "Because the loaf of bread is one, we, though many, are one body, for we all partake of the one loaf." (1 Cor 10: 17) Slightly later Paul makes explicit reference to the connection between this eating and drinking — this Eucharist — and the death of the Lord: "For as often as you eat this bread and drink the cup, you proclaim the death of the Lord until he comes." (1 Cor 11: 26) These verses have exercised a tremendous influence on how Christians have understood their Eucharist.[256] But we can ask more precisely what they mean. What does it mean to have communion in the blood of Christ, to have communion in the body of Christ? What does it mean to proclaim the death of the Lord?

It is noteworthy that neither St. Paul nor any other New Testament writer uses the word sacrifice to understand the Church's Eucharist. Indeed, apart from the Letter to the Hebrews and some of the language of the Book of Revelation, sacrifice is not used to understand the death of Christ on the cross.[257] Calling the death of Christ, and later the Eucharist, sacrifice, is a development, no less legitimate for being such. There are theological reasons why the word sacrifice would not have occurred to the first generations of Christians as an apt word for Christ's death or for the Eucharist. We do well to remember that calling the death of Christ a sacrifice is to use a metaphor to understand it. In itself Christ's death was a brutal

---

titled "All Taken into the One Sacrifice: The Sacrifice of Christ in the Church of God," pp. 83-133. The recent encyclical of John Paul II, *Ecclesia de Eucharistia*, emphasizes the sacrificial dimension of the Eucharist, using the term *sacrifice or sacrificial* more than 70 times, not counting synonymous expressions such as *offering, victim, blood poured out*. Indeed, the encyclical claims that Christ's unique sacrifice is the source of all communion. In the present context, we cannot develop more than one theme here, but other examples that could be developed with the same method I employ here would be communion in Trinitarian life, communion in the one body of Christ, communion among the churches, communion with the saints, communion in the local community, communion of all created things.
[256]See SC 6.
[257]The Letter to the Hebrews applies the word *sacrifice* to the death of Christ (10:12), to prayer (13:15) and to charity (13:16). But see Eph 5: 2. Certainly, there is much sacrificial language and imagery in the New Testament around the death of Christ. My point concerns

execution, capital punishment. To call it sacrifice is to borrow a word from cultic language and use it for some insight into the meaning of Christ's execution. The insights attached to such application have become precious to the Church and have entered so deeply into the theological talk about the death of Christ and into the euchological language used to celebrate this death liturgically that we have all but forgotten that in its initial application the term remains a metaphor. Calling it a metaphor does not weaken the term. It enables us to be precise in what we mean when we use it.

If St. Paul does not use the word sacrifice to understand the death of Christ, he does use it in other contexts; and the reasons here are also full of theological import. For St. Paul the death and resurrection of Christ and our communion in these have introduced an entirely new reality into the world, beginning from Israel and Christ's submission to the Law, but extending outward from there to include all Gentiles with a share in the promise. As a result, the Old Law and its sacrifices no longer have validity. There is a new Covenant and a new kind of sacrifice. At the end of his impressive and moving meditation on the enigma of Israel's refusal to believe in Jesus Christ in chapters 9 to 11 of the Letter to the Romans, St. Paul starts up a new line of thought in chapter 12 describing the life of Christians in clear distinction from unbelieving Israel. The first sentence of this exhortation reads: "I urge you, therefore, by the mercies of God to offer your bodies as a living sacrifice, holy and pleasing to God, your spiritual worship." (Rom 12: 1) So the new sacrifice of Christians, as opposed to the animal sacrifices offered in the Temple, is the very body of the Christian offered to God in a holy life. This is called "spiritual worship" (*logikē latreia*) as opposed to the carnal worship of animal sacrifices.

This is perhaps the clearest text where St. Paul speaks in this way, though there are others.[258] But the concept is clear and will be caught in all its clarity and developed by any number of patristic writers. The word sacrifice as used by Christians refers in a fundamental way to the sacrifice of a holy life. For reasons that are related, it will not be long before this sacrifice becomes closely associated with the Eucharist.

---

the explicit application of the word *sacrifice* to the death of Christ.

[258] Phil 2: 17; 4: 16; Rom 15: 16; 2 Cor 4: 10-11

[259] *City of God* 10, 6. CCSL 47, 279. Significantly, this text is cited in Vatican II PO, 2 in

I would like to cite St. Augustine as an example of the patristic development. In the present context, we cannot fully trace the evolution from St. Paul to St. Augustine, some 350 years later. But St. Augustine is both very close to St. Paul and representative of a great deal of developed understanding that occurred in the meantime. The context of Augustine's remark is important. It occurs in the *City of God*, that huge work of his mature years in which he envisions the distinctive nature of God's holy ones in the redeemed city, a city being built up through human history. In the course of his discussion Augustine speaks of the futility of pagan sacrifices and contrasts these with the Christian sacrifice. The Christian sacrifice, closely associated with the Eucharist, draws its force and power from the sacrifice of Christ. And that sacrifice is "... the whole redeemed city, that is, the whole assembly and community of the saints is offered as a universal sacrifice to God through the High Priest who offered himself in his passion for us in the form of a servant that we might be the body of so great a head."[259]

This is a magnificent text and representative of what Augustine says in a number of other places. Here we see the Pauline notion of the Christian people themselves being the sacrifice, and Augustine wants to say that this is the unique effective sacrifice in the whole history of the world. But we also see the development that in the Eucharist this sacrifice is offered to God through Jesus Christ. His own passion is an offering, which we can also call sacrifice. In short, we could say that the sacrifice of a holy life is offered to God by communion in the sacrifice of Christ. This communion is what the Eucharist effects and accomplishes. Year after year during his mystagogical catechesis to the newly baptized, St. Augustine insisted on this.[260]

But let us try to deepen our understanding of how this comes about. It is one thing to make the claim, another to understand in

___

speaking of the Eucharist. It is difficult to know where to end the citation. What follows says the same again in different words: "This is the sacrifice of Christians: we, though many, in Christ are one body. This is the sacrifice which the Church continually celebrates in the sacrament of the altar and which is known to the faithful, in which it is shown to the Church that in the offering which she makes to God, she herself is offered." See also *City of God* 19, 23.

[260]See Sermons 227, 228 B, 229 A, 272. See my *Theology at the Eucharistic Table, Master Themes in the Theological Tradition*, (Leominster: Gracewing, 2003): 230-231 for a discussion of these texts. For a fine synthesis of Augustine on the Eucharist, see G. Bonner, "Augus-

detail why such a claim can be made. That is, it is nice to say repeatedly things like "Eucharist is source and summit" of the Church's life, of communion, of the preaching of the gospel, or of any number of other ways of expressing it. But let us ask how actually this comes about during the course of the Eucharistic celebration.[261] To understand this we do well to employ one of the new tools for theological work much revived since the Council; namely, an examination of ritual language and ritual action as a guide for developing theological discourse. In what follows I will examine the language and the action of Eucharistic Prayer 3 in such a way as to see how that prayer is believed to accomplish our communion in the sacrifice of Christ. My choice of this prayer of the liturgy reformed after Vatican II and my way of analyzing it are evidence of the new theological climate that I spoke about at the beginning. I hope in this way to indicate some of the positive fruits of the Council.

The prayer that we rather unimaginatively call the Eucharistic Prayer — canon is a better word and *anaphora* better still — is a prayer prayed over bread and wine, accompanied by gestures that involve the bread and wine. A proper method of interpretation requires close attention to the words of the prayer as these are coordinated with the actions concerning the bread and wine.[262] If I concentrate my analysis on this prayer, we still cannot just dive into the liturgy at this point and start talking about it. It is necessary to say at least something, however briefly, about how we got this far, something about the whole context of this prayer. I reluctantly forego saying much about the Liturgy of the Word, and I do so only in the interests of space. But this much at least can be said: no matter what particular readings occur in a given liturgy, the Liturgy of the Word always has about it an event character; that is, the events of the past which are proclaimed become event for the believing community that hears them told. And all the events of the Scripture find their center in the one event that is the center of

tine's Understanding of the Church as a Eucharistic Community" in *Saint Augustine the Bishop, A Book of Essays,* eds. F. LeMoine, C. Kleinhenz; (New York: Garland, 1994): 39-63.

    [261]It is this deeper understanding that the Council urged, and it is the reason for the liturgical reforms. See the theological premise for the liturgical reform as stated in SC 47-49.

    [262]This is standard method now in liturgical theology. For a very useful discussion, see K. Irwin, *Context and Text, Method in Liturgical Theology,* (Collegeville: The Liturgical Press, 1994).

them all: the death and resurrection of Jesus. It is this about which all the Scriptures speak. This is not talk delivering ideas and concepts. It is, as I say, an event: the same event in which God once acted to save his people delivered now to this assembly by means of the word, gift of the Spirit to the Church. The words and actions of the *anaphora* say and accomplish in their own way what has already been said in the Liturgy of the Word. They intensify the event character of the one event, which is the center of all: the death and resurrection of Jesus.[263]

Among the things that the Word of God urges on the Christian people — again, speaking in summary fashion — is the offering of their lives, their bodies, as a living sacrifice, spiritual worship. The Word ultimately does not speak of the death and resurrection of Jesus without also urging this. So, one way to think of the *anaphora* is as an action of response to what has been heard in the Word. But the response is not merely the response of what any given community might be able to muster. This is a response made through Christ and in the Holy Spirit. As such it becomes fitting and adequate response, a living sacrifice, true spiritual worship. Let us examine a little more closely this response as it is articulated in word and action.

Before the bishop or priest stretches out his hands to pray over the bread and wine that lie on the altar before him, that bread and wine got there in a way that is not without significance. One of the most striking innovations of the reform of the liturgy by Vatican II is the bringing of gifts of bread and wine by the faithful and presenting these to the bishop or priest who presides at the Eucharist. Although this has been called a return to an ancient practice, it seems that there was never a rite quite like this. But even if its present form is without precedent, I think it offers one of the strongest opportunities in the rite of Paul VI for understanding the relation between the sacrifice of the Christian people and the sacrifice of Christ. What the action mean the prayers of the Presentation also say. People are bringing bread and wine, called "the fruit of the earth and work of human hands." It is worth reflecting on this simple formulation. Bread and wine are not merely raw natural symbols, as, for instance, water is.

---

[263]This notion of the event character of the word is indebted to S. Marsili. I discuss his seminal concept and develop it in my *Theology at the Eucharistic Table*, pp. 134-139.

God does not make bread and wine; people do. And that is the point here. It is true that bread and wine have their precise meaning in the context of the Passover and in Lord's Last Supper and that bread and wine are involved here in obedience to his command to do this in memory of him. But we can reflect as well on the fittingness of the Lord's choice and what the Spirit had prepared. Bread and wine in fact are extremely strong symbols, explosive in what they can set off. Perhaps nothing summarizes so well the deepest experience of what it means to be a human being and what we most desire.

We are not mere animals who snatch food from the ground or from trees with our mouths, roaming about alone until our stomachs are full enough to get us through to the next round. We produce our food together; we consume it together; we share it with one another. It is an expression of love and desire. It aims at communion. We can hardly imagine life without this — not because we are gluttons but because we were made this way. Food is both a substance needed to stay alive and a symbol needed to stay human. With food we tell one another that we love one another, that we are dependent on one another, that we desire the other to live and be well. If bread is the most fundamental end of the food spectrum, wine is its festive end. Wine testifies to the technical and aesthetic capacity of human beings. It is a refined and elegant way to say what we say more simply with bread: we love one another; we desire the other to live and be well. In a word, bread and wine aim at communion.[264]

It is not a throwaway phrase to say that we offer up our lives to God. This is a phrase full of meaning; indeed, we could say it summarizes the whole economy of salvation. But Christians do not offer up their lives by themselves. They can only do it through, with,

---

[264]See GS 38: "Christ left to his followers a pledge of this hope and food for the journey in the sacrament of faith, in which natural elements, the fruits of man's cultivation, are changed into His glorified Body and Blood, as a supper of brotherly communion (*coena communionis fraternae*) and a foretaste of the heavenly banquet." A meditation on the natural and symbolic meaning of bread and wine is a common feature of the Latin patristic tradition on the eucharist. See, for example, Cyprian, Letter 63, 13; 69, 2, 5; Augustine, *Sermon* 227, and 272; Gaudentius of Brescia, *Paschal Homily* 2. The roots of this are already found in the *Didache* n. 9 "As bread once scattered on the hillside, may your Church be gathered...." *Gaudium et spes* is the Council document which most seeks a renewal of the mission for communicating the Gospel to men and women of our times. It is striking how often the word communio is used to announce this message. See GS 3, 18, 19, 21, 32, 38. For a splendid discussion of the anthropological dimensions of human eating as the basis for our theological understanding of the eucharist, see G. Lafont, *Eucharistie, le repas et la parole,* (Paris: Cerf, 2001):13-43.

and in Christ's offering. In the course of the rite when bread and wine are brought to the hands of the bishop by some of the baptized, a magnificent exchange begins to take shape. We bring our lives — with all our efforts to produce and to be together in love, with all our desire and our willingness to share — and we place them in the hands of Christ by placing them in the hands of the bishop. (The bishop or priest is in this moment sacrament of Christ the head, who leads his whole body in offering his sacrifice.[265]) Implicitly something is said by this action that will be explicitly articulated later in the Eucharistic prayer. Basically the action is our saying to Christ, "Do something with this. Make our lives to be what your life was and is."

The action and the prayers of Presentation are simple enough. What they mean is worthy of extended reflection. But with the context of the *anaphora* now established, in however sketchy a fashion, let us look at this prayer in itself. There are a number of dimensions and approaches that would be possible. Different passes through the mystery are required, and experience shows that we cannot exhaust it. I would like to organize my own reflection around the two epiclesis prayers, in both instances keeping an eye on the dimension of sacrifice and the dimension of communion.

In the first movement of the prayer after the *Sanctus*, God the Father is praised for the gift of creation and for his plan of salvation. Significantly, this very pithy summary expresses the climax of God's plan for the world as being "so that from east to west a perfect offering (*oblatio munda*) may be made to your name." This expression echoes Malachi 1: 11, a phrase which the very first generations of Christians saw as a prophecy of the Eucharist: "From the rising of the sun, even to its setting, my name is great among the nations; and everywhere they bring sacrifice to my name and a pure offering." The Christian people were the nations; the Eucharist was their sacrifice and pure offering.[266] We note in the phrase "perfect offering" a sacrificial language. Indeed, it is legitimate to consider it synonymous with sacrifice.

---

[265]In what follows, I will refer to the bishop as president of the eucharist as a reminder of what Vatican II reminds us; namely, that every eucharist is under the local bishop. See LG 26; CD 11.

[266]This begins early. See Didache, 14; Justin Martyr, *The Dialogue with Trypho,* 41 and 117; Irenaeus, *Against the Heresies* IV, 17, 5. The verse is still be referred to the eucharist by Augustine toward the end of his life. See *City of God* 19, 23.

After this first movement of the prayer, there is a notable shift marked by the strong plea *Supplices ergo te, Domine, deprecamur.* This is rendered in the current English as, "And so we ask you..." But we want to catch the logic of the *ergo* in this phrase. What we are about to ask for in this moment is based on what God has shown his plan to be; namely, that a perfect offering be made to him. Therefore, we now ask that the bread and wine on the altar become the Body and Blood of Christ. We must remember precisely now that this bread and wine are not just static elements lying there, who-knows-why and they will become who-knows-how the body and blood of Christ. This is the bread and wine that we brought, and we say it again in the prayer: *quae detulimus.* And we dare to ask that these be changed into the body and blood of Christ because of God's own plan — it's his idea! — that a perfect offering be made to the glory of his name. This prayer is accompanied by a simple but powerful gesture. The bishop's hands are stretched out over our bread and wine. It is a rendering visible, if you will, of what is, of course, invisible: the coming of the Spirit into the bread and wine and his causing them to become Body and Blood of Christ.

Then the institution narrative follows. We know that together with the epiclesis this narrative accomplishes the transformation of the gifts we have brought. What Jesus did at the Last Supper — and what he still does now in this moment, for this is an Hour that does not pass away[267] — was to set in motion the mighty events that would be the culmination of his life. He was giving his disciples a sign together with a command to repeat it in his memory. This sign would reveal the meaning of his death, which he knew he would undergo on the morrow. The actual events surrounding his death and the long hours during which it was stretched out were too terrible to be understood by anyone, perhaps even by the one who was undergoing them. But with this sign performed before and repeated after, Jesus was revealing the meaning of his death and that he was willingly submitting to it.

Two things at least are striking to us in the sign that Jesus made: first, his use of bread and wine and the context of a meal. He is using these basic symbols of human life together — symbols of love,

---

[267]For this expression used in this way, see CCC, 1085.

desire, communion; and he is making them to say, he is declaring them to be his voluntary death. What is death for him is meant to be nourishment for us. What is death for him is even feast for us. Not only are these basic symbols of human life, but they have a specific meaning in the context of Jewish Passover. This food and drink represented Israel's Passover. And now Jesus, holding the whole history of Israel in his hands, makes it to say, declares it to be his voluntary death. All the Law and the Prophets pointed to this.

The second thing that is striking in the sign that Jesus made is the language he uses. We can certainly call it sacrificial language, even if the word sacrifice does not appear. His is "a body handed over." His is "blood poured out" to establish a "new and eternal covenant." The repetition of this sign and Jesus' words around it certainly prepare the way for the Church calling the Eucharist and the death of Jesus a sacrifice, even if this application remains metaphorical. But the mystery is so dense at this point that the metaphor flips. Christ's death in fact becomes the sacrifice against which all others are measured and consequently eclipsed. And the Eucharist, which remembers his death, becomes the same sacrifice. There can be no other.[268]

Throughout all this action and the accompanying words, it remains important for us to remember with attention that it all happens with the bread and wine that we brought; for this is how our communion in the one sacrifice is accomplished. In effect, by means of our bread and wine our lives are taken up into the one and only story in which the history of the world finds its meaning and fulfillment, the death and resurrection of Christ. It is our lives over which Jesus' once pronounced words continue to be pronounced. He makes our lives to say, he is declaring them to be his voluntary death, his sacrifice.

The prayer that follows presumes that this has been accomplished. And because it has been, the Church herself makes the offering. We are not inert matter in the hands of Jesus or for the action of the Spirit. A marvelous cooperation is occurring in which Jesus, the Spirit, and the worshipping community — the Church — all play

---

[268]Thus Augustine in *City of God* 10, 20: "To this supreme and true sacrifice, all sacrifices give way." CCSL 47, 294.

a role.[269] We are given the privilege of ourselves offering what Jesus once offered and — it must continually be repeated — which does not pass away. To make it clear that there are not two different sacrifices being offered, Jesus' and the Church's, we speak words in our offering expressing our consciousness that there is only one sacrifice, only one perfect offering. And so we remember: *memores, igitur, Domine...* We know that in the Christian dispensation "remembering" is not a weak calling to mind of a past event.[270] To remember an event of God is itself an event, the event remembered. And so we remember the death of Jesus, his resurrection, his ascension. We stand ready to greet him when he comes again in glory. And from this place, inside these events that never pass away, we say to the Father, "we offer you in thanksgiving this holy and living sacrifice." That we offer it is our communion in the sacrifice of Christ. This moment and this place in which we stand is the fulfillment of Father's plan "that a perfect offering be made to the glory of [his] name." We dared to ask for the Holy Spirit to enable us to make such an offering because it was his plan. In our communion with Christ's death and resurrection we are able to do so.

Yet the prayer does not stop there. We can say that the communion drives deeper. There is a risk that on the level of sign the bread and wine might remain too exterior to ourselves, something that we could handle at arm's length, as it were, as if it were enough somehow to have Christ's sacrifice, however mysteriously, objectively present in the bread and wine lying on the altar and say the right words of offering them up to the Father. In fact the whole rite envisions our eventually consuming the bread and wine, and this very part of the rite is called communion. The next part of the Eucharistic prayer anticipates this ritual action and makes an urgent plea that what it means come to pass in us. Using now a cultic language of sacrifice, we ask the Father to "look with favor on your Church's offering and see the Victim..." This will be the basis on which the petition which follows is made: "Grant that we, who are nourished by his body and blood, may be filled with his Holy Spirit, and become one body, one

---

[269]This is nicely described in CCC, 1091: "When the Spirit encounters in us the response of faith which he has aroused in us, he brings about genuine cooperation. Through it, the liturgy becomes the common work of the Holy Spirit and the Church."

[270]In this light it is necessary to note how misleading is the current translation of this phrase in the English version: "Father, calling to mind..."

Spirit in Christ." This is our communion with Christ's sacrifice. It will be accomplished in our reception of his body and blood. We become his body, not statically, but his body in the form or with the shape of sacrifice. The plea continues: "May he make us an everlasting gift to you." This is what St. Augustine had said: "... the whole assembly and community of the saints is offered as a universal sacrifice to God through the High Priest who offered himself ..."[271]

Such an offering is not conceived as involving only those present at a given celebration. Those present could be called the visible icon of "the whole redeemed city," which as such is invisible to the given community but nonetheless present. The words that follow acknowledge this, pray that it be so, render us aware of a presence not visible to our eyes. They are words of our communion with all the saints of the whole redeemed city: "... enable us to share in the inheritance of your saints..." Yet the communion of the given assembly is not only with the saints in heaven but also with other believers across the whole world. Our words enable us to become aware also of their presence in this sacrifice, of our communion with them. By naming the bishop of Rome and our own bishop, we are not simply deciding to pray for them because they have a rough job. Rather, the whole local church is named in the person of the bishop, and the communion of the local church with all the other churches throughout the world is named in the person of the bishop of Rome. After this we remember still others: the dead. We ask that they too be united with us in this sacrifice.[272]

This colossal prayer moves now towards its climax. It has remembered Christ's sacrifice and, by remembering, rendered it present as the event that defines the present action. It has prayed that we be joined in communion with this sacrifice, that we become one body with Christ's body, together with the people of God across time and across space. With all this "in place," we make a huge final thrust with our prayer toward the future we hope for in Christ, a future that we feel already invading the present moment of our prayer.[273] Meaning

[271]*City of God* 10, 6, as above at n. 19.

[272]For all of these gathered into the Eucharistic sacrifice and for this vision of the Church that is thereby implied, see LG 50.

[273]For this eschatological sense of the eucharist, see LG 48. Also UR 15: "... the eucharistic mystery, source of the Church's life and pledge of future glory." I develop the theme of the presence of the future in the liturgy in my *Theology at the Eucharistic Table*, pp. 179-182.

all the living and dead with whom we are now in communion, we say
"we"; and speaking for all we say to the Father, "We hope to enjoy
forever the vision of your glory, through Christ our Lord." Such
eternal enjoyment could be described, of course, as communion with
the Father. But we should not fail to notice the plural form, the "we."
Communion with the Father is something that we can only enjoy in
communion with one another. Communion with one another is not
communion of a lesser order, second to that of communion with God.
Communion with one another is an essential part of God's plan; and
having designed salvation in this form, God surely is teaching us and
causing us to participate in the tremendous regard he has for us, his
tremendous love toward us. We are made for this double communion.
St. Augustine expresses it with utter precision, again in the *City of
God* with all that that work is concerned to show. He says, "Only this
peace of the heavenly city can be truly called and esteemed the peace
of rational creatures, consisting as it does of the perfectly ordered and
harmonious enjoyment of God and of one another in God."[274]

Enjoyment of God and of one another in God — this
enjoyment is already tasted in the Eucharistic feast. The bishop lifts
up the bread and wine — bread and wine which we have brought,
bread and wine transformed into the body and blood of Christ in the
form of his sacrifice which never passes away, bread and wine which
we are shortly to consume — and lifting them up he presents them
to God the Father as the "perfect offering made to the glory of [his]
name." "Through him, with him, in him, in the unity of the Holy
Spirit, all glory and honor is yours, God almighty Father, for ever
and ever." In that moment the Church is doing what Christ did and
forever does: she offers his one body, to which she has been joined, to
the Father for the glory of his name and for the salvation of the world.
This is our communion in the sacrifice of Christ.[275]

---

[274]*City of God* 19, 17. CCSL 48, 684-685. Cited by Tillard, *Flesh of Christ,* p. 49. See also
LG 7: "Really sharing in the body of the Lord in the breaking of the Eucharistic bread,
we are taken up into communion with him and with one another." UR, 2: "In his Church,
Christ instituted the wonderful sacrament of the Eucharist by which the unity of the Church
is both signified and brought about." UR, 7: "For the closer their [the faithful's] union with
the Father, the Word, and the Spirit, the more deeply and easily will they be able to grow in
mutual brotherly love."
[275]See LG, 3: "As often as the sacrifice of the cross by which 'Christ our Pasch is
sacrificed' (1 Cor 5: 7) is celebrated on the altar, the work of our redemption is carried out.
Likewise, in the sacrament of the Eucharistic bread, the unity of believers, who form one

This moment within the whole of the rite concludes a movement and opens onto another unit of the ritual, called "communion." The communion rite begins with the joyous invocation of God by a name, which it is possible for us to call him only through our communion in the sacrifice of Christ: the name "Father." With this invocation on his lips, Jesus breathed his last: "Father, into your hands I commend my spirit." (Luke 23: 46) Empowered by the Spirit, we cry out together with Jesus this name, which never ceases to sound from the place of the cross. In this invocation there is contained all that humanity desires and all that it was made for: "hallowed be thy name; thy kingdom come; thy will be done." When we pray these words together with Jesus we enter into his same relationship with the Father. And our invocation will receive a response, the same response that Jesus received and forever receives. It is his name uttered back by the Father: "Beloved Son, in whom I am well pleased." This becomes our name as well, for we have been established in communion with Christ's sacrifice, recapitulated now in this exchange of names. This exchange of names is not merely the sound of vocables flying between heaven and earth. Rather, it is an action. If the action of Jesus' death is recapitulated in the name "Father" cried out by him, the name "Son" is enacted in the Father's raising Jesus from the dead. This is as the Psalmist mysteriously prophesied and as the Apostle wrote in the Letter to the Hebrews: "You are my beloved son. Today I have begotten you."[276]

In this way our being joined with Christ in his sacrifice and in his crying out "Father" to God also assures our being joined to him in receiving back the life offered up in resurrection when he hears the name "Son," when he hears the time, "Today." After the words of this prayer, action follows. It is the action of eating the body of the Lord and drinking his blood.[277] This action confirms in our flesh what our lips have prayed. Once again it behooves us to pay close attention to the bread and wine, which we originally brought forward.

---

body in Christ (cf. 1 Cor 10:17), is both expressed and brought about. All are called to this union with Christ..."

[276]Ps 2: 7 with Heb 1: 5, also citing 2 Sam 7:14: "I will be a father to him and he shall be a son to me."

[277]The way in which St. Augustine speaks of this theme can give us the measure of how much of this sensibility we have lost, as well an indicate a way of recovery: "So, if you want to understand the body of Christ, listen to the apostle telling the faithful, *You, though, are the*

In the same place where it was originally handed over to Christ and from the same hands that received it, it is now handed back to us. We can say that the lives we brought forward are handed back, but they are handed back completely transfigured and transformed. Into what? The simple ritual words bluntly tell us: "The Body of Christ. The Blood of Christ." We say "Amen" to express our belief but also to ratify the exchange, to say that we agree to it, that we accept its consequences. We accept becoming ourselves the body of Christ, ourselves his blood. This is not static in form. It is a body handed over, it is blood poured out in love for the sake of the world. If you will, it is the sacrifice of a holy life. It is also the risen body of Christ, for there is no other. Indeed, Christ's risen body manifests itself precisely here, in his body the Church. There are not two bodies: the historical body, crucified and risen, and another body called the Church. Christ is risen and ascended into the sacraments and through these into his Church which the sacraments have made to be his one body. "The cup of blessing that we bless, is it not communion in the blood of Christ? The bread that we break, is it not a communion in the body of Christ."

We can draw all these strands together by speaking of communion with yet a different reference; namely, communion in the life of the Trinity.[278] We began this whole ritual, we entered into it by

---

body of Christ and its members (1 Cor 12: 27). If it is you that are the Body of Christ and its members, it is the mystery meaning you that has been placed on the Lord's table; what you receive is the mystery that means you." (Augustine, Sermon 272. PL 38, 1247. English trans. from The Works of Saint Augustine, Sermons III/7 (230-272B) *on the Liturgical Seasons,* trans. and notes, Edmund Hill, O.P. (New Rochelle: New City Press, 1993), 300.) Or: "So receive the sacrament in such a way that you think about yourselves, that you retain unity in your hearts, that you always fix your hearts up above." (Augustine, Sermon 227, PL 38, 1100. English trans. Edmund Hill, *Sermons* III/6 (184-229Z), (New Rochelle: New City Press, 1993), 255. Or: "This sacrament, after all, doesn't present you with the body of Christ in such a way as to divide you from it. This, as the apostle reminds us, was foretold in holy scripture: *they shall be two in one flesh* (Gn 2: 24). *This, he says, is a great sacrament; but I mean in Christ and in the Church* (Eph 5:31-32). And in another place he says about this Eucharist itself, *We, though many, are one loaf, one body* (1 Cor 10: 17). So you are beginning to receive what you have also begun to be, provided you do not receive unworthily." (Augustine, Sermon 228 B. MA [=Miscellanea Agostiniana] 1, 18-20. English trans. Edmund Hill, *Sermons* III/6 (184-229Z), 262.) "What you receive is what you yourselves are, thanks to the grace by which you have been redeemed; you add your signature to this, when you answer Amen. What you see here is the sacrament of unity." (Augustine, Sermon 229 A: 1. MA I, 462-464 or PLS 2, 554-556. English trans. Edmund Hill, *Sermons* III/6 (184-229Z), 270.)

[278]See UR, 2: "This is the sacred mystery of the unity of the Church, in Christ and through Christ, with the Holy Spirit energizing its various functions. The highest exemplar and source of this mystery is the unity, in the Trinity of Persons, of one God, the Father and

passing through the name into which we were baptized: the name of the Father and of the Son and of the Holy Spirit. We shall be sent out from the ritual in and through the same name. What the Eucharistic celebration has accomplished is our communion in the life of the Trinity. We now share in that dynamic and joyous dance of love — the *perichoresis* — that has moved from all eternity among the Father, the Son, and the Holy Spirit. Just as each member of the Trinity is distinct from the other and yet defined by the very relation held with the others, so too we enter into Trinitarian life precisely situated. We stand in the place of the Son and have been placed there through our baptism into his death and resurrection. The Eucharist ratifies this placement and brings it to completion. In the same way that the Spirit accompanied the Son through every moment of his earthly mission, shaping it into a human expression of the Son's eternal relation with his Father, so the Spirit accompanies us and shapes our human lives into the same expression. The scriptural words and the sacraments are the Spirit's masterful tools for this shaping. This is what we mean when we say that we come to the Father through the Son and in the Holy Spirit. The Father is not the Son and the Son is not the Father, and neither of these is the Holy Spirit. But each is what he is in relation to the others. In the same way, we are not Christ and Christ is not us; we are not the Spirit and the Spirit is not us. But in the great outpouring of eternal divine life in the creation and then through the incarnate life of the eternal Son, the Son and Spirit are henceforth what they have always been now in relation to us. There is no Son that is not the whole body of the Son, the Church. And there is no Spirit but the Spirit who forms the body of the Son, the Church. And the eternal Father relates as he has related from all eternity to no other Son than the whole Son and to no other Spirit than the Spirit who forms the body of the whole Son, who is Christ come to full stature. (Eph 4: 13)

---

the Son in the Holy Spirit." Also UR, 15, which speaks of the Eucharist as the means by which the faithful are "made 'sharers of the divine nature' (2 Pet 1:4) and enter into com-munion with the most Holy Trinity." GS 19: "The dignity of man rests above all on the fact that he is called to communion with God." See also AG 2 on the trinitarian shape of God's plan.

All this is the movement, the dynamic dance of love, which is the Christian Eucharist. See how useful, then, it is to call it "Source and Summit of the Church's Communion"! "Our communion is with the Father and with his Son our Lord Jesus Christ." (1 Jn 1:3) This is the Spirit's inspired word through the Apostle John. This is the faith of the One, Holy, Catholic, and Apostolic Church.

CHAPTER 6

EXPLORING THE IDENTITY OF THE BISHOP THROUGH THE THEOLOGY OF DISCLOSURE

Msgr. Robert Sokolowski

THIS VOLUME IS DEDICATED TO the theme of ecclesiology in the light of the Second Vatican Council, and my specific topic is the identity of the bishop. I think we all are familiar with the concepts of ecclesiology, the episcopal office, and the Council. However, the title assigned to me also mentions something called the theology of disclosure. This is a term we may not be familiar with; so let me begin with a few remarks about it.

1. Theology of Disclosure

I would like to define the theology of disclosure as a form of theological thinking that makes use of phenomenology. Why should theology make use of this philosophical form? Not just in order to connect theology with a recent and contemporary type of thinking — in other words, not because it might seem to be the fashionable thing to do — but because something important can be achieved by this kind of thinking. Christian theology has always been given a certain style by the philosophy it has incorporated into itself. Patristic thinking was marked by Neoplatonism and Stoicism; and scholastic theology showed the imprint of Aristotelianism. The theology of disclosure would reflect the concern with appearance that is central to modern philosophy.

The theology of disclosure tries to reflect on the way the things of our Christian faith come to light, how they are manifested to us. It tries to reflect on the appearance of Christian things. It does not, however, take these appearances to be merely subjective or psychological or even just historical. It attempts to get to essential structures of disclosure. It tries to examine the structures of appearance, for example, in regard to the sacraments, especially the Eucharist; in regard to the Church herself; in regard to the theological virtues of faith, hope, and charity, as well as prayer; and most fundamentally, in regard to the God revealed to us in Christian faith and teaching. It tries to show what is specific and distinctive about these and other Christian things and how they are disclosed to us. It tries to show how these things must appear if they are what the Church declares them to be.

By paying attention to appearances, and by stressing the fact that appearances are public and verifiable and not merely private and subjective, the theology of disclosure comes to terms with many of the problems that modern philosophy and culture have raised in regard to Christian faith. Everyone agrees that there is a tendency in modern culture to privatize Christian faith, even to sentimentalize it, to deprive it of any truth-value. The theology of disclosure aims at countering this tendency and tries to reemphasize the publicity of Christian belief, to restore the conviction that a person could not be a Christian without publicly proclaiming the truth of that faith. As Francis Slade says when discussing Jacques Maritain and Richard Rorty, "Christianity cannot live in the privacy of the heart. It is the religion of publicness. To cease to profess it publicly is 'to lose the Faith.' This is because Christianity is the religion of truth."[279] Truth is public, not private; Christianity reveals the truth of things, and so it cannot be confined to merely internal, private sentiment. It also becomes incumbent on Christianity to show what kind of truth it deals with, and the theology of disclosure can help it to do so.

The value of the theology of disclosure is not exhausted, however, in its effort to counter the modern tendency to privatize or psychologize Christian faith; it has a further positive value in itself. It allows us to appreciate more deeply the things revealed to

---

[279]Francis Slade, "*Was Ist Aufklärung?* Notes on Maritain, Rorty, and Bloom. With Thanks but No Apologies to Immanuel Kant," in *The Common Things: Essays on Thomism and Education,* edited by Daniel McInerny (Washington, D.C.: The American Maritain Association, 1999), p. 52.

us in Christian faith. It complements, I believe, the more purely ontological style of scholastic theology, and it recovers some of the themes of patristic thought, which also spoke about the way Christian things come to light for us. Thus, the theology of disclosure comes to terms with modern problems, but it also contributes to the positive contemplation and understanding of Christian truths.

A simple and intuitive way of describing the theology of disclosure is to say that it tries to show how Christian things are distinguished from the natural things that provide their context. Most fundamentally, the theology of disclosure would attempt to show how the God revealed in Christian faith is to be distinguished from the divinities that pagan culture and thinking arrived at.[280] It would try to show how faith, hope, and charity are to be distinguished from the natural virtues of temperance, courage, justice, prudence, and friendship; it would show that they are a different kind of virtue. The theology of disclosure would try to show how the sacraments are to be distinguished from natural religious celebrations. Things are manifested when they are distinguished from things that are like them, from things that provide their context, and the theology of disclosure speaks about such distinction and manifestation in regard to what is revealed in Christian faith.[281]

2. The Bishop as Teacher

The documents of the Second Vatican Council frequently repeat the refrain that the office of the bishop involves three tasks: teaching, sanctifying, and governing.[282] *Lumen gentium* devotes three distinct sections to this triad of teaching, sanctifying, and governing (§§25–27,

---

[280]I would like to observe that pagan attitudes and pagan "gods" are not merely a matter of ancient times; they return perennially, and they are no strangers to the modern scene. Two of the ways they appear now are to be found in New Age religion and in the aestheticism that often goes along with modern rationalism. I am sure that you shared my astonishment at the widespread criticism provoked by *Dominus Iesus*, the instruction of the Congregation for the Doctrine of the Faith; many people, both within and outside the Church, did not seem to realize the distinctiveness of the understanding of God and redemption taught by the Church.

[281]We might call the theology of disclosure a kind of "theology from below," but it would not have the anthropological character so often associated with this phrase.

[282]Citations from the texts of the Council will be taken from *The Documents of Vatican II*, edited by Walter M. Abbot, S.J., and Msgr. Joseph Gallagher (New York: Guild Press, 1966).

pp. 47–52), and it goes on to say that priests also share in these tasks as they represent the bishop in the particular parishes of the diocese. (§28. See also §32) The three functions are presented as the essential obligations bishops have in their role as shepherds; the document says, "With their helpers, the priests and deacons, bishops have therefore taken up the service of the community, presiding in the place of God over the flock whose shepherds they are, as teachers of doctrine, priests of sacred worship, and officers of good order." (§20, p. 40)

Lumen gentium also notes that these tasks and this authority are given to bishops as successors of the apostles, whose mission in turn reflected the mission of Christ himself from the Father: ". . . Jesus Christ, the Eternal Shepherd, established His holy Church by sending forth the apostles as He Himself had been sent by the Father. He willed that their successors, namely the bishops, should be shepherds in His Church even to the consummation of the world." (§18, p. 37) We should notice the sequence in this action of Christ. He did not first establish a Church and then appoint its leaders, nor did he simply allow the membership to elect their rulers; after living with his disciples and forming them, he sent the apostles as the ones responsible for shaping the Church from the beginning, under the guidance of the Holy Spirit. There was no Church until it was formed around the apostles; the Church is apostolic by definition. The apostles are not an afterthought to the Church but are constitutive of it, and the way they exercise their decisive role in the Church is through teaching, sanctifying, and governing. The central role of the bishops in the Church reflects the extraordinary prominence of the apostles in the four gospels and in the Acts of the Apostles.

The triplet of teaching, sanctifying, and governing is found throughout *Lumen gentium*. It also appears in the *Decree on the Bishops' Pastoral Office in the Church, Christus Dominus*, where it is again related to the role of shepherd. The Council says, "They [the bishops] feed their sheep in the name of the Lord, and exercise in their regard the office of teaching, sanctifying, and governing" (*Christus Dominus* §11). This triplet is classical, of course, and is based on the authority of Christ as prophet, priest, and king. The identity of the bishop is defined by his role of teaching, sanctifying, and governing.

Let us look more closely at these three tasks and the relationships among them. They are not a random collection of duties. There is an order to them. The second and third functions, sanctifying and governing, are founded on the first, the office of teaching, of declaring the truth of God's revelation. Apostolic teaching establishes the possibility of sanctifying and governing, and it gives these other two tasks their sense. Teaching is related to sanctifying and governing in a way analogous to the way the theological virtue of faith is related to hope and charity. Faith opens up the whole domain of Christian life; it opens up the space in which hope and charity can take place. Likewise, apostolic teaching opens the possibility for Christian life and for the Church. It establishes the space in which sanctification and governance are to occur. Apostolic teaching is fundamental for the other two tasks.

This fundamental teaching role in the Church is described in another document from the Second Vatican Council, *Dei Verbum*, the *Dogmatic Constitution on Divine Revelation*, which says that the original preaching of the apostles "was to be preserved by a continuous succession of preachers until the end of time." (§8, p. 115) It says that, "the apostles, handing on what they themselves had received, warn the faithful to hold fast to the tradition which they have learned either by word of mouth or by letter." The document goes on to say: "This teaching office is not above the word of God, but serves it, teaching only what has been handed on, listening to it devoutly, guarding it scrupulously, and explaining it faithfully by divine commission and with the help of the Holy Spirit. . . ." (§11, p. 118) This theme is, of course, a paraphrase of the great statement of St. Paul who, in writing to the Corinthians about the Eucharist, the central act of sanctification in the Church, begins by saying, "For I received from the Lord what I also handed on to you." (II Cor 11:23) Earlier in the same letter, when he addresses a number of problems in regard to the liturgy, he begins his exercise of governance by saying, "Be imitators of me, as I am of Christ. I praise you because you remember me in everything and hold fast to the traditions, just as I handed them on to you." (II Cor 11:1-2) The deposit of faith is something we receive and assent to, not something we construct. It is not a work generated by our minds, not a theological opinion, not something we think out on our own, not a personal belief that some people have. It is the faith of the Church and it is entrusted to the bishops.[283] The most basic reason why the deposit of faith is not the product of our own intelligence is that it involves a revealed understanding of God, one that transcends human reason.

The duty to hand on the faith of the Church, which is ultimately the teaching of Christ, is the most fundamental task of the apostles and the bishops. The duties of sanctifying and governing are based on this first task. That truth has to be declared and preserved, and therefore the apostles and bishops are invested with authority to provide for the good order of the Church. The apostles and bishops do not have their authority simply because the membership and the goods of the Church have to be organized in some way or other, and someone has to be given the task of carrying out such organization. The Church is not just another human society that needs a government; the ruling authority of the apostles and bishops goes deeper than that. The identity of the bishop, therefore, rests primarily not on his governing role but on the fact that he is commissioned to receive the tradition of the Church, in her teaching and in her liturgy, and to hand it on to the people entrusted to his care. Because he must hand on the truth of Christ, he must also govern. Without the teaching, the legitimacy of his ruling is called into question.

For the sake of contrast and definition, let us try to imagine another idea of the role of the bishop, another "model," if you will, of the episcopal office. Suppose that the bishop were understood to be primarily a mediator among various groups in the Church; his

---

[283]There is a passage in the *Commonitorium* of St. Vincent of Lérins that expresses very well the role of the bishop in handing on the faith. In a commentary on St. Paul's remarks to Timothy, in which Paul exhorts Timothy to preserve the deposit of faith, St. Vincent writes, "What is 'The deposit'? That which has been intrusted to you, not that which you have yourself devised: a matter not of wit, but of learning; not of private adoption, but of public tradition; a matter brought to you, not put forth by you, wherein you are bound to be not an author but a keeper, not a teacher but a disciple, not a leader but a follower. . . ." St. Vincent continues by exhorting the bishop to present the inherited truths in a fresh and beautiful way, but always to teach what has been received, not his own innovations: "[E]ngrave the precious gems of divine doctrine, fit them in accurately, adorn them skillfully, add splendor, grace, beauty. Let that which formerly was believed, though imperfectly apprehended, be clearly understood as expounded by you. Let posterity welcome, understood through your exposition, what antiquity venerated without understanding. Yet teach still the same truths which you have learned, so that though you speak after a new fashion, what you speak may not be new." This translation is taken from *A Select Library of Nicene and Post-Nicene Fathers of the Church*, Second Series, volume 11. The translation has been slightly amended.

task would be to bring about a consensus among them, to allow them to live together and thus preserve the unity of the Church. Among the members of the Church, there are different and often differing groups. All such groups in their diversity claim to be Catholic, and it would be the role of the "overseer" to keep them all in the fold, to mediate among them and let charity prevail. You get people to give a little here, give a little there, and in the end we can all get along. Such an image of the bishop would take his governing role as primary, but it would leave him without any compass, and as a sheer mediator he would be purely formal, without any definition, without any identity. The only thing that could save him from this sort of deconstruction is a return to the tradition that he inherits and is commissioned to hand on; unity in the Church is based on the truths of Christ, not on social consensus. That tradition, as the truth of Christian teaching and liturgy, defines the bishop as well as the Church. It authorizes and also guides him in his role of governing. In other words, all the decisions that the bishop has to make are to be made in the light of the truth that he teaches, not simply on his own practical judgment.

3.   What Kind of Teaching?

Let us examine the teaching that is so central to the identity of the bishop. When we use the word, teaching, we tend to think it signifies an academic activity. The kind of teaching demanded of the bishop, however, is based on the prophetic role of Christ, who is prophet, priest, and king. The teaching in question is not scholarly or academic, but the handing on of the inherited teaching of the Church, displaying the faith of the Church. The bishop, in his formal identity as such, no longer has the right to his personal opinions; he is authorized and commissioned to represent what the Church believes.

This teaching does not occur only in what the bishop alone says and does; it also implies, obviously, that the bishop will see to it that his priests are formed in the true faith during their seminary education, and that the preaching and catechetical instruction in his diocese is orthodox. He is the teacher of teachers in his diocese. The bishop should remind his priests, deacons, and catechists of the importance of Catholic doctrine in the life of the Church. Orthodox teaching is not something to be trifled with; everything is thrown into turmoil when it is neglected. The exercise of the teaching office also means that the bishop will ensure that the liturgy will be properly performed, since the liturgy serves not only to sanctify the people but also to educate them in the faith. How could one convey a sense of the what the Eucharist really is, how could one teach the truth of the Eucharist, if the liturgy were to be celebrated in an inappropriate and unworthy manner, one that makes it seem to be something other than it is? How can the Church convey a sense of God's power, majesty, and love if the tone conveyed by the liturgy is more that of a social gathering than a prayer and sacrifice offered to God? Episcopal supervision — which, incidentally, is a redundant term — is especially centered on the teaching and the liturgy that are carried on in the diocese. Who will ensure the authenticity of teaching and liturgy if the bishop does not do so?

The core of what is to be taught is simply the Church's credo, her profession of faith: that the world we live in is not all that there is, that it is not ultimate, but has been created by God who is so perfect and good that he created it out of sheer generosity and abundance; he did not need to create; that God lives a triune life, of Father, Son, and Holy Spirit; that this God, in the person of the Son, was born a man of the Virgin Mary and suffered and died to redeem us, then rose from the dead and now lives with the Father and is present in his Church, until he comes in judgment; that he brought us forgiveness of sin and shares his resurrection and life with us; that God knows and loves each of us, and has called us, each and all, to eternal life with him; our lives are led under God's providence. There are many other things in the Catholic tradition, of course, but these are the core, the creed, and these truths are as fresh and new and illuminating now as they ever were. They are truths about God and about ourselves that God himself has revealed to us in Christ. The world looks different to us, and we look different to ourselves, when these truths are received. The teaching role of the bishop is to hand on this understanding, just as the first apostles did. All the other truths and practices in our Catholic faith take on their meaning by their relationship to these fundamental articles of faith. It is absolutely essential to the episcopal teaching office that these things not be lost from view. They are so basic that we often take them for granted and do not talk enough about them, but we need constantly to be reminded of them. Basic truths like these need to be repeated over and over again, "in season, out of season." (II Tim 4:2) It makes a great difference if they become a deep part of a person's life and the life of a community, but they can be lost, and when they are, people will not see how the Church is different from any other religious organization, or why we should make a distinction between Jesus Christ and other profound figures in human history. I think that if the bishop of a diocese brings these truths to mind in an effective way and stresses their importance, the clergy and catechists will do so as well.

I would like to say a few words about what kind of truths these are and how they come to light for us, how they can be taught. They are not just items of information; they make a difference when they are registered for us. Let us try to illustrate this by drawing an analogy. Suppose a young man has been brought up in circumstances in which the people involved in his life were selfish and abusive. He has developed in the same way. At some point, someone speaks to him about human friendship: what it is, how it is exercised, how it is a moral perfection of human beings, a great human good. The words may be only words for him; they don't really register anything. He does not see friendship or benevolence as a human possibility. But then suppose circumstances change, perhaps some people act differently toward him, or perhaps through his own intelligence he begins to see the possibility of friendship. Suppose this truth of human nature registers for him, perhaps gradually, perhaps suddenly. This event is not merely the truth of correctness; the man does not merely find out that certain claims made by others are indeed true after all. Rather, what occurs is the truth of disclosure. The reality and the truth of friendship itself becomes manifest to him. Friendship becomes distinguished for him. It is not a matter of merely matching a judgment to a fact but a matter of letting something portentous come to light. Something becomes revealed or distinguished.[284]

---

[284] A valuable contribution of phenomenology is the distinction between the truth of correctness (in which we simply match a judgment to a fact) and the truth of disclosure, in which something originally comes to light. See Edmund Husserl, *Formal and Transcendental Logic*, trans. Dorion Cairns (The Hague: Nijhoff, 1969), §46.

This is the kind of truth we deal with when we come to realize, whether gradually or suddenly, that our lives are led under God's providence, that we and the world we live in have been created by an infinitely merciful God, who took on the burden of human life and redeemed us, who showed his power over death, and who calls us to eternal life. This is not just information that is confirmed but truth that is disclosed, and it makes all the difference to us. The teaching role of the bishop is to keep that truth alive in the local Church given to his care, and to ensure that his priests, deacons, and catechists strive to do so as well. The Church, especially the apostolic part of the Church, must make this truth available so that people can respond to it. Clearly, to convey such truth involves not only words but also a way of living that bears witness to this truth; but still, it does involve words as well, along with the understanding that these words convey. Words are necessary to explain why we live as we do when we strive to live as followers of Christ. To convey such truths is already to work for the sanctification of people, and it justifies the governing authority of the bishop. Canon law, with its rights and duties, flows from this teaching office.

4. Teaching about Nature as Well as about Grace

We have been discussing the way in which the bishop is the primary teacher, the apostolic teacher, of the things revealed in our faith. God's grace, however, is not only *elevans* but also *sanans*: his grace enables us to participate in his divine life, but it also heals our human nature. The teaching of Christ and the teaching of the Church shed light on what we are in our natural way of being. Thus, the encyclical *Fides et Ratio* declares that the mission of the Church in the modern world is not only to proclaim the faith, but also "to restore faith in reason,"[285] to show people that their own rational powers are capable of attaining truth about the world, about themselves, and even about God. It should be noted that this encyclical was addressed primarily to the bishops of the Catholic Church; the Holy Father seemed to be inviting them to look more closely at this aspect of their teaching office.

[285]The phrase, "restoring faith in reason," has been used to describe a project undertaken in England in response to the encyclical *Fides et Ratio*. The first volume of studies in this project is, *Restoring Faith in Reason*, edited by Laurence Paul Hemming and Susan Parsons (London: SCM Press, and Notre Dame: University of Notre Dame Press, 2002).

This exhortation does not mean, of course, that the bishops have to become professional philosophers or scientists, but it does mean that they should help people not only to accept God's revealed word but also to discover or rediscover their own natural dignity, the truth about their own nature and the nature of the world in which they live. Such a recovery of true human nature is part of the Christian gospel. Grace builds on nature, and if nature is left in need of repair, it is difficult for grace to build on it. Consider, for example, the truth about human sexuality and the family. The Church must present not only its revealed message, say, about the sacrament of marriage, but must also clarify the nature of sexuality, its *telos*, how it finds its perfection and its excellence as a human good. Human sexuality does not disclose itself in what people call "sex," but in a network of human relationships, between husband and wife and parents and children. That is where its truth is manifested.[286] The nature and the good of sexuality must be brought to light. Only in reference to this nature and this good can the distortions and sinful uses of sexuality be defined; only in reference to the good do the prohibitions and commandments make sense. If the good is first clarified, it becomes more obvious why the aberrations are wrong and sinful. Prohibitions against an evil should always be correlated with exhortations toward the good. In this instance, how could the Church's teaching on sexual matters be presented without bringing out the natural definition of sexuality? And the natural meaning of sexuality is certainly not commonly understood in our culture; think of the way it is presented by popular music, television, and movies, in which the distinction between love and lust is almost never made. Nature itself needs to be restored.

There are many other natural truths that need to be revived if grace is to be built on them. Human friendship, social relations, society itself, the common good, political life, war and peace, human labor, human action and human responsibility, the natural virtues, even the sense of the world as having meaning and of living things as having their own integrity. Human reason itself needs to be put back into perspective. It is not just the theological and the supernatural

---

[286]Sexual hedonists are often presented as being "realists" about human desire, but in fact they live in delusion.

that needs to be proclaimed, but the natural as well. And once again, as in the case of the truths of creation and redemption, it is liberating for a person to have such natural truths registered for him when they had been previously concealed. A person who had confused sexuality with lust is given greater human freedom when he discovers that there are forms of sexuality that are not equivalent to lust. Nature itself is healed by the gospel, and one of the ways in which the truth of the gospel is made evident to people is found in the way the gospel restores nature to what it ought to be.

A beautiful doctrinal illustration of the way grace confirms nature can be found in the dogma of the Immaculate Conception, in which Mary's humanity is preserved as what humanity should be. In the Blessed Virgin we have, not wounded nature healed, but, to use a phrase of Francis Slade, innocence elevated by grace.[287] In revelation and grace the natural comes forth in its proper integrity; they allow us to see the real character of nature.

5. Problems Related to the Teaching Role of the Bishop

In this final part of my essay, I will mention a few ways in which the teaching office of the bishop might be undermined. First, the bishop might think that so many intellectual problems have arisen regard to Catholic faith in the academic and scholarly world that he, the bishop, is no longer sufficiently equipped to hand on the faith. He may be intimidated in the exercise of his office. The issues have become too complex; we now have to defer to experts in theology, scripture studies, catechetics, perhaps even psychology and history; such people would be better able to master the state of the question and determine the true content of faith. This alienation of the bishop's teaching authority, the devolution from the bishop to the scholar, is a legacy of the Enlightenment. It follows from the understanding of reason that was introduced by thinkers such as Machiavelli and Descartes some five hundred years ago, in which not prudence and tradition but scientific method is taken to be the proper avenue to truth. It is interesting to note that Spinoza, who wrote in the immediate wake of Descartes, emphasized the historical relativism of the scriptures

---

[287] I am grateful to Francis Slade for these observations about the Immaculate Conception, and for many other remarks that I have used in this paper.

and implied thereby that the true custodians of the scriptures were the historians and philologists and not the Church.[288] But the kind of truth that is taught by the bishop is not the kind that academicians and scholars are primarily responsible for. The Church's profession of faith is determined not by scholars but by the Church, primarily by the apostles and their successors, and ultimately by Christ.

Some churchmen may feel a sense of inferiority before the academy. Indeed, anyone would be awestruck by the spectacular success of science, technology, and medicine. Their methods seem almost to guarantee truth and to move us unstoppably toward more and more discovery. How can anyone compete with this? How feeble it may seem, in contrast, to simply repeat something inherited from the past. But still, science, technology, and medicine are human achievements, and to be expert in them does not guarantee that one will use them well; another kind of truth is required for that, one based on a knowledge of both nature and human nature, and it is this kind of truth that Christian faith addresses, in the realms of both nature and grace. Furthermore, the humanities and social sciences, which deal more directly with human goods, have not enjoyed the same unquestionable success as the hard sciences; in fact, it is not unreasonable to say that they are in a particularly confused state right now, so much so that the academy would be one of the last places one would look for guidance on important human questions. I should also add that there is a very strong bias against Christianity in the Western intellectual and academic world, even within Catholic institutions, and the Church should not be naive about this hostility. This world has practically declared war on Christianity and it specifically attacks its claims to truth, and as we move into the domain of human biological and social engineering the conflict will probably get worse.[289]

The bishop should have confidence that the faith of the Church bears witness to itself if it is persistently and confidently proclaimed.

---

[288]Spinoza *Theological-Political Treatise*, chapters 7–10, discusses the authorship of the books of the Old Testament.

[289]Kenneth Minogue has described the sharp conflict between modern rationalism and Christianity: "At both the popular and the elite levels, American secularists are becoming increasingly hostile to Christian believers. The same is true in Europe, where such hostility is even more puzzling because there is a strong feeling among European rationalists that they have already 'won the argument'." "Religion, Reason, and Conflict in the 21st Century," *The National Interest* (Summer, 2003): 131. He says that "Western secularism," which

Certainly the teacher of the faith and the members of the Church must testify to the gospel by their own way of living, but Christian truths also bear witness to themselves; in themselves they shed light on human existence and on the nature of things, to anyone who is willing to come into this light. There is no reason for the Church or the bishops to be intimidated by academic experts. What Christ has taught us about our destiny as human beings does not need to yield to the pictures presented by our intellectual elites.

I should also add that the bishop does not need to be a great writer or a television star to fulfill his teaching role, nor does he have to address crowds of thousands. It is a matter of persistent and consistent restatement of basic truths. The apostles, after all, spoke to small groups. St. Thomas Aquinas says that direct oral teaching is superior to written because it imprints the teaching on the hearts of the hearers.[290]

Secondly, the bishop's teaching role may be given over to the various committees and offices within the diocese or within national Church conferences. The bishop may think it necessary to defer to their expertise, much as he might be inclined to trust the judgment of scholars over his own. He may defer to the bureaucracy. Of course, councils, committees, and offices may be very helpful to the bishop and even necessary, but they do not take the place of the apostles, and they too must be subordinated to the essentials of the Church's faith. We can't really imagine a committee making a report at the Areopagus, and it was the apostles and Peter who spoke at Pentecost, not their staffs. The bishops run the risk of losing control over their institutions, especially their educational institutions, if they trust the experts more than their own judgment.[291]

The third and final challenge to the identity of the bishop that I wish to mention is more in the realm of ideas. It is the substitution

is "entrenched in the universities," takes pains "to assail Christianity . . . with everything from rational argument to satirical mockery." (p. 128) He observes that secular thinkers do not show the same hostility toward other religions, because they see them as expressions of culture, while Christianity makes claims to truth that compete with modern rationalism. This article by Minogue is a review of Phillip Jenkins, *The Next Christendom. The Coming of Global Christianity.*

[290]St. Thomas Aquinas, *Summa Theologiae III*, q. 42, a. 4. I am grateful to Kevin White for this reference, and for many other comments on my paper. I wish also to thank John Smolko for observations that I have used.

[291]On Catholic colleges and universities and their task of handing on the faith, see Robert Sokolowski, "Church Tradition and the Catholic University," *Homiletic and Pastoral Review* 96 (February 1996): 22–31.

of a religion of humanity for the Christian faith. We often think of Marxism or scientism as the main challenges to Christian thought, but I would claim that the greatest popular influence on our contemporary Western culture has been exercised by John Stuart Mill and Auguste Comte, both of whom lived in the middle of the 19th century, and both of whom thought that Christianity had outlived its time and should be replaced by a religion of humanity. They respected Christianity and wanted to accept its teaching of charity, of benevolence and peace, but they also thought that such benevolence should be based on a love of mankind, not on doctrines about God and not on the hope for eternal life. As Nietzsche said about them, they wanted to "outchristian Christianity" by demanding that we sacrifice everything for others, for humanity at large, and that we do so without any hope of salvation for ourselves, that is, that we should do so with no self-interest whatever. They call for charity without hope for redemption. In Nietzsche's words, "The more one liberated oneself from the dogmas, the more one sought as it were a justification of this liberation in a cult of philanthropy: not to fall short of the Christian ideal in this, but where possible to outdo it, was a secret spur with all French thinkers from Voltaire up to Auguste Comte: and the latter did in fact, with his moral formula *vivre pour autrui*, outchristian Christianity."[292] Nietzsche clearly shows that it is specifically the truth of Christianity, the dogmas, that the religion of humanity wishes to deny, and that it does so while claiming to possess an even more noble sense of Christian charity. This point is often shown in a practical way: our secular culture will often accept and even praise the Church to the extent that she is serving the religion of humanity, but it will become very hostile to the Church when she publicly presents her own teaching, her own faith.[293]

But Christian charity is not just an amplified human benevolence. Christian charity is based entirely on the belief in God

---

[292]Nietzsche, *Daybreak:* §132.

[293]It is true that the Christian message involves, as an immediate inference, concern for the poor; St. Paul in the Letter to the Galatians describes the Council of Jerusalem and says that he and Barnabas were commissioned to preach to the Gentiles, with the following provision: "Only, we were to be mindful of the poor, which is the very thing I was eager to do." (Galatians 2:10) Concern for the poor follows from the Christian message. In the modern alternative, concern for the poor becomes primary and the message is seen as an ideological contribution. But when this reversal occurs, the concern for the poor becomes more like a partisan political exercise of what Aristotle called democracy.

as the supremely charitable Creator and Redeemer, the one whose Trinitarian life is even more intensely generous than are his actions of creation and redemption. It is because God is the way he is, it is because of the way God has revealed himself to us, that we are called to Christian charity. You cannot have the theological virtues without the theological truths. We hope for eternal life not because of some striving we experience in ourselves, but because we have been told that God is life, and this life is the light for men, and this light has shone in the darkness. To the Christian, the world looks the way it does, and the human person looks the way he does, because God is the way he is. Christ has revealed this to us, and the Church, through the apostles, hands on this understanding and this living presence of God; she makes it known to all men and confirms it in those who already believe. The identity of the bishop is determined by the mission, given him by Christ in the Holy Spirit, to teach these truths about the Father, and to sanctify and govern the Church that is built upon them.

I would like to close with a more general comment on the Second Vatican Council. It may seem trivial to say this, but I think it has to be said: The Second Vatican Council was not the only ecumenical council in the history of Church. Regrettably, what became known as "the spirit of Vatican II" gave the impression that this council somehow negated all the others, or at least that it was different from all the others and provided a unique interpretation on all the rest. If I may use a metaphor from football, the impression was given that the tradition of the Church was not a continuous handing on, through the centuries, of something received; it was more like a long pass from the apostolic age to the Second Vatican Council, with only distortions in between, whether Byzantine, medieval, or baroque. But in fact, the Second Vatican Council is only one council among many, and all the others — including the First Vatican Council and the Council of Trent — as well as the tradition of the Church retain their force and importance. I think the sudden and radical change in the liturgy of the Western Church contributed to this popular idea of the uniqueness of the Second Vatican Council. One of the greatest challenges to the Church is to reestablish the continuity between the present Church and the Church throughout the centuries, to revalidate the tradition of the Church. This is a challenge for all the educational institutions in the Church, from elementary catechetics to colleges to seminaries to universities and research centers, but it is a challenge for the bishops most of all, since they are entrusted with preserving the definition of the Church. Indeed, as a colleague of mine once put it,[294] it may be necessary for the entire papacy of some future pope to be devoted to a single goal: the comprehensive restoration of tradition and especially the liturgy, to make it obvious that the changes in the liturgy and in theology begun in the 1960s were not the radical break they are so often taken to be. Without episcopal teaching in continuity with the apostles and with Christ, there is no sanctification and government, and there can be no Catholic Church.

---

[294]Kevin White.

CHAPTER 7

The Petrine Ministry and the Indefectibility of the Church

Robert Fastiggi

Nous trouverons dans L'Évangile que Jésus-Christ voulant commencer le mystère de l'unité dans son Église, parmi tous les disciples il en choisit douze: mais que voulant conserver le mystère de l'unité dans la même Église, parmi les douze il en choisit un.

J.B. Bossuet (1627-1704), *Sermon sur l unité de L Église, premier point*

For it is through Christ's Catholic Church alone, which is the universal help towards salvation, that the fullness of the means of salvation can be obtained. It was to the apostolic college alone, of which Peter is the head, that we believe that our Lord entrusted all the blessings of the New Covenant, in order to establish on earth the one Body of Christ into which all those should be fully incorporated who belong in any way to the people of God.

Vatican II, *Unitatis Redintegratio*, 3

INTRODUCTION

THE PETRINE MINISTRY IS CENTRAL to the nature and identity of the Catholic Church. This essay will seek to examine this ministry as it relates to the indefectibility of the Church. The teachings of Vatican II and the post-conciliar Church will be given special consideration, but these teachings will be interpreted in continuity with earlier magisterial interventions. As Cardinals Joseph Ratzinger and Avery Dulles, S.J. have emphasized, the documents of Vatican II must be interpreted in the light of the great tradition of the Church,

especially earlier ecumenical councils.[295] This is what I hope to do
with respect to the issues of the papal office and the indefectibility
of the Church. Seven major topics will be explored: 1) the divine
institution of the episcopacy and the papacy; 2) the meaning of the
Church's indefectibility; 3) the indefectibility of the Church's essential
structure; 4) the Petrine ministry and the preservation of unity in
faith and morals; 5) indefectibility and infallibility; 6) the exercise and
expression of the Petrine office since Vatican II; 7) conclusion: the
Petrine office as essential for the nature and mission of the Church,
especially for the ecclesiology of communion.

1) The Divine Institution of the Episcopacy and the Petrine Office

Although he had Gallican leanings, the French bishop and
preacher, Jacques Bénigne Bossuet (1627–1704) understood the central
point of the Petrine office, viz., it is established by Jesus Christ Himself
to preserve unity in the Church. In his 1681 *"Sermon on the Unity of the
Church,"* Bossuet notes:

> We will find in the Gospel that Jesus Christ, wishing to
> inaugurate the mystery of unity in His Church, chose twelve
> among all the disciples: but wishing to conserve the mystery of
> unity in the same Church, he chose one among the twelve.[296]

Among all the disciples, Jesus chose twelve, and, among the
twelve, he chose one. The witness of Bossuet is direct and lucid. The
choice of Peter among the twelve is not due to historical or political
factors. It is due to the free and sovereign will of Christ. This is how
the Catholic tradition understands the matter. As Cardinal Ratzinger
observed: "the Church is not *our* Church, which we could dispose of
as we please. She is, rather, *his* Church."[297]

The selection of Peter as the head of the primordial apostolic
college is attested to in Scripture and Tradition. When the Twelve

---

[295]See *The Ratzinger Report,* translated by S. Attanasio and Graham Harrison (San Francisco: Ignatius Press, 1985), 28 and Avery Dulles, "Vatican II: The Myth and the Reality," *America* (Feb. 24, 2003) 9. Dulles is using the Second Extraordinary Synod of Bishops of 1985 as his point of departure. The Final Report of this Synod of Bishops can be found in *Origins* Vol. 15: No. 27 (1985): 444-450.

[296]J.B. Bossuet, *Sermon sur l'unité de L'Église, premier point* in *Sermons de Bossuet, tome quatrième* (Paris: Garnier Frères, Libraires, 1973), 427 (my translation; in the remainder of this essay, all translations are my own unless otherwise cited).

[297]*The Ratzinger Report,* 48.

chosen by Jesus are listed, Peter's name is always given first (cf. Mt 10:2; Lk 6:13-16 and Acts 1:13). In the Gospels, Peter is mentioned 114 times. In Acts, his name appears 57 times. By comparison, John (probably the next most prominent member of the Twelve) is mentioned 38 times in the Gospels and 8 times in Acts.[298] According to one account, Peter is referred to by name (sometimes as Simon or Cephas) at least 195 times in the New Testament while the mention of all the rest of the Twelve combined comes to 130.[299] The prominence of Peter in the New Testament is undeniable. It has been recognized by ecumenical groups of Catholics and Protestants and Catholics and Anglicans.[300] Eastern Orthodox scholars have likewise recognized the special importance of Peter in Scripture.[301]

The Catholic position, however, goes beyond a simple recognition of Peter as the most prominent member of the Twelve. Instead, we believe that Christ's choice of Peter constitutes an essential moment in the foundation of the Church and her permanent structure. This Catholic belief is based not only on the witness of Scripture but also from the historical testimony of tradition and the Magisterium. According to the Catholic faith, the Petrine office does not exist because of church law only (*ius mere ecclesiasticum*); rather it exists by divine law (*de iure divino*) and by divine institution (*ex institutione divina*).[302]

The Catholic understanding of the Petrine ministry is rooted in Scripture. In the Gospels, Christs calls Peter as the rock upon which his Church will be built (Mt 16:18). Peter is given "the keys to the kingdom of heaven" (Mt 16:19), a symbol of his distinct

---

[298]Johann Auer, *Dogmatic Theology 8: The Church, the Universal Sacrament of Salvation*, trans. Michael Waldstein (Washington, D.C.: The Catholic University of America Press, 1993), 228.

[299]Scott Butler, Norman Dahlgreen and David Hess, *Jesus, Peter & the Keys: A Scriptural Handbook on the Papacy* (Santa Barbara, CA, 1996), 3-4.

[300]See Raymond E. Brown, K.P. Donfried and J. Reumann, eds, *Peter in the New Testament* (Minneapolis, MN: Augsburg Publishing, 1973) and J. Michael Miller, CSB, *What Are They Saying about Papal Primacy?* (New York: Paulist Press, 1983) and *The Gift of Authority* issued in 1999 by Anglican-Roman Catholic International Commission [ARCIC]. This latter document can be found under the Pontifical Council for Promoting Christian Unity on the Vatican web site (vatican.va).

[301]See J. Meyendorrf, A Schmemann, N. Afanassief, and N. Koulomzine, *The Primacy of Peter* (Aylesbury, UK: The Faith Press, 1973) and J. Meyendorrf, ed. *The Primacy of Peter* (Crestwood, N.Y.: St. Vladimir's Seminary Press, 1992).

[302]See J. Michael Miller, CSB, *The Divine Right of the Papacy in Recent Ecumenical Theology* (Roma: Università Gregoriana Editrice, 1980) and Avery Dulles, SJ, "*Ius Divinum* As An Ecumenical Problem" *Theological Studies* 38 (1977) 681-708.

authority as the Vicar of Christ.[303] Moreover, the Lord instructs Peter to strengthen his brethren in the faith (Lk 22:32) and to feed and tend the flock (Jn 21:15-17).

What is revealed in the Gospels is supported by Tradition. "A revelation is not given," Newman tells us, "if there be no authority to decide what it is that is given."[304] Consequently, the classic Petrine texts must be read "within the living Tradition of the whole Church."[305] Moreover, "the task of giving an authentic interpretation of the Word of God, whether written or handed down in Tradition, has been entrusted only to the living Magisterium of the Church (*soli vivo Ecclesiae Magisterio concreditum est*).[306] Therefore, although the Catholic belief in the divine institution of the Petrine office rests on the authority of divine revelation, this revelation can only be received and properly understood within "the living Tradition of the whole Church" and the authority of the "living Magisterium." Just as the Catholic Church has judged the Trinity and the divinity of Christ to be truths revealed by God so also has the same Church discerned the divine establishment of the Petrine office.

Since the Church emerges from "the utterly gratuitous and mysterious design" of the eternal Father's "wisdom and goodness,"[307] it follows that the structure of the Church is not accidental. As "founded by the words and actions of Jesus Christ" and "fulfilled by his redeeming cross and his Resurrection,"[308] the Church, in her very origins, shows the signs of divine Providence and protection. Just as Jesus was "delivered up by the set plan and foreknowledge of God" (Acts 2:23), so also has the Church been established according to God's wisdom and providence. Indeed, the Church was "prefigured in creation" and "prepared for in the Old Covenant."[309] The words and actions of Jesus towards Peter and the Twelve, therefore, reflect a "plan born in the Father's heart."[310]

---

[303]See Butler, et. al., 39-68 on the authority of the keys and the power of binding and loosing as interpreted in the light of the Old Testament passages such as Isa 22:22.
[304]J.H. Newman, *An Essay on the Development of Christian Doctrine* (1878) II, 2, 12.
[305]*Catechism of the Catholic Church* [CCC], 113
[306]*Dei Verbum*, 10.
[307]*Lumen Gentium*, [LG] 2; CCC, 759.
[308]CCC, 778.
[309]Ibid.; cf. LG, 2.
[310]CCC, 759.

It is only within this theological recognition of the Church's providential ordering that the following declaration of *Lumen gentium*, 18 can be understood:

> This sacred synod, following in the steps of the First Vatican Council, teaches and declares with it that Jesus Christ, the eternal Pastor, set up the holy Church by entrusting the apostles with their mission as he himself had been sent by the Father (cf. Jn 20:21). He willed that their successors, the bishops namely, should be shepherds in his Church until the end of the world. In order that the episcopate itself, however, might be one and undivided he put Peter at the head of the other apostles, and in him he set up a lasting and visible source of the unity both of faith and of communion.[311]

Clearly the Fathers of Vatican II understood the Petrine office, along with the episcopacy, to be divinely instituted by Christ Himself. Thus, we are told that the Lord Jesus "having prayed at length to the Father, called to himself those he willed and appointed twelve to be with him."[312] Jesus made the choice of the Twelve within the context of prayer and in union with the Father. Furthermore, these twelve apostles "he constituted in the form of a college or permanent assembly, at the head of which he placed Peter, chosen from amongst them (cf. Jn 21:15-17)."[313] The sovereign will of Jesus, therefore, in accordance with "the utterly gratuitous and mysterious design"[314] of the Father, is the true source of "the institution, the permanence, the nature and import of the sacred primacy of the Roman Pontiff and his infallible teaching office."[315]

Vatican II's declaration of the divine establishment of the Petrine ministry is consistent with the historical witness of the Church from the beginning. Even within the first century (c. 96 A.D.), we find evidence of the successor of Peter, namely Clement I, speaking with authority to the Church of Corinth. In reaction to the unjust removal of some presbyters from their functions, Clement warns the Corinthians of the dangers of disobedience from his instructions:

---

[311]LG, 18 (all Vatican II translations are taken from the Flannery edition, unless otherwise noted).
[312]LG, 19.
[313]Ibid.
[314]LG, 2.
[315]LG, 18.

> If, on the other hand, there be some who fail to obey what God has told them through us, they must realize they will enmesh themselves in sin and in no insignificant danger (c.59, n. 1)...Yes, you will make us exceedingly happy if you prove to be obedient to what we, prompted by the Holy Spirit, have written, and if, following the plea of our letter for peace and harmony, you rid yourselves of your wicked and passionate rivalry (c. 63, n. 2).[316]

Clement, as the Bishop of Rome, assumes an authority over the Church of Corinth that demands obedience.

Further testimony of the preeminence of the Church of Rome is to be found in other early Patristic writings. In his letter to the Romans (c. 107 A.D.), Ignatius of Antioch speaks of the Roman Church as enjoying "the presidency" (προκάθημένη) of love.[317] Irenaeus, in his *Adversus haereses* (c. A.D. 180-199) praises "that very great, oldest and well-known Church, founded and established at Rome by those two glorious apostles Peter and Paul."[318] Furthermore, he teaches that, "every Church must be in harmony with this Church because of its outstanding pre-eminence (*propter potentiorem principalitatem*), that is, the faithful from everywhere, since the apostolic tradition is preserved in it by those from everywhere."[319] The phrase *"potentiorem principalitatem"* has been variously translated as "superior authority," "superior origin;" "more-exalted origin," and "more powerful principality." All of these communicate the sense of preeminence over all the other churches, a preeminence that demands harmony or agreement in doctrine.[320]

Cyprian of Carthage provides another witness to the importance of the Petrine office. In a letter to all his people written, c. A.D. 251, the African bishop notes that "there is one God and one Christ, and one Church, and one Chair founded on Peter by the word of the Lord."[321] In the first edition of his treatise on *The Unity of the Catholic Church*, Cyprian points to "the chair of Peter" as the mark of Church unity:

---

[316]*Clement's First Letter,* 59,1 and 63,2 in Cyril Richardson, ed. *Early Christian Fathers* (New York: Touchstone, 1996), 70 and 75; these selections can also be found in Denzinger-Hünermann [D-H](37th ed.), *102

[317]Ignatius, To the Romans in E. Giles, ed. *Documents Illustrating Papal Authority, A.D. 96-454* (London: SPCK, 1952), 4.

[318]*Adversus haereses,* III, 3, 3 in Richardson, 372.

[319]Ibid, III, 3, 2.

[320]The importance of this passage of Irenaeus is manifested by its citation in Vatican I's *Pastor Aeternus,* D-H, *3057.

[321]William A. Jurgens, ed. *The Faith of the Early Fathers, Volume I* (Collegeville, MN: The Liturgical Press), 229.

> Indeed, the others were that also which Peter was; but a primacy is given to Peter, whereby it is made clear that there is but one Church and one chair...If someone does not hold fast to this unity of Peter, can he imagine that he still holds the faith? If he desert the chair of Peter upon whom the Church was built, can he still be confident that he is in the Church.[322]

Along with these written testimonies to papal primacy, there is also the witness of doctrinal interventions. Thus, Pope Victor I (r. 189-198) censured the Quatrodecimans, Callistus I (r. 217-22) condemned Sabellianism, and Stephen I (r. 254-257) opposed the re-baptism of heretics. Speaking of the third century pontiffs, Cardinal Newman observed:

> The Popes acted as if they were infallible in doctrine — with a very high hand, peremptorily, magisterially, fiercely. But when we come to the question of the *analysis* of such conduct, I think they had as vague ideas on the subject as many of the early Fathers had upon portions of the doctrine of the Holy Trinity. *They acted in a way which needed infallibility as an explanation* [emphasis in original].[323]

In the fourth and fifth centuries, testimonies to the preeminence of Bishop of Rome continue, along with the recognition that this preeminence comes from Christ Himself. Thus, Ambrose, (c. A.D. 340-397) writes:

> That is Peter to whom [Christ] said, "Thou art Peter, and upon this rock I will build my Church." Where therefore Peter is there is the Church. Where the Church is, there is no death, but life eternal. And he also adds, "And the gates of hades shall not prevail against it, and I will give to thee the keys of the kingdom of heaven." Against blessed Peter, neither has the gate of hades prevailed, nor the gate of heaven shut, but on the contrary he has destroyed the forecourt of hades and thrown open the heavenly one.[324]

In a similar manner, Jerome (c. A.D. 342-420) highlights the role of Peter as the head of the apostolic college. In *Adversus Jovinianum*, he observes:

> But you say that the Church was founded upon Peter: although elsewhere the same is attributed to all the apostles, and they all

---

[322]Ibid., 220-221; the second edition of this treatise (sometimes called the episcopal text as opposed to the primacy text) seems to highlight the equality of the other bishops with Peter. Scholars continue to debate whether the "episcopal text" or "the primacy text" best reflects the mind of Cyprian. It is now generally believed, however, that both versions are the work of Cyprian; cf. Henry Bettenson, ed. *The Early Christian Fathers* (Oxford and New York: Oxford University Press, 1984), 263.

[323]From Newman's letter to Mrs. H. Froude (March, 1871), quoted in full in W. Ward, *The Life of John Henry Cardinal Newman* (London: Longmans, Green and Co., 1912), vol. 2, 378-379.

[324]*Ambrose, Enarratio in Psalmum* XL; Migne PL, 14, 1082; Giles, Document 111, 144-145.

receive the keys to the kingdom of heaven, and the strength of the Church depends on them all alike, yet one among the twelve is chosen so that when a head has been appointed, there may be no occasion for schism.[325]

There are numerous Magisterial documents from the fourth and fifth centuries that support the primacy and authority of Roman See and its divine institution. Many selections from Denzinger's *Enchiridion* for this time period can be cited.[326] The impression, though, is sometimes given that belief in papal primacy and authority was a purely Western position. This, however, was not the case. For example, John Chrysostom (c. 344-407), an Eastern contemporary of Ambrose and Jerome, finds evidence in the Gospels of Christ's bestowal of universal government on Peter:

> After this lamentable fall — for no evil can equal denial — after, I say, such an enormous fault, Jesus restores Peter to his prior dignity and entrusts to him the government of the universal Church.[327]

The attitude of Flavian, the Patriarch of Constantinople from 446-449, towards the See of Rome reflects a remarkable confidence in the ability of the Roman Pontiff to resolve doctrinal questions. Writing to Leo I (Pope from 440-461) about the error of Eutyches, Flavian, the Bishop of the "New Rome," believes that an intervention by the Bishop of the "Old Rome" is sufficient to settle the question:

> The whole question needs only your single decision and all will be settled in peace and quietness. Your sacred letter will with God's help completely suppress the heresy which has arisen and the disturbance it has caused; and so the convening of a council which is in any case difficult will be rendered superfluous.[328]

Thus, a doctrinal pronouncement by the Pope can resolve a theological dispute for the universal Church and render an ecumenical council superfluous. A stronger witness to the Pope's universal magisterial authority is difficult to imagine.

Flavian's deference to the Roman See is reflected in the writings other Eastern theologians of the seventh, eight and ninth

---

[325] *Jerome, Adversus Jovinianum*, Book I; Migne, PL 23, 247; Giles, 155.

[326] D-H *132-133; 181; 217-218; 221; 233-235; 282 and 350-351.

[327] John Chrysostom, *Homelia 5 de poenitentia;* Migne, PG 49, 308.

[328] J.D. Mansi, *Sanctorum conciliorum nova et amplissima collectio...*(Lucca 1748-1752), vol. 5. Col. 1356. Translation taken from Vladimir Soloviev, *Russia and the Universal Church*, trans. H. Rees. (London: Geoffrey Bles/The Centenary Press, 1948),134. This same text by Flavian is cited in Stephen K. Ray, *Upon This Rock: St. Peter and the Primacy in Scripture and the Early Church* (San Francisco: Ignatius Press, 1999), 242.

centuries. Sophronius (c. 560-638), the Patriarch of Jerusalem from 634-638, instructed Bishop Stephen of Dora (who spoke Latin) to go "to the apostolic See, where are the foundations of orthodox doctrine" in order to destroy the new heresy of Monotheletism."[329] After Sophoronius' death, Bishop Stephen appealed in person to Pope Martin I (r.649-655) at the opening of the Lateran Synod of 649 in these words:

> I would like to denounce Monothelitism before the eminent Chair, the teacher of all the chairs; I mean your superior and divine chair, since it may completely heal the wound. Your chair has been accustomed from the beginning to rule with apostolic and canonical authority. It is very evident, indeed, that it is not only the keys to the kingdom of heaven that Peter, alone among all, received. Besides the keys of heaven, by which he can open and shut for the well-being of believers and the misfortune of unbelievers, this true head and director of the apostles, was the first entrusted with the feeding the sheep of the entire Catholic Church ... and the only one authorized to strengthen his colleagues and spiritual brothers when they become shaken, on account of the foreknowledge of God Incarnate who, for our sake, gave him power and priestly authority over them all.[330]

Witness to the primacy and divine origin of the Roman See is given by Maximus the Confessor (c. 580-662). He notes that, "since the Incarnation of the Word, all the Christian Churches of the entire world have not had, and still do not have, any but this most sublime Church as a base and foundation."[331] Speaking of the Roman See, he likewise observes that

> This Apostolic See, which, from the incarnate Word of God Himself, as well as all the holy synods, according to the sacred canons and decisions, has received the sovereignty, authority and power (*imperium, auctoritatem et potestatem*) of binding and loosing over all the holy Churches of God in the entire world, in and through all things.[332]

A final Eastern Father worthy of mention is Theodore of Studium (759-806). Not only does he affirm the divine origin of papal

---

[329]Mansi, vol. 10, col. 896; cited in Martin Jugie, AA, *Le Schisme Byzantin* (Paris: Lethielleux, 1941), 77; see also Stanley L. Jaki, *Eastern Orthodoxy's Witness to Papal Primacy* (Port Huron, MI: Real View Books, 2004), 7.

[330]Mansi, vol. 10, col. 896; cited in Martin Jugie, AA, *Le Schisme Byzantin*, 78; see Jaki, p. 7 for a slightly different translation.

[331]Migne, PG, vol. 91, col 137-140; Cited in Jugie, 79.

[332]Migne, PG 91, 144 (in Latin only); Mansi, vol. 10. col. 692; Jugie, 79.

primacy, he also recognizes the Pope as the final judge of all heresies. As he writes:

> Since Christ our God gave to Peter, after the keys to the kingdom of heaven, the dignity of supreme pastor, it is necessary to submit to Peter, that is to say, to his successor (πρός Πέτρον ἤτοι τον διάδοχον), all the novelties introduced into the Church by those who deviate from the truth.[333]

In another passage, Theodore refers to the Pope as "the limpid and always inalterable source of orthodoxy" and "the tranquil port and judge of the universal Church against all the storms of heresy.[334]

Eastern Fathers such as Flavian, Sophronius, Maximus the Confessor and Theodore the Studite manifest an understanding of papal authority that is completely Catholic and in accord with the teachings of Vatican I and Vatican II. The seeds of an alternative Eastern ecclesiology, however, are manifest in Canon 3 of Constantinople I (A.D. 381) and Canon 28 of Chalcedon (A.D. 451). When Canon 3 teaches that, "the bishop of Constantinople is to enjoy the privileges of honour after the bishop of Rome,"[335] the reason given is that it is the "new Rome." Here secular and political stature becomes a criterion for ecclesiastical honor rather divine decree or apostolic tradition. When Canon 28 of Chalcedon bestows "equal privileges" to Constantinople, the "new Rome" as those enjoyed by the "older Rome," the reason is that the "new Rome" "is honoured by the imperial power and senate and enjoying privileges equalling older imperial Rome."[336] The papal rejection of Canon 3 of Constantinople[337] and Canon 28 of Chalcedon[338] reveals a Roman resistance to this emerging Eastern ecclesiology.

As is well known, those Eastern Christians who wished to downplay the universal authority of the See of Rome developed the concept of the Pentarchy of the five primal Sees, viz., Rome, Constantinople, Alexandria and Antioch and Jerusalem. These five Sees were compared to the "five senses" of the Mystical Body of Christ.[339] After the schism, though, the theory of the Pentarchy could

---

[333]Ibid., PG 99, 1017; Jugie, 94.
[334]Ibid., PG 99, 1156; Jugie, 95.
[335]Norman Tanner, S.J., ed. *Decrees of the Ecumencial Councils*, Vol. I (London and Washington, D.C.: Sheed & Ward and Georgetown University Press, 1990), 32.
[336]Ibid., 100.
[337]Ibid., 23.
[338]Ibid., 76.
[339]See M. Jugie,"Primauté D'Après Les Byzantines," in *Dictionnaire de Théologie Catholique,*

no longer be sustained. The argument was that, following Rome's defection from Orthodoxy, Constantinople assumed the position as the primal See.[340] The new structure of authority in the Church was the Tetrarchy. The comparison was now made, not to the five senses of the body, but to an edifice sustained by the four columns of the four Patriarchal Sees.[341]

The Catholic Church has great respect for the historical importance of the five ancient Patriarchal Sees and the subsequent Patriarchates. This is evident in canon 21 of Constantinople IV (A.D. 869-870),[342] the "Decree for the Greeks of Florence (A.D. 1439)[343] and the "Decree for Catholic Eastern Churches" of Vatican II (A.D. 1964).[344] It is clear, however, that the Catholic Church would never describe such Patriarchates as being established *de iure divino*. Instead, the order of these venerable Patriarchal Sees has been "transmitted in the canons" (*ordinem traditum in canonibus*).[345] The rights and privileges according to the Patriarchates come from "the ancient traditions of each church and the decrees of the ecumenical councils."[346] These traditions and decrees, however, pertain only to ecclesiastical law (*ius mere ecclesiasticum*) and not to divine law (*ius divinum*).

It follows, therefore, that the Catholic hierarchical structure of the Pope and the college of bishops is perceived as divinely established while the special privileges accorded to certain Patriachates emerge from ecclesiastical tradition. This is seen in the Catholic *Code of the Eastern Churches* (1995). The institution of the Patriarchates exists "according to the most ancient tradition of the Church" (*secudum antiquissimam Ecclesiae traditionem*),[347] but the Petrine office, came into being "by the Lord's decision" (*statuente Domino*).[348] The fact that Patriarchates can be established and abolished (as in the case

---

[DTC] vol. 13, part 1 (Paris: Letouzey et Ané, 1936), 376 and Martin Jugie, A.A. *Theologia Dogmatica Christianorum Orientalium ab Ecclesia Catholica Dissidentium, vol. IV (Paris: Letouzey et Ané, 1931)*, 451-461.

[340]DTC, 376.

[341]Ibid., 378 and Jugie, *Theologia Dogmatica*, 461-462.

[342]Tanner, Vol. I, 182; D-H, 661.

[343]Tanner, Vol. I, 528; D-H, 1308.

[344]*Orientalium Ecclesiarum*, 7-11; see also *Unitatis Redintegratio*, 14.

[345]Council of Florence; D-H, 1308.

[346]*Orientalium Ecclesiarum*, 9.

[347]Canon 55 of the *Codex Canonum Ecclesiarum Orientaliu*m [CCEO] (Roma: Liberia Editrice Vaticana, 1995).

[348]Canon 42 of the CCEO.

of Moscow)[349] is a sign of their inability to claim divine institution. All this shows that, according to Catholic doctrine, the primacy and authority of the papal office exists, not as an accident of ancient imperial power, nor simply by ecclesiastical law, but according to the will of Christ. The theological note attached to this teaching would be *de fide definita*. This is evident from the following canon of Vatican I" *Pastor Aeternus*:

> Therefore, if anyone should say that it is not by the institution of Christ the Lord, Himself, that is, by divine law (*non esse ex ipsius Christi Domini institutione seu iure divino*) that Blessed Peter should always possess successors in the primacy over the universal Church; or that the Roman Pontiff is not the successor of Blessed Peter in this primacy: let him be anathema.[350]

Following Vatican I, the divine institution of the Petrine office has been reaffirmed on numerous occasions, most notably by Leo XIII in *Satis cognitum* [1896],12-13 and Pius XII in *Mystici corporis* [1943], 40. Vatican II likewise teaches that the Petrine ministry has been established, *de iure divino*, by Christ Himself (cf. *Lumen gentium*, 18-19, *Orientalium Ecclesiarum*, 3, *Unitatis redintegratio*, 2 and *Christus Dominus*, 2). In the years since Vatican II, the Congregation for the Doctrine of the Faith has underscored the divine institution of the Petrine office on several occasions,[351] and John Paul II has taught that, "the office of the Bishop of Rome corresponds to the will of Christ."[352]

2. The Meaning of the Church's Indefectibility

The indefectibility of the Church has become a topic of increased interest in recent decades. Although the concept of the Church's indefectibility is rooted in Scripture and Tradition,[353] it was Hans Küng's 1970 book entitled *Unfehlbar? Eine Anfrage* [*Infallible?An*

---

[349]See Ronald Roberson, CSP, *The Eastern Christian Churches: A Brief Survey*, 6th ed. (Rome: Edizioni Orientalia Christiana, 1999), 61: "A Russian Orthodox Patriarchate was officially established by Constantinople in 1589, but it was abolished by Peter the Great in 1721. Mention could also be made of the suppression of the Patriarchate of Aquileia of Grado by Pope Nicholas V in 1451 and the establishment of the Patriarchate of Venice in the same year. See *New Catholic Encyclopedia* (Washington, D.C: CUA Press, 1967), S.v. "Grado, Patriarchate," vol. VI, 685.

[350]D-H, 3058.

[351]Cf. *Mysterium Ecclesiae* (1973), 1-3; *Reflections on the Primacy of Peter* (1998), 3-5 and *Dominus Iesus* (2000), 16-17.

[352]*Ut unum sint* (1995), 95.

[353]Cf. DTC, volume 14, part 2, S.v. "Église," 2145-2150.

Inquiry] that brought the term into greater prominence. Küng timed the publication of his work with the 100th anniversary of the solemn definition of papal infallibility at Vatican I (1870). Finding the doctrine of Vatican I problematical, Küng's proposed speaking of "the indefectibility of the Church" rather than her "infallibility." His central thesis is stated in these words:

> We should therefore like to substitute for "infallibility" the term "indefectibility" or "perpetuity in truth." The concept of "indefectibility" (indestructibility, permanence) and the positive concept of "perpetuity" (imperishability, endurance) are ecclesiological concepts just as traditional as that of infallibility, and in practice it is often hardly possible to distinguish them. And though in textbook theology perpetuity or indefectibility tend to be more closely linked to the existence than with the truth of the Church, it should be borne in mind that the Church's being and the Church's truth are inseparable. If the Church ceases to be in the truth, it ceases to be the Church. But the truth of the Church is not dependent on any fixed, infallible propositions, but on her remaining in the truth throughout all her propositions, including erroneous ones.[354]

What, though, is the "truth" of the Church in which she remains indefectible? For Küng, it is the Christian message or the Gospel. As he writes: "The gospel remains invariably the source, norm and the driving force of the faith and the perpetuity and the indefectibility of the Church in the truth."[355] Skeptical about claims of infallibility for either the Bible or the Church, Küng still upholds the indefectibility of the community of the faithful. Thus, he observes: "The Church as the community of the faithful cannot make infallible propositions, but possesses a fundamental indefectibility in the truth."[356] This means that the Christ and the Holy Spirit will preserve the Church in the truth of the Gospel even though "there is no inherently infallible teaching office" and "no inherently infallible teaching book in Christendom."[357]

Küng's perspective on the Church's indefectibility appears to have an ecumenical purpose. He believes that the Reformed traditions could accept his proposal of "an indefectibility or perpetuity of the Church that depends on the presence of the Spirit, the proclamation

---

[354]Hans Kung, *Infallible?* trans. E. Mosbacher (London: Collins, 1971), 150.
[355]Ibid., 156.
[356]Ibid., 180.
[357]Ibid.

of the word, the community of believers, but not on infallible propositions."[358]

A similar ecumenical concern for "indefectiblility" is to be found in the 1978 "Common Statement" produced by the USA National Committee of the Lutheran World Federation and the USA Catholic Bishops' Committee for Ecumenical and Interreligious Affairs. Although this statement does not embody Küng's hostility towards infallible propositions, it does, at one point, affirm that, "the perpetuity of the Church includes its indefectibility, i.e. its perseverance in the truth of the gospel, in its mission, and in its life of faith."[359]

From a Catholic perspective, it must be asked whether the indefectibility of the Church can be reduced to phrases like "perseverance in the truth of the Gospel." Certainly, the Church will persevere in her proclamation of the Gospel, but is there more to her indefectibility than just that? In order to answer this question, it is important to note that indefectibility, from a linguistic perspective, can take on different senses. The Latin root is the verb, *deficere*, which originally meant, "to loosen" or "set free" (from "*de*" "*facere*" or "undo") but gradually came to mean, "to leave," "to desert," "to cease," "to fail" as well as "to forsake," "to abandon" and "to revolt."[360] In ecclesiastical Latin, another meaning is "to be wanting."[361] There are two nouns derived from *deficere*. First, there is *defectio*, which can mean either a "defection" or "desertion," a "failing" or "deficiency."[362] And there is also *defectus*, which in ecclesiastical Latin refers to a "defect" or "failing," or the "lack of something needed," as in "defect of form" (*defectus formae*).[363]

The various connotations of these Latin roots suggest three basic meanings of the "indefectibility of the Church." In the *first sense*, the Church is indefectible because she will never cease to be; she is

[358]Ibid., 162.
[359]Paul C. Empire, T. Austin Murphy and Joseph A. Burgess, eds. *Teaching Authority & Infallibility in the Church: Lutherans and Catholics in Dialogue VI* (Minneapolis: Augsburg, 1978), 31.
[360]Cf. C.T. Lewis and C. Short, *A Latin Dictionary* (Oxford: Clarendon Press, 1955), 529-530.
[361]Leo F. Stelton, *Dictionary of Ecclesiastical Latin* (Peabody, MA: Hendrickson Pub., 1995), 68.
[362]Lewis and Short, 528.
[363]Cf. Stelton, 67 and 302.

enduring and indestructible. In the *second sense*, she is indefectible because she will never desert Christ and His truth, and Christ will never desert her. In the *third sense*, the Church is indefectible because she will never be lacking in what she needs to fulfill her mission; she is complete and without any deficiency in terms of her basic constitution and identity. Put in positive terms, these three senses can be summarized as *permanence, fidelity* and *completeness*.

These three meanings often merge together and support each other. Because the Church lacks nothing to achieve her God-given purpose, she will never disappear or desert Christ and His truth. Moreover, the Church will never cease to be who she was meant to be, viz., the Body of Christ and "the pillar and foundation of truth" (1 Tim. 3:15). As such, she is also indestructible and incapable of desertion.

The Scriptural foundations of the Church's indefectibility likewise reflect these different, but interconnected, senses. When Jesus tells Peter that the gates of hell will not prevail against His Church (Mt 16:18), we perceive her indestructibility or permanence. When Jesus commissions His disciples to teach all nations and He promises to be with them always (Mt 28:19-20), we know that the Church is indefectible or ever faithful in doctrine. Among other New Testament passages, mention should be made of Ephesians 4:11-14 where Paul links the offices of apostles, pastors, teachers etc. to the building up of the Church in order to withstand the waves and winds of false teaching and deceit. Finally, there is Jesus' promise to protect Peter's faith from failing in Lk 22;32, a passage whose significance for indefectibility is clearest in the Latin of the Vulgate: "*Ego autem rogavi pro te ut non deficiat fides tua.*" Thus, supported by the promise of Christ, Peter's faith can never fail or be deficient, and this is why he is authorized to strengthen[364] or confirm his brethren in the faith (Lk 22:32). From a Catholic perspective, this means that the Church, united with Peter's successor, will never fail in her witness to the truth. Since the Church has been commissioned by Christ to teach the truth

---

[364]The verb, *sterizein,* and its compound, episterizein, can mean either to strengthen or confirm. As used elsewhere in the New Testament, this verb is used in connection with the gift of grace and prophetic confirmation (e.g. 1 Thess 3:2 and Acts 15:32). See S. Bulter, et. al., 142-143 and R.E. Brown, et. al., 121.

(cf. Mt 28:19-20), the Petrine ministry pertains to the very essence of the Church's being (*ad esse ecclesiae*) and not merely to her well-being (*ad bene esse*).[365]

In the history of the Church, testimony to indefectibility is both implicit and explicit.[366] In the early symbols of the faith, there is an implicit confidence in the divine protection of the Church in her solemn professions of faith. If there were no visible Church with authoritative teachers capable of distinguishing truth from error, it would be impossible to locate the "One, Holy, Catholic and Apostolic Church."[367] Along these lines, Irenaeus maintains that, in the Catholic Church, "there is a firm system directed to the salvation of men," and "in the Church, God has placed apostles, prophets and doctors, and all the other means through which the Spirit works."[368] Because the Spirit of Truth guides and protects the Church, she is indefectible. As Irenaeus observes: "For where the Church is, there is the Spirit of God; and where the Spirit of God, there the Church and every grace."[369]

The essential role of the See of Rome in the indefectibility of the Church is consistently affirmed in the Patristic and medieval eras. For example, Pope Hormisdas (r. 514-523) proclaims the necessity of guarding "the rule of the correct faith" in the "manner constituted by the Fathers."[370]

For Hormisdas, the words of Mt 16:18, by which Jesus promised to build His Church, have been confirmed by the course of historical events "because the Catholic religion has always been preserved as immaculate in the Apostolic See" (*quia in Sede Apostolica immaculata est semper catholica servata religio*).[371] Therefore, union with Rome is a mark of true Catholicity, since this See is the one "in which

---

[365]Cf. Dulles, *Ius Divium*, 707 and J. Michael Miller, C.S.B., *What Are They Saying About Papal Primacy?* (New York: Paulist Press, 1983), 59 and 63-67. The other possibility is that the Petrine office is necessary for the fullness or perfection of the Church (*ad plene esse Ecclesiae*) but not for her existence in the strict or absolute sense. To my mind, though, what belongs to the Church's essence must also pertain to her fullness or perfection. Otherwise, the fullness of the Church exists only *per accidens*.
[366]DTC, vol. 4, part 2, S.v. "Église," 2136.
[367]*Symbolum Constantinopolitanum;* D-H, 150.
[368]Irenaeus, *Adversus haereses*, 3, 24,1; Jurgens, vol. 1, 226.
[369]Ibid.
[370]D-H, 363.
[371]Ibid.

the solidity of the Christian religion is whole and true" (*in qua est integra et vera christianae religionis soliditas*).[372]

This "Formula of Hormisdas," was affirmed by the Fathers of the Fourth Council of Constantinople in 869 (and repeated at Vatican I in 1870).[373] In the Middle Ages, union with the See of Rome continued to be proclaimed as an essential sign of Catholicity. Among the most notable magisterial documents in this regard are "The Profession of Faith of Michael Palaeologus" (read out at Lyons II in 1274),[374] the bull, *Unam sanctam* of Boniface VIII (1302),[375] and the *Decretum pro Graecis* of the Council of Florence (1439).[376] During this era, there is also the testimony of Thomas Aquinas (c. 1225-1274), who taught that it pertains to the Pope, as the head of the whole Church, to convoke an ecumenical council and to draw up a symbol of the faith.[377]

In the post-Tridentine era, theologians such as Bellarmine (1542–1621) and Suárez (154–1617) affirm both the indefectibility of the Church as a whole and the necessity of the Petrine office for maintaining this indefectibility in doctrine. In *De Ecclesia militante*, Bellarmine closely links the Church's indefectibility with her infallibility. Thus, after showing that the Church must be visible, he goes on to demonstrate that the visible Church is also indefectible (*Ecclesiam visibilem non posse deficere*).[378] Moreover, because the Church is indefectible, she is unable to err (*Ecclesiam non posse errare*).[379]

In *De Conciliorum auctoritate*, Bellarmine maintains that general or ecumenical councils must be infallible in teaching matters of faith and morals. "If such councils could err," he writes, " there would be no firm judgment by which controversies could be settled and Church unity preserved."[380] For Bellarmine, however, such councils must be confirmed by the Supreme Pontiff because he is "the head of

---

[372]As cited in D-H, 3066 (*Pastor Aeternus*, chap. 4). In D-H, 365, the text is slightly different, viz. "in qua est integra et verax christinae religionis *[et perfecta] soliditas*" (in which the solidity of the Christian religion is whole and true [and perfect]].

[373]SeeTanner, vol. 1, 157 and D-H, 3066.

[374]D-H, 861.

[375]D-H, 874-875.

[376]D-H, 1307.

[377]*Summa theologica* II-II, q. 1, art. 10.

[378]Robert Bellarmine, S.J., *Disputationes de Controversiis Christiane Fidei Adversus Huius Temporis Haereticos* (Cologne: Joannes Gymnicus & Anthony Hierat, 1615), Volume Two, I, book III: *De Ecclesia miliante toto orbe diffusa,* chapter XIII, 59-60.

[379]Ibid., chapter XIV, 60-61.

[380]Ibid., book II, *De Concilorum auctoritate*, chapter III, 24.

the whole Church" (*Summum Pontificem caput esse totius Ecclesiae*).[381]
Moreover, the Pope occupies "the first See which will be judged by no
one" (*Prima sedes a nemine iudicabitur*).[382]

Bellarmine's fellow Jesuit and contemporary, Francisco Suárez,
argues that the Church's indefectibility is a logical consequence of her
establishment by Christ. As he writes:

> The Church of Christ the Lord, that is, insofar as she was
> instituted by Him, never defects from her institution (*numquam
> a sua institutione deficit*), nor will she ever defect from it (*neque in
> aeternum deficiet*).[383]

This doctrine, Suárez maintains, is *de fide*.[384]

The Doctor Eximius[385] likewise upholds the indispensability
of the Petrine office for the Church's indefectibility. He observes that
"the Roman Church" can refer either to the particular Church of Rome
or to the See of the Roman Pontiff who, when assuming the posture
of the teacher of the universal Church, can never err or depart from
the faith.[386] For this reason, "the faith of the Roman Church is the
Catholic faith, and the Roman Church has never departed from this
faith nor could she ever so depart because the chair of Peter presides
over her."[387] Suárez, believes the papal office is a necessary aspect of
the Church's structure, and it is based on Sacred Scripture and upheld
by Tradition. Furthermore, he maintains that the faith of the See of
Peter is indefectible, and he offers the following syllogism:

> The faith of Peter was Catholic and unable to fail; but the faith
> of the Roman Church is the faith of Peter. Therefore, the faith of
> the Roman Church is the Catholic faith, from which this See can
> never defect (*Fides Petri catholica fuit, et deficere non potest; sed fides
> Ecclesiae Romanae est fides Petri; ergo fides Ecclesiae Romanae est fides
> catholica a qua numquam illa sedes potest deficere*).[388]

---

[381]Ibid. chapter XV.
[382]Ibid., chapter XVII, 39. This Latin phrase cited by Bellarmine is thought to have been
first invoked by Pope Sylvester I (r. 314-335). It appears in a slightly different form in the
letter of Pope Nicholas I to the Emperor Michael of A.D. 865 (cf. D-H, 638) and in Vatican
I's *Pastor Aeternus* of 1870 (D-H, 3063).
[383]Francisco Suárez, *De Fide*, disp.9 (*De Ecclesia*) sect 3, n..4 in Suárez, *Opera Omina*
(Paris, Vivès, 1858), volume 12, 256.
[384]Ibid.
[385]Pope Paul V (r. 1605-1621) bestowed upon Suárez the title of Doctor Eximius, the
Exceptional or Uncommon Doctor.
[386]Cf. Suárez, *Defensio Fidei Catholicae Adversus Anglicanae Sectae Errores*, chap. 5, no. 5-6
in Vivès ed., vol. 24, 21-22.
[387]Ibid., chap. 5, no. 7; Vivès, vol. 24, 22.
[388]Ibid.

We see that for Bellarmine and Suárez, the indefectibility of the Church refers both to the permanence of her institution and her unfailing preservation of the true faith. This is a far richer concept of indefectibility than the "fidelity to the truth of the Gospel" offered by Küng and others. From the viewpoint of traditional Catholic theology, the Church's indefectibility concerns not only her fidelity to the Gospel but also "her essential identity in all that concerns her divine constitution."[389] This identity will endure until the consummation of the world and includes all the "divine prerogatives" of the Church as well as her "immutability" in structure and "perpetuity" in doctrine.[390]

Whenever the Church's indefectibility has been challenged, the Magisterium has responded. Thus, Pope Pius VI, in 1794, condemned as heretical the proposition of the Synod of Pistoia that "in these latter times there has been diffused a general obscuring of truths of major importance concerning religion which are the basis of the faith and moral doctrine of Jesus Christ."[391] To suggest that the Catholic Church could obscure the truths of the Jesus Christ is to deny her indefectibility. This indefectibility, however, is found not only in the Church's doctrinal fidelity but also in the permanence and fullness of her divinely established structure and nature. This richer and more complete understanding of the Church's indefectibility is found in the original *Schema* on the Church drawn up for Vatican I. The relevant section reads as follows:

> We declare, moreover, that the Church, considered in her existence as in her constitution, is a perpetual and indefectible society, and that no other economy of salvation, more finished or more perfect, can be expected in this world since the establishment of the Church. Since in fact it is to Christ that mortal men pilgrimaging here below owe their salvation, his Church, which is the only society of salvation, will last until the end of the world, unchangeable and immutable in her constitution.
>
> Therefore, although the Church shows increase — and please God she will constantly increase in faith and charity — for the edification of the body of Christ; although she develops differently according to the diverse periods of her age and the very circumstances in which she continues to live and struggle; she nonetheless remains identical with herself and in her constitution, which she received from Christ.

---

[389]DTC, vol. 14, part 2, S.v. *"Église,"* 2149.
[390]Ibid.
[391]D-H, 2601.

> And so the Church of Christ can never be dispossessed of her properties and of her endowments, of her sacred Magisterium, of her ministry and her government, so that Christ, by means of his visible body, will ever be for men the way, the truth, and the life.[392]

The political situation of 1869–1870 prompted the Fathers of Vatican I to focus their discussion on papal infallibility rather than the Church in general. Nevertheless, there are several passages within this Council's decrees that capture some aspects of the Church's indefectibility as articulated in the *Schema*. In *Dei Filius*, the Catholic Church is described as the indefectible protector of revelation in these words:

> To the sole Catholic Church belong all the manifold and wonderful endowments, which, by divine disposition, are meant to put into light the credibility of the Christian faith. Nay more, the Church, by herself, with her marvelous propagation, eminent holiness and inexhaustible fruitfulness in everything that is good, with her Catholic unity and invincible stability (*invictamque stabilitatem*), is a great and perpetual motive of credibility and an irrefutable testimony of her divine mission.[393]

In *Pastor Aeternus*, the Church's indefectibility is recognized in a particular way in the special gift given to Peter and his successors:

> Therefore, this charism of truth and of faith which can never fail (*veritatis et fidei numquam deficientis charisma*) was conferred upon Peter and his successors in this Chair so they may exercise their exalted office for the salvation of all; in order that the universal flock of Christ might be protected from the poison of error and be nourished by the food of celestial doctrine, and, eliminating any occasion of schism, the whole Church might be preserved as one, and, fixed securely in her foundation, she might stand firm against the gates of hell.[394]

After Vatican I, one of the clearest presentations of the divine institution and indefectibility of the Catholic Church is found in the 1896 encyclical, *Satis cognitum*, of Leo XIII. Speaking of the Church as the Mystical Body of Christ, Leo teaches that "this Church, therefore, is one and perpetual (*unica et perpetua*)" and "those who separate themselves from her deviate from the will and prescription of Christ our Lord...."[395] After expounding on the unity of the Church

---

[392]The Benedictine Monks of Solesmes, *Papal Teachings on the Church*, trans., Mother E. O'Gorman, R.S.C.J., (Boston: Daughters of St. Paul, 1962), 815.
[393]D-H, 3013; translation from J. Neuner and J. Dupuis, *The Christian Faith in the Doctrinal Documents of the Catholic Church*, revised ed. (New York: Alba House, 1982), 43.
[394]D-H, 3071.
[395]D-H, 3304.

in faith, government and liturgy, Leo points to the Petrine ministry as the divinely established source of ecclesial unity. Commenting on the text of Mt 16:18-19, Leo notes:

> From this text it is clear that by the will and command of God the Church rests upon St. Peter, just as a building rests on its foundation. Now the proper nature of a foundation is to be a principle of cohesion for the various parts of the building. It must be the necessary condition of stability and strength. Remove it and the whole building falls. It is consequently the office of St. Peter to support the Church and to guard it in all strength and indestructible unity. How could he fulfill this office without the power of commanding, forbidding and judging, which is properly called *jurisdiction*? It is only by this power of jurisdiction that nations and commonwealths are held together. A primacy of honor and the shadowy right of giving advice and admonition, which is called *direction*, could never secure to any society of men unity or strength.[396]

Pius XII, in his 1943 encyclical, *Mystici corporis*, locates the Church's indefectibility in the presence of Christ and the Holy Spirit within the body of the Church. But since the Church is a visible society, Christ, who is "all wise...could not leave the body of the Church He founded ... without a visible head."[397] The Pope, however, is only "the Vicar of Christ," and "there is only one chief Head of this Body, namely Christ, who never ceases Himself to guide the Church invisibly."[398] But, at the same time, Christ rules the Church in a visible manner though the Pope who is His "representative on earth."[399] The Petrine office, therefore, supports the indefectibility of the Church by the hidden presence of Christ. Pius XII appeals to the authority of Bellarmine who "with acumen and accuracy" notes that,

> this appellation of the Body of Christ is not to be explained solely by the fact that Christ must be called the Head of His Mystical Body, but also by the fact that He so sustains the Church, and so in a certain sense lives in the Church, that she is, as it were, another Christ.[400]

The mystical ecclesiology of Pius XII prepares the way for the "ecclesiology of communion" of Vatican II. There are numerous passages in Vatican II which affirm the indefectibility of the Church

[396] *Satis cognitum*, 12; *Papal Teachings on the Church*, 321.
[397] Mystici corporis, 40; *On the Mystical Body of Christ and Our Union With It in Christ* (Boston: St. Paul Books & Media, nd), 25.
[398] Ibid.
[399] Ibid.
[400] *Mystici corporis*, 53; *On the Mystical Body*, 32; cf. Bellarmine, *De Rom. Pont.* 1, 9; *De*

168 CALLED TO HOLINESS AND COMMUNION

as one, holy, Catholic and apostolic. The Church is indefectibly one because Christ, the one Mediator, "unceasingly sustains" (*indesinenter sustentat*) His holy Church, constituted on earth as "a visible organism" (*ut compaginem visibilem*) and a "community of faith, hope and love (*Lumen gentium*, 8)."[401] The unity "which Christ bestowed on His Church from the beginning... subsists in the Catholic Church as something she can never lose" (*Unitatis redintegratio*, 4).

In a similar manner, *Lumen gentium*, 39 describes the Church as "indefectibly holy" (*indefectibilter sancta*)[402] because Christ has joined the Church to Himself as His Bride and His Body "and endowed her with the gift of the Holy Spirit for the glory of God."

The Church is indefectible in her apostolicity since the "divine mission, which was entrusted by Christ to the apostles, is destined to last until the end of the world (cf. Mt. 28:20)" [*Lumen gentium*, 20]. Moreover, the apostolic preaching, "which is expressed in a special way in the inspired books" is preserved "in a continuous line of succession until the end of time" (*Dei Verbum*, 8). Thus, "the Church, in her doctrine, life and worship, perpetuates and transmits to every generation all that she herself is, and all that she believes" (Ibid.).

Finally, the Church is indefectibily Catholic since she is "the universal sacrament of salvation" (*Lumen gentium*, 48), and it is "through Christ's Catholic Church alone...that the fullness of the means of salvation can be obtained" (*Unitatis redintegratio*, 3). To serve the Church's catholicity and unity, Christ willed that the bishops "should be shepherds in His Chuch until the end of the world" (*Lumen gentium*, 18). Furthermore, He established the Petrine office as "a lasting and a visible source and foundation of the unity both of faith and communion" (Ibid.).

Since Vatican II, the Magisterium has sought to uphold the authentic meaning of the Church's indefectibility as expressed in both Vatican I and Vatican II. A number of interventions have been occasioned by the attempt to substitute a generic "indefectibility in

---

Concil. 2, 19. This citation helps to offset the inaccurate perception that Bellarmine's ecclesiology is overly juridical, apologetic and "narrow", which is the view expressed by Christopher O'Donnell, O.Carm., *Ecclesia: A Theological Encyclopedia of the Church* (Collegeville, MN: The Liturgical Press, 1996), 51.

[401] D-H, 4118.

[402] D-H, 4165.

truth" for infallibility in faith and morals. Along these lines, the declaration, *Mysterium ecclesiae*, issued by the Congregation for the Doctrine of the Faith (CDF) in 1973, seemed to have Küng's position in mind[403] when it taught that

> the faithful are in no way permitted to see in the Church merely a fundamental permanence in truth which, as some assert, could be reconciled with errors contained here and there in the propositions that the Church's Magisterium teaches to be held irrevocably.[404]

In 1982, the CDF likewise recognized a difference in the use of the term "indefectible" as found in the "Final Report of the Anglican Roman Catholic International Commission (ARCIC)" and the meaning of "indefectible" as found in Vatican I. As the CDF notes:

> For ARCIC, the assurance the faithful have of the truth of the teaching of the Church's Magisterium, in the last analysis, lies in the fidelity to the Gospel they recognize in it rather than the authority of the person who expresses it.[405]

The CDF further observes that, according to the Catholic faith, infallibility refers immediately not to truth but to certitude; for it says that the certitude of the Church about the truth of the Gospel is present without any doubt in the testimony of the successor of St. Peter when he exercises his office of 'strengthening his brethren' " (Lk 22:32; cf. constitution, *Lumen gentium*, no. 25; DS 3065, 3074).

Clearly, the Magisterium has ruled out any reductionist understanding of the Church's indefectibility that limits it to a basic "permanence in truth" or "fidelity to the Gospel." The more complete understanding of indefectibility requires a sense of the essential structure and purpose of the Church as divinely constituted. It also includes recognition of the Petrine office as a lasting foundation for ecclesial communion, established *de iure divino*. Finally, the indefectibility of the Church logically demands an infallible teaching office.

---

[403]Cf. Introduction to D-H, 4530-4541.

[404]D-H, 4537; Austin Flannery, O.P., ed., *Vatican Collection, Volume 2, Vatican II: More Postconciliar Documents* (Northport, N.Y. Costello Publishing Co., 1982), 432. The introduction to *Mysterium ecclesiae* in Denzinger-Hünermann, 4530-4541 states that this document was issued with Küng in mind.

[405]*Enchiridion Vaticanum* (1982), # 164, p. 142.

3. The Indefectible Constitution of the Catholic Church

As we have seen, the original *Schema de Ecclesia* for Vatican I understood indefectibility not only in terms of the Church's fidelity to Christ but also in terms of her permanence and completeness in structure and constitution. What, though, is the constitution of the Church that remains indefectible? To answer this question, a good point of departure is the definition of the Catholic Church provided by Bellarmine:

> The one and true [Church] is the assembly of human beings joined together by the profession of the same Christian faith and the communion of the same sacraments under the government of legitimate pastors, especially the one Vicar of Christ on earth, the Roman Pontiff.[406]

Bellarmine's definition embodies the three characteristics of visible communion in the Catholic Church: faith, sacraments and government. In his 1959 encyclical, *Ad Petri cathedram*, Pope John XXIII points to these "three unities" — faith, sacraments and ecclesiastical government — as the characteristic signs of Catholic identity. As he observes, the Catholic Church is such that "she is adorned and distinguished by these three characteristics: namely, unity of doctrine, government and worship" (*unitate nempe doctrinae, regiminis et cultus*).[407]

In several places, Vatican II likewise affirms these three marks of unity. In the *Decree on the Eastern Catholic Churches*, *Orientalium Ecclesiarum*, the following definition of the Church is given:

> The holy Catholic Church, which is the Mystical Body of Christ, is made up of the faithful who are organically united in the Holy Spirit by the same faith, the same sacraments and the same government.[408]

Here we find a description of the Church that combines Bellarmine's definition with that of Pius XII in *Mystici corporis*. The underlying image is the Church as a mystical *communio*, within which the faithful are united by a common faith, sacramental life and hierarchical structure.

---

[406]Bellarmine, *De controversiis, De conciliis et ecclesia, liber tertius, cap.* II, 44. The Latin reads: *illam [Ecclesiam] unam, & veram esse coetum hominu eiusdem Christinae fidei professione, & eorundem Sacramentorum communione colligatum, sub regimine legitmorum pastorum, ac praecipue unius Christi in terris Vicarii Romani Pontificis.*
[407]John XXIII, *Ad Petri cathedram*, 67.
[408]*Orientalium ecclesiarum*, 2.

In *Lumen gentium*, 14, there is a similar invocation of the three marks of visible unity. Thus, we read:

> Fully incorporated into the Church are those who, possessing the Spirit of Christ, accept all the means of salvation given to the Church together with her entire organization, and who — by the bonds constituted by the profession of faith, the sacraments, ecclesiastical government, and communion — are joined in the visible structure of the Church, who rules her through the Supreme Pontiff and the bishops.[409]

Once again, the three marks of unity are presented as the indications of full membership in the Church. In addition to the bonds of faith, worship and ecclesial government, there is also mention of "communion." The word "communion" does not add anything in content to the other three signs of unity. It does, however, remind us that these marks of unity are not merely juridical or external but pertain to the interior life of love, solidarity and fidelity present among the members of Christ's Church. The word "communion" also underscores the Eucharistic nature of the Church by which the faithful, joined in the Paschal sacrifice, "are taken up into communion with [Christ] and with one another."[410] The centrality of the Eucharist to the very identity of the Catholic Church has been emphasized by Pius XII in *Mystici corporis* [1943], 81-84, by the Congregation for the Doctrine of the Faith in *Communionis notio* [1992], 5, and more recently by John Paul II in *Ecclesia de Eucharistia* [2003].

These documents either anticipate or highlight what Vatican II teaches about the Eucharist and the Church. In *Sacrosanctum concilium*, 2, we are taught that it is through the liturgy, most especially the divine sacrifice of the Eucharist, that "the work of our salvation is accomplished" and the faithful manifest to others "the mystery of Christ and the real nature of the Church." In addition, *Lumen gentium*, 11 describes the Eucharistic sacrifice as "the source and summit of the entire Christian life"[411]

The bond of the sacramental life of the Church, most especially the Eucharist, is a major aspect of Vatican II's ecclesiology. This is why the Congregation for the Doctrine of the Faith has stressed

---

[409] *Lumen gentium*, 14.

[410] *Lumen gentium*, 7.

[411] The Latin phrase is *"totius vitae christianae fontem et culmen."* For some reason, the *totius* is ignored in the Flannery translation, but I have included it as "entire" here.

that, "the ecclesial communities which have not preserved the valid Episcopate and the genuine and integral substance of the Eucharistic mystery, are not churches in the proper sense."[412] On the other hand, the separated Orthodox churches, because they have preserved a true Episcopate and Eucharist, are true particular sister churches in relation to the particular churches of the Catholic Church.[413] Since these separated particular churches have preserved one of the essential bonds of ecclesial communion, viz., the full integrity of the Eucharist and the other sacraments, some theologians believe they should not be considered in complete schism from the Catholic Church but only in partial schism.[414] Full communion, however, would demand total unity in faith and ecclesial government, the other two signs of Catholic communion according to Bellarmine and Vatican II.

The Church's indefectibility, therefore, requires permanence and completeness in faith, worship and government. This is the proper context in which to understand the traditional concept of the Church as a "perfect society." The understanding of the Church as a *societas perfecta* is usually linked with the Ultramontaninsm movement of the 19th century and with the "Roman school" of theologians like Perrone and Franzelin.[415] This is certainly true, but I think it would be inaccurate to claim that the concept of the Church as a *societas perfecta* has been totally abandoned by Vatican II. Part of the confusion is that the phrase "perfect society" seems to contradict Vatican II's recognition of the Church as "clasping sinners to her bosom" and "at once holy and always in need of purification" (*sancta simul et semper purificanda*).[416] The concept of "perfect society," however, refers to the Church's essential structure not to the perfect holiness of all her members. Perfect in this sense means complete or full. In other words, the Church, as a "perfect society" is endowed with the "fullness of the means of salvation" (*omnis salutarium mediorum plenitudo*),[417] as Vatican II teaches.

---

[412]CDF, *Dominus Iesus* [2000], 17. See *Unitatis redintegratio*, 22.

[413]CDF, "Doctrinal Note on the Expression 'Sister Churches,'" *Origins* (Sept. 14, 2000), 223-224.

[414]See Aidan Nichols, O.P., *Rome and the Eastern Churches* (Collegeville, MN: The Liturgical Press, 1992) 1-25 and 25 in particular.

[415]Johann Auer, *The Church; The Universal Sacrament of Salvation*, 69.

[416]LG, 8.

[417]UR, 3.

The recognition of the Church as a perfect society is intimately connected to her indefectibility. To deny that the Church has been given all the means necessary to carry out her divinely instituted mission is to deny the Church's indefectibility. This is why one of the errors listed in the 1864 *Syllabus of Errors* of Pius IX is that "the Church is not a perfect society, completely free and able to operate according to her own proper and permanent rights that have been conferred on her by her divine founder."[418] Leo XIII provides further elaboration on the meaning of the Church as a perfect society in his 1885 encyclical, *Immortale Dei*:

> This society, although it is made up of men just like a civil society, nevertheless, is supernatural and spiritual because of the end for which it was founded and the means by which it pursues that end. Therefore, it is distinct and different from civil society, and, what is more, it is a society perfect in its nature and its law (*societas est genere et iure perfecta*), possessing, by the will and grace of its Founder, in itself and through itself, all the assistance needed for its well-being and action.[419]

As can be seen, Leo XIII understands the Church as endowed with all the means needed for her proper identity and mission. What, though, is the mission of the Church? As Pius XI explains in his 1929 encyclical, *Divini illius magistri*, the mission or goal of the Church is the "eternal salvation of men."[420] To achieve this goal, "the Church is a supernatural society embracing all mankind, and it is perfect in itself, having within itself all the means sufficient for its end" (*Ecclesia est, supernaturalis quidem societas universum humanum genus complectens, atque in se perfecta, cum sibi omnia suppetant ad finem suum*).[421]

The recognition of the Church as a complete or perfect society is another way of affirming her indefectibility. As a *societas perfecta*, the Church lacks nothing that pertains to the fulfillment of her God-given mission.[422] This aspect of indefectibility is manifested in the four marks of the Church as one, holy, Catholic and apostolic, and it is likewise expressed by her unity in faith, worship and ecclesiastical government.

---

[418]D-H, 2919.
[419]D-H, 3167.
[420]D-H, 3685.
[421]Ibid.
[422]When understood in this way, it is clear that the concept of the Church as a "perfect society" has not been rejected but rather affirmed by Vatican II, in spite of what some

Although Vatican II does not explicitly speak of the Church as a "perfect society," the concept of her indefectible fullness is communicated in several passages. We have already noted that *Unitatis redintegratio,* 3 teaches that, it is "through Christ's Catholic alone, which is he universal help towards salvation, that the fullness of the means of salvation is obtained." In the same Decree, the Petrine ministry is presented as a divinely established feature of the Church's indefectible constitution:

> In order to establish this, his holy Church everywhere in the world till the end of time, Christ entrusted to the College of the Twelve the task of teaching, ruling faith, he determined that upon him he would build his Church; to him he promised the and sanctifying. Among their number he chose Peter. And after Peter's confession of keys of the kingdom of heaven, and after his profession of love, entrusted all his sheep to him to be confirmed in faith and shepherded in perfect unity, with himself, Christ Jesus, remaining the chief cornerstone and shepherd of souls.
>
> It is through the faithful preaching of the Gospel by the Apostles and their successors—the bishops with Peter's successor as their head—through their administering the sacraments, and through their governing in love, that Jesus Christ wishes his people to increase, under the action of the Holy Spirit; and he perfects its fellowship in unity: in the confession of one faith; in the common celebration of divine worship, and in the fraternal harmony of the family of God.[423]

We see from this passage that the Petrine ministry is an essential feature of the Church's indefectible structure. The Church of Christ on earth will always retain this structure because it has been willed and established by the Divine Savior to last till the end of time. This is why *Lumen gentium,* 8 teaches that the sole Church of Christ, professed in the Creed as one, holy, Catholic and apostolic, "constituted and organized as a society in the present world, subsists in the Catholic Church, which is governed by the successor of Peter and the bishops in communion with him." Consequently, those particular churches and ecclesial bodies separated from the See of Peter, cannot be understood as part of the one, holy, Catholic and apostolic Church subsisting as a visible society in the present world.

---

commentators have said, e.g. Gerald O'Collins, S.J. and Mario Farrugia, S.J., *Catholicism: The Story of Catholic Christianity* (Oxford: Oxford University Press, 2003), 328; and Maureen Sullivan, O.P. *Vatican II: 101 Questions & Answers on* (Mahwah, N.J.: Paulist Press, 2002), 110.

[423]UR, 2.

To a greater or lesser extent, they retain true Catholic elements, but these elements "belong by right to the one Church of Christ"[424] and "are forces impelling towards Catholic unity."[425]

In the case of the separated Eastern churches, these Catholic elements are most prominent, especially by virtue of their authentic apostolic succession, priesthood and Eucharist. As a result, these separated Eastern churches, as particular churches, are true sister churches to the particular churches in full communion with the See of Peter.[426] They are joined to the Catholic Church "in closest intimacy" and "some worship in common (*communicatio in sacris*), given suitable circumstances, and the approval of Church authority, is not merely possible but is encouraged."[427] Although the one Church of Christ is "present and operative"[428] in these separated Eastern churches in their sacramental mysteries, they "lack full communion with the Catholic Church, since they do not accept the Catholic doctrine of the Primacy, which, according to the will of God, the Bishop of Rome objectively has and exercises over the entire Church."[429]

From a Catholic perspective, lack of full communion with the See of Peter means that a church is missing an essential element of the ecclesial structure established by Christ. As a result, such churches cannot claim indefectibility in the sense of fullness or completeness. This is why the single Church of Christ "subsists in the Catholic Church, governed by the Successor of Peter and the Bishops in communion with him."[430]

Unfortunately, some Catholic theologians have obscured this teaching by claiming that the sole Church of Christ also subsists in some churches lacking full communion with the Roman Pontiff.[431]

---

[424]UR, 3.
[425]LG, 8.
[426]Cf. the CDF's "Doctrinal Note on the Expression 'Sister Churches'" of June 30, 2000 in Origins ((Sept. 14, 2000), 223-224.
[427]UR, 15.
[428]CDF, *Dominus Iesus*, 17 (translation from Vatican website).
[429]Ibid.
[430]Ibid.; cf. *Lumen gentium*, 8 and the CDF's declaration, Mysterium Ecclesiae, of June 24, 1973 in D-H, 4530.
[431]See the CDF's Notification on the Book "Church Charism and Power" by Father Leonardo Boff: AAS 77 [1985], 756-762 and *Enchiridion Vaticanum* 9 [1985], no.1525-1526, pp.1386-1387. Some theologians seem ambiguous about this matter. For example, Auer, on p. 347, observes: "The statement that the Church 'subsists in' the Catholic Church implies

Cardinal Ratzinger, however, notes that, by using the word, "subsists," in *Lumen gentium*, 8, Vatican II wished to explain, "that the Church of Jesus Christ as a concrete subject in this world can be found in the Catholic Church."[432] Furthermore, this subsistence takes place only once and cannot be multiplied.[433] In other words, the single Church of Christ does not *subsist* in those churches and ecclesial bodies that lack communion with the Roman Pontiff, even though many authentic "elements" of the Catholic Church can be found be in these congregations.[434]

Vatican II clearly teaches that: "the Catholic Church has been endowed with all divinely revealed truth and with all means of grace."[435] Furthermore, only those are fully incorporated in the Catholic Church "who accept all the means of salvation given to the Church, together with her entire organization."[436] This organization, of course, refers to "the visible structure of the Church of the Church of Christ, who rules her through the Supreme Pontiff and the Bishops." This means that the hierarchical structure of the episcopacy and the papacy is essential to the divinely established constitution of the Church. The Catholic Church is indefectible in her structure and essence. The Church will never defect from her divinely constituted structure, and this structure will insure that the Church will never defect from Christ.

---

that the true Church can be found in the Catholic Church, which is not to deny that it can be found in other churches, especially the ancient Eastern Churches." Richard McBrien, in *Catholicism*, New Edition (San Francisco: HarperCollins, 1994), correctly observes: "the Catholic Church alone has all the institutional elements which are necessary for the integrity of the Body of Christ..." (p. 732). But he also asserts that the Church spoken of at Vatican II "is the whole Body of Christ: Catholics, Orthodox, Anglicans, Protestants, and Oriental Christians alike" (p. 684; cf. also p. 735). Theological discussion of the meaning of *"subsistit in"* still continues. See Karl Becker, S.J., "An Examination of *Subsistit in*," *L'Osservatore Romano* [Eng. ed.] (December 14, 2005), 11 and Francis A. Sullivan, S.J., *"Quaestio Disputata:* Response to Karl Becker, S.J. on the Meaning of *Subsistit in*," *Theological Studies* (2006) 67:2, 395-409.

[432]Joseph Cardinal Ratzinger, "Ecclesiology of the Constitution of the Church," *L'Osservatore Romano* [Eng. ed.] No. 38, Sept. 19, 2001, 8. More recently, the CDF has addressed the issue of the one subsistence taught by LG, 8 in "Responses to Some Questions Regarding Certain Aspects of the Doctrine on the Church" (June 29, 2007) http://www.vatican.va/roman_curia/congregations/cfaith/documents/rc_cfaith_doc_20070629_responsa
...

[433]Ibid.

[434]Cf., CDF, *Notification on the Book, "Church: Charism and Power"* by Father Leonardo Boff, AAS 77 [1985], 756-762.

[435]UR, 4.

[436]LG, 14.

4) The Petrine Ministry and the
Preservation of Unity in Faith and Morals

The Petrine office is directed towards the unity of the Church. Peter is called by Christ to tend and feed His sheep (cf. Jn 21:16-18), and Christ wishes there to be one flock and one shepherd (cf. Jn 10:16). This is why Catholic theologians have always linked the Petrine office with the unity of the Church. Bellarmine, for example, readily acknowledges that the Church is the Body of Christ and not the Body of Peter or Paul.[437] Nevertheless, Christ also wished there to be one head of the visible Church on earth, serving the unity of the entire body of the faithful. The seventh of Bellarmine's fifteen "notes" of the Church "is the union of the members among themselves and with the head, for the Church is one body, one spouse, one flock as Scripture teaches in Rom. 12, Cant. 6, John 10 and likewise the Symbol of Constantinople."[438] Since this one head of the Church on earth is the Pope, "it has always been held that union with the Roman Pontiff is a sign of the true Church" (*semper fuisse habitam pro nota verae Ecclesiae coniunctionem cum Romano Pontifice*).[439]

Suárez affirms this principle of unity by noting that "it is necessary that there be in the Church some supreme power to which belongs the government of Christ's universal Church."[440] This, he observes, is a *de fide* doctrine that the heretics deny. Making use of citations from Scripture, the Fathers and Councils, Suárez goes on to demonstrate that Christ gave pastoral authority over the universal Church to Peter and his successors.[441] The authority of the Pope, therefore, exists by divine law, i.e. *de iure divino*. Moreover, God insures that papal definitions can never be erroneous.[442] Even if a Pope, as a private person, might fall into error out of ignorance (though not contumacy), God, in His divine Providence, would graciously insure

---

[437]*De Romano Pontifice,* book 1, chap. 9.
[438]*De notis Ecclesiae,* book 4, chap. 10.
[439]Ibid.
[440]*De Fide,* disp. 9, sect. 6, no. 2; Vivès, vol. 12, 263.
[441]Cf. Ibid., disp. 10, sect. 1-6; Vivès, 280-322.
[442]Cf. Ibid., disp. 10, sect. 6, no. 10; Vivès, 319: *"Deus promisit Papam definientem numquam erraturum..."*

that this heretical Pope would not harm the Church.[443] In other words, God will never allow such a Pontiff to impose an erroneous teaching on the universal Church. For Suárez, this is a sign of the indefectibility and infallibility of the Pope as the successor of Peter. As he writes: "For if Peter or his successor could deceive the Church, it would not be a firm and stable edifice."[444] Christ, though, prays that Peter's faith will not fail (cf. Lk 22: "*ut non deficiat fides tua*"), therefore, the See of Peter will remain indefectible by divine protection.

Vatican II affirms the same principles taught Bellarmine and Suárez. God established the Petrine office as the means for insuring ecclesial unity and communion. *Lumen gentium*, 18, as we have seen, teaches that Christ set up in Peter and his successors "a lasting and visible source and foundation of the unity of both faith and of communion."

In *Lumen gentium*, 22-25, the Council explains how the Petrine office works in harmony with the divinely established authority of the bishops to proclaim the Gospel faithfully until the end of the world. The Roman Pontiff, as the successor of Peter, "is the perpetual and visible source and foundation of unity both of the bishops and the whole company of the faithful."[445] All the bishops, of course, "have the obligation of fostering and safeguarding the unity of faith and of upholding the discipline which is common to the whole Church."[446] The ministry of the Pope is to insure that the bishops teach with a unified voice in explaining matters of faith and morals. The bishops "have supreme and full authority over the universal Church,"[447] but this authority must be exercised "together with their head, the Supreme Pontiff, and never apart from him."[448]

5. Indefectibility and Infallibility

Since Christ wishes His Church to proclaim the truth, the Church cannot fail in her witness to the truth, at least in her universal

---

[443]Ibid.: "*Quamvis enim efficere Deus possit ut haereticus Papa non noceat Ecclesiae, suavior tamen modus divinae providentiae est, ut, quia Deus promissit Papam definientem numquam erraturum, consequenter provideat ne unquam ille haereticus sit.*"
[444]Ibid., disp. 5, sect. 8, no.4; Vivès, vol. 12,162.
[445]*Lumen gentium*, 23.
[446]Ibid.
[447]*Lumen gentium*, 22
[448]Ibid.

and solemn Magisterium. Thus, indefectibility logically leads to infallibility, for if the Church were to teach error and impose this error upon all the faithful, she could not be said to be indefectible in her teaching office.

Vatican I solemnly taught the dogma of papal infallibility, viz., the Roman Pontiff possesses a divine protection from error when, speaking and acting in his office as the shepherd and teacher of all the Christians, he defines a doctrine on faith or morals to be held by the universal Church.[449] Vatican II reaffirms the dogma of papal infallibility, but strives to place papal infallibility within the context of the infallibility of the universal Magisterium of the episcopal college. The Petrine office, though, cannot be separated from the collegial infallibility of the bishops. As Vatican II explains:

> Although the bishops, taken individually, do not enjoy the privilege of infallibility, they do, however, proclaim infallibly the doctrine of Christ on the following conditions: namely, when, even though dispersed throughout the world but preserving amongst themselves and with Peter's successor the bond of communion, in their authoritative teaching concerning matters of faith and morals, they are in agreement that a particular teaching is to be held definitively and absolutely. This is still more clearly the case when, assembled in an ecumenical council, they are, for the universal Church, teachers of and judges in matters of faith and morals, whose decisions must be adhered to with the loyal and obedient assent of faith.[450]

The bishops, therefore, are protected by the gift of infallibility, when they come to a common agreement that a particular teaching on faith and morals is be held definitively by the universal Church. In light of Catholic history, we can observe that the vast majority of our dogmas have been proclaimed or confirmed as infallible either by the universal and ordinary Magisterium of the bishops or by their solemn teachings and pronouncements at ecumenical councils. The collegial exercise of infallibility, however, must include "the bond of communion among themselves and with the successor of Peter" (*communionis nexum inter se et cum Successore Petri*).[451]

This is why "there is never an ecumenical council which is not confirmed or at least recognized as such by Peter's successor."[452] The

---

[449]D-H, 3074.
[450]*Lumen gentium*, 25
[451]*Lumen gentium*, 25; D-H,4149.

requirement of papal endorsement of ecumenical councils is witnessed to in the ancient Church. Even the controversial canon 28 of the Council of Chalcedon was sent to Pope Leo I for his confirmation (which he refused to give).[453] A ninth century Slavonic commentary on the 28th canon notes that,

> without [the Pope's] participation manifested by the sending of some of his subordinates, every Ecumenical Council is non-existent, and it is he who renders legal what has been decided in the Council.[454]

The Arab Bishop of Haran, Theodore Abou-Qurra, provides further testimony (c. A.D. 820) of the need for papal confirmation of ecumenical councils:

> By the grace of the Holy Spirit, in every circumstance our recourse is simply to build ourselves on the foundation of St. Peter, who administered the six holy Councils [the Seventh Ecumenical Council was not yet received in parts of the East], which were convened by the order of the Bishop of Rome, the capital of the world. Whoever is established on her throne is the one entrusted by Christ, to turn to the people of Christ his Ecumenical Council, and then to confirm them, as we have established in a number of others places.[455]

These ancient sources affirm what is found in Vatican II. When the bishops teach in communion with the Roman Pontiff, they are "to be revered by all as witnesses of divine and Catholic truth."[456] Outside this communion with the Pope, the college of bishops, "has no authority" over the universal Church.[457]

In addition to the collegial infallibility of the bishops, Vatican II upholds the special role of the Roman Pontiff as the one who "confirms his brethren in the faith" (cf. *Lumen gentium*, 25 and Lk

---

[452]*Lumen gentium*, 22.

[453]See Tanner, vol. I, 76 and James Likoudis, *The Divine Primacy of the Bishop of Rome and Modern Eastern Orthodoxy* (New Hope, KY:St. Martin de Porres Lay Dominican Community, 2002), 79.

[454]This is from an ancient Slavonic *Nomocanon* possibly edited by St. Methodius himself in the 9th century. The whole text is found in *Vizantitskit Vremennik* (1897), ed. A. Pavlov, t. IV, 150-152, and cited in French by Michel d'Herbigny, S.J., *Theologia de Ecclesia*, vol. II (Paris: Beauchesne, 1921), 151. It is also cited in Likoudis, 98-99.

[455]From Theodore Abou-Qurra's essay, "On the Death of Christ," cited by Fr. Sidney H. Griffith, S.T. in "Councils in the Church: An Apologetic View from the Christian Orient," 24-25 (paper given at the June, 1987 Orthodox-Catholic Dialogue in Brookline, MA); also cited in Likoudis, 97.

[456]*Lumen gentium*, 25

[457]*Lumen gentium*, 22.

22:32). This is usually done by his confirmation of what the college of bishops teaches, as in the case of ecumenical councils. Vatican II, however, incorporates this role of the Pope in its description of papal infallibility:

> The Roman Pontiff, head of the college of bishops, enjoys this infallibility when, as supreme pastor and teacher of all the faithful — who confirms his brethren in the faith (cf. Lk 22:32) — he proclaims in an absolute decision a doctrine pertaining to faith and morals. For that reason his definitions are rightly said to be irreformable by their very nature and not by reason of the assent of the Church, in as much as they were made with the assistance of the Holy Spirit promised to him in the person of blessed Peter himself; and as a consequence they are in no way in need of approval by others, and do not admit an appeal to any other tribunal.[458]

In this passage, we see that the Pope confirms his brethren not only as the head of the college of bishops but also as the one "in whom the Church's charism of infallibility is present in a singular way (*singulariter*)."[459] The Pope, therefore, is not simply the one who confirms what the college of bishops teaches, but he is also the one who can confirm his brother bishops in the faith by teaching infallibly "in a singular way." As Umberto Betti, O.F.M., a *peritus* of Vatican II, observes:

> The college also remains a body hierarchically structured, in which the Pope, therefore, maintains completely all his personal prerogatives. Hence, he is not bound to decide in conformity with the majority of the members; on the contrary, exercising also his role as the principle and center of the unity of the episcopal body, he invites the other members to agree with his own judgment.[460]

In other words, the Pope can confirm what the college as a whole has taught, or he can, as the head of the college, confirm or strengthen his brother bishops in what they, as a college, should teach. This can be done in a definitive or non-definitive manner. The

---

[458]Ibid..

[459]Ibid.

[460]Umberto Betti, O.F.M., "Il Papa e gli altri membri del Collegio," in *La Chiesa del Vaticano II,* ed. G. Barauna, O.F.M. (Firenze: Vallechi Editore, 1965), 769. The Italian reads: *"Il collegio rimane anche allora un corpo gerarchicamente strutturato, nel quale perciò il Papa mantiene integre tutte le sue perogative personali. Egli quindi non è tenuto a decidere in conformità della maggioranza dei membri; al contrario, esercitando anche allora la sua funzione di principio e centro dell'unità del corpo episcopale, invita gli altri membri a concordare nello stesso giudizio."*

Roman Pontiff, thus, retains his office of Vicar of Christ by which he, as universal pastor, "has full, supreme and universal power over the whole Church."[461] If the Pope confirms his brother bishops on a matter of faith and morals by a definitive judgment, the college of bishops cannot exercise a "veto power." On the contrary, the college, in communion with the Roman Pontiff, will embrace the judgment of the Pope as its own.

The Scriptural point of reference is Lk 22:32. Vatican I cites this text in *Pastor aeternus*[462] in order to emphasize the promise of the Lord to pray that Peter's faith may not fail. In *Lumen gentium*, 25, though, the text is cited to show how the Successor of Peter, in confirming his brethren, teaches infallible doctrine. Vatican I's use of the text highlights the indefectibility of the See of Peter. Vatican II's usage underscores how the infallibility of the Pope can be exercised precisely in confirming his brother bishops (and all Catholics) in the faith. The two uses, though, are complementary, and they show how closely linked indefectibility is to infallibility.

6. The Exercise and the Expression of the Petrine Office Since Vatican II

A survey of magisterial teachings concerning the Petrine office since Vatican II reveals two main trajectories. On the one hand, interventions have been made to correct erroneous opinions about the papacy and the Church. On the other hand, the Magisterium has sought to present the Catholic doctrine of the papacy with an ecumenical purpose in mind. In other words, the role of the Roman Pontiff as the servant of Christian unity is offered in a positive light for the separated brethren to consider.

With regard to interventions of the CDF, the cases of four theologians can be mentioned: Hans Küng, Edward Schillebeeckx, O.P., Leonardo Boff, O.F.M. and Reinhard Messner.[463] Küng was initially censured in 1975 for, *inter alia*, denying the dogma of papal infallibility. In 1979, the CDF ruled that he could no longer teach

---

[461] *Lumen gentium*, 22.
[462] D-H, 3070.
[463] The first three cases are summarized by Patrick Granfield, *The Limits of the Papacy: Authority and Autonomy in the Church* (New York: Crossroad, 1987), 11-14.

with the status of a Catholic theologian.[464] It is widely believed that 1973 declaration of the CDF entitled, *Mysterium Ecclesiae*, was issued with Küng's errors in mind.[465]

In 1984, Schillebeeckx received a warning from the CDF concerning his thesis that, in extraordinary circumstances, someone other than an ordained priest could offer the Eucharist. A year earlier, in 1983, the CDF had issued a letter entitled *Sacerdotium ministeriale*, which reaffirmed the Catholic teaching that only an ordained priest could offer a valid Eucharist.[466] Schillebeeckx was asked to clarify his position, but he never did so adequately. In 1986, the CDF issued a subsequent notification stating that the Dominican's views on ministry were not in harmony with the teachings of the Church.[467]

In response to Leonardo Boff's 1982 book, *Church: Charism and Power*, the CDF, in 1985, issued a notification.[468] Boff's book was criticized for obscuring the hierarchical nature and unicity of the Church. Later, the CDF would refer to this notification in footnote #56 of its declaration, *Dominus Iesus* (2000). Boff's view that the one Church of Christ "could subsist also in non-Catholic Churches and ecclesial communities" was judged to be unacceptable.

On Nov. 30, 2000, the CDF issued a Notification on some publications of Prof. Dr. Reinhard Messner.[469] In this case, the problem was the obfuscation of apostolic succession and the divine institution of the sacrament of holy orders. Since Messner's view is found in other books on "ministry" published by contemporary theologians, the Notification is particularly significant.[470] If Jesus did not intend to institute the priesthood and the hierarchy of the Church, then the teaching of *Lumen gentium*, 18 on the permanence of the episcopacy and the papacy is certainly obscured.

---

[464] Ibid., 11, cf. *Enchiridion Vaticanum* (1979), no. 1942-1951.

[465] See introduction to D-H, 4530-4541.

[466] *Enchiridion Vaticanum* (1983), no .380-393; see also AAS 75 (1983) pars I, 1001-1009.

[467] Granfield, 12.

[468] Ibid., 13.

[469] The notification can be found in Italian and German on the Vatican website under the doctrinal documents of the CDF.

[470] Cf. Paul Bernier, S.S.S., *Ministry in the Church* (Twenty-Third Publications,1992 and 2000) pp. 3, 5, 21 and 40; Thomas O'Meara, O.P. *Theology of Ministry* (Paulist Press, 1983) pp. 87, 101-102; and Kenan Osborne, O.F.M, *Priesthood: A History of the Ordained Ministry in the Roman Catholic Church* (Paulist, 1988), pp. 70, 348 and 353. All these authors seem to

The teachings of John Paul II, most notably *Ut unum sint* (1995), as well other documents of the CDF, viz. *Communionis notio* (1992) *Reflections on the Primacy of Peter* (1998) and *Dominus Iesus* (2000), have tried to underscore the Pope as the servant of unity. It is in within this context, that the Holy Father invites the Church leaders and theologians of the separated Christian bodies to join with him "in a patient and fraternal dialogue on this subject,"[471] namely, how the Petrine ministry can be at the service of Christian unity. To be sure, the present Pontiff understands that "the office of the Bishop of Rome corresponds to the will of Christ," but this office is not separate "from the mission entrusted to the whole body of Bishops, who are also 'vicars and ambassadors of Christ.'" [472]

In the exercise of his Petrine authority, John Paul II has been careful to reaffirm definitive teachings in virtue of his ministry "to confirm the brethren in the faith" (cf. Lk 22:32). The appeal to the Lucan text is found in his definitive reaffirmation of the Church's inability to confer priestly ordination on women in *Ordinatio sacerdotalis* (1994).[473] An implicit appeal to the Lucan text is also found in John Paul II's definitive condemnations of direct abortion and euthanasia in *Evangelium Vitae* (1995), no. 62 and 65. In the case of abortion, he appeals to "the authority which Christ conferred on Peter and his successors" and makes it clear that he is teaching "in communion with the bishops."[474] The definitive judgments issued in *Ordinatio sacerdotalis* and *Evangelium vitae* seem to reflect the type of papal infallibility articulated in *Lumen gentium*, 25. The Pope, as the head of the college of bishops, confirms his brethren on a point of faith and morals that is to be held in a definitive and irreformable manner. Such judgments are, according to the CDF, infallible.[475] It may be that future infallible judgments of the Pope will follow this model.

---

suggest that Jesus only instituted generic "ministry." The hierarchal order of bishop, priest and deacon, as well as papal and episcopal jurisdiction, developed later (circa 3rd century).

[471] *Ut unum sint*, 96.

[472] Ibid.,96; cf. *Lumen Gentium*, 27.

[473] J. Dupuis, ed. *The Christian Faith in the Doctrinal Documents of the Catholic Church*, 7th ed. (New York: Alba House, 2002), 761; the Latin text can be found in *Enchiridion Vaticanum* (1994-1995), no. 1348, p. 740.

[474] Cf. Ibid., 1008.

[475] Cf., the CDF's *Commentary on the Concluding Formula of the 'Professio Fidei*,"

The importance of Lk 22:32 to the Petrine ministry is manifested in John Paul II's General Audience of Dec. 2, 1992. In his judgment,

> The basic elements of the Petrine mission are found in these words [Lk 22:32]: first of all, that of strengthening his brothers by expounding the faith, exhorting to faith, as well as all the measures necessary for the development of the faith. This activity is addressed to those whom Jesus, speaking to Peter, calls "your brothers." In context the expression first applies to the other apostles, but it does not rule out a wider sense embracing all the members of the Christian community (cf. Acts 1:15)...These words of the evangelist Luke (22:31-33) are very significant for all who exercise the *munus Petrinum* in the Church. They continually remind them of the kind of original paradox that Christ himself placed in them, with the certitude that in their ministry, as in Peter's, a special grace is at work which supports human weakness and allows him to "strengthen his brothers."[476]

The weakness of Peter is a sign that "the surpassing power" that upholds his ministry "belongs to God" and not to him (cf. 2 Cor. 4:7). As Bossuet notes, "the mystery of the Gospel is infirmity and strength united, grandeur and weakness assembled."[477] Just as Jesus Christ, in His earthly life, combined divine power and human weakness so also does His body, the Church. With respect to the divine and the human, Bossuet (citing Pope Leo I) observes: "One shines forth in miracles, the other succumbs to injuries: *Unum horum coruscat miraculis, aliud succumbit injuriis.*"[478] In regard to the Petrine ministry, this means that the Popes, with all their human frailties, are able to strengthen their brothers in the faith precisely and only because of supernatural support. The Petrine office is indefectible because God, who cannot fail, is its hidden but ever-present strength.

L'Osservatore Romano [Eng. Ed.] No. 28, 15 July, 1998, 3-4.; See also José Pereira, "Infallible Papal Pronouncements," *Homiletic & Pastoral Review* (March, 1996), 55-60.

[476]"Peter Strengthens His Brothers in Faith," General Audience of Dec. 2, 1992 in John Paul II, *A Catechesis on the Creed, vol. 4: The Church, Mystery, Sacrament, Community* (Boston: Pauline Books & Media, 1998), 251-252.

[477]J.B. Bossuet, *Sermon Sur L'Église* (1660) in *Sermons de Bossuet,* Vol. 1 (Paris: Garnier Frères, 1872), 705.

[478]Ibid., 706; cf. Tome of St. Leo, D-H, 294.

7. Summary and Conclusions

From what has been presented, it should be clear that the link between the Petrine office and the indefectibility of the Church depends on the institution of this office, *de iure divino*. Indefectibility cannot be reduced to a mere "fidelity to the Gospel." In light of Scripture and Tradition, it is also evident that indefectibility includes fidelity and stability in the essential structure and identity of the Church as established by Christ. In the words of Pope Paul VI, "we believe that the Church founded by Jesus Christ and for which he prayed is indefectibly one in faith, worship and the bond of hierarchical communion" (*unam...indeficienter esse*).[479] A true ecclesiology of communion must recognize and support the means for achieving communion established by Christ Himself. When we realize that the Petrine ministry is a gift given to the Church *de iure divino*, we will understand that the Catholic Church, united in communion with the See of Peter, is indefectible — she will never be lacking the fullness of the means of salvation.

To be sure, the Petrine ministry is not the only means for insuring ecclesial unity. Much could also be said about the indispensable role of Mary who is "intimately united to the Church"[480] and who cares for the faithful "by her maternal charity."[481] The central point of this essay, however, is that the Petrine office is essential to the indefectible structure of the Catholic Church. As a "visible source and foundation"[482] of ecclesial communion, the Roman Pontiff fulfills a divinely ordained service of unity. Without the Petrine ministry, the Church would be lacking an essential aspect of what Christ willed for His Church on earth. Without the Petrine office, the Church ceases to be indefectible.

---

[479]Paul VI, *Credo of the People of God* (1968), no. 21; Enchiridion Vaticanum (1968-1970) no. 557, pp. 264-265.

[480]*Lumen gentium,* 63

[481]Ibid., 62.

CHAPTER 8

Pastores Dabo Vobis: Establishing an Ecclesial Culture for the Clergy

Most Rev. Allen H. Vigneron, Bishop of Oakland

My task in this essay is to explore how in *Pastores dabo vobis*[483] Pope John Paul II establishes an ecclesial culture for the Church's pastors. Because I have devoted so many years of my ministry to the work of priestly formation, I am grateful for the opportunity to offer these reflections in a volume on the theme "Called to Holiness and Communion." I want to begin with a few prefatory remarks on some of the presuppositions, which are embedded in this theme, because these will have an effect on the way I develop my argument.

First, I want to note that one of the significant aims of the Second Vatican Council was to call the Church to a renewal of holiness and a strengthening of communion. While there are some who read the Council through a very different lens — e.g., seeing the Fathers as engaged in a more political process of shifting power from one group to another — my own reading and study of the Council's documents shows that the above presupposition is accurate.

Second, in my essay I will bracket the task of spelling out the relationship of the two dimensions of the Council's aim. For example, which is the means and which is the end? Are we to grow in holiness for the sake of strengthening communion? Or does a stronger communion among the Church's members bear fruit in a holier Church? Or perhaps — and this is, I think, the direction in which the answer lies — each is a means to the other, because in the

---

[483]Post-Synodal Apostolic Exhortation *Pastores dabo vobis On the Formation of Priests in the Circumstances of the Present Day* [Vatican City: Libreria Editrice Vaticana, 1992 (hereafter cited as PDF)].

New Covenant holiness and communion are essentially ordered to each other. Perhaps being holy and living in communion is the same thing seen from different perspectives.

Third, I take it for granted that the examination of a text published some twenty-seven years after the close of the Council is subject matter suitably included in a study on Vatican II's ecclesiology. That is, the theme of this volume presupposes that PDV has an intrinsic connection with that achievement to which we give the summary title "Vatican II." Another way to say this is that PDV is one of the elements in what we can call the "Johanno-Pauline Project" through which the Holy Spirit has been directing the Church for these last four decades.

Working off of these presuppositions I have just articulated, I am able to specify further my task. My aim is to consider how PDV, by establishing an ecclesial culture for the clergy advances the aims of the Johanno-Pauline project of strengthening the Church's communion and increasing her holiness.

I will attempt to achieve this aim in three basic moves. The first is more formal. In that section I will offer an account of how it is possible for a text to establish or foster a culture. For this I will draw upon the resources of Husserlian phenomenology. In the second section, which is the longest of my essay, I will identify two key distinctions at play in PDV and consider how these distinctions establish an ecclesial culture and then discuss how, according to PDV, this ecclesial culture for the clergy will advance the growth of the Church in holiness and communion. In the final section of my talk I will evaluate the usefulness of this ecclesial culture in forwarding the aims of the Second Vatican Council and offer some observations on the tasks we must be about in renewing priestly formation in order to bring about the renewal of the Church that is the promise of Vatican II.

I. TEXT AND CULTURE

To begin this section on the capacity of a text to establish a culture, I want to go to the Second Vatican Council to find a description of what a culture is. It appears in the *Constitution on the Church in the Modern World, Gaudium et spes.* In the first lines of number 53, the Fathers, with a view to the etymology of the term, explain that culture (*cultura*) is the activity of "cultivating (*colendo*) natural goods and values, which, while contrasted with nature (*natura*) is "intimately connected with [it]." Culture is, then, what results from what we do with what nature gives us. The Constitution fills in this very formal delineation of culture by going on to say that the term "culture," in its general sense, indicates everything by which man refines and unfolds his manifold spiritual and corporeal endowments. And this is spelled out in a series of appositional clauses:

- Devoting himself to directing the world by his knowledge and effort;
- Making social life, both in the family and in the civic community, more human, by improving customs and institutions;
- Over the course of time, expressing, communicating and conserving in his work great spiritual experiences and aspirations, so that these may be of advantage to the progress of the many even of the whole human race.

It is the last of these three clauses that points us on the road to understanding how a text can establish a culture.

Let us, then, simply phrase our question in terms borrowed from *Gaudium et spes*: How is possible for a text to function as a foundational resource for that cultivation of natural goods which occurs when we express, communicate and conserve great spiritual expressions and aspirations? When the question is phrased that way the answer seems to come *per definitionem*. How is it possible for a text, by its very nature, not to express, communicate and conserve great spiritual experiences and aspirations? Isn't that precisely what texts do? Not that all texts deal with *great* spiritual matters. The fourth grade doggerel of "Roses are red / Violets are blue" does not measure up to *The Divine Comedy*. The Monday night sit-com does not belong in the canon along side of *King Lear*. And my business letter, with its mandatory three paragraphs of introduction, body and conclusion will never be mistaken for Paul's Epistle to the Romans. But every well-written text, precisely to the degree it succeeds in achieving the aim of speech as such, established or enhances human culture.

Husserl proposes a richly connotative term to highlight the capacity of a text to advance human culture. He suggests that we think of a text as a "sediment."[484] That is to say that in a text we are presented with a judgment achieved through the insightful thinking of the author. Because of the permanence of writing, that insight can remain available and be transmitted embodied in the text across continents and over centuries. For example, Socrates' insight that a citizens' faithful service to the city may require breaking his city's laws is sedimented into the text of the Platonic dialogue, *The Apology*. Through that medium this insight that loyalty is not always the same as conformity continues to be handed on as a foundational conviction available for reappropriation by each new generation.

A text can establish a culture by preserving a judgment or insight concerning a strategic distinction achieved by a skilled thinker regarding an important matter or good that is significant for human living. Sedimented within the text that piece of wisdom is available to the skillful reader, who, using the text as a sort of map, follows the author's lead in thinking through along with him the truth he has put into words. By appropriating the insight the reader comes to share in the foundational convictions of a people.

Having our reading of PDV informed by Husserl's observations on how culture's founding insights are sedimented in texts will assist us in identifying the "moves" in that text, which serve as the foundation stones for an ecclesial culture.

II. PASTORES DABO VOBIS AND ECCLESIAL CULTURE

A cursory review of PDV shows that the exhortation situates the theme of the priesthood and priestly formation squarely within an ecclesial context. The Church is the reason for the existence of the priesthood: "Without priests the Church would not be able to live that

---

[484]All of the essential elements of Husserl's analysis of how a text presents a "sedimented" judgment appear in his essay, *Die Frage nach dem Ursprung der Geometrie als intentional-historische Problem, "Beilage III," Die Krisis der europäische Wissenscaften und die transzendentale Phänomenologie: Einleitung in die Phänomenologische Philosophie* (Husserliana: Gesammelte Werke VI, ed. Walter Biemel, The Hague: Martinus Nijhoff, 1976) pp. 365-386.) [The English translation appears as *The Origin of Geometry, "Appendix VI," The Crisis of European Sciences and Transcendental Phenomenonolog,* trans. David Carr (Evanston, IL: Northwestern University Press, 1970): 353-378.]

For an important parallel treatment of this theme by Husserl, see his *Erfahrung und Urteil* (ed. Ludwig Landgrebe, Hamburg: Claassen, 1954), pp.136-139. [The English translation is found in *Experience and Judgment,* trans. James S. Churchill and Karl Ameriks, (Evanston, IL: Northwestern University Press, 1973): 121-124.]

fundamental obedience [to evangelize and to celebrate the Eucharist] which is at the very heart of her existence and her mission in history" (n.1). And the future of the Church depends on priests.[485] Thus the Church has the authority and the duty to form her priests.

That these themes announced in the "Introduction" of PDV serve as foundational axioms for its full presentation on priestly formation is confirmed by the fact that the whole of Chapter II's exposition on "The Nature and Mission of the Ministerial Priesthood" is ecclesiologically grounded: "It is within the Church's mystery, as a mystery of Trinitarian communion in missionary tension, that every Christian identity is revealed, and likewise the specific identity of the priest and his ministry" (no. 12).

My summary recap in the paragraph above can serve to represent the much longer exposition that would result from a thorough examination of the ecclesiological themes which PDV takes up to explain the priesthood and to chart the course for priestly formation in the future. That way of reading the text is one obviously valid way to consider how PDV seeks to foster the ecclesial culture of the clergy. However, invoking what I said earlier, I want to read PDV with the interpretative resources provided by phenomenology, and that's the direction I want to take us in now.

As reported earlier, Husserl saw that a text established a culture by preserving an insight. A text is the sediment of the fruit of thinking, the perduring embodiment of those moves of distinguishing and joining that go into seeing a state of affairs for what it is.[486]

Texts that have the capacity to ground a culture are those sediments of insightful judgments about significant matters that can support common convictions and common actions. Husserl teaches us that it is the important distinctions embedded in a text that will serve as the sort of genetic code for the unfolding of a culture. Instructed thus by Husserl, I propose that we read PDV to identify the "strategic distinctions"[487] that will blossom into the ecclesial culture of the clergy.

---

[485]PDV, n. 4.

[486]Husserl's most polished analysis of the act of judging is his *Formale und tanszendentale Logik. Husserliana: Gesammelte Werke XVII*, ed. Paul Janssen (The Hague: Martinus Nijhoff, 1974). The English translation appears as *Formal and Transcendental Logic*, trans. Dorian Cairns (The Hague, Martinus Nijhoff, 1969).

[487]I am indebted to Robert Sokolowski for teaching me the importance of identifying

In a volume such as this it is not possible to catalogue all the distinctions PDV makes, much less to subject them all to a thorough examination. Rather, what I want to do is to focus on two:

- The distinction between the Priest Jesus Christ and the Church
- The distinction between human formation and the other three aspects of priestly formation, viz., intellectual, spiritual and pastoral formation.

Focusing our attention on these two particular distinctions embedded in PDV is worth our attention because each of them serves as a kind of lever upon which a significant portion of the argument of PDV is moved forward. Distinguishing Christ the Priest from the Church is strategic for PDV's explanation of the identity and mission of the ordained priesthood. Setting up human formation as a distinct task in seminary education is a key strategy in PDV's articulating the program of priestly formation that will help to ensure that the lives of the ordained are consistent with that identity. The first distinction is indispensable for grasping the essence of the priesthood. PDV requires the second to treat the qualities that are rooted in the identity.

In its second chapter PDV established the identity of the ordained priest by distinguishing Christ from the Church on the analogy of the distinction between a body and its head, a flock and its leader, a wife and her husband. Christ is not the Church because he is her head, her shepherd and her bridegroom. This distinction, however, is not a divorce. To say that being Christ is different from being the Church is not, for example, like saying that being Christ is different from being a parallelogram. That our distinction is not a divorce is precisely the point of differentiating Christ from the Church *as* her head, shepherd and bridegroom — all names that denote beings whose very essence is relational.

As PDV affirms, the identity given to a man at his priestly ordination is grounded in the distinction between Christ and the Church. Through the Sacrament of Holy Orders a man is configured

---

"strategic distinctions" in order to read a text intelligently. See his "Making Distinctions," *Pictures, Quotations and Distinctions: Fourteen Essays in Phenomenology* (Notre Dame, IN: University of Notre Dame Press, 1992): 55-91.

to Christ the Priest, the Head (-not-the-Body), the Shepherd (-not-the-flock), the Bridegroom (-not-the-bride).

Now on to PDV's second strategic distinction: between human formation and the other three dimensions of formation in this set of four. By way of an aside, I want to point out that spending time examining this distinction is not only important for our purposes today, but also give us a chance to become better acquainted with one of the original contributions of PDV, since setting out human formation as a distinct field of concern in the seminary curriculum is a new move.

The first mention of "human formation" occurs at n. 43 in PDV, where it is characterized a the "necessary foundation" for "the whole work of priestly formation." PDV gives only the briefest sketch of the nature of this dimension of formation: it is the "cultiva[tion of] a series of human qualities" (n. 43). To fill in this sketch we need to look at the three lists PDV offers to illustrate what some of these "human qualities" are.

The first two lists work in tandem. The earlier is original to the text; the latter is taken from St. Paul's Epistle to the Philippians. Each contains a set of qualities that we would generally recognize as needed for anyone that could be characterized as a good man as such. The third list is more specific. It lists a set of qualities, which the good man as such needs in order to be able to relate to others. In this list PDV places particular importance on "affective maturity," the capacity for love and friendship, whether these are expressed within marriage or outside of it, the latter being the case in all instances of the celibate clergy. This human quality is so important that the whole of section n. 44 is devoted to discussing it.

The text of PDV contains several other indications that can help us see what distinguishes human formation from the other dimensions of priestly formation. The qualities to be cultivated here are, PDV tells us, reflections of the "human perfections of Christ" (n.43), since, as PDV says later, "Jesus Christ offers the most complete, genuine and perfect expression of what it means to be human" (n. 72). Thus, by foiling, at least implicitly, the qualities a priest needs with the perfections that are proper to Christ as divine, PDV is underscoring that the qualities to be cultivated specifically by human formation are excellences rooted in human nature. This point is confirmed by PDV's affirming that these desired qualities are needed by a priest because of the nature of those whom he serves, or as PDV says, "the human formation of the priest shows its special importance when related to the receiver of the mission" (n. 43). Human formation according to PDV is, then, we can conclude, the cultivation of those qualities that enable a man to relate well with others. PDV contrasts this effort with spiritual formation, intellectual formation and pastoral formation.

Earlier I made the claim that distinguishing human formation, as a specifically different dimension of seminary training is an original move. At this point, however, some may wish to challenge the claim. Responding to that challenge will, I believe, help clarify further the nature of human formation.

The challenge I mention might go something like this: "Isn't the distinction between human formation and its foils just a new presentation of the classic distinction between moral virtue and the virtues of intellect and making? The intellectual virtues are a perfect match, and the professionally required qualities cultivated by pastoral formation seem to fit under the heading of poetical virtues understood in a justifiably extended sense. That seems to leave us with no choice but to say that the qualities to be cultivated by human formation are identical to the moral virtues spoken of by the Ancients."

The solution to the challenge starts with a closer examination of the dimension of formation that would be left unaccounted for were we to attempt to laminate PDV's distinction on top of the Ancients', namely, "spiritual formation" (treated in nn. 45-50).

A plausible first effort for dealing with the question might well be to say that spiritual formation, as an item that has no parallel in the list of thinkers who relied on natural reason alone, means formation in grace. The implication of this approach is that the virtues to be cultivated in human formation are natural and the virtues to be cultivated in spiritual formation are supernatural. For a first indication that this not what PDV has in mind we look to its affirmation that "in the task of bringing his human formation to maturity, the priest receives special assistance from the grace of Jesus Christ" (n. 72). So clearly for PDV, human formation is not separate from that grace-directed formation that leads to supernatural excellence. The distinction between human formation and spiritual formation is not the same as the distinction between natural moral virtue and holiness.

Getting it right about how human formation relates to spiritual formation requires that we turn to PDV for a closer look at the matter. PDV, n. 45, says that spiritual formation "completes" human formation. Spiritual formation focuses on the specifically "religious dimension of the human person" and seeks, PDV says, citing *Optatam totius*, to foster those qualities needed for living "in intimate and unceasing union with God" (n. 45). The work of spiritual formation is fostering a deep communion with Jesus Christ" (n. 43). So then, both human formation and spiritual formation seek to cultivate what the ancients would call moral virtues, virtues that are dispositions to use our freedom well. And efforts in both spheres are sustained by grace. What distinguishes the two dimensions is the object to which the free acts are directed. The qualities cultivated in a seminarian's spiritual formation are moral virtues conducive to his sound relationship with the Three Divine Persons. The qualities cultivated in human formation are moral virtues conducive to sound relationships with other human persons.

Having followed the path indicated by PDV toward seeing for ourselves the strategic distinctions it makes, we come to apprehend what we are looking for; we can identify what human formation is. It is the cultivating of that series of moral qualities that are human as such and are needed for good relationships with other men.

Having worked through PDV's two key distinctions we can now consider the sort of culture to which each would give rise.

To set up the identity of the priest by distinguishing between Christ, the Head, and the Church, His Body, is to locate the priest within an explicitly correlative context. That is, his identity is based on that to which he stands in a necessary relationship. More specifically, the context is nuptial-covenantal.[488] The patterns of understanding and behavior coherent with this context are

- Respect for irreducible differentiation
- Mutual self-giving, to the ideal point of self-sacrifice

---

[488]On this theme, see Pope John Paul II, *Man and Woman He Created Them: A Theology of the Body*, trans. Michael Waldstein (Boston, MA: Pauline Books and Media, 2006). For a

- And a dependence on the other which is neither servile nor tyrannical on the part of either, but is liberating for both.

These patterns are the elements of what I will call, for now, a culture of mutuality.

The identification of human formation as a distinct dimension in the training of the clergy establishes that, among the qualities needed for living out one's priestly identity, are those that foster authentic human transactions. That is, the ecclesial culture within which priests trained according to the vision of PDV is a "relational culture."

Clearly this culture, which we have called by the names "mutual" and "relational," is one. It is, to use a more theological term than either of the earlier two, "a culture of communion. This culture is a settled way of thinking and acting wherein the basic pattern is of two becoming a one without ceasing to be two. And because the ecclesial culture that PDV establishes for the priest is a culture of communion, PDV describes him as "a man of communion" (nn. 18.2 and 43.3).

PDV further indicates that this culture of communion is a culture of charity, namely that species of charity specified as "pastoral."[489] According to PDV the pastoral charity of a priest is a participation in Christ's pastoral charity (n. 23). It is that way of thinking and acting proper to Christ as Head, Shepherd and Bridegroom of the Church (n. 21). Pastoral charity is, then, PDV affirms, the priest's total gift of self to the Church (n. 23). Its source is the configuration of a man to Christ the Head in Holy Orders. The Eucharist, the efficacious sign of communion, is the expression and nourishment of pastoral charity. Pastoral charity is, therefore, the over-arching quality or virtue that enables a priest to think and act according to the nuptial-covenantal communion he has with the Church through Christ. The future priest's initiation into the culture of communion fosters the development of this virtue of pastoral charity, and his attainment of that virtue reinforces and enhances that culture.[490]

---

systematic discussion that complements the Pope's presentation, see Angelo Scola, The *Nuptial Mystery*, trans. Michelle K. Borras (Grand Rapids, MI: William B. Eerdmans Publishing Company, 2005).

[489]The discussion of pastoral charity is found in nn. 21-23.

[490]It is worthy of note that one of the results of a priest's pastoral charity is, according to

On the basis of the identity between charity and holiness in the Christian vision of life, we can conclude this section by noting that in fostering a culture of communion for the Church's clergy, PDV is, in effect, making the fostering of a culture of holiness a central aim in the seminary curriculum. The middle term here is charity. And this observation leads us to see how the topic being explored contributes to the overall goal of this volume, viz., examining afresh the doctrine of the Second Vatican Council on the Church in order to understand more deeply how that teaching is, necessarily, a call to communion and holiness. Indeed, according to the ecclesiology of the Council, as we see it in PDV, setting the direction for the work of priestly formation, the call to communion is the call to holiness; and such a summons is another name for the call to renew the Church, to intensify what it is for the Church to be the Church.

III. ASSESSMENT

In this concluding section of my essay I would like to do two things:

- First, after identifying the challenge or difficulty to which PDV is responding in insisting on a culture of communion as essential for priestly formation today, offer an initial assessment of the adequacy of that response.
- Second, discuss some of the areas for further theological reflection that must take place if PDV's sense of a culture of communion is to be better understood, and, by that fuller understanding gain in credibility.

As to the first point: It is a hermeneutical truism that themes emerge to take center stage in our thinking because something or someone provokes a shift in our attention. For example, understanding the conditions for the stability of the earth preoccupies us after we've been through an earthquake. So, our question here is: "What's been rocking the world of priestly formation to the point that PDV must underscore the need for a culture of communion?"

PDV, the establishment of a communion within the priest's own self. That is, one of the effects of pastoral charity is the "unity between the priest's interior life and all his external actions and the obligations of the ministry" (n. 23).

[491]A phenomenological First Philosophy offers theology rich resources for exploring

The Exhortation itself begins by articulating some of the questions or problems for priestly formation to which it seeks to respond. Among those catalogued in section n. 7 are:

- The trend to compensate for loneliness through hedonism or flight from responsibility;
- A sufficiency of material goods that results in a practical atheism;
- A distorted sense of human sexuality, which often gives rise to a break-up of families;
- The spread of social injustice through a loss of concern with the common good;
- A relativistic response to the authoritatively presented faith.

And the section offers a summary formulation of the challenge it will address, viz., "a desperate defense of personal subjectivity which tends to close it off in individualism, rendering it incapable of true human relationships" (n. 7).

Given this read of the difficulties to be faced in our seminaries today, we understand why the ecclesial culture, which PDV seeks to offer the clergy, is a culture of communion. It is precisely this culture of communion, established by PDV's distinguishing Christ from the Church, and human formation from other aspects of seminary education, which will remedy the ills that follow from the triumph of the "imperial self" in our contemporary values and mores.

About the adequacy of this strategy, two comments: First, in calling for a culture of communion PDV is directing us to the very antithesis of the culture of the autonomous self. PDV has the merit of eschewing half measures that only seek to diminish the presenting symptoms of the problem. Rather PDV aims to cure a culture which "renders [us] incapable of true relationships" (n. 7) by fostering the virtue of charity, which is the capacity for the deepest of relationships, covenantal self-giving.

Second, insofar as the culture of communion is accurately identified as a necessary consequence of the Church's very essence, a judgment about its adequacy as a remedy will be the same as one's judgment about the adequacy of Christ's grace to heal and elevate our nature. All of the arguments of the old and new apologetics, now transposed into this particular "key" of "Christian life as existence in communion," will have here the same probative force as those accounts exercise in their original formulations. Those of us who hear in the statement of *Gaudium et spes* that "in reality, the mystery of man is only really made clear in the mystery of the Word incarnate" (n. 22) the authentic witness of our faith and who recognize that the work of the Savior is the restoration of communion lost by sin, will see that PDV hits the mark.

Perhaps the most effective way for the culture of communion to vindicate its claim over the culture of radical autonomy is for that culture to be manifested in the thinking and acting of its adherents. The assent of seminarians to the superiority of the culture of communion will, in great part, depend on their living in such a culture, living with those who are adept at self-giving and experiencing the rightness of their own thinking and acting in charity.

Such a practical case for a culture of communion needs, however, the reinforcement of a theoretical account. And this is where I want to identify some properly theological tasks that must be undertaken in order to provide a coherent understanding of communion.

To this end speculative theologians will have to discover in ontology the resources (a) for explaining the way differences play themselves out within identities, i.e., how multiplicity and unity do not contradict each other; and (b) for articulating the relationship between parts and wholes. We rightly look to ontology for such resources since considering "the one" and "the one and the many" is the long-established competence of that science.

A third theme for exploration in speculative theology's reflection on communion is to tease out the relationship between participation and representation. Here we seek an answer to the question of how something that shares in another makes manifest that other in which it shares. That is, we need to know what are the principles on the basis of which the play of identity and difference in participation displays itself in image and imaged.[491] Such an investigation is important for the theology of communion precisely insofar as Christian communion is fundamentally and irreducibly sacramental. The reason for this is that in the sacramental economy representation causes participation, and participation makes representation possible. That is, the way that the sign is same and other to the signified not only parallels the way participant and the participated in are same and other, but, in the sacramental economy, cultivating and enriching these approaches carries us forward toward achieving the aims set for us by the Second Vatican Council.

CHAPTER TEN: THE RENEWAL OF RELIGIOUS LIFE:

themes such as the three I have mentioned here. See, for example, Robert Sokolowski, *Presence and Absence: A Philosophical Investigation of Language and Being* (Bloomington, IN: Indiana University Press, 1978), especially pp. 144-171.
    [492]*Perfectae caritatis*, 2e, in Flannery, Austin, ed., Vatican Council II: *The Conciliar and Post*

CHAPTER 9

THE RENEWAL OF RELIGIOUS LIFE: STRENGTHENING THE TRINITARIAN *COMMUNIO* IN THE CHURCH

Rev. Gabriel O'Donnell, OP,
Dominican House of Studies, Washington, D.C.

Introduction

A BRIEF SURVEY OF THE HISTORY of religious life in the United State since the close of the Second Vatican Council reveals much about the Council's hoped-for renewal of religious orders and congregations. The clarion call to renewal was embodied in the conciliar "Decree on the Appropriate Renewal and Adaptation of the Religious Life," *Perfectae caritatis*, which cast that renewal and updating in lofty terms indeed:

> Before all else the religious life is ordered to the following of Christ by its members and to their becoming united with God by the profession of the evangelical counsels. For this reason, it must be seriously and carefully considered that even the best-contrived adaptations to the needs of our time will be to no avail unless they are animated by a spiritual renewal, which must always be assigned primary importance even in the active ministry.[492]

While the council itself was careful to situate the call for renewal and adaptation within a theological framework, post-Conciliar directives and commentators tended to focus on the practical need for change, experimentation, and wide-ranging consultation among the members and outside secular experts. So thoroughgoing

---

[492] *Perfectae caritatis*, 2e, in Flannery, Austin, ed., Vatican Council II: *The Conciliar and Post Conciliar Documents*, Vol. I (New York: Costello Publishing, 1992): 613.

was this movement that it entailed the re-writing of each institute's constitutions. "It is the institutes themselves which have the main responsibility for renewal and adaptation."[493] The "general chapter has the right to alter, temporarily, ... by way of experiment, provided that the purpose, nature and character of the institute are safeguarded. Experiments which run counter to the common law ... will be readily authorized by the Holy See as the need arises."[494] Perhaps naively, many religious became convinced that only through a courageous conformity to modernity, would their communities become more authentic, more capable of carrying out their mission, and being thus "renewed" would attract new members. In actuality, the encounter with modernity did not produce the new life intimated in the teaching of the Constitution of the Church in the Modern World, *Gaudium et spes*.[495]

This notion of renewal and adaptation to the modern world as a kind of inculturation into modernity was in the air even before the Council was called. The Congregation for Religious had been calling for the modernization of religious communities, particularly those of women, for twenty years prior to the Council.[496] The consequent confusion among religious was due, largely, to the lack of precise explanations as to the meaning of such phrases as "modern man," "modern society" and the "modern world." Having embraced a way of life rooted in a counter-cultural withdrawal from the world in order to effect a more radical following of Christ, the religious was now summoned to become adapted to the culture. Just where the counter-cultural character of the religious life ended and the secular world began was never addressed in the documents of the Council. Indeed, as Tracey Rowland suggests in an important recent study on the period following the Council, "the fathers of the Second Vatican Council lacked an adequate hermeneutic of culture."[497] The consequences of this critique are far-reaching.

---

[493]"Norms for Implementing the Decree: on the Up-to-Date Renewal of Religious Life," *Ecclesiae sanctae II* in Flannery, Vol. I, 624.

[494]Ibid. 6.

[495]Cf. *Gaudium et spes*, especially paragraphs 40-44 where the text speaks optimistically of what the secular culture of the twentieth century has to offer to the Christian faithful.

[496]Wulf, Frederick, "Decree on the Appropriate Renewal and Adaptation of Religious Life," in Vorgrimler, Herbert et al, eds., *Commentary on the Documents of Vatican II*, Vol. II, (New York: Herder & Herder, 1968), 303.

[497]Rowland, Tracey, *Culture and the Thomist Tradition: After Vatican II*, (New York: Routledge, 2003), 33.

Rowland's focus is the world of theological and philosophical discourse after the Council. In another recent study, Lauren Pristas has addressed related issues with regard to the creation of the *Missale Romanum* by the *Consilium* for the Implementation" of the Constitution on the Liturgy.[498] In tracing the selection and editing of collects for the *editio typica* of the Roman Missal, Pristas encounters a similar problematic in the adaptation of liturgical texts to modern sensibilities: a liturgical inculturation in progress.

A parallel observation might be made in reflecting on the renewal of the religious life called for by the Second Vatican Council. The lack of clarity on the part of the fathers and *periti* of the Council regarding a proper understanding of culture and modernity may well be a major contributing factor to the difficulties facing religious men and women in the United State early in the twenty-first century.

My contention in this essay is that the failure of the renewal of religious life as envisioned by Vatican Council II to become a reality is due, in large measure, to the failure to understand the necessarily theological nature of that renewal. In considering religious life, there has been a failure to reflect, reason, analyze and evaluate, theologically. While Pope Paul VI and Pope John Paul II were articulating a fuller theology of the religious life, religious themselves were engaged in "renewal" at another level, what is sometimes referred to as the "grassroots." In one sense there have been two distinct paths of renewal in operation without reference to one another: the one proposed by the Council and fostered by the ongoing teachings of the Church, and the other engaged in at the grassroots level among religious in the United States. For this reason I have entitled the first section of my essay "Vatican II and the Theology of the Religious Life," followed by the section entitled "Vatican II and the Life of Religious."

Vatican II and the Theology of the Religious Life

Theological reflection on the religious life at the time of the Council was often cast in the form of commentaries on the three vows of poverty, chastity and obedience, understood as constituting

---

[498]Pristas, Lauren, "The Redaction of the Roman Missal (1970)" *The Thomist,* Vol. 67, 2, (April, 2003), 157-195.

a person in "the state of perfection." Not strongly biblical or patristic in approach, these reflections represented, by and large, a spirituality of post-Reformation Catholicism. Almost exclusively Christological, these writings embodied a certain theological narrowness that prevailed after the restoration of religious life in Europe in the wake of the French Revolution. As a result, there emerged a certain a nineteenth century legalism among many religious in the United States. In the first half of the twentieth century exhortations to greater fidelity to the holy rule and the commands of superiors, as well as the canonical implications of the 1917 Code of Canon Law, were typical of the literature on religious life and affirmed in ecclesiastical directives. Religious were constantly urged to fulfill the obligations imposed by their profession. This, in part, explains the "lack of genuinely theological, spiritual thought" in the preparatory documents for Council in regard to religious life.[499]

In spite of careful preparation for the consideration of religious life by council fathers, it was a topic somewhat contentious from the first. In the initial draft of the Constitution on the Church, issued on November 10, 1962, the chapter treating of the religious life was titled, "The States of Life Devoted to Acquiring Evangelical Perfection." The revised draft issued a year later signaled a shift in attitude. Rather than a separate chapter on the religious life, the revised schema absorbed the treatment of religious into the chapters entitled, respectively, "The People of God with Special Reference to the Laity," and "The Call to Holiness in the Church."[500] While this change did not go unchallenged, particularly by the fathers of the council who were superiors general, in the end their proposals to highlight the role of religious in Church life and structures were rejected.[501] Further, unable to distinguish clearly between "religious" and "secular" consecrated life, all forms of "consecrated life" were eventually considered under the rubric of the laity and the universal call to holiness in the Church. This emphasis on the role of the laity became a byword of the Council and had serious effects on theological reflection concerning the religious life and

[499]Wulf, 303.
[500]Wiltgen, Ralph, S.V.D., ed. *The Religious Life Defined: An official Commentary on the Second Vatican Council Deliberations,* (Techney: Divine Word Publications, 1970), 6-7.
[501]Ibid., 9

practical consequences among those religious attempting to respond to the call for renewal and adaptation.

Regardless of any evaluation of the Council's theological account of the religious life, this decision effected a certain "muting" of its central role and importance within the Church. Seemingly, this was done to emphasize the role of the laity and the centrality of the doctrine of the universal call to holiness in the Constitution on the Church. As a consequence, the Council might be judged somewhat ambivalent about the religious life, its role in the Church's mission and its witness to the mystery of the transcendent in the modern world. *Perfectae caritatis*, one theologian claims, "represents a search for identity within this renewal [of the Church]."[502]

While the topic of religious life is treated in four other Council documents, the actual decree on religious life, *Perfectae caritatis*, is best read between the two "bookends" of *Lumen gentium*, the Dogmatic Constitution on the Church, which sets religious life in a new ecclesiological framework, and *Gaudium et spes*, the Constitution on the Church in the Modern World, which, although lacking a specific treatment of religious life, was frequently appealed to as providing a hermeneutic in understanding the meaning of renewal and adaptation in the modern world.[503] In Chapter V of *Lumen gentium*, the highlighting of the role of the evangelical counsels in regard to the universal vocation to holiness seems to bring about a certain diminution of the unique character of consecration through the vowing of these same counsels in religious life. The act of religious profession was understood by many to constitute the specific nature and identity of the religious. In addition, the movement within the text to identify different types of "consecrated life" gave rise to a number of questions regarding the various forms of Christian life that have yet to be addressed in the Church today.

In the face of these theological limits, there has still been significant theological development in the theology of the religious

---

[502]Beyer, Jean, S.J., "Life Consecrated by the Evangelical Counsels: Conciliar Teaching and Later Developments," in Rene Latourelle, S.J., ed., *Vatican II: Assessment and Perspectives*, Vol. II (New York: Paulist Press, 1989), 73.

[503]*Lumen gentium, Ad gentes, Christius Dominus* and *Presbyterorum ordinis* all discuss the religious life.

life, particularly in the writings of the popes since the Council. Paul VI, enthusiastic concerning the emergence of secular institutes, nevertheless, held religious life in high esteem and proclaimed the excellence of this freely given response to the call of the Spirit in his 1971 exhortation, *Evangelica testificatio.* The meaning of consecration, its ecclesial nature and the call to mission are well outlined there. It is in this document that the term "charism" as applied to religious life appears for the first time.[504] Although never applied to religious life in the documents of Vatican II, "starting with Paul VI, it would become normal in Church documents, and John Paul II uses it very frequently."[505]

The Contribution of John Paul II

It is clearly John Paul II, building on the teaching of Vatican II and the theology of Paul VI, who offers the most comprehensive view of religious life in the twentieth century, most especially in his post-synodal exhortation *Vita consecrata.*[506] His contribution to the theology of the religious life is but one aspect of his remarkable vision of the Christian faith, particularly his teleological focus on Trinitarian *communio* as the source and goal of all life and his consequent anthropology. The latter forms a large part of the foundation for his Christian humanism and his convictions about the civilization of love, which is set against the culture of death. Clearly, *Vita consecrate* is a document of theological renewal.

The Christological emphasis of earlier decades is, in the teaching of John Paul II, broadened to a new Trinitarian awareness indicated by the title of chapter I of *Vita consecrata,* "*Confessio Trinitatis: The Origins of the Consecrated Life in the Mystery of Christ and of the Trinity.*" While his point of departure is the account of the transfiguration in St. Matthew's gospel, his explanation of the evangelical counsels as "a gift of the Holy Trinity," is unique in the tradition. (VC, 20) "The deepest meaning of the evangelical counsels is revealed when they are

---

[504] *Evangelica testificatio,* AAS, 63 (1971) 11. The term, *charismata,* however, is used in other contexts within the documents of Vatican II, e.g. LG, 12; PO, 9, and AA, 3.
[505] Beyer, 76.
[506] *Vita consecrata,* March 25, 1996; my interest is specifically that of religious life and so have retained that term almost exclusively throughout.

viewed in relation to the Holy Trinity, the source of holiness." (VC, 21) Thus, the vows are understood as a reflection of Trinitarian life and the path for the religious to Trinitarian *communion*, through the following of Jesus Christ. Each of the vows is considered as coming from the Trinity and leading back to the Trinity.

The *sequela Christi*, Pope John Paul insists, defines the religious life and marks it out from other forms of Christian existence. Though all Christians are called to full discipleship, the religious not only follows the Lord, but attempts to live the very life that Christ lived. Living his virginity, his poverty and his obedience mark the religious out from other Christians who "follow" Christ and live the counsels according to the demands of their proper vocation. This living "more closely" the life that Christ lived through the vows of chastity, poverty and obedience not only prepares the religious for Trinitarian communion, but constitutes "the most radical way of living the Gospel on this earth, a way which may be called divine, because it was embraced by him ..." (VC, 18) Christ's earthly life, lived in chastity, poverty and obedience, was an expression "of his relationship as the Only-Begotten Son with the Father and with the Holy Spirit." (VC, 18) For the religious, the way of the evangelical counsels is the way to the Trinity.

One of the important theological suppositions of *Vita consecrata*, as indeed all his teaching on the religious life, is the Holy Father's Christian anthropology. The sacredness of all life, coming from the hand of the Creator, requires the recognition of the dignity of each person, a centerpiece of the John Paul II's theological vision from the earliest moments of his pontificate. It is in virtue of our humanity, now transformed through the sacred humanity of Jesus Christ, that we lay claim to a Trinitarian destiny. "The human person is created in the image of God (*imago Dei*) in order to grow into the image of Christ (*imago Christi*)."[507] Quoting *Gaudium et spes*, the Constitution of the Church in the Modern World, the Pope often insists on the Christocentric nature of this anthropology: "In reality it is only in the mystery of the Word made flesh that the mystery of man truly

[507]DiNoia, J. Augustine, O.P. *"Imago Dei-Imago Christi:* The Theological Foundations of Christian Humanism," Paper presented to the International Congress of the Pontifical Academy of St. Thomas Aquinas, Rome, Sept. 22, 2003.

becomes clear."[508] Ironically, the document so often used as a warrant for renewal at the "grassroots" level, also provides the anthropological foundation basis for the Pope's theology of the religious life. It is this lofty view of the human person that pervades the Holy Father's theological understanding of the religious life in *Vita consecrata*. Indeed, it is his Christian humanism that allows him to posit that a life of renunciation can satisfy the deepest longings of the human spirit. The mystery of the Incarnation has changed the human situation and invested it with new possibilities only comprehensible through the mystery of the sacred humanity of Christ, most especially his Paschal Mystery (VC, 24).

This mystical communion with Christ and the Blessed Trinity finds its expression in a fraternal life that mirrors the inner life of the triune Godhead — the "*Signum fraternitatis*." The fraternity of the religious community is a communion in love that reflects the life of the Trinity and witnesses to the *communio* of the Church. (VC, 41-42)

Finally, drawn into the circle of love, the religious shares in the mission of Christ. In virtue of their consecration, religious are called to live and die for others (VC 72-73). Whether completely dedicated to the contemplative life or immersed in the work of the new evangelization, the consecrated person is living out the reality of that life which Christ himself lived in his offering of himself to the Father for the salvation of souls — the "*Servitium caritatis*" (VC, 86)

Serving in some ways as a corrective for the possible marginalisation of the religious life in the structure of *Lumen gentium*, Pope John Paul reiterates that the "Christian tradition has always spoken of the *objective superiority of the consecrated life*." (VC, 18) With this in mind he does not hesitate to adopt the comparative language of *Lumen gentium* 44, indicating that consecrated life "constitutes a closer imitation and abiding re-enactment in the Church," of the way in which Jesus himself lived. (VC, 22)

Pope John Paul's teaching is the beginning of a renewed theology of the religious life. Oddly, few theological treatments on the religious life seem to have appeared in the English-speaking world since the close of the Council. Aside from the work of Basil

---

[508] *Gaudium et spes*, 22.

Cole and Paul Conners, I am not aware of any attempts to integrate the teachings of Vatican II and Pope John Paul into a comprehensive theology of religious life.[509]

There are, of course, certain challenges presented by *Vita consecrata*, to the religious and to the theologian of the religious life. Some examples: the use of the term "consecrated life," coined at the Second Vatican Council and taken up into the 1983 Code of Canon Law, requires clarification. It is intended to include a wide range of forms of Christian life. While everything in VC applies to religious life, it does not necessarily apply equally to all other forms of consecrated life. Also, the precise meaning of "consecration" continues to require greater precision. Are profession and consecration two theologically distinct acts? Is consecration an act of the individual and received by the Church, or does the Church herself effect this consecration? What of those forms of consecrated life without any public act of dedication or profession? Finally, taking up the new ordering of the vows employed by Vatican II, John Paul II lays great stress on the meaning and beauty of chastity. Is there need for greater attention to the classical notion that all three vows are, in the end, an expression of Christ's obedience and the holocaust of his will in his Paschal Mystery?

Vatican II and the Life of Religious

It must be admitted, at the outset, that the hoped-for renewal of religious life did not take place. It is, perhaps, a still-to-be-hoped for grace for the Church in the United States. On the contrary, institutes of religious life are diminishing to the point of disappearance and death. This failure to flourish in the face of such concerted efforts to respond with alacrity to the Church's call to renewal and adaptation is one of the conundrums inherent in our discussion.

Two themes guided the work of the Second Vatican Council: a return to the sources, *ressourcement*, and adaptation to modern life, *aggiornamento*, more literally, updating. From the first, among religious of the United States, it was the second theme, updating, that

---

[509]Cole, Basil, O.P. and Conner, Paul, O.P., *Christian Totality: Theology of the Consecrated Life*, rev. ed. (New York: Alba House, 1997).

210 CALLED TO HOLINESS AND COMMUNION

gained the ascendancy. The notion of returning to the sources was itself often misunderstood to refer exclusively to the sources of one's own religious family; the re-appropriation of what came to be called the "charism" of one's founder. The broader theological meaning of *ressourcement* as a return to foundations of Christian life, as a call to become yet more authentically Catholic, was often overlooked.

Influenced in large measure by the emergence of the social sciences in the mid-twentieth century, particularly psychology and sociology, and operating out of an inadequate ecclesiology based on an eclectic cluster of ideas drawn from various European theologians, religious institutes set about the work of renewal with a spirit of optimism and autonomy unprecedented in the post-medieval Church. It was not foreseen that gradually, for many religious, renewal and modernization would become synonymous.

Convinced that updating required a break with the past, and believing that this was the intention of the Council, many religious entered into this process reluctantly but with every hope that a true renewal would result. Considerations of the history of each institute and a study of the "charism" of the founder often became a search for patterns of discontinuity to be discovered there. The emphasis was too often on what was "new" or "revolutionary" in the beginnings of a particular order or society. A more theological methodology was either never considered or, if considered, set aside, with little regard for a critique of modernity, much less a concern for continuity with the broader and more ancient tradition of religious life.

A quick perusal of the issues published through the 1970s of *Review for Religious*, the main organ for the discussion on religious life at that time, reveals that renewal and adaptation was understood primarily as a call to change, i.e., to discontinue, to leave off, to omit, even to reject, those elements that were judged to be out of sync with modern life or injurious to the psychological and spiritual health of the religious themselves. Convenience, efficiency, suitability to the mentality of the modern world and practicality became watchwords of that period of experimentation and change. Religious clothing, community life, external exercises of piety, common apostolates, even the three evangelical counsels were subject to evaluation and revision according to these normative ideas. While generally held that future form of religious life could not be determined given the need for such radical overhauling, it was suggested that it would be unlike anything known in the past.[510] This became a theme for commentators on the religious life and continues among the more popular writers and presenters for the religious life today. Anything reminiscent of the remembered past, i.e., the past half-century, is dismissed as "culturally inappropriate."[511] These dispositions informed the rewriting of constitutions and directories mandated by the post-Conciliar norms for adaptation and renewal.

In some circles the very definition of the religious life was blurred by the appearance of secular institutes, new movements that included lay members, clerics and vowed religious, a wide range of associations of Christ's faithful and the introduction of the contradictory category of "non-canonical" communities.

The justification for this radical revision of religious life in all its aspects was seen as provided by the documents coming directly from the Holy See. The publication of *Renovationis causam* by the then Sacred Congregation for Religious and Secular Institutes in 1969, for example, attempted to address some of the serious misinterpretations of the Church's notion of renewal.[512] Nonetheless, the need for accommodation to the demands of the modern world was strongly emphasized in this document that it provided great latitude in the restructuring of formation programs among religious institutes. More to the point, there was no provision for an accountability whereby some evaluation of each institute's adherence to these norms could be monitored.

The puzzling aspect of this situation is that it went unchecked by Church authorities. Indeed, the tragic case of the Immaculate Heart of Mary Sisters of Los Angeles stands as a notable exception, which has yet to be fully documented.[513] While the theological understanding

---

[510]Chittister, Joan, *The Fire in These Ashes: A Spirituality of Contemporary Religious Life,* (New York: Rowan & Littlefield, 1995), 6.

[511]Schneiders, Sandra, *Finding the Treasure: Locating Religious Life in a New Ecclesial and Cultural Context,* (Mahwah: Paulist Pess, 2000); see also by the same author, *Selling All: Commitment, Consecrated Celibacy, and Community in Catholic Religious Life,* (Mahwah: Paulis Press, 2001).

[512]*Renovationis causam,* 13 February, 1969,:AAS, 51 (1969):103-120.

[513]Anita Caspery, *Witness to Integrity: The Crisis of the Immaculate Heart Community of California,* (Collegeville, Liturgical Press, 2003).

of the religious life was being proclaimed by Pope John Paul in his addresses to gatherings of religious superiors, general chapters and various celebrations focused on the vocation to the consecrated life, the newly-named Congregation for Institutes of Consecrated Life and Societies of Common Life, was approving constitutions that appeared to be in contradiction to the Holy Father's theological vision. Some of the documents issued by the same dicastery are not representative of the legislation it approved for institutes of religious life.[514] Perhaps the most obvious instances of the lack of congruence are the religious habit, residence in a religious house with a local superior, and engagement in a community ministry.

Early on the Second Vatican Council was spoken of as pastoral rather than doctrinal. This led many religious to the false notion that serious theological reflection was not an integral part of pastoral renewal in the Church. The generally anti-intellectual mood of clerics and religious in the United States in the second half of the twentieth century buttressed this perception and left many communities vulnerable to contemporary movements such as those of womens' rights, feminism, social radicalism, ecological preservation and a host of special interest groups whose influence helped to alienate many religious from the magisterium.

In fact, it is likely that the current crisis facing religious life in the United States is not limited to institutes of consecrated life but is symptomatic of wider ecclesial problems. The misunderstanding of the work and message of Vatican II might almost be seen as inevitable given theological developments in the post-medieval world and particularly in the post-Reformation and post-Enlightenments Church. The movement in Christian spirituality to an increasing emphasis on interiority is well documented.[515] The turn toward the subject, intensified by the Enlightenment, and the decided focus on interiority prepared the ground for many twentieth century attitudes.

---

[514]Cf. The Contemplative Dimension of Religious Life, March, 1980; *Essential Elements in the Church's Teaching on Religious Life as Applied to Institutes Dedicated toe Works of the Apostolate*, May, 1983.
[515]Leclercq, Vanderbroucke & Bouyer, eds., *History of Christian Spirituality: The Spirituality of the Middle Ages*, Vol. II (New York: Seabury, 1968); Raitt, McGinn & Meyendorff, eds., *Christian Spirituality: High Middle Ages and Reformation*, Vol. 17, (New York: Crossroads, 1991).

Regarding the religious life as precisely that, a *way of life*, rather than as an interior commitment or attachment, was compromised. What might be called the "sacramental" principle of the religious life was eclipsed by a kind of disembodied notion of dedication and service. It became more important to be in tune with the wide world than to offer it a counter-cultural critique, one of the fundamental functions of any religious movement of tradition. Ours is an age that has glamorized the human body and placed material possessions high on the list of society's wish list. The denial of the appropriateness of incarnating the religious life in external forms was a serious mistake.

The Church has long understood religious life itself as constituting a kind of culture, a sub-culture, if you will, within the wider Church, and set prophetically against the culture of the modern world. When religious were confronted with the language concerning modernity in the documents of the Second Vatican Council a crisis in meaning and direction was set in motion. The ethos of the religious life has always embodied certain values; the loss of which commentators recognize as a great impoverishment as religious life disappears from the cultural horizon.[516]

To think that progress is made in discontinuity from tradition and from history — a growing conviction among some Catholic theologians — has not been tenable in the event. Anthony Levi's recent study suggests the limits of a notion of modernity based in this notion of discontinuity.[517] In the areas of spirituality and moral theology this has taken the form of increased focus on what is demanded of the human person in order to obtain intimacy with God rather than the ideal of human flourishing under the influence of grace as preparation for a life of Trinitarian communion.

The loss of confidence among religious that their way of life has the potential to lead them to holiness and to a certain human fulfillment has produced a certain sourness that has not gone unnoticed. Once separated from the tradition, it is difficult to believe that religious life is a sure way to God, a sure way to happiness and

---

[516]Fialka, John, J., *Sisters: Catholic Nuns and the Making of America*, (New York: St. Martin's Press, 2003).

[517]Levi, Anthony, *Renaissance and Reformation: The Intellectual Genesis*, (New York: Yale University, 2002).

a sure way to contribute mightily to the transformation of the world through the announcement of the Good News of Jesus Christ.

Conclusion

For the renewal of the religious life to come about there will have to be, of necessity, a re-discovery of the ancient tradition of religious life among religious orders and congregations, and their place in it according to the mind and spirit of their founder. This in turn, must be situated within the ecclesial teaching regarding the meaning and purpose of religious life. Any methodology for renewal must be fundamentally theological. In this way each religious community will be prepared to critique its own recent history and will be provided with theological and spiritual principles necessary to discern what adaptation to the modern world, in any period, will require.

CHAPTER 10

Disciples in the Midst of the World: Collaboration of the Lay Faithful in the Sacred Ministry of Their Pastors

Peter Casarella

I. Introduction

WRITING ALMOST A DECADE *prior* to the Second Vatican Council, the theologian Hans Urs von Balthasar likened the arrival of the "hour of the laity" to the awakening of a slumbering giant.[519] The Council then introduced a radically new understanding of lay participation in the Church. In its wake the laity were seen as central to the ecclesial communion and co-participants in Christ's universal call to holiness. Discerning the genuine novelty of the conciliar position has not been easy. The Council Fathers were not primarily interested in treating the question of the laity in terms of "more" or "less" participation although the discussion in the ensuing years has sometimes gotten side-tracked by this quantitative way of thinking. Lay people did not require a Council to legitimize their status as a valid ecclesial reality. To the question "Who are the laity?" Cardinal Newman likewise responded with the quip, "the Church would look foolish without them."[520] The Church in the United States is experiencing rapid changes with regard to the image and function of the laity, but if we content ourselves simply to marvel at the statistics of growing

---

[519]Hans Urs von Balthasar, *Razing the Bastions* (San Francisco: Ignatius Press, 1993), 39ff. The German original is *Schleifung der Bastionen: von der Kirche in dieser Zeit* (Einsiedeln: Johannes, 1952).
[520]*Letters and Diaries of John Henry Newman*, vol. XIX (London: Nelson, 1969), 141. Cf. Michael Sharkey, "Newman on the Laity," *Gregorianum* 68, 1-2 (1987), 339-346.

lay involvement in different ecclesial functions, we will surely miss the real point of a conciliar theology of the laity. The real novelty of the Council concerns the *meaning* of the lay presence within the ecclesial communion. The deeper question then and today remains that of the ecclesiological significance and theological identity of a lay witness. "Lay witness" is an elastic concept that includes a broad spectrum of activities, e.g., daily work at home and in the workplace, work in the public sphere for social justice, prayer (including liturgical prayer), and those more official roles today known as "lay ecclesial ministries." This essay will explore the question: "What is the real ecclesial meaning in each of these instances of the lay witness?"

A. Theology and pastoral practice

The question of collaboration between laity and their pastors has taken on a new urgency in light of recent developments, and these new contexts for ministry demand new ways of thinking. One common issue concerns the relationship between theological reflection and pastoral practice. A strict separation between theology and ministry is difficult to imagine if one teaches in a setting that involves the training of candidates for ministry. In such contexts practical wisdom is cherished above all else. Likewise, on those occasions when I have lectured to lay audiences on the theology of the laity, a question such as the following arises: "My pastor will not let me do such and such in the parish school." In these cases I always refer to questioner back to his or her pastor even though I know this answer never satisfies the questioner. In most the cases in which people in the Church think about the role of the laity the matter can or should be settled by a practical solution rather than an abstract theological principle. As in all collaborative ventures there is no "theology" of the laity that can substitute for mutual respect, a willingness to listen, and a faithful witness to Christ.[521] Married persons know the difference between a theology of marriage and the daily living out of one's vocation. A

---

[521]Cf. *Apostolicam actuositatem* 29: "If good human relations are to be cultivated, then it is nece8ssary for genuine human values to stand at a premium, especially the art of living and working on friendly terms with others and entering into dialogue with them." All documents from the Council are cited according to: *Vatican Council II: The Conciliar and Post Conciliar Documents,* ed. Austin Flannery, O.P. (Northport, N.Y.: Costello Publishing Company, 1988), p. 794.

similar caveat applies to the theology of the laity. In all matters, human decency, respect, and genuine Christian charity must prevail on both sides. Christ prayed for unity in the Church, and ultimately his intercession on the behalf of conflicted parties is the only solution that applies to all cases all of the time.[522] The practical priority of concrete guidance by no means vitiates the need for theological reflection. On the contrary, all members of the body of Christ need first principles to face the challenges of the everyday. Christian practice pursued thoughtlessly and without meditative prayer threatens to become self-serving, not to mention tedious.

B. Lay Ecclesial Ministry

The issue of "lay ecclesial ministry" is also very topical. The preliminary conclusions published by the United States Catholic Conference's Subcommittee on Lay Ministry represent the fruit of wide consultation and much labor. They served as important steps towards a "foundational" document promulgated by the U.S. bishops' conference in November 2005 entitled *Co-Workers in the Vineyard of the Lord: A Resource for Guiding the Development of Lay Ecclesial Ministry.*[523] The prior 1999 report, *Lay Ecclesial Ministry: The State of the Question,* had made several definitive strides forward in the elaboration of a theology of lay ministry. It advocated using the term "ecclesial lay ministers" as a generic way of identifying lay persons who are adequately trained for lay ministry and who have been authorized by a "competent ecclesiastical authority" to play "a formal and public role" in the Church's

---

[522]Jn 17: 22.
[523]This document is available online at http://www.usccb.org/laity/laymin/index.shtml. Prior documents on the subject include, Lay Ecclesial Ministry: *The State of the Questions (Washington, D.C.: United States Catholic Conference,* 1999), also available online at http://www.usccb.org/laity/laymin/layecclesial.htm. As background on the USCC's efforts to develop a theology of the laity, one should also consult *Called and Gifted: The American Catholic Laity* (Washington, D.C.: United States Catholic Conference, 1980); *Called and Gifted for the Third Millennium: Reflection of the U.S. Catholic Bishops on the Thirtieth Anniversary of the Decree on the Apostolate of the Laity and the Fifteenth Anniversary of Called and Gifted* (Washington, D.C.: United States Catholic Conference, 1995); and *Together in God's Service: Toward a Theology of Ecclesial Lay Ministry* (Washington, D.C.: United States Catholic Conference, 1998). The USCC also sponsored two research studies by Msgr. Philip Murnion, a pioneer in the advocacy of lay leadership: Philip J. Murnion, New Parish Ministers: *Laity and Religious on Parish Staffs* (New York: National Pastoral Life Center, 1992) and Philip J. Murnion and David DeLambo, *Parishes and Parish Ministers* (New York: National Pastoral Life Center, 1999).

ministry. It defined "ecclesial lay ministers" as "professionally prepared men and women, including vowed religious, who are in positions of service and leadership in the Church."[524]

The specifically theological reflections of the 1999 report are "offered not as the final word, but as a faithful beginning."[525] These consist of twenty-eight points, many of which will be treated below. Above all, the report emphasizes the rootedness of lay ministries "in sacraments of initiation, which incorporate individuals into the body of Christ and call them to mission."[526] Moreover, the document states that,

> lay ecclesial ministry should not be seen as a retreat by the laity from their role in the secular realm. Rather lay ecclesial ministry is an affirmation that the Spirit can call the lay faithful to participation in the building of the Church in various ways.[527]

Even though the issue comes to the fore when parts of the Church are experiencing a decline in priestly vocations, lay ecclesial ministry is not to be seen as an emergency response. Each share in the one ministry of Christ — lay and ordained — "is needed in its full dignity and strength if the Church is to be fully alive in its communion and mission."[528] Both the sacramental character of priestly ordination and the secular character of the lay vocation are reinforced through the genuine collaboration of priests and laity.[529]

Lay Ecclesial Ministry moves the question of the laity forward in decisive ways by highlighting a specific form of lay witness in the Church.[530] On the other hand, the collaboration of the lay faithful is not limited to these roles. As the report acknowledges, the theology of the laity cannot focus mainly on the work of paid and volunteer participants in the official life of the parish. The laity are universally called to serve the Church whether or not they ever fulfill such formal roles, a point that does not go unnoticed in the Subcommittee's report.[531]

---

[524]*Lay Ecclesial Ministry*, 8.
[525]Ibid., 9.
[523]Ibid., 9, conclusion 3.
[527]Ibid., 10, conclusion 7.
[528]Ibid., 11, conclusion 13, with reference to *Lumen Gentium 10, Christifideles Laici* 20, and *Ecclesia in America* 39.
[529]*Lay Ecclesial Ministry*, 11, conclusion 16.
[530]Cf. ibid., 14.
[531]Ibid., 8, in which it is mentioned that some bishops responded to the report's definition of ecclesial lay ministry by asking for a clarification of the distinction between ecclesial ministry and universal service.

By addressing "the modality of being" of the layperson in the Church, this essay is a propaedeutic and complement to a theology of ecclesial lay ministry.[532] In other words, apart from all the specific services and resources that lay people offer the institution, one still needs to consider the gift that a layperson represents simply as a faithful Christian.[533] *Lay Ecclesial Ministry* offers some indications of how the ontological approach can be undertaken based upon the baptismal calling of the laity and their share of the gifts of the Spirit, but even more reflection on the theological identity of the lay witness is needed.

C. Lay Boards

The lay review boards that have received a great deal of attention recently represent an altogether different form of lay witness. They are playing an important role in resolving the present crisis regarding the sexual abuse of minors, but they have a strictly advisory status and no canonical legitimation. On the diocesan level bishops can choose to handle their input as they wish. On the national level the review board is at best a kind of "bully pulpit" that can cajole the bishops to conform to its standards of conduct but cannot mandate sanctions in a formally recognized fashion.[534] Contrary to what one sometimes reads in the secular press, it is not clear that the lay boards represent a radical shift in the way that the Catholic Church is being governed or in the way that its power is delegated. Some groups in fact have criticized them precisely on these grounds. In spite of their critics, the work of the lay boards represents a meaningful way in which the secular character of the lay vocation can help to build up the Church. The presence of legal, psychological and other professional experts on these boards is indispensable. When these individuals properly exercise their authentic lay vocation to discipleship, the Church can truly be reformed from within.

---

[532]In the background of this remark is a concern to distinguish between constitutive and voluntarist ideas of ecclesial communion. In other words, the lay faithful always *are* in ecclesial communion. Their ecclesial communion is not somehow "activated" by training or signing up for a specific form of ministry. Cf. David Schindler, "Toward a Culture of Life: The Eucharist, the 'Restoration' of Creation, and the 'Worldly' Task of the Laity in Liberal Societies," *Communio: International Catholic Review* 29, no. 4 (2002): 679-90, here at 684-85.

[533]Cf. ibid., 14.

[534]I would like to thank my colleague Fr. John Beal for pointing this out to me.

The crisis regarding the sexual abuse of minors and the revelations of episcopal misconduct represent a new phase in the legitimation of a lay perspective in the Catholic Church within the USA. Lay voices are being taken more seriously not just by the press but also by Church officials themselves, and this positive sign of progress should not be dismissed as *Schadenfreude* or a subtle power ploy on the part of the Church's detractors. On the other hand, I tend to agree with Peter Steinfels, who in his most recent book, *A People Adrift: The Crisis of the Roman Catholic Church in America*, states that that the American Catholic Church would still be grappling with impending decline or a serious overhaul even if the sexual abuse crisis had never found its way into newspaper headlines.[535] Even without the sex abuse crisis, we in the American Catholic Church would still be facing a pivotal moment in our own history, one in which the future contribution of the laity to the Church is both undeniable and in desperate need of theological reflection. Lay people are more visible in the American Church than ever before. The real problem today is that far too many Catholics in the United States are still "adrift" as to the spiritual foundations of a lay apostolate.

Each of these three contemporary issues — the renewal of pastoral theology, lay ecclesial ministry, and the review boards — brings out a different aspect of the collaboration between the lay faithful and the ministry of their pastors. None of these starting points, however, uncovers the theological meaning of the collaboration. This essay will therefore proceed in three steps to develop a theology and spirituality of lay collaboration. First, I will show that there has been from Yves Congar to Pope John Paul II an ever-deepening awareness not only that lay persons are in ecclesial communion but also that this communion contributes essentially to the nature and mission of the Church. Second, I will argue that the lay communion has a particular shape and character, one that can be identified with the Church's Marian profile. Third, I will show that the question of collaboration in both

---

[535]Peter Steinfels, *A People Adrift: The Crisis of the Roman Catholic Church in America* (New York: Simon & Schuster, 2003). Steinfels' analysis of the current crisis in American Catholicism and the specific solutions that he proposes go outside the scope of this essay. The point here is that a veteran Catholic journalist who has thoroughly investigated the sex abuse crisis over a long period of time could come to the conclusion that the question of the laity needs to be treated in the context of broader, ecclesial concerns.

its theological and pastoral dimensions can be fruitfully addressed in terms of a Marian spirituality of communion.

II. The Laity in Ecclesial Communion: From Yves Congar to *Christifideles Laici*

The twin themes of a universal call to holiness and a Church as communion have dominated the theological discussion of the last two decades and can readily be characterized as the new marks of the Church in the current postconciliar epoch. Both themes highlight that the vocation of the laity is not somehow of a rank inferior to the vocation of ordained priests. A decisive step was already taken in Pope Paul VI's 1972 motu proprio *Ministeria quaedam,* which freed the ministries of lector and acolyte from the designation "minor orders" so that they could now be exercised by lay people in virtue of their share in the priesthood of Christ through baptism.[536] Of greater importance than the new roles was the accentuation of a universal baptismal priesthood. Without erasing distinctions between priests and laity, the new orientation proposes the lay vocation as a central path to holiness within the Church. The holiness of the Church depends as much on the exercise of discipleship by the lay faithful as it does on the clergy. With this decisive volte-face, the Church can no longer be conceived along the lines of either a ghetto or a bureaucracy. It is no wonder that von Balthasar associated the arrival of the hour of the laity with "a razing of the bastions."

Many, many scholarly books and one letter of the Congregation for the Doctrine of the Faith have been dedicated to explicating the meaning and significance of the conciliar theme of communion.[537] "*Communio* ecclesiology" is frankly a weasel word, and its present proliferation under a diversity of guises is a sign either that the concept

---

[536]This was just a first step in a gradual expanding of the role of the ministry of the laity that took place under Paul VI. See David Power, *Gifts That Differ: Lay Ministries Established and Unestablished* (New York: Pueblo Publishing Company, 1980), 5ff.

[537]The bibliography here is immense. A representative selection of Roman Catholic contributions available in English might include: Dennis M. Doyle, *Communio Ecclesiology: Vision and Versions* (Maryknoll, N.Y.: Orbis, 2000); Avery Cardinal Dulles, "The Church as Communion," in New Perspectives in Historical Theology, ed. Bardley Nassif (Grand Rapids, MI: Eerdmans, 1996), 125-39; Walter Cardinal Kasper, "The Church as Communion: Reflections on the Guiding Ecclesiological Idea of the Second Vatican Council," in *Theology and Church* (New York: Crossroad, 1989), 148-165; Joseph A. Komonchak, "Conceptions of

has become unmoored from its roots in the teachings of the Council or that the conciliar articulation of the principle was not without ambiguity.[538] In order then to establish a notion of communion grounded in the reality and teachings of the Council, I will begin with a preliminary definition of what it means to conceive of the laity in ecclesial communion and then sketch out a brief history of how this notion developed from the period immediately preceding the Council to the present.

The notion of communion can be understood in either a vertical or horizontal sense.[539] Vertically, the people of God are in communion with the divine communion of Father, Son, and Holy Spirit. There is no trace of egoism in God. The bond of love that joins the three persons of the Trinity flows outward for the sake of the world's salvation. The Christian life in its everyday expression consists of a vocation to participate in this divine communion. We are not talking about a special path reserved for the Olympic athletes of Catholic spirituality. We are talking about a universal invitation to experience God as communion and share in these divine rhythms. By the same token, the very notion of communion implies a new form of relationality on the horizontal level. If the Church as communion is portrayed as personal and Spirit-filled rather than juridical or institutional, a false dichotomy is introduced. Communion is rooted in the concrete history of the pilgrim people rather than an abstract, merely otherworldly destiny. Communion embraces the social web that comprises the fabric of daily life. In this web and from this vital center communities of faith seek intimacy, acceptance, forgiveness, and justice. Most

---

Communion, Past and Present," *Cristianesimo nella storia* 16 (1995): 321-40; John J. Markey, O.P., *Creating Communion: The Theology of the Constitutions of the Church* (Hyde Park, N.Y.: New City Press, 2003); David Schindler, *Heart of the World, Center of the Church: Communio Ecclesiology, Liberalism, and Liberation* (Grand Rapids, MI: Eerdmans, 1996); J.M.R. Tillard, *Church of Churches: An Ecclesiology of Communion*, trans. R.C. Peaux (Collegeville, MN: Liturgical Press, 1992); and Joseph Cardinal Ratzinger, *Called to Communion: Understanding the Church Today*, trans. Adrian Walker (San Francisco: Ignatius Press, 1996). The letter of the Congregation is entitled "Some Aspects of the Church Understood as Communion," *Acta Apostolica Sedis* 85 (September 1993), 838-50; Origins 22/7 (June 25, 1992): 108-12. Also important is the final report of the 1985 Extraordinary Synod of Bishops, which is entitled "The Church, in the Word of God, celebrates the Mysteries of Christ for the Salvation of the World." This document highlighted the paramount importance of a theology of communion to the reading of the conciliar documents.

[538]Dennis Doyle, for example, identifies six "contemporary Catholic versions of communion ecclesiology." Dennis Doyle, *Communion Ecclesiology*, 19ff.

[539]Cf. Joseph Cardinal Ratzinger. *"Communio: A Program," Communio: International Catholic Review* 19, no. 3 (1992): 436-49.

important of all, the reality of communion counters the tendency in our culture to treat faith as the private possession of an individual, a trend that augments the alienation experienced by many of the faithful even when they are regularly participating in the sacramental life of the Church. These two aspects of communion, the vertical and the horizontal, are not separable. One could not say, for example, that the first is operative when we partake of the sacraments, and the second when we meet with parishioners for coffee afterwards or work together in a soup kitchen. The laity are called to partake of both forms of communion simultaneously and with equal fervor. The vocation of the laity, no less than that of the ordained, lies at the intersection of the vertical and horizontal dimensions of communion. In that sense, the vocation of those called to live out their baptismal priesthood is cruciform, i.e., its very shape and form exist in conformity with the human agony of Christ that is undergone for the sake of the salvation of the entire world.[540]

A. Yves Congar

A conciliar theology of the laity was not built in a day; however, to delve into the history of preconciliar developments would take us far afield from our subject.[541] It is still appropriate to single out the achievement of the French Dominican Yves Congar and in particular his ground-breaking work, *Jalons pour une théologie du laicat* (1953; English translation, *Lay People in the Church*, 1957 and revised ed. in 1965). He begins this monumental work with the rather straightforward question, "What is a layperson?"[542] To pose such a question may seem jejune given the self-evidence of lay people in the Church today. To answer such a question, one might say today, one need only to itemize the manifold tasks accomplished by lay persons in the Church today — the lay person is the lector, the school teacher, the parish administrator, the nurse, doctor, lawyer, etc. But this functional approach is shortsighted.

---

[540]Cf. *Christfideles laici* 9, 12, and 54.

[241]See, for example, Eugenio Zanetti, *La nozione di "laico" nel dibattito preconciliare. Alle radici di una svolta significativa e problematica* (Rome: Editrice Pontificia Università Gregoriana, 1998) and Joseph Komonchak, "Conceptions of Communion, Past and Present."

[542]Yves Congar, *Lay People in the Church* (London: Bloomsbury, 1957), 1-21. In what follows I cite from the translation from the first edition in order to lay out the connections to the Council.

Although building upon the historical research of a number of contemporaries, there is little doubt that Congar's basic conception broke new ground. The word supply in the New Testament, he notes, does not refer to the laity. It is a word used to designate the Jews as a people of God. Thus, a distinction between clergy and laity such as we conceive of it today is absent from the New Testament. From this philological point, Congar is not going to chart the origins of a fully de-clericalized people's Church, as nineteenth century Protestant historians began to do. He is quicker to note the emergence of three, not two, classifications of Christians by the third century, viz., clergy, laity, and monks. In this view only a lay condition can be defined, not an office or role in the Church. Here too, however, the definitions are primarily negative. Clerics and monks are given over to holy things; the laity lives among earthly things. Isolated instances of lay holiness and apostolic initiatives by the laity are both duly recognized, but there is also a sense that to choose the lay state is a concession to human weakness. Too often in the Middle Ages, Congar writes, the theologians forced a separation between, on the one hand, the Pope, bishops, monks, and clergy, and, on the other, the emperor, princes, knights, peasants, lay men, and lay women. They could, at least for a time, still invoke the spiritual and the temporal being united into a single body, for they were, after all, operating under the assumption of a single *Respublica christiana*. Nonetheless, the damage had already been done. What was for the scholastics only a conceptual distinction would eventually become embodied as an ecclesiological rift. By the time of Martin Luther in the sixteenth century, it was too easy to feel compelled to choose between either a priesthood without a people or vice versa.[543] Congar also notes an important shift that takes place beginning in the thirteenth century away from associating the clergy too narrowly with monastic orders.[544] In the monastic hermeneutic, Congar opines, lay people exist as a concession to the worldliness of

---

[543]Luther attacks the medieval notion of dividing spiritual and temporal estates in the Church in "To the Christian Nobility of the German Nation Concerning the Reform of the Christian Estate (1520)," in Martin Luther, *The Christian in Society*, I, ed. James Atkinson, vol. 44 of *Luther's Works*, ed. Helmut T. Lehmann (Philadelphia: Fortress Press, 1966), 115-217, here at 126-33.

[544]Yves Congar, *Lay People in the Church*, 14.

the world.[545] In the new clerical view the laity were primarily recipients of instruction given through the prophetical office of the mendicants and other clergy.[546] We are still left with a primarily negative determination of the lay state.

Drawing upon the full witness of the New Testament and the earliest Christian community, Congar then develops two positive "approximations" of the identity of the layperson. It is important to see the tentativeness of the formulation. Congar himself would later criticize this attempt rather severely. I nonetheless think that the early view of Congar merits careful study. If nothing else, the *joining* of the two approximations contains real insight into the theological issues at stake.

According to the first approximation:

> Lay people are called to the same end as clergy or monks — to the enjoyment of our inheritance as sons of God; but they have to pursue and attain this end without cutting down their involvement in the activities of this world, in the realities of the primal creation, in the disappointments, the achievements, the stuff of history. The laity is called to do God's work in the world; not merely in the sense that its members should move heaven and earth to introduce into lay life what monks and nuns do in the cloister. . . they *in addition* do the work of the world, which religious don't have to do. . . [T]he total mission of the Church, corresponding to God's design, requires that the Lord's reign be prepared in and through that creation in the perfecting of which man must co-operate. Therefore do God's design and the Church's mission call for the existence of

---

[545]Congar's account of the origins of Christian monasticism is one-sided, and the implication that monks were uniformly disdainful of the world is misleading. The current historiographical trend looks at the monks not so much as a caste set wholly apart but as unique representatives of a total ascetical culture that promoted holiness of diverse sorts. This trend, while deeply ambivalent vis-à-vis the spiritual core of monastic life, offers an important corrective to Congar's approach. Cf. Columba Stewart, OSB, "Asceticism and Spirituality: New Vision, Impasse or Hiatus?" *Christian Spirituality Bulletin* 4 (1996): 11-15 and Armand Veilleux, "Les origines du monachisme chrétien," *Louvain* 97 (April 1999), available on-line at http://users.skynet.be/bs775533/Armand/wri/origines.html. There was a greater flow of ideas between monks (both coenobitic and eremitical) and the world than Congar acknowledges, and the elitism professed by the monks was co-determined by worldly ideas, financial exigencies, and pastoral needs. See, for example, Philip Rousseau, *Ascetics, Authority, and the Church in the Age of Jerome and Cassian* (Oxford: Oxford University Press, 1978), 199-220. Recent scholarship has even found a surprisingly dialectical attitude towards the family in monastic ascetical writings. See Andrew S. Jacobs and Rebecca Krawiec, "Fathers Know Best? Christian Families in the Age of Asceticism,"*Journal of Early Christian Studies* 11,3 (2003): 257-63 as well as the fine articles by each of these authors in the same volume.
[546]In this chapter Congar omits the important history of the third orders that arose shortly after the mendicant revolution of the thirteenth century. These along with the confraternities that developed in the high and late Middle Ages become essential to the development of a spirituality of the laity. See, for example, *Lay Sanctity, Medieval and Modern: A Search for Models*, ed. Ann W. Astell (Notre Dame, IN: Notre Dame, 2000).

lay faithful; they need a laity which, in its wholeness, is called to glorify God without lessening its engagement in the work of the world.[547]

In other words, the lay state signifies neither a concession to mortal weakness nor a guarantee of an attentive audience. The laity have no less an obligation than the ordained to hand themselves over to heavenly things. Unlike the clergy, they do not have the privilege to exclude themselves from worldly ones. The work done by the laity in and for the sake of the world belongs to both "God's design" and the mission of the Church.[548] In sharp contrast to the preoccupation of medieval royalty with disputes over Church property, episcopal governance of civil territories, and their own investing of Church officials, Congar portrays the autonomous apostolate of the laity as the Church's investment in the world. The laity are commissioned by the Church to struggle in and for the world. Without this lay commitment (which, by the way, requires no official endorsement on the part of the hierarchy), the mission of the entire Church to prepare for the kingdom of God remains incomplete.

The second approximation is quite interesting, for it deals with the kind of knowledge proper to the two states. Most Catholic universities today retain requirements in the areas of philosophy and theology, and one might expect Congar to delineate complementary curricula of some sort. In fact, he takes a different tack altogether. He builds upon a distinction to be found in the works of St. Thomas Aquinas between a philosopher and a faithful Christian (*fidelis*).[549] Basically, the lay person is supposed to be able to look at the world with the same detachment and curiosity that St. Thomas found in Aristotle. The world for the lay person is an object of wonder that can be examined in terms of both its mechanical functioning and metaphysical purpose. One might

---

[547]Yves Congar, *Lay People in the Church*, 16.

[548]Congar recognizes, of course, that the worldliness of the lay vocation is "in the world and not of the world." See *Lay People in the Church*, 379-428 and the discussion of the secular character of the laity below.

[549]Cf. Aquinas' *Prologus to II Sent. and Summa contra Gentiles*, ii, 4, as cited in Lay People in the Church, 17n26. Thomas Aquinas, Congar would be the first to point out, had rare capacities in both areas, for he stands "at the junction of the ancient world, sacral and monastic (but also feudal), with the modern world, scientific and positive." Regarding the exemplarity of Thomas' wisdom for the modern Church, Congar opines: "He is a model and a peerless guide for a world given over to technique and particular explanations without any unifying references, and suffering accordingly. He may be said to have been authentically lay, even though a cleric." *Lay People in the Church*, 21.

think, for example, of the way that even today a true natural scientist must investigate nature for its own sake and, in doing so, set aside all personal prejudices and concerns related to the exercise of daily life. The Aristotelian philosopher and the modern scientist pursue truth analogous in their theoretical expression to what Congar terms "the true inwardness of things."[550] The cleric (or monk), on the other hand, turns his gaze directly to the transcendent end of earthly things, i.e., their First Cause in the language of the scholastics. He submits all things to God not as a speculative maneuver but in order to distil their meaning for everyday Christian life. By analogy, consider the example of a pediatrician. She has, one hopes, a great storehouse of scientific learning, but in the end her role is eminently practical, i.e., to diagnose the particular illness of a particular child. A successful homily, to offer a different example, requires the learning of a *fidelis,* which is not untutored piety but wisdom translated into practical advice. The difference between the two perspectives is not between an earthly and a heavenly orientation. Both states presuppose a dual commitment to God and the world. The difference is one of emphasis. The layperson seeks detached knowledge; the pastor shares practical wisdom.

Congar's point, of course, is to integrate the two perspectives. He is worried, for example, about an overly theoretical clerical mindset that ignores an engagement with the real world and prefers instead to proliferate vague generalities or advance self-interest. By the same token, Congar is concerned about an overt "laicism" (what we today might call secularization) in the lay perspective. The lay mindset needs to engage the world on its own terms not only for the advancement of science but also for the establishment of a just society. "To be secular is to use all the resources within us in that pursuit of justice and truth for which we hunger, the very stuff of human history."[551] Yet this noble cause can be pursued without reference to the First Cause, and this omission represents an equally grave danger.[552] In sum, the wisdom of the lay person complements that of the cleric. Alone neither has a monopoly on the

---

[550]*Lay People in the Church,* 19.
[551]Ibid., 20. Congar defended Catholic Action, a lay movement with whom he had had contact as a young priest in the 1930's.
[552]Ramiro Pellitero thinks that Congar in his second approximation concedes too much to modern secularism: ". . . it is understandable that Congar might want to concede everything possible to modern laicism, but perhaps he goes too far, or his expression of the idea is

truth. True Christian wisdom consists of the perfect synthesis of these two viewpoints. We miss the mark altogether if we, for example, in the name of a more public theology listen only to "the priesthoods of a second causes"[553] or, alternatively, in the name of a more spiritual theology consider the ways of the world as "simply occasions or starting-points for an affirmation of the sovereignty of the Principle, or as mere means towards the carry-out of some religious programme."[554]

In spite of its real penetration of the theological problem, Congar believed that the chapter on the identity of a lay person in *Lay People in the Church* was tied to a certain dualism. Inasmuch as he focused on the integration of a notion of community into a hierarchical ecclesial structure, Congar himself came to the recognition of an "inappropriate element" in his early procedure.[555] Congar detects an unnecessary (but not altogether unwelcome) residue of the Scholastic capacity to make overly fine distinctions. Congar maintains that the early work defines "the ministerial priesthood purely in itself" and because of its focus on the instrumental causality of the hierarchical priesthood reduces "the building of the community to the action of the hierarchical ministry."[556] With regard to the definition of the laity, Congar drops the idea of investigating "things in themselves" from his later writings.[557] He also moved away from the underscoring the distinction between priesthood

ambiguous. He gives the impression that he leaves in the layperson in the 'territory' of laicism, without emphasizing sufficiently his condition as a Christian." Ramiro Pellitero, "Congar's Developing Understanding of the Laity and their Mission," *The Thomist* 65, 3 (July 2001): 340. I myself see less cause for concern than Pellitero on this point but agree with him that Congar's thought on the laity developed significantly and not always in a linear fashion.

[553] *Lay People in the Church*, 17.
[554] Ibid., 18.
[555] Yves Congar, O.P., "My Path-Findings in the Theology of Laity and Ministries," *The Jurist* 32 (1972): 169-88, here at 174. The interpretation of Congar's self-critique is a matter of some debate. Pellitero, for example, concludes: "Congar tried to define the mission of the laity in relation to the priest, and saw the lay mission as developing within earthly realities. But the lay faithful remained too 'lay' and not 'faithful' enough." Ramiro Pellitero, "Congar's Developing Understanding of the Laity and their Mission," 358. Paul Lakeland, on the other hand, says: "At this time in his development, Congar did not see the sacredness of the autonomy of the secular." Idem, *The Liberation of the Laity: In Search of an Accountable Church* (New York: Continuum, 2003), 156. Thus, Pellitero claims that in *Lay People in the Church* Congar may have inadvertently paved the way to a secularization of the lay apostolate by underscoring lay worldliness, and Lakeland maintains that Congar ignored in that early work the inherently spiritual dimension of life in a secular world come of age. Neither author, in my estimation, grasps the legitimate core of Congar's early dualism. The early Congar rightly insisted that the integration of love of God and involvement in worldly affairs is arrived at differently depending on one's state of life in the Church but that the ecclesial integration requires the joining of these two profoundly different perspectives.
[556] Yves Congar, O.P., "My Path-Findings in the Theology of Laity and Ministries," 175.
[557] Ramiro Pellitero, "Congar's Developing Understanding of the Laity and their Mission," 345.

and laity and turned to the relationship and distinction between ministries and modes of community service, indicating, inter alia, a renewed
respect for the engagement of the laity in the work of social justice.[558]
Without advocating "a democratism of the sort which is not in fact
professed by Protestants," he sometimes also substituted the notion of
a "Christian ontology" for the baptismal priesthood, following a path
that had been laid out by Karl Rahner and others.[559] These developments represent a real change in Congar's thinking about the theology
of the laity. One constant that remains throughout his career was the
conviction that the lay people, precisely as members of the People of
God, are called to seek out "the holiness of earthly existence itself" and
thereby consecrate the secular world to God.[560]

B. The Laity in Communion according to the Second Vatican Council

Congar's *Lay People in the Church* was among the sources that
influenced the Fathers of the Second Vatican Council with respect to
the theology of the laity.[561] Without getting into the details and leaving aside other important influences such as Johann Adam Möhler (a
theologian from the nineteenth century favored by Congar) or Jerome
Hamer, O.P. (a student of Congar), one can easily see — as Congar
himself would later remark — a line of development that links Congar's breakthrough to the documents of the Council.[562] The Fathers of
the Council were able to effect a shift of perspective. The laity can no
longer be viewed as second-class citizens in the Church; the distinction between clergy and laity is cast in a new light. The vocation of
lay people has its own non-derivative spirituality. The laity participate
in the mission of the Church through their own distinct "apostolate."

---

[558]Yves Congar, O.P., "My Path-Findings in the Theology of Laity and Ministries," 176.
Cf. Ramiro Pellitero, "Congar's Developing Understanding of the Laity and their Mission,"
348.

[559]Yves Congar, O.P., "My Path-Findings," 177. Cf. Ramiro Pellitero, "Congar's Developing Understanding of the Laity and their Mission," 348.

[560]Ibid., 345-46.

[561]On Congar's theology of the laity and the Council, see Eugenio Zanetti, *La nozione
di "laico,"* 77-128 and Ramiro Pellitero, *La Teología del Laicado en la Obra de Yves Congar*
(Pamplona: Navarra Gráfica Ediciones, 1996), 323-350. Less satisfying, I found, was the
treatment of this issue in Paul Lakeland, *The Liberation of the Laity,* 49ff., which also sees a
close connection between Congar's proposals and the Council's treatment of the laity.

[562]Yves Congar, O.P., "My Path-Findings," 172 et passim. On Hamer, see John Markey,
Creating Communion, 48-50.

Their contribution as individuals, in small groups, and as a whole is a fully organic and by no means passive part of the Mystical Body of Christ.[563] The model of purely passive recipients of prophetical instruction is replaced by the image of active participants. The lay apostolate complements that of the ordained and is just as essential to the mission of the Church as that of the clergy.

There are separate conciliar documents that treat the subject of the laity, most notably, The Dogmatic Constitution on the Church, *Lumen gentium* (Nov. 21, 1964); The Decree on the Apostolate of the Laity, *Apostolicam actuositatem* (Nov. 18, 1965); and The Constitution on the Church in the Modern World, *Gaudium et spes* (Dec. 7, 1965). Rather than attempt a comprehensive analysis of each, my focus is on common themes.[564]

The very image of the Church changed in the course of the Council.[565] The question about whether this is a whole new image or an ecclesiological renewal with new conceptual categories is probably not decisive.[566] Innovativeness of some sort is certainly present in Lumen gentium, which begins with (and affirms in its very title) the Church as a mystery illuminated by Christ the light of humanity. Regarding the relationship of the heavenly and earthly elements of this mystery, the constitution on the Church famously remarks:

> The one mediator, Christ, established and ever sustains here on earth this holy Church, the community of faith, hope, and charity, as a visible organization through which he communicates truth and grace to all men. But, the society structured with hierarchical organs and the mystical body of Christ, the visible society and the spiritual community, the earthly Church and the Church endowed with riches, are not to be thought of as two realities. On the contrary, they form *one complex reality*, which comes together from a human and divine element. For this reason the Church is compared, not without significance, to the mystery of the incarnate Word.[567]

The comparison between the human and divine elements in the Church and in the person of God the Word is not without ambiguity

[563] *Apostolicam actuositatem* 2.
[564] Angel Antón provides a useful overview in "Principios fundamentales para una teología del Laicado en la ecclesiología del Vaticano II," *Gregorianum* 68,1-2 (1987): 103-55. Antón correctly notes that it is necessary to review basic ecclesiological principles before addressing the theology of the laity. The topic is also treated in Paul Lakeland, *Liberation of the Laity*, 78-110 and David Power, Gifts that Differ, 52-63.
[565] David Power, *Gifts that Differ*, 52.
[566] Angel Antón, "Teología del Laicado," 111.
[567] *Lumen gentium* 8. Italics added.

and has provoked intense debate. Highlighting the terms "one complex reality" allows us to consider some basic points regarding both
the unity and the complexity of the Church. According to *Lumen gentium*, the union between the Church as a sociological datum with all
too clay feet and the spiritual reality of a spotless Bride is as intimate
as that between the human and divine natures of Christ. The distinction between the two is hardly obliterated and is underscored at key
points later in the document. Nonetheless, the union is real and not
notional. We are not permitted to bracket either aspect of the Church
in considering the identity and mission of the laity. The laity inherit a
share in a human institution and the Mystical Body all at once.

The single, complex reality of the Church cannot be reduced to its
social function and sociological appearance. Nor can the ecclesial reality be elevated to a domain above that of the daily business of the lay
faithful. Likewise, the Church like Christ remains "holy, innocent,
and undefiled" but at the same time is "clasping sinners to her bosom"
and "always in need of purification."[568] Just as the sinless One paved a
path that offered penance and sought the renewal of hearts and corporate bodies, so too does the Church enter into the sorrows of the world
and even the agony of its own confession of fault. Although tension
may arise in imitating the One without sin and welcoming the sin-
ner, the Church must always exemplify "humility and self-denial."[569]
In this sense, the Pope's calls for forgiveness and the U.S. bishops'
struggle to admit fault in the sexual abuse crisis do not represent a
fundamentally new theological orientiation.[570]

The second chapter of *Lumen gentium* identifies the Church as the
"people of God." The human element is contained in the noun, and the
non-reductive spiritual element derives from the prepositional phrase.
The Church, however, is — once again — both simultaneously. God
establishes and elects his people through a covenant, which already
clarifies the vertical, grace-filled dimension of God's prior action.[571]
"It is Christ indeed who had purchased it with his own blood."[572] The
horizontal innovation derives from the fact that "the chosen race"
and "holy nation" are also on an earthly pilgrimage. There is a crucial

---

[568]Ibid. The first phrase is taken from Heb 7:26.
[569]*Lumen gentium* 8.
[570]On the former, see Luigi Accatoli, *When the Pope Asks for Forgiveness: The Mea Culpa's of
John Paul II*, trans. Jordan Aumann (Boston: Pauline Books & Media, 1998).
[571]*Lumen gentium* 9.

symbolic dimension to the duality (and union) between being simultaneously "from above" and "from below." As God sends his chosen
People "into human history" (and also endures its "trials and tribula-
tions"), the Church serves through Christ and his Spirit as "the visible
sacrament of this saving unity."[573] In other words, as the Church incorporates God's saving message into its own visible forms of existence
and communication, the Church itself gives expression to the hope for
ecclesial and human solidarity that Christ himself preached.[574]

Conceiving the notion of the Church as communion entails a far
more radical idea of unity than we normally envision.[575] The unity of the
Church extends both outward across the globe (hence, its catholicity)
and inward into the hearts of all believers (hence, its organic character).
Normally, I think that we conceive of unity in a fairly literal fashion.
Everyone is gathered together in a single place (room, home, parish,
city, diocese, etc.). The whole in this view is assembled from distinct
parts, and the unity lies in the placing of the parts together into a single
conglomerate. The actualization of this unity may extend as far as dialogue, exchange, or cooperative projects, but the concept of unity is still
drawn from the external features of the assemblage. When the model
of unity is an assemblage, it is possible to maintain a properly functioning mechanism and accomplish a successful plan of action. Organic
communion, however, has not necessarily been realized.

The Council, by contrast, posits a conception of internal unity, one
that depends completely on the gift of love given by God's Spirit.
The people of God are never homogenous. Their unity lies in their diver-

> All the faithful scattered throughout the world are in communion
> with each other in the Holy Spirit so that "he who dwells in Rome
> knows those in most distant parts to be his members ... In virtue
> of this catholicity each part contributes its own gifts to other parts
> and to the whole Church, so that the whole and each of the parts
> are strengthened by the common sharing of all things and by the
> common effort to find fullness in unity."[576]

---

[572]Ibid., with reference to Acts 20:28.
[573]Ibid.
[574]Cf. Peter Casarella, *"Solidarity as the Fruit of Communio: Ecclesia in America,* 'Post-
Liberation Theology,' and the Earth," *Communio: International Catholic Review* 27 (Spring
2000), 98-123.
[575]Cf. John J. Markey, *Creating Communion,* 126-147.
[576]*Lumen gentium* 13. Cf. ibid. 30: "For from [Christ] the whole body—being closely

sity. The offices in the Church, including the Petrine office, are bound to uphold "legitimate variety while at the same time taking care that these differences do not hinder unity, but rather contribute to it."[577]

Where do the laity fit into this picture? According to *Lumen gentium* 31, the term "laity" refers to "all the faithful except those in Holy Orders and those who belong to a religious state approved by the Church."[578] The laity are further defined in terms of their incorporation into the body of Christ through baptism, their place among the People of God, and their unique share in the priestly, prophetic, and kingly office of Christ as well as the mission of the whole Christian people in the Church and in the world.

Lumen gentium then goes on to draw a distinction between the laity and "those in Holy Orders" on the basis of a "secular character" that is "proper and peculiar to the laity."[579] Moreover, "by reason of their special vocation it belongs to the laity to seek the kingdom of God by engaging in temporal affairs and directing them according to God's will."[580] The secular character of the laity is likewise stressed in *Apostolicam actuositatem*, which speaks of lay persons as "citizens among citizens"[581] and enjoins them, pace Congar's "second approximation," to "make sound judgments on the true meaning and value of temporal realities both in themselves *and* in relation to man's end."[582]

What then is the secular character of the laity? This is not a simple question to answer, and even Congar had to struggle to achieve clarity on this issue. As far as I can tell, there are two general claims being made in the documents of the Council, namely, that there is a properly secular character to the lay vocation and that this secularity in some fashion differentiates the lay apostolate from that of the ordained. Both of these contentions belong to the enduring legacy of conciliar

---

joined and knit together through every joint of the system according to the functioning in due measure of each single part — derives its increase to the building up of itself in love" (Eph. 4:15-16).

[577]Ibid.

[578]*Lumen gentium*, 31. This is a different definition than that employed by the U.S. bishops' Subcommittee in Lay Ecclesial Ministries. The question of whether non-ordained religious should be considered as lay persons obviously needs to be addressed even though I am not taking it up in this paper.

[579]*Lumen gentium*, 31.

[580]Ibid.

[581]*Apostolicam actuositatem*, 7.

[582]Ibid. 4. Italics added.

theology and are also the subject of varied interpretation.[583] Congar wrote in his 1972 essay, "My Path-Findings in the Theology of Laity and Ministries": ". . . the formula, 'To the cleric the spiritual, to the laic [layperson] the temporal,' could only be a caricature or a betrayal of my position."[584] The same statement, I believe, applies to what the Second Vatican Council says about the secularity of the laity. The Council never denies that the laity can be delegated to assume some official, non-clerical positions in the institutional Church. Such provisions are, in fact explicitly endorsed.[585] Nor does the Council treat either the lay or ordained apostolate in a self-contained, "extrinsicist," or two-tiered manner. The distinction introduced in *Lumen gentium*, 31 is not meant to be a separation. There is nothing in that paragraph or elsewhere in the conciliar documents that allows one to conceive of the differentiation between laity and clergy in terms of a superior or inferior rank. They are, quite simply, different and complementary kinds of vocation.

By the same token, the distinction between the secular profession of the laity and the sacred ministry of the ordained is important and needs to be retained. The first clue to a proper interpretation lies, as with so much of the theological content of *Lumen gentium*, in an image: To be leaven in the world is very different from being a mole or a secret agent. To leaven is "to mingle or permeate with some modify-

> [The laity] are called by God that, being led by the spirit to the Gospel, they may contribute to the sanctification of the world, *as from within like leaven,* by fulfilling their own particular duties. Thus, especially by the witness of their life, resplendent in faith, hope, and charity they must manifest Christ to others.[586]

---

[583]David Power, for example, links these teachings to Pope John Paul's insistence that the clergy in Latin America stay out of civil politics: "John Paul II continues to interpret the lay vocation in light of *Lumen gentium*, 31 and to insist on its essentially secular character. This accompanies an ever-growing stress on the special nature of the priestly calling and on the essential difference between ordained priesthood and the common priesthood of all the faithful." *Gifts that Differ*, 53ff., here at 58. Power, whose book was published prior to the promulgation of *Christifideles laici*, is not denying that the Pope is mainly interested in accentuating and promoting the positive character of lay involvement in the affairs of the world but seems suspicious of too sharp a distinction between Church and world, ordained and baptismal priesthood. Paul Lakeland's proposal regarding secularity is far more radical than Power's. See idem, *The Liberation of the Laity*, 149–85.

[584]"My Pathfindings," 173.

[585]*Lumen gentium*, 33; *Apostolicam actuositatem*, 22.

[586]*Lumen gentium* 31. Italics added. See also *Actuositatem Apostolicam* 2. Yves Congar used this same image prior to is appearance in either of these documents. See his entry "Laie" in *Handbuch theologischer Grundbegriffe, vol. II* (Munich: Kösel-Verlag, 1963), 23.

ing, alleviating, or vivifying element."[587] The leaven, in other words, cannot flee from the dough that it raises once the bread is baked. The fate of the leaven lies with the fate of the entire world. But the tools for leavening, so to speak, are not altogether different from the tools for sacred ministry. At least one can say that the leavening agent like the ordained minister is called to preach the gospel and "manifest Christ to others." The point of the lay involvement of the world is not to simply carry on a worldly existence or to interject a more secular perspective into Catholic affairs but quite precisely to "consecrate the world itself to God."[588] There is a decidedly evangelical thrust to the mission of the laity in the world as conceived by *Lumen gentium*. Were the laity to abandon their apostolate in the world, there would be little hope that the norms for justice, goodness, peace, and equality that were preached by Christ himself could ever be announced, far less implemented, in the public square.

But that is just the first step. The real heart of the theology of the laity in *Lumen gentium* derives from the laity's share in the threefold office of Christ as prophet, priest, and king. This conception, originally deriving from nineteenth century Protestant theology but also present in Congar's *Lay People in the Church,* was first articulated as a conciliar doctrine in paragraphs 10-13 of *Lumen gentium* with respect to the entire people of God.[589] Significantly, the Council Fathers underscore the fact that "everything that has been said of the People of God is addressed equally to laity, religious and clergy."[590]

In what sense are lay people called to realize their priesthood in the Church? The term itself causes some confusion even among well-informed Catholics. Christ alone remains the "supreme and eternal priest" in the Church.[591] Christ's priesthood is marked by sacrifice, a sacrifice of his very person for the sake of the salvation of the world. "All disciples of Christ, persevering in prayer and praising God,[592]

---

[587] *Webster's Ninth New Collegiate Dictionary* (Springhill, MA: Merriam-Webster, 1987), 681.

[588] *Lumen gentium*, 34.

[589] Ibid. 10-13. Cf. Walter Kasper, "Christology and Anthropology," in *Theology and Church,* 84-85. This schema was also incorporated into the new *Code of Canon Law* (1983), Canon 204.

[590] *Lumen gentium*, 30. This point has been reiterated by Pope John Paul II in the Apostolic Constitution *Sacrae disciplinae leges* (Jan. 15, 1983) in *Acta Apostolica Sedis* 75 (1983), p. XI.

[591] *Lumen gentium* 34.

[592] Cf. Acts 2:42-47.

should present themselves as a sacrifice, living, holy, and pleasing to God."[593]The language of sacrifice is not so easy to swallow for people today. I am not speaking about a cultural libertinism whereby individuals only seek comfort and convenience at all costs. The very notion — so central to the witness of the New Testament and the earliest Christian community — that Christ died as our representative and "for the sake of our salvation" is often shunted to the side in Christian discourse. But there is an anthropological truth regarding sacrifice that extends to the sphere of biological activity and is essential to our humanity as such.[594] Self-offering is a form of life that expresses love in a wide variety of forms. It comprises miniscule, barely visible gestures and actual martyrdom. It involves the personal confession of sin as well as the bending over backwards to help one's neighbor, spouse, child, parent, and even the unknown stranger who happens across one's path. But these personal acts also reflect a natural phenomenon described in the Scriptural verse: "Unless a grain of wheat falls into the earth and dies, it remains alone; but if it dies, it bears much fruit."[595] The share of the laity in Christ's priestly office points to a mode of existence whereby the very things of creation can be made holy again.[596]

"The manifestation of the Spirit is given to everyone for profit."[597] This Biblical passage is cited as a confirmation of the universality of the prophetic office among the holy People of God. Here is not the place to engage the question of how such charismatic gifts are to be preserved and tested in the Church. Suffice it to say that the Council affirms that these "extraordinary gifts" are present among all of God's faithful and that "they are to be received with thanksgiving and consolation since they are fitting and useful for the needs of the Church."[598] These specific fields of activities are mentioned as legiti-

---

[593]Ibid. 10. Cf. Rom 12:1.
[594]Walter Kasper, *"Christology and Anthropology,"* 88.
[595]John 12:24. On cosmic self-offering see also my "Waiting for a Cosmic Christ in an Uncreated World," *Communio: International Catholic Review* 28 (Summer 2001), 254-9.
[596]On this point Catholics can learn a lot from the Eastern Orthodox. See, for example, Alexander Schmemann, *For the Life of the World: Sacraments and Orthodoxy* (Crestwood, N.Y.: St. Vladimir's Seminary Press, rev. ed., 1977) and *Cosmic Grace, Humble Prayer: The Ecological Vision of Green Patriarch Bartholomew I,* ed. John Chryssavgis (Grand Rapids: Eerdmans, 2003).
[597]1 Cor 12:7, as cited in *Lumen gentium,* 12.
[598]*Lumen gentium,* 12.

mate domains of a lay prophetical office: married,[599] family, and social life, evangelization by word and deed in the ordinary circumstances of the world, and some "sacred functions to the best of their ability" (but only in cases "when there are no sacred ministers or when these are impeded under persecution").[600]

But none of these individual specifications gets to the heart of the lay prophetic office. One key is found in the claim that the universal share in Christ the prophet is "aroused and sustained by the Spirit of truth."[601] To be sure, *Lumen gentium* ties this arousal to obedience to the Church's magisterium, which is an hardly an undesired outcome. But there is, as Walter Kasper points out, a deeper, human meaning to the prophetic ministry.[602] Sometimes we believe that the Church provides truth in the way that we go about looking for a lost household item or remembering the address of an old friend. In this view, we know that an entirely recognizable thing will eventually present itself to us. The discovered truth remains wholly outside of ourselves. But Christian revelation is different. In fact, Christ is the light of the world precisely in the sense that "among the many will o' the wisps and illusions found in the world, Christ has shown human beings the truth about themselves and about the world in which they live.[603] In the life of the laity, light is a symbol for salvation in a variety of ways. The grace of Christ illuminates daily life by making us grateful for our very existence, by providing a moral law, and by helping us to sift through what in our culture is good and true and what is false or ideological. As in Christ's parables, which "often contain wholly unexpected and improbable features," the prophetic path can often illuminate things in an entirely new light.[604]

What is the lay share in Christ's kingship? Unless you are an heir to an actual crown like, say, Prince William of Great Britain, it may seem more than a little implausible to characterize the laity as sharers

---

[599]The family as a "domestic Church" is a key term developed by the Council and figures prominently in the postconciliar developments such as *Familiaris Consortio*, the 1981 Apostolic Exhortation on the role of the Christian family in the modern world. The consecration of the world and the formation of the Christian that takes place within the domestic Church are a key conciliar themes, but there is unfortunately no space to go into this here.

[600]*Lumen Gentium* 35.

[601]Ibid. 12.

[602]Walter Kasper, "Christology and Anthropology," 85.

[603]Ibid. Cf. *Gaudium et Spes* 22.

[604]Walter Kasper, "Christology and Anthropology," 87.

in a royal office. This obstacle together with the close association of shepherd and king in the symbolisms of the Old and New Testament prompted Walter Kasper to rename this office "Christ's pastoral office."[605] In any case, Christ is a king who rules from the cross.[606] This Biblical truth establishes that the kingship of Christ is "not of this world" and that its task is "to bear witness to the truth."[607] It shows that the revelation of a whole new order of things can be disclosed through the service, poverty, suffering, powerlessness, and sacrificial death of the anointed one on the cross. It also shows that all human activity finds its fulfillment in the paschal mystery of Christ, a theme taken up again in *Gaudium et spes, 38*. This hardly seems consoling if the norm for achievement and productivity follows a worldly standard of self-advancement, increased productivity, technological progress, or material output. On the other hand, the movement towards the realization of a genuine "civilization of love" in our midst is often slow, halting, and filled with setbacks.

A key achievement of the Council is embodied in the message that "all Christians in any state or walk of life are called to the fullness of Christian life and to the perfection of love, and by this holiness a more human manner of life is fostered also in earthly society."[608] The call to holiness can be misunderstood. Too often the question of holiness has been encumbered by syrupy accounts of prudish detachment. The Council shifted the notion of holiness: holiness is the vocation of all Christians rather than the possession of an elite caste. In his life, death, and resurrection, Christ preached holiness as a way of life for all Christians to follow. The Council simultaneously raises the bar in that all — not just the ordained and religious — are called to follow Christ, the Holy One, and make this path more accessible in that the humble and cross-bearing carpenter is now our guide. In order to receive their royal inheritance, lay people are therefore encouraged "to aid one another to greater holiness of life."[609] For the laity, holiness is not just about one's relationship to the parish. The path to holiness is also pursued through a specific technical competence as well as a

---

[605]Ibid., 89.
[606]Ibid., 90.
[607]Jn 18:33-37. Cf. Mk 15:2,9,12,18,26.
[608]*Lumen gentium* 40.
[609]Ibid. 36.

commitment to bring the light of Christ to bear in the betterment of society. Holiness is not a part-time job; properly understood, it is a task to be undertaken seven days a week.

Given that the laity and clergy are both equally exhorted to a life of holiness, there must be a complementarity to their tasks. There are of courses instances in which the roles of shepherd and sheep are not interchangeable. The Council makes it clear that a pastor can claim that the buck stops here.[610] But this does not mean that the style of management in a parish or elsewhere must proceed in a bureaucratic fashion. *Lumen gentium* is equally clear on this point:

> The pastors, indeed should recognize and promote the dignity and responsibility of the laity in the Church. They should willingly use their prudent advice and confidently assign duties to them in the service of the Church, leaving them freedom and scope for acting. Indeed, they should give them the courage to undertake works on their own initiative. They should with paternal love consider attentively in Christ initial moves, suggestions and desires proposed by the laity. Moreover the pastors must respect and recognize the liberty, which belongs to all in the terrestrial city.[611]

In practical terms the organic model of communion anathematizes both micro-management and ruling with a heavy hand. Lay people are in the Church to further the mission of the Church, and pastors need to recognize that lay initiatives contribute as much to this mission as the pastor's own personal agenda. The role of pastor and the role of lay person are meant to be mutually reinforcing, which by no means obliterates the distinctiveness of each role. On the contrary, through a model of organic communion the priest's identity as a shepherd of the faithful and the lay person's participation in God's own redemptive mission in Christ are each positively enhanced.

Finally, the royal road prepared by Christ's suffering and death on the cross does not end with the goals of good parish management, solid family values, and a plea for social justice. "Christ, made obedient unto death and because of this exalted by the Father,[612] has

---

[610]*Lumen gentium* 37: "Like all Christians, the laity should promptly accept in Christian obedience what is decided by the pastors who, as teachers and rulers of the Church, represent Christ."

[611]Ibid. Cf. *Apostolicam actuositatem* 6. Below we also consider the question of lay obedience to the pastors, which is not antithetical to the spirit of freedom enunciated here.

[612]Cf. Phil 2:8-9.

entered into the glory of his kingdom."[613] The promise of a share in
Christ's kingdom is a promise of eternal life with God as Father, Son,
and Holy Spirit. This Trinitarian, eschatological truth should not be
bracketed in considering the lay apostolate. Whether or not lay persons engage in official collaborative ventures with their pastors, their
one goal, which is already proclaimed and realized in liturgical acts of
thanksgiving, is to partake of divine life.[614]

C. *Christifideles laici*

Christifideles laici ("The Vocation and the Mission of the Lay
Faithful in the Church and in the World") was promulgated by John
Paul II a little over a year after the 1987 Synod of Bishops in which
members of the episcopacy as well as lay representatives discussed
"Vocation and Mission in the Church and in the World Twenty Years
after the Second Vatican Council." The document thus bears the
Pope's stamp and conveys the *Lineamenta to the Instrumentum Laboris*
as well as the many synodal reports and propositions. Above all, the
document aims to translate the "rich 'theory' on the lay state expressed
by the [Second Vatican] Council" into "authentic Church 'practice'."[615]
Many conciliar themes are reprised, e.g., the Church as communion,
the secular character of the laity, the unity of spiritual and secular life,
and the inheritance of Christ's threefold mission. But the document
also raises issues and challenges either ignored or treated inadequately
by the Fathers of the Council.

Christifideles laici may be the most exhaustive theology of the
laity ever attempted in the history of the magisterium. The gospel image of the vine and the branches is the metaphor around which the
different chapters are organized.[616] By fusing the images of working
the vineyard of the Lord together with the baptismal grafting of the
faithful branches onto the one vine of Christ, the document identifies vocation and mission to communion with the Lord. Service is a
response to an unexpected personal invitation from the Lord. One

[613]*Lumen gentium* 36.
[614]Cf. *Sacrosanctum Concilium* 8 and *Gaudium et spes* 38.
[615]John Paul II, *The Vocation and the Mission of the Lay Faithful in the Church and in the
World* [hereafter: *Christifideles laici*] (Washington, D.C.: United States Catholic Conference,
1988), 2.
[616]Mt 20:1ff; Mk 12:1; Jn 15:1ff.; Jer 2:21; Ez 19:10; Is 5:1-2; and Ps 80: 15-16.

becomes a new person upon entering the Lord's vineyard, and vocation develops by growing closer to God.[617]

I will focus on what I take to be new in the document with respect to the prior tradition. In this regard, one can distinguish between the new questions raised by the document and the new approaches taken to old issues. The document addresses a wealth of new "temptations," problems, issues, and questions. Depending on where one looks, one could easily get the impression that the laity were either underutilized or overcommitted. In fact, the document makes strong remarks against both unnecessary utilization and a willful ignorance of the gifts to the Church represented by lay women and men. Congar was so concerned about partial readings that he recommended a hermeneutical approach based upon "the principle of totality" in the reading of magisterium.[618]

The document criticizes the growing "clericalization" of the lay apostolate.[619] One major temptation for the laity is to be "so strongly interested in Church services and tasks that some fail to become actively engaged in their responsibilities in the professional, social, cultural and political world."[620] The document urges that "pastors guard against a facile yet abusive recourse to a presumed 'situation of emergency' or to 'supply by necessity', where objectively this does not exist or where alternative possibilities could exist through better pastoral planning."[621] The terms, drawn from the Code of Canon Law, by no means rule out lay ecclesial ministry.[622] The idea that laity "supply for" certain offices of the Church but not in cases when there is no necessity is not altogether clear. The general concern, however, is unambiguous. Lay ministry is not "an ecclesial structure of parallel service to that founded on the Sacrament of Orders."[623] Furthermore, lay people cannot shirk their duties and responsibilities of being leaven in the world through involvement in Church offices.

---

[617]Mt 20:4.

[618]Ramiro Pellitero, "Congar's Developing Understanding of the Laity and their Mission," 357.

[619]Christifideles laici 23.

[620]Ibid. 2.

[621]Ibid. 23.

[622]Code of Canon Law, Can. 230 § 3 (as cited in Christifideles laici 23): ""When the necessity of the church warrants it and when ministers are lacking, lay persons, even if they are not lectors or acolytes, can also supply for certain of their offices, namely, to exercise the ministry of the word, to preside over liturgical prayers, to confer Baptism, and to distribute Holy Communion in accord with the prescriptions of the law."

[623]Christifideles laici, 23.

> There are still some strikingly positive words about the exercise of lay ministry:
> Following the liturgical renewal promoted by the Council, the lay faithful themselves have acquired a more lively awareness of the tasks that they fulfill in the liturgical assembly and its preparation, and have become more widely disposed to fulfill them: the liturgical celebration, in fact, is a sacred action not simply of the clergy, but of the entire assembly. It is, therefore, natural that the tasks not proper to the ordained ministers be fulfilled by the lay faithful.[624]

Thus, a smooth transition is still possible between the development of a new conciliar theology and the implementation of lay involvement in the organized structures of the Church as envisioned not only by the Council but also in the 1983 revision of the *Code of Canon Law*. In spite of the concern raised by some synodal participants that there was a risk of confusing the roles of laity and clergy in the postconciliar Church, *Christifideles laici* nonetheless supports the judicious and properly deputed implementation of new roles, even liturgical roles, for the laity in the institutional Church. There is no possibility, therefore, of retreating back to a position in which the liturgy is viewed as an activity performed solely by the clergy. The postconciliar Mass is an assembly in which all are called to participate, and some lay people will even be formally recognized as ecclesial ministers. In sum, *Christifideles laici* reaffirms the difference between baptismal priesthood and the ordained priesthood (and between those ministries that flow from the sacraments of initiation and those that flow from Holy Orders) but also with equal fervor the necessity for conceiving of their relation in terms of an organic communion. Communion is central to collaboration.

Besides clericalization equal attention is paid to another problem, namely, the secularization of the laity's function in society. Secularization refers not only to the cultural and political forces that place limits on religious discourse but also to the tendency of believers to compartmentalize beliefs, even deeply held ones. The Council Fathers, as we saw above, wanted lay people to spread the gospel throughout the world. Thus, the second major temptation of the laity is that "of legitimizing the unwarranted separation of faith from life, that is, a separation of the Gospel's acceptance from the actual living of the Gospel in various situations in the world."[625] The laity are disciples in

[624]Ibid.
[625]Ibid. 2.

the midst of the world. Their worldliness is not just a sociological fact but "a theological and ecclesiological reality as well."[626] Speaking of the special applicability of the gospel images of salt, light, and leaven, the document suggests that secularity begets "radical newness." Lay people, in other words, should not view their baptismal calling as a kind of insulation from or parallel existence to the ways of the world. The lay person becomes immersed in the *saeculum* precisely for the purpose of bringing about its conversion to Christ. To separate one's commitment to the Gospel from "secular" life is a grave mistake. "Every activity, every situation, every precise responsibility. . . are the precise responsibilities ordained by Providence for a 'continuous exercise of faith, hope, and charity.'"[627] The branch that is engrafted onto the vine of Christ "bears its fruit in every sphere of existence and activity."[628]

The Fathers of the Council cannot be said to have treated the question of women as a serious theological concern, but *Christifideles laici* seeks to remedy this blind spot.[629] First of all, the document not only follows a synod of bishops but was also promulgated in the immediate wake of the Apostolic Letter *Mulieris dignitatem* ("The Dignity and Vocation of Women") and thus refers to one of the Pope's signature issues.[630] Moreover, the document makes repeated reference to "the fuller and meaningful participation of women in the development of society" and is not referring exclusively to their roles as wives and mothers.[631] Women are also considered as actors in culture, politics, and society. The exclusion of women from the ministerial priesthood is repeated, but an effort is made to conscientize men and women to acknowledge openly "the personal dignity of women" as "the first step taken to promote the full participation of women in Church life as well as in social and public

---

[626]Ibid. 15.

[627]Ibid. 59, citing *Apostolicam actuositatem* 4.

[628]*Christifideles laici* 59. See also the exhortation in *Apostolicam actuositatem* 33: "It is the Lord himself who is once more inviting all the laity to unite themselves to him ever more intimately. . ."

[629]Nothing is said about the changing roles of women in the chapter of *Lumen gentium* on the laity, but *Apostolicam actuositatem* 9 contains this remark: "Since in our days women are taking an increasingly active share in the whole life of society, it is very important that their participation in the various sectors of the Church's apostolate should likewise develop." Cf. *Christifideles laici*, 49.

[630]*Mulieris dignitatem* was issued on August 15,1988 and *Christifideles laici* on December 30, 1988. Cf. Michele M. Schumacher, ed., *Women in Christ: Toward a New Feminism* (Grand Rapids, MI: Eerdmans, 2004).

[631]*Christifideles laici* 2, 5.

life."[632] The history of the contribution of women to the Church is invoked not only that it may continue but "indeed that it be expanded and intensified in the face of the growing and widespread awareness of the personal dignity of woman and her vocation. . ."[633] Affirming a synodal *propositio*, the document resolves to put into practice "all the gifts of men and women" for the life and mission of the Church.[634]

Vatican II made it clear that the laity are to be active participants in the evangelization of peoples. *Christifideles laici*, however, raises a concern that had begun to be seriously addressed under Pope Paul VI in *Evangelii nuntiandi*, namely, the re-evangelization of Christians.[635]

> Without doubt a mending of the Christian fabric of society is urgently needed in all parts of the world. But for this to come about what is needed is to first remake the Christian fabric of the ecclesial community itself present in these countries and nations.[636]

The Pope's "new evangelization" is part of the development of a theology of the laity, for *Christifideles laici* presents lay involvement as the fruit of a spiritual transformation. This is not simply a matter of maintaining good public relations with fellow Catholics but of re-inviting them to a faithful commitment to the person of Christ. In the words of Paul VI, the Church must be both an evangelizing and evangelized community.[637] Lay people no less than the ordained are not going to be able to serve the Church or proclaim Christ's message in the world unless they challenge themselves in a radical fashion to encounter the person of Christ. This simple but often very difficult process of conversion is at the heart of the whole document.

"We can speak of a *new era of group endeavours* of the lay faithful."[638] Vatican II mentions various types of group apostolates and pays close attention to one form of lay association that was very much on the minds of Catholics in the 1960s, viz., Catholic Action.[639] Christifideles laici calls attention to new groups in the Church and sets

---

[632]Ibid. 49.

[633]Ibid.

[634]Ibid.

[635]*Evangelii nuntiandi* ("On Evangelization in the Modern World"), Apostolic Exhortation of Dec. 8, 1975 by Pope Paul VI. See especially 52.

[636]Ibid. 34.

[637]Ibid. 36. Cf. *Evangelii nuntiandi*, 15, 71.

[638]*Christifideles laici* 29.

[639]*Apostolicam actuositatem* 20.

up norms and regulations for supporting their development.[640] In a certain sense, *Christifideles laici* is a charter document for the new ecclesial movements.[641] In sanctioning lay associations, the hierarchy has no need to cede a portion of its authority, for the freedom of the laity to form such associations flows directly from the sacrament of baptism. The goal and requirement of groups and movements is to serve the Church's life of communion and realize the task of being a missionary presence in midst of the world. Josef Cardinal Ratzinger, whose definition of what constitutes an ecclesial movement takes the "Franciscan awakening of the thirteenth century" as a point of departure, writes:

> Only when the person is struck and opened up by Christ in his inmost depth can the other also be inwardly touched, can there be reconciliation in the Holy Spirit, can true community grow. With this basic christological-pneumatological and existential structure, there can be a great diversity of accents and emphases, in which Christianity is a perpetually new event and the Spirit unceasingly renews the Church "like the youth of the eagle."[642]

The movements and other new group endeavors signal a concrete "method" for following Christ in the context of the postconciliar renewal of an ecclesiology of communion.

Some old questions also need to be addressed with renewed vigor and a new way of thinking. For example, *Christifideles laici* replants the seeds for a notion of the parish that overcomes the usual focus on "a structure, a territory, or a building."[643] The parish is in the first instance a personal reality and site of organic communion. "Plainly and simply," it says, "the parish is founded on a theological reality, because it is a Eucharistic community."[644] The document promotes lay involvement in the local parish. Although not all aspects of the lay apostolate

---

[640]*Christifideles laici* 29-30.

[641]The question of the new ecclesial movements was the topic of a meeting of the Holy Father on Pentecost of 1998 (May 30). His homily from that event likens the presence of new movements and new communities to the "outpouring" of the Spirit of Pentecost and of the Second Vatican Council. He also admonished adherence to the criteria of ecclesiality detailed in *Christifideles laici*. See also Joseph Ratzinger, "The Theological Locus of Ecclesial Movements," *Communio: International Catholic Review* 25,3 (1998): 480-504 and Paul Josef Cordes, *In the Midst of our World: Forces of Spiritual Renewal*, trans. Peter Spring (San Francisco: Ignatius Press, 1988).

[642]Joseph Ratzinger, "The Theological Locus of Ecclesial Movements," 502. The citation is from Ps 103:5.

[643]Ibid., 26-28.

[644]Ibid. 26. Representative conciliar teachings on the parish structure are found in *Sacrosanctum concilium* 42 and *Lumen gentium* 28. The document also references Paul VI,

originate in the parish, "in our day the parish still enjoys a new and promising season."[645] Affirming a synodal *propositio,* several specific efforts at the renewal of parish life are endorsed: adaptation of parish structures (especially in poor urban centers or mission territories) "according to the full flexibility granted by canon law," establishment of "small, basic or so-called 'living' communities" among the faithful to foster the sharing and living out of the Word of God, and cooperation among diverse parishes in the same area.[646]

Christifideles laici highlights the diversity of lay vocations. This is evident in the attention to the role of women and to the non-parish based lay apostolates already mentioned. Respect for diversity enhances the Church as communion.

> ["Organic communion"] is characterized by a *diversity* and a *complementarity* of vocations and states in life, of ministries, of charisms and responsibilities. Because of this diversity and complementarity every member of the lay faithful is seen *in relation to the whole body* and offers a *totally unique* contribution on behalf of the whole body.[647]

There are some surprising aspects to the plea to maintain diversity. The sick and suffering are not only to be considered as mere recipients of Christian charity but also as agents of evangelization.[648] Likewise, children, adolescents, and the elderly are treated as vibrant and essential contributors.[649] In stark contrast to the rest of the world, the standard for participation is not productivity. In this fashion, the hope and grace of youth as well as the eloquent wisdom of older people should lead the way in discipleship. The document likewise maintains that "attention should be paid to diverse cultures which can exist in one and the same people or nation at the same time."[650] Thus, the contribution of minority communities are not added to the mix as an act of pastoral largesse or expedient multiculturalism. They are rather a blessing from God and rich symbol of the diversity of gifts bestowed upon the local communion.[651]

"Discourse to the Roman Clergy," (June 24, 1963): *Acta Apostolica Sedis* 55 (1963), 674.
[645] *Christifideles laici* 26.
[646] Ibid.
[647] Ibid. 20.
[648] Ibid. 53: ". . . the sick are called to live their human and Christian vocation and to participate in the growth of the Kingdom of God *in a new and even more valuable manner.*"
[649] Ibid. 46-48.
[650] Ibid. 63.
[651] Cf. the section "Multicultural Issues" in *Lay Ecclesial Ministry.*

The document unites themes that challenge the Catholic Church in the USA. For example, the document's missionary thrust to promote evangelization and re-evangelization is joined to a renewed plea for "the defense and promotion of justice."[652] In the sphere of ethical and social life, the laity are dealing with dilemmas of which there was only a dim awareness at the Second Vatican Council. The promotion of the dignity of the person, respect for the inviolable right to life, confronting the "challenge" posed by new problems in bioethics, addressing "the so-called 'ecological' question" and alerting our consciences to the *moral dimension* of development, defending religious liberty as well as the social value of the family — these are just some of the difficult social issues that confront lay people today. *Gaudium et spes*, for example, provided a blueprint for confronting offenses against life itself and grave injustices to humanity and human dignity, but, astonishingly, many lay people today are still largely ignorant of the moral and theological principles that comprise the Church's social teaching. Not all are aware that this centenary of Catholic doctrine differs in kind from all existing political agendas or social movements and calls them to seek the Christian wisdom that will "take up the task of calling culture back to the principles of an authentic humanism, giving a dynamic and sure foundation to the promotion and defense of the rights of the human being in one's very essence, an essence which the preaching of the Gospel reveals to all."[653] All lay persons must incorporate this wisdom into the complex spheres of daily existence. It is not a question of training an elite corps of specialists in Catholic social teaching. The charge to call the culture back to the principles of an authentic humanism is allotted to mothers, fathers, grandparents, teachers, workers in the healthcare industry, scientists and technological innovators, wielders of political and economic power, manual laborers and trade union organizers, members of the press, and owners of mass media.

According to *Christifideles laici*, social justice is not attained just by realizing a list of social policies but is also linked to the renewal of a theological anthropology.[654] The view of the person who is free to enter into communion is, as it were, the hidden center of the Church's social

---

[652]*Christifideles laici* 42. Cf. Peter Casarella, "Solidarity as the Fruit of Communio," 98-118.
[653]Ibid. 38.
[654]Ibid. 36ff.

agenda. In this sense, the document bears the unmistakable stamp of John Paul II, whose very first encyclical proposed a Christologically grounded view of the human person.[655] This anthropology is the thread in *Christifideles laici* that joins such diverse issues as the respect for life, the organization of work, the evangelization of the family and culture, and even the thorny question of the reciprocity of male and female.[656] Basically, this thread has to do with the Pope's disavowal of the notion of the person as a disembodied center of individual consciousness and development of a Christological and trinitarian anthropology that explicates the mutual reinforcement of person and community as well as the profound expressivity of gender.[657]

How does this view of Christian anthropology relate to collaboration? In the Church no woman or man is an island. The Lord calls us to work in his vineyard without renouncing our distinct charisms as men and women, without tying us to rigid and narrow-minded social roles that developed in earlier generations of Church and society, and without expecting Herculean results based solely on individual efforts. The many ministers in the Church — lay and clerical — who feel trapped or frustrated by the inordinate demands placed upon them appreciate this point. Persons in communion, by contrast, must pool their resources. According to this view, persons are unique creations of expressed love. In *Redemptor hominis* the Pope states that through Christ's mystery of redemption, each one of us becomes "'expressed' and, in a way, is newly

---

[655]"The man who wishes to understand himself thoroughly — and not just in accordance with immediate, partial, often superficial, and even illusory standards and measures of his being -- he must with his unrest, uncertainty and even his weakness and sinfulness, with his life and death, draw near to Christ. He must, so to speak, enter into Him with all his own self, he must "appropriate" and assimilate the whole of the reality of the Incarnation and Redemption in order to find himself." John Paul II, *Redemptor hominis, Encyclical Letter on the Redeemer of Man* (Washington, D.C.: United States Catholic Conference, 1979), here at 10.

[656]On this last point, see *Christifideles Laici* 50: "The Synod Fathers have deeply felt this requirement, maintaining that "the anthropological and theological foundations for resolving questions about the true significance and dignity of each sex require deeper study."

[657]The literature here is immense and growing. Foundational, however, is his *Person and Community: Selected Essays*, trans. Theresa Sandok (New York: Peter Lang, 1993) and *The Theology of the Body: Human Love in the Divine Plan* (Boston: Pauline Books and Media, 1997). Some of the relevant secondary literature includes: Sara Butler, "Personhood, Sexuality, and Complementarity in the Teaching of Pope John Paul II," Chicago Studies 32 (April 1993): 43-53; Rocco Buttiglione, *Karol Wojtyla: The Thought of the Man who Became Pope John Paul II* (Grand Rapids, MI: Eerdmans, 1997); Leonie Caldecott, "Sincere Gift: The Pope's New Feminism," in *John Paul II and Moral Theology*, ed. Charles E. Curran and Richard A. McCormick, S.J., (Mahwah, N.J.: Paulist Press, 1998); Avery Dulles, *The Splendor of the Faith. The Theological Vision of Pope John Paul II* (New York: The Crossroad Publishing Company, 1999); Mary Rousseau, "Pope John Paul II's Letter on the Dignity and Vocation of Women: the call to communio," *Communio: International Catholic Review* 16 (1989): 212-

created."[658] By giving himself up for the sake of humanity, Christ created a new idea of human personhood, one based upon self-giving love. There is no immediate recipe for social reform or the resolution of disputes in this formula. But the starting point in theological anthropology contains a new way to think about lay discipleship in the face of the degradation of human dignity in the world today.

In sum, the renewed theological identification of the laity that began with Yves Congar and the Second Vatican Council can be traced back to the idea of the Church as a communion that emerges from an organic, Spirit-filled unity of diverse charisms.[659] Ecclesial communion represents a whole greater than its constituent parts. Theology of communion is also a matter of seeing how God allows "radical newness" to emerge from the center of the Church.[660] Union with Christ bears fruit.

> As the branch cannot bear fruit by itself, unless it abides in the vine, neither can you, unless you abide in me. I am the vine, you are the branches. He who abides in me, and I in him, he it is that bears much fruit, for apart from me you can do nothing.[661]

When the many, diverse charisms of lay men and women are grafted onto the vine of Christ, this union simultaneously fulfills baptismal promises and expresses a sign of the immense fecundity emanating from within the triune life of God. In the face of this gift, Christians are universally called to a life of holiness. Neither the ordained nor the laity have a monopoly on the holiness of the Church. Ecclesial sanctity is no longer the possession of an individual to pursue moral perfection but a corporate task of God's people to follow the Holy One.

232; John Saward, "The Christocentricity of John Paul II," *Communio: International Catholic Review* (Fall 1991): 332-355; ibid. Christ is the Answer: *The Christ-Centered Teaching of Pope John Paul II* (Staten Island, N.Y.: Alba House, 1995); David L. Schindler, *The Heart of the World, Center of the Church;* Kenneth L. Schmitz, *At the Center of the Human Drama. The Philosophical Anthropology of Karol Wojtyla/Pope John Paul II* (Washington: The Catholic University of America Press, 1993); Angelo Scola, "'Claim' of Christ, 'claim' of the world: On the trinitarian encyclicals of John Paul II," *Communio: International Catholic Review* (Fall 1991): 322-331; Jeffrey Tranzillo, "'The Silent Language of a Profound of a Profound Sharing of Affection': The Agency of the Vulnerable in Selected Writings of Pope John Paul II" (PhD diss., The Catholic University of America, 2003); George H. Williams, *The Mind of John Paul II: Origins of His Thought and Action* (New York: Seabury, 1981); Elzbieta Wolicka, "Participation in Community: Wojtyla's Social Anthropology," *Communio: International Catholic Review* 8 (Summer 1981):108-118.
[658] *Redemptor hominis* 10.
[659] Cf. *Christifideles laici* 28, 31.
[660] Ibid. 15.
[661] Jn 15:4-5. Cf. *Christifideles laici* 17.

III   Lay Trinitarian Communion
and the Church's Marian Profile

This sketch still remains too abstract, too removed from the concrete form of the lay apostolate. It is thus necessary to introduce the "ecclesial profile" of the laity. What is a "profile?" The term is used by Hans Urs von Balthasar.[662] Its Balthasarian sense was taken up virtually verbatim by Pope John Paul II and repeated in *The Catechism of the Catholic Church*.[663] The precise term used in these documents is *ratio*, which is translated into Italian as *"principio"* and into English, French, and German as "dimension." Ratio here is a reckoning, account, or scheme. A *ratio* is not an isolatable part. It refers to a mode of being without which the whole cannot survive. The Latin term refers to an abiding aspect or way of looking at the Church and in this sense is synonymous with "profile." One profile may be more evident among a certain group, but no individual or group can do without the complementary presence and activity of another profile. Likewise, an ecclesial profile is rooted in history and invested with an institutional and legal form. The profile concerns the actual embodiment of the lay response to God's word in the midst of the lived Trinitarian communion. Lay people do not somehow "activate" their participation in the Church by volunteering in a parish or becoming professionally licensed. These commitments follow from a personal stance and cannot be separated from the question of the formation of the person. From this profile we can consider the lay act of participation as a spiritual act of a distinct sort, eschewing the relegation of the spiritual to private devotion, personal inwardness, or voluntaristic choice.[664] The spirituality of the lay profile has a concrete, visible, and sacramental form.[665] It is lived out in one's baptismal vocation to die with Christ by handing over one's very self to God.

The distinctive profile of the laity follows a Marian pattern. This approach is found in nuce in the documents of the Second Vatican

---

[662]See Brendan Leahy, *The Marian Profile in the Ecclesiology of Hans Urs von Balthasar* (Hyde Park, N.Y.: New City Press, 2000).

[663]*Mulieris dignitatem* 27; *Catechism of the Catholic Church* [hereafter=CCC] 772.

[664]See Charles Taylor, *Varieties of Religion Today: William James Revisited* (Harvard University Press, 2002) on the present popularity and inherent limits of conceiving of religion along the lines of personal inwardness.

[665]On the question of interior and exterior form, one may consult my "The Expression and Form of the Word: Trinitarian Hermeneutics and the Sacramentality of Language in the Theology of Hans Urs von Balthasar," *Renascence* 48 (Winter 1996): 111-135.

Council and is entirely compatible with the main lines of the conciliar theology.[666] The specific point of departure for the Marian profile is this passage in *Mulieris dignitatem:*

> Although the Church possesses a "hierarchical" structure, nevertheless this structure is totally ordered to the holiness of Christ's members. And holiness is measured according to the "great mystery" in which the Bride responds to the gift of love to the Bridegroom. . . . The second Vatican Council, confirming the teaching of the whole tradition, recalled that in the hierarchy of holiness it is precisely the "woman," Mary of Nazareth, who is the "figure" of the Church. She "precedes" everyone on the path to holiness; in her person "the Church has already reached that perfection whereby she exists without spot or wrinkle." In this sense, one can say that the Church is both "Marian" and "Apostolic-Petrine."[667]

The role of the laity in the Church is to be likened to the figure of Mary, and the role of the ordained priest to that of Peter. The Petrine profile of the Church is different from the Petrine ministry, for its *terminus a quo* is the Biblical figure of Peter and not the office held by the bishop of Rome. We are all called through our baptism to imitate Mary's stance of faith, and this vocation is nothing less an empowerment of human freedom. The Marian stance enhances the dignity of all Christians — male and female, lay and clerical — baptized into the universal priesthood of Christ's body. Finally, because Mary goes before us all in the holiness that is the Church's mystery as "the bride without spot or wrinkle," the Marian profile precedes the Petrine.[668] The Marian and Petrine profiles need to be examined individually and in terms of their complementarity.

The Marian profile is not a plea for more devotions, feast-days, or special prayers and is not tied to particular Marian doctrines.[669] Nor is it a special possession of Marian movements. Moreover, while Hans Urs von Balthasar and Adrienne von Speyr link it to various senses of feminine figures in the Church, men too are encouraged to adopt the stance.[670] The use of a feminine model of the Church introduces

---

[666]See, for example, *Apostolicam actuositatem* 4: "Perfect model of this apostolic spiritual life is the Blessed Virgin Mary, Queen of Apostles." Ties to the conciliar theology, and especially to the inclusion of Mary in the constitution on the Church, are defended in Brendan Leahy, *The Marian Profile*, 33-36.

[667]*Mulieris dignitatem* 27. The Biblical citation is from Eph 5:27.

[668]Ibid.; CCC 772.

[669]Brendan Leahy, *The Marian Profile*, 10.

[670]On the "comprehensive femininity of the Church" according to von Balthasar, see Brendan Leahy, *The Marian Profile*, 119-22.

questions of sexual difference that require a much fuller elaboration than is possible here. The Marian profile is part and parcel of a theological work in progress known as the nuptial mystery.[671] The stance of all of God's people within the nuptial mystery is one of testimony or bearing witness.[672] One cannot bear witness as a disembodied disciple of the Lord. On the other hand, the claim that sexual difference is important for expressing embodied discipleship involves no imposition of an abstract (e.g., Jungian or Goethean) archetype or culturally biased sense of maleness or femaleness. At issue rather is the freedom whereby men and women symbolically disclose a radically other God who embraces the goodness of ontological difference within the divine mystery while fully transcending the univocal predication of gendered attributes.[673]

The Marian profile starts with the Marian experience of God and is fundamentally Biblical in origin. Mary, for example, has been called the daughter Zion.[674] She has the faith of Abraham and carries forward into the rest of history the covenantal love that binds Yahweh with his people. Mary's *fiat*, a free self-offering to the Lord, is exemplary. She is "full of grace," which means she is disposed to carry out the will of the Lord. The words "let it be to me according to your word" in no way imply that she is created to be trampled upon.[675] There is no place here for the flaccid sort of Marianism whereby one loses sight of one's dignity or individuality. Rather Mary is the one who offers body and soul to God without being absorbed into an indistinct whole. In giving glory to God ("My soul magnifies the Lord, and my spirit rejoices in God my saviour" [676]), she echoes the words of the mighty one who "has shown strength in his arm, he has scattered the proud in the imagination of their hearts, he has put down the mighty from their thrones, and exalted those of low degree; he has filled the hungry with good things, and the rich he has sent empty away."[677] Through this powerful form of self-dispossession, she is free

---

[671]Angelo Cardinal Scola, "The Nuptial Mystery: A Perspective for Systematic Theology?" *Communio: International Catholic Review* 30,2 (Summer 2003): 210-234.

[672]Ibid., 222-24.

[673]Ibid., 221-22.

[674]Zep 3:14ff. and Zec 9:9. Cf. *Lumen gentium* 55 and Joseph Ratzinger, *Daughter Zion: Meditations on the Church's Marian Belief* (San Francisco: Ignatius, 1983).

[675]Lk 1:38.

[676]Lk 1:46-17.

[677]Lk 1:51-53.

to be of service to others. Third, she is "a human mother, with all her maternal feelings and experiences, joys and especially sorrows, [who] is taken into God's service in order to bear the mystery of the Incarnate God and the redeemer of the world.[678] Her maternal form encloses all Christians within herself.[679]

The Petrine profile is not to be confused with the Petrine office since the former pertains to all who have partaken of the sacrament of Holy Orders.[680] We might think of the Petrine profile in terms of a Biblical and spiritual ecclesiology of the vocation to the ordained priesthood. Above all, this profile too derives from Peter's faith as an experience of God.[681] Peter has already seen the glory of the Lord at Mount Tabor. While Peter seems to lack the boldness of Paul's preaching, he nonetheless serves as a firm moral compass to the Christian community. Peter in a sense translates the prophetic disclosure of being an eyewitness to the glory of the Lord into terms that all members of the Church can grasp and follow. There is no question here of dumbing-down the gospel message. Peter is a guide to all who face the cost of discipleship.

> For this reason, the archetype of Christ in Peter has a certain tendency to become a moral example or be reduced to such:[682] the believer possesses the truth in its hierarchical proclamation; his firm conviction concerning this truth[683] leads to his alienation from the world[684]and to his unjust persecution.[685] But through this his destiny the believer 'experiences' his 'annexation' to Christ and his 'inbuilding'[686] into him."[687]

In other words, Peter holds and communicates firm convictions by offering discrete but unmistakable clues to the flock. By following his lead, the members are brought closer to Christ.

Peter is of course also the representative of the twelve apostles and embodies apostolic faith in a unique way. Jesus' decision to grant

---

[678]Hans Urs von Balthasar, *The Glory of the Lord, I* (San Francisco: Ignatius Press, 1982), 341

[679]Cf. *Christifideles laici* 54.

[680]For some thoughts on how the pairing of Marian profile and Petrine profile may relate to the exercise of the Petrine office, see Hans Urs von Balthasar, *The Office of Peter and the Structure of the Church* (San Francisco: Ignatius Press, 1986), 183-225.

[681]Hans Urs von Balthasar, *The Glory of the Lord, I*, 352-4.

[682]1 Pt 2:21.

[683]2 Pt 1:12.

[684]1 Pt 1:1, 17; 2:11.

[685]1 Pt 2:18ff.; 3:9, 13-17; 4:12-19.

[686]1 Pt 2:4ff.

[687]Hans Urs von Balthasar, *The Glory of the Lord, I*, 353.

the keys to the kingdom to Peter in Matthew 16:18-19 reflects this primacy. Peter is not alone in his experience of God. His corporate role as the first among equals belongs to the Petrine profile. By the same token, Peter represents *the good shepherd* par excellence. According to von Balthasar, "Peter strives to be a good shepherd according to the Lord's command, and he exhorts the hierarchy to tend the flock with the attitude of Christ, the supreme Shepherd, and so to be a *"typos* [archetype] for the flock," a model which impresses its form and makes the archetype visible. For doing this they are promised a crown of glory.[688] Preaching, in its essence, involves "arming, strengthening, fortifying, and confirming" the people on behalf of God.[689]

The Marian and the Petrine experiences both come from God. Mary is the one who embodies the state of life and vocation of the laity in the Church. All men and women are called to live out this essentially receptive vocation. Peter is the archetype of the state of life of the ordained clergy. Men who receive the gift of the priesthood are called to live his example of being a "good shepherd."

How is actual collaboration between the two profiles possible? Here the nuptial imagery of the New Testament can be illuminating. According to 1 Corinthians 11:11-12: "...in the Lord woman is not independent of man nor man of woman; for woman was made from man, so man is now born of woman. And all things are from God." Competing roles are ruled out. God calls all members of the body of Christ to recognize that their vocations emanate from God. Christ's love for the Church is not an empty promise. This love has the strength to permeate the institution at every level and be a model of fidelity and communion for all forms of collaboration.

The complementarity of Mary and Peter thus points to the ecclesial reality of the nuptial mystery that binds Christ to his Church. There is a long tradition of spousal imagery in the Church running from the books of Hosea and Song of Songs in the Old Testament and the book of Revelation in the New Testament to the medieval commentaries of St. Bernard of Clairvaux or the modern readings of Matthias Scheeben, Adrienne von Speyr, and Hans Urs von Balthasar.[690]To see that

---

[688]1 Pt 5:2ff.
[689]1 Pt 5:10.
[690]For a brief survey, see Brendan Leahy, *The Marian Profile*, 17-38.

God's relationship to his people is that of a Bridegroom wedded to his Bride is more a question of analogical wisdom than science.[691] This is not to say that we are abandoning a rational faith for something more pleasing to our aesthetic sensibilities. In a world dimmed to Biblical theophany and wonder of spousal generativity the Marian profile still cannot be reduced to that of a beautiful adornment. Aestheticizing Christian faith impairs a genuine retrieval of the Church's inner spousal form. On the contrary, we are discussing a set of analogies that require a great deal of systematic reflection if they are not to be presented in a distorted fashion. This symbolic way of theologizing was quite common in the early Church but lately has fallen into desuetude. Congar, in a sketch of a theology of Catholic Action from 1957, turned precisely to this way of thinking. The ecclesial identity of the laity, he writes, is analogous to a mother's womb:

> We are accustomed to envisaging this maternity hardly at all, [as if] it only happens through the carrying out of the particular means of divinely instituted grace: sacraments, priesthood, official preaching. But Holy Scripture, the Fathers, and the facts of ecclesial life of every age teaches us that all the faithful also exercise this motherhood through faith, charity, prayer, and through the entire *vita in Christo (in Spiritu Sancto)*, with which it also worthily includes satisfaction, merit, and cooperation in Redemption. This motherhood, the Virgin Mary is the first to employ, under the totally exceptional conditions of her predestination as the Mother of the Incarnate Word-Savior and of her grace. But it is this very motherhood that she uses for the benefit of all of humanity, she who has no hierarchical power and who is in a matter of speaking the first lay person. The Fathers never tired of showing in Mary the actualization of the spiritual maternity that they also attributed to all the faithful: *"concepit de fide"* ["she conceived by faith"], *"cooperata est caritate ut fideles in ecclesia nascerentur"* ["she cooperated out of love so that the faithful would be engendered in the Church"]. . .[According to St. Augustine,] if we consider Christians individually and in isolation from one another, we must call them sons of the Church. If we consider them in the unity that they form through *caritas*, we must accord them the value and role of mother. As a matter of fact, it's in this unity, in this caritas that souls are begotten by God, that sins are forgiven, and that sacraments bear the fruit of grace.[692]

---

[691]See Pope John Paul II, *Novo Millennio Ineunte* 30 and Angelo Cardinal Scola, "The Nuptial Mystery," 7-11.

[692]Yves Congar, O.P., "Esquisse d'une théologie de l'Action Catholique," in idem, *Sacerdoce et laïcat devant leurs tâches d'évangélisation et de civilisation* (Paris: Cerf, 1962), 329-56, here 343. In order to avoid any sense of abstractness to this remark, Congar also invokes in the

It is difficult to capture the analogical relationship between God and the world in just the right terms. There is the temptation to project onto God a merely finite conception of the spousal bond as well as the equally dangerous possibility of banishing the idea of divine love to a realm wholly unrecognizable to us. By invoking the exemplarity of the nuptial mystery in Mary, Congar maintains an equilibrium that avoids the importation of anthropomorphic sexuality into God and the evisceration of the analogical mystery.[693] Moreover, he proposes the Marian profile not as a kind of spiritual bouquet but as the concrete ecclesial basis for lay engagement with the world.

One additional perspective is needed to introduce the Marian profile. Ecclesial profiles emerge from within the Church's sacramental life. The wedding feast celebrated at the Eucharist, for example, discloses the spousal relationship of Christ and the Church. In the celebration of the Mass, the priest stands *in persona* Christi and therefore represents Christ, the high priest, in a unique way. By virtue of Christ's commandment "Where two or three are gathered in my name, I shall be there with them," the community of believers also discloses a distinct manifestation of the body of Christ.[694] The gathered assembly brings with them a share in Christ's priesthood by virtue of their baptismal priesthood. What type of relationship exists sacramentally between the priest as head and pastor and the lay faithful? Since I have attempted to address this question elsewhere, my remarks on this point can be brief.[695] There are duties such as proclaiming the Word of God, administering the sacraments, and directing the faithful pastorally that pertain uniquely to the ordained priest. Even according to the 1997 instruction that underscores the difference between ordained and baptized priesthood, these duties bear with them a frightening mandate and proscribe any abuse of rightful authority by the clergy.[696] The relationship between ordained priests and the laity is ordered, but it does

---

same context the exemplary spiritual maternity and Christian witness of St. Thérèse de Liseux.

[693]Angelo Cardinal Scola, "The Nuptial Mystery," 221-22.

[694]Mt 18:20.

[695]See my "Eucharist: Presence of a Gift" in *Rediscovering the Eucharist: Ecumenical Considerations,* ed. Roch A. Kereszty (New York: Paulist, 2003), 215-19.

[696]See Congregation for the Clergy and seven other curial dicasteries, "On Certain Questions Regarding the Collaboration of the Non-Ordained Faithful in the Sacred Ministry of the Priest"(1997), 29-35 and Joseph Cardinal Ratzinger, *A New Song for the Lord* (New York: Crossroad, 1996), 176.

not involve a placing of the priest on a higher path to holiness than the lay person. To be sure, the latter assertion stands in tension with that venerable and ancient tradition whereby "holy virginity surpasses marriage in excellence... because it has a higher aim."[697] But there is no need to place the hierarchical ordering proposed by Pius XII at odds with the conciliar definition of corporate unity so long as there is an equal recognition of the mutual pitfalls and benefits of the two states of life. The clergy and the laity are called by God to distinct, equally challenging states of life. Since Augustine the Church has proscribed the life of celibacy for those who "shun the burdens of marriage or because like the Pharisees they proudly flaunt their physical integrity."[698] There is also a practical benefit to maintaining a complementarity of the two states. In the cautious words of Pius XII, the "zealous efforts [of the laity] can often touch souls that priests and religious cannot gain."[699] On this last point there is real continuity in the tradition.

The matter of states of life is nonetheless caste in a new light in the postconciliar period. Following Congar and the Council, the focus shifts from the still valid question of which state of life offers more freedom to dedicate oneself body and soul to God to the now more pressing issue of what establishes the Church as the one body of Christ. Accordingly, the laity and the ordained priest are both called to holiness and to share in the one priesthood of Christ. Lay persons, such as myself, are not hindered in their vocation to holiness by the essentially different role of the ordained priest.[700] Christ's priesthood cannot be divided into parts. No one is given just a part of the person. Christ encounters each one of us in the totality of his personhood. Lay people and clergy alike are called to partake wholly of the sacrificial love that pours out from Christ's priesthood.

The baptismal priesthood of the laity carries with it no less of a frightening mandate. Elsewhere I have (following Balthasar) identified this mandate with the spirituality of a doxological act or "kneeling

---

[697]Pope Pius XII, *Sacra virginitas* (encyclical of March 25, 1954), par. 24 (AAS 46 [1954]). Pius XII forcefully rejects the arguments of those who take celibacy as functional disorder of the human person as well as those who impede the proposal of celibacy by advancing the merits of the married life. He does not, however, maintain that virginity is a requirement for Christian perfection. Ibid., 45.
[698]Ibid., 13.
[699]Ibid., 26. In this passage, Pius XII is specifically acknowledging the merits and apostolic fruits of Catholic Action.
[700]Cf. CCC, 1546.

theology."[701] The act of consecration performed by the laity is not less spiritual than the priest's consecration in the Mass even though the two acts are radically distinct. What makes the laity's patient labors of everyday life into spiritual sacrifices acceptable to God (and therefore like kneeling) is a concerted attachment to prayer, a prayer offered up for the sake of the entire world. There are therefore two, complementary activities of consecration. These two modes of participating in Christ's priesthood are not in competition with one another.[702] One might also ask whether the lay state remains in the ordained priest. If it does, then one can speak of a simultaneity of standing in persona Christi and kneeling in his heart within the presider.[703] If, as others have maintained, the lay state does not remain in the ordained priest, then an intense bond of unity still joins the two acts within the one body of Christ.[704]

The idea of a Marian profile as such has developed quite recently in the tradition, and many of its nuances are still in need of greater scrutiny. Although closely related to developments spanning from the Fathers of the Church to the Second Vatican Council, its recent genesis lay in the collaborative venture that marked the lives of the Hans Urs von Balthasar and Adrienne von Speyr.[705] Pope John Paul II's mention of the term in his 1988 encyclical *Mulieris dignitatem* and its inclusion in the *Catechism of the Catholic Church* represent the first official sanctioning of this way of thinking.[706] The short life of this relatively new concept seems to have flourished mostly in the new ecclesial movements. The Pope was quick to draw the connection, and Chiara Lubich, founder of the Focolare Movement, eagerly notes his approval of this characterization of the movement that she founded, which also carries the official title of "The Work of Mary."[707] The future of the Marian profile, however, need not be restricted to the ecclesial movements. By considering the Marian aspect of eccle-

---

[701]Peter Casarella, "Eucharist: Presence of a Gift," 216-17.
[702]Cf. "On Certain Questions Regarding the Collaboration of the Non-Ordained Faithful," 26.
[703]This at least is what I speculated in "Eucharist: Presence of a Gift," 218-19.
[704]See Ramiro Pellitero, "Congar's Developing Understanding of the Laity and Their Mission," 354n76.
[705]Cf. Johann Roten, S.M., "The Two Halves of the Moon," *Communio: International Catholic Review 16*, 3 (1989): 419-45. The article was reprinted in *Hans Urs von Balthasar: His Life and Work*, ed. David Schindler (San Francisco: Ignatius Press, 1991).
[706]CCC, 773.

sial ontology through the lens of the Council's call for a theology of communion and a universal call to holiness, its fruitfulness for the whole Church can perhaps be brought to light.

IV On the Collaboration of the Lay Faithful in the Sacred Ministry of their Pastors

Given its origins in the ecclesial movements, could the Marian profile flourish in the parish? One charism of the ecclesial movements is to nourish in everyday existence an embodied lay spirituality of communion. Catholics who are unfamiliar with the structures or style of the movements might be tempted to shy away from a commitment of this sort, which is understandable given the little attention paid to the movements in the United States. Elsewhere I posed the question of the relationship between the spirituality of the ecclesial movements and that of parish ministry, for a dialogue that has barely begun.[708]

In *Novo millennio ineunte,* the Pope promotes the spirituality of communion.[709] The spirituality of communion belongs exclusively to neither movement nor parish. Nor is it to be misconstrued as a fruit-less quest for "planned" holiness.[710] It is rather

The structures and mechanisms of the Church cannot contain the

> the guiding principle of education wherever individuals and Christians are formed, wherever ministers of the altar, consecrated persons, and pastoral workers are trained, wherever families and communities are being built up. A spirituality of communion indicates above all the heart's contemplation of the mystery of the Trinity dwelling in us, and whose light we must also be able to see shining on the face of the brothers and sisters around us. A spirituality of communion also means an ability to think of our brothers and sisters in faith within the profound unity of the Mystical Body, and therefore as "those who are a part of me." This makes us able to share their joys and sufferings, to sense their desires and attend to their needs, to offer them deep and genuine friendship. A spirituality of communion implies also the ability to see what is

---

[707]In 1987 the Pope said that "The Church therefore possesses an irreplaceable Marian profile alongside the Petrine profile. . . " in a discourse to the Roman Curia (*Insegnamenti* X:3 [1987], p. 1484) and repeated this remark in 1998 address to a group of bishops and friends of the Focolare Movement (*L'Osservatore Romano,* February 16-17, 1998, p. 6). See also Chiara Lubich, *The Cry of Jesus Crucified and Forsaken* (Hyde Park, N.Y. : New City Press, 2001), 122.

[708]Peter Casarella, "Not a Fusion of Liberal and Conservative," *Initiative Report: Catholic Common Ground Initiative* 7,2 (June 2003): 3-6, here at 5.

[709]Pope John Paul II, Apostolic Letter *Novo millennio ineunte* (January 6, 2001), 43-45. I would like to thank Fr. Daniel McClellan, O.F.M. for bringing this to my attention.

[710]Ibid. 31.

positive in others, to welcome it and prize it as a gift from God: not only as a gift for the brother or sister who has received it directly, but also as a "gift for me." A spirituality of communion means, finally, to know how to "make room" for our brothers and sisters, bearing "each other's burdens" (*Gal* 6:2) and resisting the selfish temptations which constantly beset us and provoke competition, careerism, distrust and jealousy. Let us have no illusions: unless we follow this spiritual path, external structures of communion will serve very little purpose. They would become mechanisms without a soul, "masks" of communion rather than its means of expression and growth.[711]

depth of love that flows outward from the harmonious union of Father, Son, and Holy Spirit. In the light of that boundless love, the other members of the one body are no longer just fellow collaborators with whom one shares a common goal. Communion indwells and binds the hearts of those dedicated to a Trinitarian spirituality. Communion cannot be planned or structured. To pursue its path one must make a daily commitment to nurturing the soul of the Church as a truly organic, Spirit-filled reality.

The Marian profile can deepen the reality of the parish as site of communion.[712] A priest of the Focolare movement recounts parish experiences in which lay people and priests have incorporated it into parish life.[713] The "animators of communion," to use his term, need not seek a charismatic renewal of the parish or promote the agenda of any particular group or movement. Prudent pastors recognize that parish unity can be threatened by intra-Church proselytism. The parish is a more stable unit of communion than are the movements, and it needs by definition to remain open to a wide variety of individual tastes and needs. To promote a Marian spirituality of communion in a parish setting cannot be seen as either a merely liturgical reality or as need that will be satisfied by adding yet another program for adult education. Instead the Marian profile unlocks the transcendent dimension of parish life.

Mary gave Jesus to the world. This is their commitment: that of generating Jesus mystically in the community, and that of fulfilling

---

[711]Ibid. 43.

[712]Ibid., 45: "The theology and spirituality of communion encourage a fruitful dialogue between Pastors and faithful: on the one hand uniting them a priori in all that is essential, and on the other leading them to pondered agreement in matters open to discussion."

[713]Adolfo Raggio, "*The Parish: A Community of Communion*," in *The Parish Community: a Path to Communion,* ed. Fr. Adolfo Raggio (Hyde Park, N.Y. : New City Press, 2000).

the wish that Chiara [Lubich] expressed when she said: "My wish
for you is that the Mother of God may live in each one of you, so
that you may help her and give life again to that part of the world
entrusted to you." [714]

The Marian profile of the parish allows the parishioners to experience
Jesus in their midst. "Generating Jesus mystically in the community"
reflects and nurtures the task of building up unity in the parish. Real
parish life is filled with rancor, misunderstanding, disappointment,
and conflicting approaches to serving God and the Church. If the lay
people and priests were committed to generating Jesus in the parish,
then the communities would not only be able to bear the burden of
such troubles but would even be able to see the inevitable obstacles as
springboards to ever deepening love.[715]

Can the spirituality of communion alleviate all the real tensions
that exist in the U.S. Church today? Probably not. Catholic laity are
better informed on matters relating to theology and the Church than
ever before and more willing to speak up in the face of outright abuse.
Hispanics, Asians, and other minorities who are not treated with dignity by Catholic pastors can almost always find a welcome embrace
in a Pentecostal or non-denominational setting. The priesthood, by
contrast, is steadily aging and subject to greater public scrutiny than
at any time in recent history. Of greater concern than its diminished
manpower are the reports of widespread loneliness.[716]

The new challenges need to be met head-on. The question of power,
for example, need not be swept under the rug. It is naïve and theologically unhelpful to think that no one in the Church is trying to grasp
for power. The sexual abuse crisis has only sharpened our awareness of
this reality. Neither the priests nor the laity have a monopoly on the
power in the Church, and neither group is free from that original sin
whereby we seek to gather a little bit of power just for ourselves. In
the end, however, neither the Marian nor the Petrine ministries are

[714]Ibid., 57.
[715]Ibid., 71-74, which describes such an experience in a parish in which the lay people were
initially quite adverse to the style of a new pastor.
[716]According to the latest information available, the average age at ordination for a priest
in the United States increased from 32 to 36 in the period between 1984 and 2001. See Dean
R. Hoge, *The First Five Years of the Priesthood: A Study of Newly Ordained Catholic Priests*
(Collegeville, MN: Liturgical Press, 2002).

about power. They do, however, acknowledge rightful "authority" in a hierarchical form. Pastors are called to exercise authority without squelching new initiatives: "It is for the pastors to pass judgment on the authenticity and good use of these gifts, not certainly with a view to quenching the Spirit but to testing everything and keeping what is good."[717] Pastors need to be firm in their exercise of authority and encourage a fruitful dialogue with the faithful.[718] A priest who fails to exercise proper authority is no pastor. A pastor who repudiates all dialogue ruptures the communion given by Christ in the Spirit.

The real problem for theology concerns the relationship of authority and freedom. How is real human freedom affirmed in the spousal reality of the Church? How do we avoid a bad marriage? It would be easier, it seems, to circumvent this complicated reality or to translate it into terms not directly related to our embodied ecclesiality, but that option is not available to us in the living Church. Lay women and men, as we have seen, enjoy equal dignity in the Church even though not all the roles are interchangeable. If one leaves aside the juridical question of the exclusion of women from the ordained priesthood, one really arrives at the more fundamental question of how the Marian stance of a lay person can truly embody freedom. In some important sense, this stance never generates its own proposal, at least not in terms of an individual plan. But the withdrawal of some sense of autonomy does not evacuate the content of self-determination. The spirit of the laity remains that of a self-determining agent working towards the fulfillment of the mission of the Church. From the Marian standpoint freedom perdures in obedience and not even of a shallow, partial sort. Claudia Consenza, a lay Focolarina, writes: "Obedience lived in reciprocal charity (with Jesus in the midst) is an enlightened obedience."[719] Enlightened obedience is the fruit of a path chosen without duress or coercion. To be sure, a free communion is no guarantor of sanctity as when a manipulative pastor fails to respect to dignity of his associates and treats them as agents in the fulfillment of his own personal

---

[717]*Apostolicam actuositatem* 3, making reference to 1 Thes 5:12, 19, 21.
[718]*Novo millennio ineunte* 45.
[719]Claudia Consenza, "Authority and Participation in the light of the Lay Experience of the Focolare Movement" (presentation, Catholic Common Ground Initiative Conference, Serra Retreat Center, Malibu, CA, March 2002), 3.

agenda.[720] A pastor can expect obedience from a lay person, but only because that person freely abides within a structured communion of grace.[721] This order does not simply permit the individual to flourish as a kind of concession. Self-determination and communion reinforce one another without restrictions.

In the end, a sharp distinction between power and authority must be maintained. Authority is not earned; it is given as a sacred trust and as a reflection of the gratuitousness of God's grace. Peter is called to be firm in his convictions so that his flock may be incorporated into the body of Christ. Christ never authorized Peter to stop listening to his sheep or ignore their very human needs. In the parable of the fishermen, for example, Peter says to the Lord: "At your word I will let down the nets."[722] In this sense, the Petrine office is as much about being a handmaiden of the Lord except that here self-dispossession takes the form of safeguarding the truth.[723]

The complementarity of the Marian and Petrine offers a profoundly theological insight into the nature of collaboration. Distinct roles are assigned to laity and priests, but they together form one body. Unity brings together into a real whole the diverse charisms given by the Spirit. St. Paul said it best:

> Now there are varieties of gifts, but the same Spirit; and there are varieties of service, but the same Lord; and there are varieties of working, but it is the same God who inspires them all in every one. To each is given the manifestation of the Spirit for the common good. ... All these are inspired by one and the same Spirit, who apportions to each one individually as he wills. For just as the body is one and has many members, and all the members of the body, though many, are one body, so it is with Christ. For by one Spirit we were all baptized into one body — Jews or Greeks, slaves or free — and all were made to drink of one Spirit."[724] (1 Cor 12:4-12)[724]

---

[720]Of course, lay people can also be manipulative.

[721]Cf. *Apostolicam actuositatem* 25.

[722]Luke 5:5. Cf. *Novo Millennio Ineunte* 38.

[723]Safeguarding means indwelling and preserving what is truly Christ's in preparation for the coming of his kingdom. It does not mean deflecting all criticisms made against the institution or being less than forthcoming with the faithful when, God forbid, the other workers in the vineyard betray the Lord's own commandments.

[724]1 Cor 12:4-12.

CHAPTER 11

THE FAMILY:
SIGN OF COMMUNION
IN THE NEW EVANGELIZATION

Carl A. Anderson

THE TOPIC OF THIS ESSAY, "The Family: Sign of Communion in the New Evangelization" is precisely right for a volume dealing with "The Call to Holiness and Communion: Vatican II on the Church." In promulgating the *Catechism of the Catholic Church* in 1992, Pope John Paul II stated, "For me ...Vatican II has always been, and especially during these years of my Pontificate, the constant reference point of my every pastoral action, in the conscious commitment to implement its directives concretely and faithfully."[725] It is not surprising then, that Pope John Paul II would begin his *Letter to Families* [1994] with a meditation on *Gaudium et spes*. He writes, if "man is the way of the Church,"[726] then "the family is the first and the most important way" of the Church.[727] The pope is clear about this fundamental insight of the Council itself, that unlike the various ideologies of the modern age, the human person cannot be successfully understood as an abstraction — that is, isolated from the context of family life. Instead, each person must be seen in the concrete reality of his daily life. As the Council itself says in the opening paragraphs of *Gaudium et spes*: "It is man ... who is the key... man considered whole and entire, with body and soul, heart and conscience, mind and will."[728] And for John Paul II, this must include consideration of man as he lives in the family.

---

[725]John Paul II, Apostolic Constitution, *Fidei Depositum*.
[726]John Paul II, *Redemptor hominis*, no. 14.
[727]John Paul II, *Letter to Families*, no. 2.
[728]*Gaudium et spes*, no. 3.

266 CALLED TO HOLINESS AND COMMUNION

At the conclusion of the *Letter to Families*, the pope emphasizes, "the family is placed at the center of the great struggle between good and evil, between life and death, between love and all that is opposed to love."[729] In Evangelium vitae he wrote, "The role of the family in building a culture of life is *decisive and irreplaceable*."[730] Less publicly, he has observed that the family is the fundamental point of encounter between the Church and contemporary culture.

With these points in mind, it is clear that the family must be seen as both subject and object of the "new evangelization." Indeed, the evangelization of the family is a hallmark of the new evangelization and is at its center. It is hardly possible to conceptualize a "new evangelization" faithful to the thought of John Paul II that is not centered upon the Church's mission to marriage and family.

If it is true that John Paul II saw the family at the center of the great encounter between the Church and the modern world, it is equally true that critics of the Judeo-Christian tradition understand the family as central to their efforts. During the last century, Western politics embraced (in differing degrees) one of two radically opposed ideological visions of community and person — the radical collectivism of communism, Nazism and fascism or the radical individualism of social Darwinism and libertarianism. These competing ideologies understood they had a common obstacle — the stable family based upon marriage. For the collectivist, the family is an institution that promotes individuality; it takes a person out of anonymity and gives him a unique environment, unique experiences and ultimately, a unique personality, thus making it impossible to successfully incorporate him as part of the collectivist "mass." For the radical individualist, the family is an institution that prevents a person from fully realizing his own individuality—marriage and procreation become burdens limiting one's freedom to choose.

Concurrently, nineteenth century secular thought — epitomized by Marx, Nietzsche and Freud — provided a framework that left no room for Christianity and very little room for its view of the family. As Paul Ricoeur pointed out, these thinkers succeeded in

---

[729]Id., no. 23.
[730]John Paul II, *Evangelium vitae*, no. 92.

placing Christianity under suspicion and especially distrusted what it had to say about such matters as human dignity and freedom.[731] These thinkers contended that Christianity was simply not to be trusted to provide an adequate answer about the nature, dignity and freedom of the human person.

The diversity of American culture has mixed together all these dynamics. Today, the family is assaulted from many points on the political compass. While the welfare state continues to drain social and economic functions from the family as an institution, the family is directly challenged by an individualism, which asserts that only with complete autonomy is a person fully able to realize his moral, spiritual and intellectual capacities. Moreover, it has become increasingly clear that according to this view complete autonomy is not possible without absolute freedom of choice in regard to decisions to enter or remain in the workforce and procreation. Therefore the feminist agenda insists both on the absolute control of fertility through unrestricted access to both abortion and divorce. At the same time, a jurisprudence that combines autonomy with equality professes to see no unique place in the legal horizon for marriage and the family based upon it. In Europe these trends have combined with socialist economic policies, which posit the full introduction of women into the labor force and therefore by necessity require the legalization of both divorce and abortion as prerequisites to an equalitarian economic order. The convergence of socialist economic policy with feminist social policy has been an important factor in the astonishingly rapid secularization of Western Europe.

The post-synodal apostolic exhortation, *Ecclesia in Europa* [2003], acknowledges "an increasingly evident crisis of the family" in Europe.[732] What is also increasingly evident is that Western Europe, by and large, no longer possesses (nor is interested in possessing) a Christian family social order. The answer *Ecclesia in Europa* proposes is that Europe must rediscover "the truth" about the family. But what is this truth? According to the text, Europe must recover a vision

---

[731]Paul Ricoeur, *Freud and Philosophy: An Essay on Interpretation* (New Haven: Yale University Press, 1970), 32.
[732]John Paul II, *Ecclesia in Europa*, no. 90.

that understands the family as "an intimate communion of life and love open to the procreation of new persons, as well as its dignity as a 'domestic Church'."[733]

Increasingly in the United States as well, (and recently with an accelerated pace) the Christian view of the family is regarded as a social anachronism at best and with outright hostility at other times. Many signs indicate that the United States is well on its way in following Europe as a society hostile to Christian family life. The Second Vatican Council anticipated this situation by developing in the first chapter of *Gaudium et spes* the foundation for an adequate response to our family crisis. This chapter entitled, "The Dignity of the Human Person," concludes with the often cited section 22 that it is only through the Incarnation that the mystery of man is made clear. Already in the first section of the chapter, the idea of family and communion is introduced as absolutely necessary to understand the true nature of human existence. The Council states that "God did not create man a solitary being [to the contrary] male and female he created them. This partnership of man and woman constitutes the first form of communion between persons."[734] Thus, the family as a sign of communion is introduced at the very beginning of *Gaudium et spes*.

In its first chapter, *Gaudium et spes* boldly challenges secular anthropologies of the nineteenth and twentieth centuries as inadequate. Moreover, it asserts that only Christianity provides an understanding of the human person that is adequate to support both human dignity and human freedom. And this Christian understanding of the person is inseparable from the understanding of the role of the person in the family.

In *Familiaris consortio* [1981], John Paul II puts forward with great clarity this anthropology — founded on the communion of persons and therefore founded upon the family. He writes, "God created man in His own image and likeness, calling him to existence through love. He called him at the same time for love. God is love," the Holy Father continued, "and in Himself lives a mystery of personal loving communion. Creating the human race in His own image and

[733]Ibid.
[734]*Gaudium et spes*, no. 12.

continually keeping it in being, God inscribed in the humanity of man and woman the vocation, and thus the capacity and responsibility, of love and communion. Love is therefore the fundamental and innate vocation of every human being."[735]

If this is so, then it follows that only the capacity to love, only the responsibility to love and only the vocation to love is adequate to understand and to protect the dignity of every person. This is why the pope would later write, that the family must be the way of the Church. The family is the first school in which the way of this communion is taught — a way in which the vocation to love is learned. We see in the theological understanding of the family a model of community life that transcends those we establish ourselves. In the family, as a sign of this communion, we see manifest in history the life of the Holy Trinity.

While it is only through revelation that the mystery of the Trinity can be understood, John Paul II has written that, "Nevertheless, this mystery which infinitely transcends us is also the reality closest to us, because it is the very source of our being.... In the depths of our being, where not even our gaze can penetrate, the Father, the Son and the Holy Spirit, one God in three Persons, are present through grace. Far from being a dry intellectual truth, the mystery of the Trinity is the life that dwells in us and sustains us."

The family mirrors the community of the Trinity as it realizes its vocation to love as the first culture of life and the first culture of love that each person experiences. John Paul II describes the family as "an eloquent and living image" of the Trinity.[736] Thus, the Trinitarian dimension of the family provides a fundamental point of reference for the evangelization of family life.

This is also why the Holy Father has called marriage the primordial sacrament, because within the very structure of human existence there exists a spousal dimension, which we might say directs each person's vocation to love. In this way the very structure of the marital community too has been imprinted by the Creator with a real image of the community of love that radiates from within the Holy Trinity.

---

[735]John Paul II, *The Role of the Family in the Modern World, Familiaris consortio*, no. 11.
[736]John Paul II, *"Yours Must be a Witness of Love," L'Osservatore Romano* (English ed., Oct. 12, 1994), p.2.

The family as a sign of communion in the new evangelization also may be understood as the key to the renewal of society at large. In this sense, the community of the Trinity is the first form and model of all human community — including in a special way the first human community — the family. Because the family is in a sense a primordial reflection of the life and communion of the Trinity woven into the very framework of all human existence, the family, understood as a school of communion, is a model for all other associations in society. Secular analysis, to the contrary, increasingly employs business concepts of association to redefine relationships within the family; for example, as in the tendency by many in the legal community to refer to marriage now as essentially a "joint venture for profit" or "joint tenancy" to which little more than the general rules of contract law apply. Privacy has replaced procreation as the fundamental societal interest to be protected in the marriage relationship. Little wonder then, that there is increasing pressure to open up this "joint venture for profit" to persons of the same gender.

To the degree to which the new evangelization is directed toward the evangelization of culture and therefore toward the renewal of society, what we have said about the importance of the family is fundamental to this aspect of the new evangelization as well. In other words, if the vocation of the person is to love, then there can only be one way human community and culture can provide for an environment in which the spiritual, moral and intellectual capacities of the person can be realized to the fullest. And that, as John Paul II said so often, is to build a civilization of love, since only a civilization of love is worthy of the dignity of a person whose vocation is to love. But a civilization of love is possible only in a society that respects the truth of marriage and family.

The Christian family — that privileged community where the culture of life and the culture of love are united — is the first and indispensable building stone of the civilization of love. And this is also why the Holy Father has called abortion the primordial evil. Abortion takes the life of an innocent human being, but it also strikes at the primordial structure of human existence where life and love must be united if human dignity is to be preserved and a civilization of love achieved.

When we are physically born we enter into the community of the family. When we are born again in baptism we enter a new communion of persons that transcends any model of earthly community.

These two models of community life — the community of faith and the community of family — are the models of community life that should guide and direct and inspire us in the work of the new evangelization. The *Catechism of the Catholic Church* quotes *Familiaris consortio* to state that "The Christian family constitutes a specific revelation and realization of ecclesial communion, and for this reason it can and should be called a *domestic church*."[737] Furthermore, it continues to describe the Christian family as "a communion of persons, a sign and image of the communion of the Father and the Son in the Holy Spirit."[738]

How, therefore, are we to understand the Christian family as a sign of communion apart from understanding it as "a specific revelation and realization of ecclesial communion" and as a community called to be a "domestic" church? Within the space of this essay, I cannot discuss the whole history of the concept of the "domestic" church, but I can empaszie that an understanding of the family as "domestic" church is absolutely essential to understanding the family's role within the new evangelization. Any adequate pastoral care of the Christian family in contemporary society, therefore, must keep the "domestic church" in mind.

The Christian family as subject of the new evangelization must also be an active principle of the new evangelization. In democratic societies it may indeed be the principal agent of evangelization. The Christian family in the concrete reality of day-to-day living becomes a community, which as *Familiaris consortio* noted, is one in which "all the members evangelize and are evangelized."[739]

Thus, in large measure, the new evangelization will proceed in its mission to evangelize culture by means of many millions of small cultures of evangelization, that is to say, by means of millions of Christian families.

---

[737] *Catechism of the Catholic Church*, no. 2204; quoting *Familiaris consortio*, no. 21.
[738] *Catechism of the Catholic Church*, no. 2205.
[739] No. 52.

From what has been said already it should be clear that the care of the family must be of the highest priority in the Church's mission of evangelization. The fact that we have made such little headway in fulfilling the promise of the new evangelization is not unrelated to the failure to adequately understand family as both subject and object of the new evangelization, and to deal with the family as such. We might ask, for example, the degree to which the two great pastoral documents on the care of the family, that is, *Familiaris consortio* and *The Letter to Families* currently provide the basis for diocesan pre-cana programs or the degree to which they actually guide pastoral activity on the parish level. Addressing the challenges facing the family, John Paul II, in *Ecclesia in America* [1999], wrote, "Also required is a serious preparation of young people for marriage, one which clearly presents Catholic teaching on this sacrament at the theological, anthropological and spiritual levels."[740]   No more urgent task faces us than the preparation of a serious and clear program of studies for those intending marriage derived from the teaching of *Familiaris consortio* and *The Letter to Families*.

In 1994, John Paul II indicated that *Familiaris consortio* was intended to be the primary pastoral document for the care of the family in the parish when he wrote that Familiaris consortio provides "an organized context for the pastoral care of the family as a priority and the basis of the new evangelization."[741] More than twenty years after the promulgation of *Familiaris consortio,* in how many dioceses may it be said that this document provides the "context for the pastoral care of the family?"

In his 1994 Holy Thursday letter to priests throughout the world, John Paul II wrote that, "The pastoral care of the family — and this I know from personal experience — is in a way the quintessence of priestly activity at every level."[742] Indeed, this view would appear entirely consistent, if not mandated, by the understanding of the importance of marriage and family developed in *Gaudium et spes,* numbers

---

[740]John Paul II, *Ecclesia in America,* no. 46.
[741]*L'Osservatore Romano* (English ed., October 12, 1994), p. 2.
[742]*L'Osservatore Romano* (English ed., March 30, 1994), p. 3.

47-52. If this is true, then one may rightly ask whether the current level of priestly formation is adequate to this task.

In 1995, the Congregation for Catholic Education promulgated new *Directives on the Formation of Seminaries Concerning Problems Related to Marriage and the Family.* The Directives constitute one of the most important initiatives for the pastoral care of the family. They recognize that there now exists a distinct *corpus* of magisterial teaching on marriage and family and that this *corpus* must be taught with confidence and without qualification or apology. Moreover, the *Directives* realize that this *corpus* is not unrelated to questions of Christian anthropology, ecclesiology and Christology and that therefore it is not adequate to simply add one more course on the subject of marriage and family to the seminary curriculum without taking into due consideration the implications of this teaching on the seminarian's entire program of studies. However, once again one suspects that we have far to go in the consideration and practical implementation of the *Directives* by seminaries in the United States.

Given the present concern regarding seminary education and priestly formation — especially as it affects the priest's relationships with families, few considerations should have a higher priority than a reconsideration of seminary formation based upon the *Directives*. Recent events concerning the conduct of some clergy may yet have an enduring effect upon seminary enrollment and a future downturn in the number of men answering the call to the priesthood. Indeed, such a development would seem not unlikely should an ancillary problem also develop, namely, the increasing alienation of families from their bishops and local pastors. Providentially, it may be precisely in giving a new and heightened priority to the pastoral care of families as envisioned by *Familiaris consortio and The Letter to Families* that a way out of this difficulty may be found.

Now is the time for greater unity between families and priests, not less. The family is a sign of communion not only within itself — as an expression of the relationships of husband and wife, parents and children. It is also sign of communion outside of itself and this is especially true regarding its life within the Church.

John Paul II first called the Church to the task of evangelization that is "new in its ardor, methods and expression" more than twenty years ago.[743] In *Ecclesia in America* he maintained that the task of evangelization "calls for a new program which can be defined overall as a 'new evangelization'."[744] Part of what is "new" about the new evangelization is that it is inseparable from the Second Vatican Council's universal call to holiness, especially as it affects the role of the laity. This is not to say that prior to the Council there was not such a call to holiness, but that there is now a shift in emphasis. Especially in light of the Council's teaching and that of John Paul II, it is clear that the tendency to see the married state of life as in some sense an obstacle to holiness is no longer appropriate. Instead, if we have understood marriage correctly as a sign of Trinitarian communion and the family as "domestic Church," then the married state of life is not only an appropriate vehicle, but also a privileged place for Christians to pursue the path of holiness.

In addressing the task of the new evangelization, John Paul II states in *Ecclesia in America,* "In accepting this mission, everyone should keep in mind that the vital core of the new evangelization must be a clear and unequivocal proclamation of the person of Jesus Christ, that is, the preaching of his name, his teaching, his life, his promises."[745] In *Christifideles laici,* John Paul II speaks of the new evangelization in terms of the re-evangelization of the First World. He says this: "Without doubt a mending of the Christian fabric of society is urgently needed in all parts of the world. But for this to come about what is needed is to first remake the Christian fabric of the ecclesial community itself.... At this moment the lay faithful, in virtue of their participation in the prophetic mission of Christ, are fully part of this work of the Church. Their responsibility, in particular, is to testify how the Christian faith constitutes the only fully valid response — consciously perceived and stated by all in varying degrees — to the problems and hopes that life poses to every person and society. This will be possible if the lay faithful will know how to overcome in them-

[743]John Paul II, Address to the Assembly of CELAM (March 9, 1983); cited in Ecclesia in America, no 66.
[744]*Ibid.*
[745]No. 66.

selves the separation of the Gospel from life, to again take up in their daily activities in family, work and society, an integrated approach to life that is fully brought about by the inspiration and strength of the Gospel."[746] It is precisely to accomplish such an integrated approach to life that the pastoral concern for the family as a sign of communion is presented within the context of the new evangelization.

While the challenges which our families and our Church face may now be greater than at any other time in the history in the United States, the renewal of the Church begun by the Second Vatican Council and continued by the pontificate of John Paul II offers the possibility that those entrusted with its ministries may make an adequate response — a response that offers the promise of a new springtime of the Gospel.

---

[746]John Paul II, *Christifideles laici*, 34.

CHAPTER 12

THE AUTHORITY OF WOMEN IN THE CHURCH AND *ORDINATIO SACERDOTALIS*

Pia de Solenni, STD

THE QUESTION OF WOMEN'S ORDINATION provokes an impassioned response from almost every part of the Catholic Church. Too often, the supernatural is constricted strictly to the lens of the natural. Whatever happens in society or the culture at large is superimposed on the Church and the Church is read through societal constructs. In reality, the Church exceeds the bounds of any contemporary society. While the natural is necessary to understand the supernatural, there is a danger of confusing the things that are natural in their essence with things that are a natural result of sin.

Although several contexts might serve as a point of departure; one in particular comes to mind. In the fall of 1994, the Vatican was holding the Synod for Religious. Women religious from around the world, most particularly from the western part, addressed their role within the Church and asked for more power. Mother Teresa responded simply that these women needed to fall in love with their spouse who is Jesus. Apparently, her analysis caused consternation. Yet it speaks volumes. Within the context of sincere and authentic love, issues of power rarely, if ever, are left unresolved. Authority, too, can be understood and accepted within the context of love. Outside this context, it takes on a wholly different perspective.

The reexamination of the role of women in the Church has coincided with the mainstreaming of radical feminist thought. Those who identify themselves as "conservative" are often quick to dismiss many feminist thinkers. But even if one disagrees with their conclusions, this in no way reduces the significance of the questions the feminists have addressed. These questions arose within a particular time, concerning real individuals and real situations. To dismiss them would be to deny them the respect owed to human persons. The context of these questions, very frequently, arose from situations that can be objectively recognized as wounding, perhaps even traumatic, and definitely hurtful.

Based on Aquinas's presupposition that grace builds upon nature, a consideration of the Church and the priesthood could be conducted first from the perspective of the natural complementarity between men and women.

Aside from the biological aspects of procreation, natural complementarity is perhaps most clearly indicated in a succinct response that Aquinas makes to the question of whether it was fitting that Eve was created from Adam's side. Aquinas explains that woman was not created from man's head to rule over him, or from his foot to be ruled by him, but from his side to rule with him.[747] The order of creation and our sexually differentiated bodies confirms this sameness and difference.

Ecclesiology and Christology, in which the relationship between Christ and the Church is seen as the spousal relationship *par excellence* from which we borrow our notions of spousal relations, further develops the image of man and woman in complementary roles.[748] Ironically, what is known first and best, namely the relation between husband and wife, is not the most perfect spousal relationship. Rather these notions are derivatives.

Scripture develops the notion of the spousal relation between Christ and the Church, perhaps starting most memorably with the Canticle of Canticles and further developed almost infamously with Ephesians 5,20-33.[749] Frequently, the only reference to this passage is a hurried reading of the line, "Wives be submissive to your husbands." Sometimes the reading is even abridged so as not

---

[747] *Summa Theologiae*, I, q. 92, a.3.
[748] Cf. St. John Chrysostom's *Homily On Ephesians 5*, in *On Marriage and Family Life* (Crestwood, N.Y.: St. Vladimir Seminary Press, 1997).
[749] Francis Martin, "The New Feminism: Biblical Foundations and Some Lines of Development," in *Women in Christ: Towards a New Feminism*, Michele Schumacher, ed. (Grand Rapids, MI: William B. Eerdmans Publishing Company, 2004): 141-168.

to offend. Unfortunately, such temptations only cloud the dynamic reality that is the relationship between Christ and the Church and the exhortation that husbands love their wives *"as Christ loves the Church, giving himself unto death for her."* This passage indicates substantial aspects of ecclesiology, Christology, and sexual complementarity. The passage rests on the reality that sexual differentiation is an essential part of our identity, an essential accident if you will.

In the paradigm offered by St. Paul, there are no power struggles because he situates masculinity and femininity within the context of authentic love. Considering the passage from Ephesians, John Paul II explains,

> At the same time Christ emphasized the originality which distinguishes women from men, all the richness lavished upon women in the mystery of creation. Christ's attitude towards women serves as a model of what the Letter to the Ephesians expresses with the concept "bridegroom." Precisely because Christ's divine love is the love of a Bridegroom, it is the model and pattern of all human love, men's love in particular....[*The Eucharist*] *is the sacrament of the Bridegroom and of the Bride.* The Eucharist makes present and realizes anew in a sacramental manner the redemptive act of Christ, who "creates" the Church, his body. Christ is united with this "body" as the bridegroom with the bride.[750]

Essentially, both Paul and John Paul II describe the perfect marriage that exists between Christ and the Church. From this perfect marriage, men and women learn and understand what marriage is. However, it becomes quite a challenging feat when either or both realities are missing from the human experience. In a certain sense, this is reminiscent of the initial remarks on some forms of radical feminism and its ensuing inquiries. Born from an experience of greatly flawed human relations, especially the most intimate relationship of marriage, certain generalizations are generated which demonstrate a lack of the experience of the reality that is marriage, whether perfectly as it exists between Christ and the Church, or less perfectly as it exists between men and women. Regardless of whether they are ultimately correct or not, they arose because of particular and actual situations for which we, as members of the Church, may have been responsible indirectly if not directly.

---

[750] *Mulieris dignitatem*, nn 25-26.

There can be no doubt that the Church has passed through great difficulties in the past century, not limited to persecution or to the sexual scandals that broke in 2002. Indeed, Councils are not convened because everything is going well. They are convened to address a particular crisis. Vatican II may have been the exception to this pattern, but among the various issues addressed by the Council documents, the emerging question could be summed up as an identity crisis of the Church, her members, and her priests. The apparent newness of lay spirituality and the dissemination of the message of the universal call to holiness subsequent to the Council indicate that such understandings were sorely lacking. In some respects, the settling out of the Council is just beginning to occur. One pastor explained, "When you upset an old lady, it takes her a while to settle down. Well, the Church is a 2000-year old woman. It will take her a while to settle down after Vatican II."

Questions of power and authority affect not only the Church, but civil society as well. The two are intricately united and what affects one, affects the other as well because they share the same members. In the secular world, there have clearly been abuses of power, not just between men and women, but also between entire peoples. When power becomes the issue of contention, it is only natural that those involved in the conflict should seek power because they are looking to correct an inequality. For the purpose of this essay it is important to consider the notions of power and authority. Strictly speaking, power resides in God, *omnipotente*. Authority is the right to use power and it is a right that is given by the One who is Love. Outside of this context, when power is humanly sought, it becomes a love of force. Whereas, in an authentic theological context, authority is the force of love. Authority is given; power is taken.

Power today means being able to do what one wants, as willed, and being able to have one's say. This understanding of power has no relevance in the economy of the Church. Our bishops, our priests, our religious, our laity, no matter what authority they have been given, they do not have a *right* to say and do what they want if it is not in accord with God's design for the Church. A parish priest explained, "If a priest gets up to preach and starts to tell you what he thinks, turn him off. He ought to be telling you what the Church thinks." Granted, one would hope that these would be the same. But most can attest to struggles where one is called to put aside what "I think" and take up what the Church "thinks". It happens every time a penitent enters the confessional. At the end of the day, authority has an essential sense of service. Even if notions of power and authority have been skewed, the authentic concepts must be kept in mind and serve as a matrix.

This said, some groundwork has been laid for an initial look at the 1994 Apostolic Letter *Ordinatio sacerdotalis, On Reserving Priestly Ordination to Men Alone*. When the document was first released, many were disappointed. After all, it was such a little document for such a big question.

Ordinatio sacerdotalis is a summary document. It is short because nothing new has been introduced. It simply articulates what the Church has always taught and will always teach. The exposition of the topic was done in the earlier declaration, *Inter insigniores*, published by the Congregation for the Doctrine of the Faith in 1976. In a sense, *Inter insigniores* provides the discussion that explains the conclusion set forth in *Ordinatio sacerdotalis*.

Ordinatio sacerdotalis makes three basic points:
1. Christ, in ordaining only men, acted freely without constraint by cultural norms.
2. Nonadmission to the priestly ordination is not a sign of lesser dignity.
3. The Church does not have the faculty to ordain women.

Perhaps the most frequently used argument in favor of the ordination of women is that of cultural norms. The argument maintains that Christ did not ordain women because to do so would have gone against cultural norms and standards. Women, allegedly, did not have an active role in society and, therefore, Christ was only respecting the cultural norms and mirroring them in his own choice of the male apostles. Given the changes in the role of women in our culture, where women excel at the same education and professional realms as men, it would seem that the Church ought to reflect this cultural change in the priesthood, allowing women to be ordained just as they have been allowed into other professional realms.

The problem with the argument lies in the very premise that Christ maintained the cultural norms of the time. In fact, the Gospels indicate that he repeatedly broke with tradition, particularly in his regard for and rapport with women.[751] One of the Gospel narratives which can further our understanding is Christ's encounter with the Samaritan woman at the well.[752]

> Jesus said to her, "Believe me, woman, the hour is coming when you will worship the Father neither on this mountain nor in Jerusalem. You people worship what you do not understand; we worship what we understand, because salvation is from the Jews. But the hour is coming, and is now here, when true worshipers will worship the Father in Spirit and truth; and indeed the Father seeks such people to worship him. God is Spirit, and those who worship him must worship in Spirit and truth." The woman said to him, "I know that the Messiah is coming, the one called the Anointed; when he comes, he will tell us everything." Jesus said to her, "I am he, the one who is speaking with you."

The Gospels do not report Jesus revealing himself as Messiah so directly and with such clarity to anyone but this woman. Remarkably, not even to the apostles who subsequently question his encounter with the Samaritan woman does he reveal himself with such clarity as he did to her.

Secondly, *Ordinatio sacerdotalis* explains that the non-admission to priestly ordination is not a sign that women are of lesser dignity.[753] The whole history of the Church witnesses to the presence and active participation of women. It was the consent, understanding, and devotion of a woman that brought the Church to us. It is a woman, in the room of the last supper, who on the Sunday of Pentecost is the authority of grace for the apostles. Her active openness to grace is essential for salvation history. It becomes the example for each member of the Church, whether man or woman. Mary, the mother of God, the authentic model of feminine virtue, provides the understanding for the place of women and their authority in the Church. The fact that she was not chosen by her son to receive priestly ordination indicates that the sacrament does not discriminate on the basis of dignity or merit. Her role of authority is one to which all priests, all men, and all women are subject.[754] For this she is recognized as the Queen of

---

[751] Jn 4,27; Mt 9,20-22; Lk 7,37; Jn 8,11. Cf. *Inter insigniores*, 4: "No one however has ever proved – and it is clearly impossible to prove – that this attitude is inspired only by social and cultural reasons."
[752] Jn 4,21-26.
[753] *Ordinatio sacerdotalis*, n. 3.

Heaven. This title represents a permanent reality, not a mere pious sentiment. *Ordinatio sacerdotalis* extends an invitation to discover or perhaps rediscover this reality.

At the same time, the reality of Mary's maternal and regal authority over all the members of the Church, and through her maternal authority even over the Head of the Church, indicates another reality, namely that the Church does not have the faculty to ordain women.[755] If it were a question of holiness or understanding, no one would have been more suited for ordination than Mary. The ordination of women is not a matter of opinion. The fact that women cannot be ordained will not change regardless of our personal convictions. Like all matters referring to the deposit of faith, the reality remains such no matter what we may think based on our human experience.

Ordinatio sacerdotalis refers to the reality of the spousal relationship that is most obviously indicated by human bodies and, in turn, by their souls. This relationship is characterized as that of either the bridegroom or the bride. Despite whatever gifts a particular woman or man may have, she or he will always be a woman or a man and, as such, called to be either bride or groom. In essence, the apostolic letter is a call to reexamine *Inter insigniores* and a challenge to not confine the question of the vocation of women to the discussion of ordination. Woman will never be the bridegroom, in any form. The temptation to force upon woman a masculine paradigm arises from our confused notions of power and authority, which, in turn, devalue her vocation as bride, which is clearly illustrated by Mary, even if she has not been given serious consideration or she has been viewed obscurely. At the same time, the letter affirms what has always been the authentic tradition of the Church also reiterated by *Inter insigniores*, "The greatest in the kingdom of heaven are not the ministers but the saints" (no. 6).

Inter insigniores launches into the discussion of the ordination of women by first precluding any misconceptions regarding the Church's estimation of the dignity of women and the equality of the

---

[754] Cf. Jn 2,5, the wedding at Cana, "Do whatever he tells you."

[755] *Ordinatio sacerdotalis, n. 4*: "*Ut igitur omne dubium auferatur circa rem magni momenti, quae ad ipsam Ecclesiae divinam constitutionem pertinet, virtute ministerii Nostri confirmandi fratres (cf. Lc 22,32), declaramus Ecclesiam facultatem nullatenus habere ordinationem sacerdotalem mulieribus conferendi, hancque sententiam ab omnibus Ecclesia fidelibus esse definitive tenendam.*"

sexes.[756] At the same time the document is explicit in affirming the active role of women in society just as Paul VI commented at the close of Vatican II, "Women, the peace of the world depends upon you."

The notion of complementarity developed by the declaration might be further illumined by a consideration from Thomas Aquinas in the *Third Part of the Summa Teologiae,* question 27, article 5, ad 3, where Aquinas asks whether Mary, by virtue of her sanctification in the womb, received the fullness of grace:

> There is no doubt that the Blessed Virgin received in a high degree both the gift of wisdom and the grace of miracles and even of prophecy, just as Christ had them. But she did not so receive them, as to put them and such like graces to every use, as did Christ: but accordingly as it befitted her condition of life. For she had the use of wisdom in contemplation, according to Lk. 2:19: "But Mary kept all these words, pondering them in her heart." But she had not the use of wisdom as to teaching: since this befitted not the female sex, according to 1 Tim. 2:12: "But I suffer not a woman to teach." The use of miracles did not become her while she lived: because at that time the Teaching of Christ was to be confirmed by miracles, and therefore it was befitting that Christ alone, and His disciples who were the bearers of His doctrine, should work miracles. Hence of John the Baptist it is written (John 10:41) that he "did no sign"; that is, in order that all might fix their attention on Christ. As to the use of prophecy, it is clear that she had it, from the canticle spoken by her: "My soul doth magnify the Lord" (Lk. 1:46, etc.).[757]

Aquinas's insights can help greatly. First, he clearly explains that she had the gifts of wisdom, miracles, and prophecy as Christ had them. There can be no more emphatic statement of her dignity and capability. Despite the similarity of their gifts, she still had a different role from that of her son. While she had the same gifts, she did not use them as Christ did nor was she intended to do so. Perhaps Aquinas could have said more about what Mary did, especially regarding her maternal pedagogy, but he explicitly maintained that she was not lacking in capability. Again, Aquinas's description of Mary's perfect gifts reinforces the idea that priestly ordination does not depend on merit, but on something else.

Inter insigniores develops the notion of complementarity by referring to the Pauline letters. As the declaration explains, biblical exegetes put forth the differences in the two formulae used by Paul in his addresses. He uses two formulae: "my fellow workers" (Rom 16,3; Phil 4,2-3) and "God's fellow workers" (1 Cor 3,9; cf. 1 Thess 3,2). When he uses

---

[756] Cf. *Gaudium et spes,* 29.
[757] St. Thomas Aquinas, *Summa Theologica* Volume IV trans. Fathers of the English Dominican Province (Allen, TX: Christian Classics; reprint, 1981), pp. 2162-2163.

"my fellow workers", Paul addresses both the men and women helping him in God's work. Paul uses the phrase, "God's fellow workers" when referring to Apollos, Timothy, and himself because they are specifically apostolic ministers entrusted with the preaching of the Word in the specific manner of Christ. As ordained ministers they act on Christ's behalf and with his divine power.[758] The declaration also addresses the argument of fundamental equality: if men and women are fundamentally equal, should not they be able to receive the same sacrament of priestly ordination? Citing Galations 3,28: "There is neither Jew nor Greek, there is neither slave nor free person, there is not male and female; for you are all one in Christ Jesus." On face value, it appears that even sexual differentiation does not create such a significant difference that it would preclude women from receiving that which men may receive. In fact, the Pauline teaching confirms the fundamental equality, which is based on divine filiation, not on ministry. In other words, men and women are equal in so far as they are made in the image of God, which allows them to be able to share in divine filiation through the marvelous gift of sanctifying grace. Divine filiation is equally available to both sexes. The basis for this equality is not ministry. Ministry is something apart from the underlying shared equality.

The declaration then turns to the discussion of sacrament. This lays the basis for the affimation in *Ordinatio sacerdotalis* that the Church does not possess the faculty of ordaining women. While the sacrament has superhuman power, it is not without limits. The limits of the power are not the power itself which is divine omnipotence and, therefore, unlimited. Human nature, on the other hand, is limited in its capacity to receive. It isn't that God lacks the power to ordain women. Rather, human nature does not include this particular capacity to receive except among men. The declaration cites Pius XII's 1947 apostolic constitution *Sacramentum ordinis:* "The Church has no power over the substance of the sacraments, that is to say, over what Christ the Lord, as the sources of revelation bear witness, determined should be maintained in the sacramental sign."[759] The sacraments precisely represent actions and things. Priestly ordination represents the reality

---

[758] *Inter insigniores*, 3.
[759] *Inter insigniores*, 4. Cf. Martimort, A.G., "The Value of a Theological Formula '*In Persona Christi*'". Martimort citing Aquinas: "[T]he priest himself is and must be a sign, and

of the relationship of Christ to the Church. That relationship, no matter the moral character of the priest, is that of a bridegroom to a bride. Just as there can be bad husbands, there can be bad priests but they will still be priests. A woman, on the other hand, will never be a husband, good or otherwise. No matter her personal dispositions, tendencies or gifts, she is and represents a different spousal reality: bride. Similarly, although man may need to learn from woman what it is to be bride and part of the Church who is bride, no man will ever be a bride. In the end, respect for the sacrament is also respect for the reality signified and actualized by the sacrament. To ordain a woman would be in essence to show complete disregard for the reality she is as a woman, as a bride. In fact, contrary to the current commonplace attitude, to promote the ordination of women is a sign of misunderstanding and even disrespect for the dignity of woman. Upon reflection, Christian women might even feel offended by the proposal of women's ordination.

The reality signified by the sacrament of ordination is a reality tied to the supreme event of salvation history: the nuptial covenant and the nuptial mystery. The sexual differences reflect a greater difference than other differences that are only skin deep or due to social status, such as differences of race or social status. Cardinal Ratzinger explains that the concept of a sacrament is the symbolic representation, which makes and impregnates symbols with a concealed reality. Man and woman have a symbolic place in the Christian understanding of relation, each having equal rights and equal dignity. They differ in their testimony. Ratzinger identifies two challenges to the Church in promoting the equality of women and the understanding of the sacrament of ordination. He explains, "Though it may not seem so at first sight, it is a question here of woman's right to be herself, not in an equivocal equality which considers the sacrament as a career and so changes it into a dish of lentils which is not worth buying."[760]

---

therefore he must confirm the conditions required for that: *'cum sacramentum sit signum, in his quae in sacramento aguntur requiritur non solum res sed signum rei.'* [*In IV Sent.*, Dist. 25, q. 2, art. 2, quaestiuncula 1, corp.] The principal condition is that the sign should have a natural resemblance with what is signified: *'Signa sacramentalia ex naturali similitudine repraesentant.'* [Ibid., ad 4um]. These two principles are invoked by St. Thomas, as is known, to explain that women cannot receive holy orders."

[760]Ratzinger, Joseph, "The Male Priesthood: A Violation of Women's Rights?" *L'Osservatore Romano*, May 12, 1977, 6-7.

Inter insigniores provides a superb overview of the historical and theological aspects of the question at hand. The fact that Christ is a man is essential; it plays a distinct role in salvation history. The document puts forth:

> That is why we can never ignore the fact that Christ is a man. And therefore, unless one is to disregard the importance of this symbolism for the economy of revelation, it must be admitted that, in actions which demand the character of ordination and in which Christ himself, the author of the covenant, the bridegroom and the head of the Church, is represented, exercising his ministry of salvation — which is in the highest degree the case of the Eucharist — his role (this is the original sense of the word persona) must be taken by a man. This does not stem from any personal superiority of the latter in the order of values, but only from a difference of fact on the level of functions and service.[761]

From this discussion of symbolic reality follows the need to also consider the mystery of the Church. The priest symbolizes Christ. Woman, no matter who she is, is a bride and as such symbolizes the Church. The fact that we are at a point where the significance of feminine identity is so largely misunderstood or even disregarded, indicates that our very notion of Church is in peril. For many, the Church has ceased to signify bride and mother. For these people, she has, in a very real way, lost her personality. She has become an "it", a mere institution rather than a living being. It is no wonder then, that the authority of women is understood only in terms of the all-male priesthood. At the same time, women have also lost their place in the natural world as the family has gradually begun to disappear, particularly in much of the Western world. What a woman contributed as wife and mother has been underestimated because her contribution cannot be empirically measured in monetary quantities.[762] (Aside, when this has been measured for academic consideration, the results have shown that most could not afford salaried wives and mothers).

In fact, at the risk of sounding extreme, the discussion of women's ordination has been an "overestimation of the masculine", as if the feminine had no real value, as if the Church has no intrinsic

---

[761]*Inter insigniores*, 5.
[762]Cf. *Familiaris consortio*, n. 86: "The future of the family passes by way of the family."; *Mulieris dignitatem*, n. 29; Joyce Little, "Women Are Called to Bear Christ into Their Families and the World," *L'Osservatore Romano* 22:47, November 1995, 2-3;

288 CALLED TO HOLINESS AND COMMUNION

value. Instead of an atmosphere of complementarity, the masculine and the feminine have been pitted against each other.

Inter insigniores provided the historical and theological framework for addressing the question of whether women could be ordained. *Ordinatio sacerdotalis* was the definitive statement that the teaching that women cannot be ordained belongs to the deposit of the faith. Still, doubts remained for some and the Congregation for the Doctrine of Faith issued an affirmative reply to this "Dubium" on October 28, 1995.

After 1994, Pope John Paul II took the discussion in a different direction. He no longer discussed whether women could be ordained priests. While it may be difficult for some to accept, the question had been settled. John Paul II moved on. After 1994, rather than continuing to discuss whether or not women may be ordained, he dedicated all of his relevant magisterium to explaining why she cannot be ordained. In particular, he shifted the discussion to the unique role of Mary. After writing several excellent works on the dignity of women, the Pope perhaps made his most intriguing comment, even if rarely noticed, in the encyclical *Fides et ratio*, n. 108.[763] He concludes the encyclical with his customary invocation of Mary. In the invocation, however, he exalts Mary as the paradigm of all philosophers.[764]

After teaching the need to contemplate the face of Christ in *Novo Millennio ineunte* [2001], John Paul II provided a specific way to do so in *Rosarium Virginis Mariae* [2002].[765] Christ is the supreme teacher, and it is Mary who teaches him to us.[766] Her power lies in her intercession,

---

[763]Pia de Solenni, *"Fides et Ratio:* A Context for Developing the New Feminism", given at the Fellowship of Catholic Scholars' Annual Convention, 28 September 2002 and published in convention proceedings of 2004.

[764]*Fides et ratio*, n. 108: "I turn in the end to the woman whom the prayer of the Church invokes as *Seat of Wisdom*, and whose life itself is a true parable illuminating the reflection contained in these pages. For between the vocation of the Blessed Virgin and the vocation of true philosophy there is a deep harmony. Just as the Virgin was called to offer herself entirely as human being and as woman that God's Word might take flesh and come among us, so too philosophy is called to offer its rational and critical resources that theology, as the understanding of faith, may be fruitful and creative. And just as in giving her assent to Gabriel's word, Mary lost nothing of her true humanity and freedom, so too when philosophy heeds the summons of the Gospel's truth its autonomy is in no way impaired. Indeed, it is then that philosophy sees all its enquiries rise to their highest expression. This was a truth, which the holy monks of Christian antiquity understood well when they called Mary 'the table at which faith sits in thought'. In her they saw a lucid image of true philosophy and they were convinced of the need to *philosophari in Maria;"*cf. *Ecclesia de Eucaristia*, n. 7.

[765]*Rosarium Virginis Mariae*, n. 10-11.

[766]*Rosarium Virginis Mariae*, n. 14.

as demonstrated by the wedding at Cana.[767] The Pope clearly credits Mary with the miracle of Cana when he explains, "…Christ changes water into wine and opens the hearts of the disciples to faith, thanks to the intervention of Mary, the first among believers."[268] As John Paul II notes, "her presence remains in the background." There is nothing front and center about her. Still, her intercessory role is necessary according to the economy of grace:

> Yet the role she assumed at Cana in some way accompanies Christ throughout his ministry. The revelation made directly by the Father at the Baptism in the Jordan and echoed by John the Baptist is placed upon Mary's lips at Cana, and it becomes the great maternal counsel which Mary addresses to the Church of every age: "Do whatever he tells you" (Jn 2:5). This counsel is a fitting introduction to the words and signs of Christ's public ministry and it forms the Marian foundation of all the "mysteries of light".[769]

In his 2003 encyclical *Ecclesia de Eucharistia*, John Paul II looks to the School of Mary. Although there is no record that she was present at the Last Supper, she has a "profound relationship with the Eucharist….*Mary is a 'woman of the Eucharist' in her whole life.* The Church, which looks to Mary as a model, is also called to imitate her in her relationship with this most holy mystery."[770] The challenge, then, is to recover the sense of the relation between the feminine vocation and the priesthood. While not the same, they certainly are not at odds. *Ecclesia de Eucharistia* was given on April 17, 2003, which was also Holy Thursday. Given the unique correlation between the feminine vocation and the Church, the fact that an encyclical describing the central aspect of the Church was given on a day which celebrates the institution of the Mass and the priesthood indicates a tremendous union between the Church and the priesthood, between the feminine and the masculine.

Modern challenges to the feminine vocation include the loss of the sense of family, the loss of the sense of the Church as Mother, and confusion surrounding the concepts of maternity and paternity. No doubt, women need a voice in the Church, but it must be an authentic voice and not their voice made to sound like a man's. At the

---

[767] *Rosarium Virginis Mariae*, n. 16; Jn 2–3.
[768] *Rosarium Virginis Mariae*, n. 21.
[769] *Rosarium Virginis Mariae*, n. 21.
[770] *Ecclesia de Eucharistia*, n. 53. Cf. n. 55.

same time, it would be presumptuous to say that women do not have a voice. Although different, it already exists even if often unused.

In various writings and discourses, John Paul II outlined a unique feminine authority expressed in the person of Mary. More needs to be done to understand her and to understand the Church. As the papal preacher, Fr. Cantalamessa, explained in a Lenten retreat, "The Church is a mystery of maternity and Mary is her model."[771] Developing this insight will help us better understand the vocation and authority of woman, along with the vocation of man, and the specific male vocation of priesthood.

---

[771]April 11, 2003; Source - ZENIT News Service ZE03041111.

CHAPTER 13

THE SENSUS FIDELIUM
AND HUMANAE VITAE[772]

Dr. Janet E. Smith

FOR SOME THEOLOGIANS the fact that the vast majority of Catholics both approve of contraception and also practice contraception is powerful evidence that, by the criteria of the *sensus fidelium* [sense of the faithful], the Church's teaching against contraception may or must be wrong.[773] John E. Thiel argues that the principle of the *sensus fidelium* can be used to help discern which teachings of the magisterium are in what he calls a state of "dramatic development". A "dramatically developing doctrine" is one "that is developing in such a way that its

---

[772]In this essay I am going to prescind from the question whether the Church's teaching on contraception has been taught infallibly by virtue of the ordinary universal magisterium, which would render any consultation with the *sensus fidelium* moot. The literature on the subject is extensive; here let me note that the argument that the teaching of Humanae vitae is infallible can be found in John C. Ford, S. J., and Germain Grisez, Contraception and the Infallibility of the Ordinary Magisterium," *Theological Studies* 39:2 (June 1978). 258-312. For a response to this article, see Garth L. Hallett, S. J., "Contraception and Prescriptive Infallibility," *Theological Studies* 43:4 (December 1982), 629-650. See also, Ermenegildo Lio, *Humanae Vitae e Infallibilità* (Vatican: Libreria Editrice Vaticana, 1986). Monsignor Cormac Burke argues that the fact that the *sensus fidelium* "for centuries right up to the post-conciliar period" along with the teachings of the ordinary and universal Magisterium understood contraception to be wrong, is a sign of the infallibility of the teaching, *Authority in the Church*, (San Francisco: Ignatius Press, 1988) 172.

[773]An earlier exploration of this possibility can be found in Joseph Komonchak, *"Humanae vitae* and Its Reception: Ecclesiological Reflections," Theological Studies 39:2 (June 1978) 221-257. A recent statement of this position can be found in John E. Thiel, "Tradition and reasoning: a nonfoundationalist perspective" *Theological Studies* 56 (Dec. 1995) 627-51; see also, Philip S. Kaufman, *Why You Can Disagree and Remain a Faithful Catholic*, (New York; Crossroad, 1992) and Luke Timothy Johnson, "Sex, Women and the Church: The need for prophetic change," *Commonweal* (June 20, 2003), an excerpted version is available online at http://www.commonwealmagazine.org/2003/june202003/6202003ar.htm/ ; and his "Abortion, sexuality and Catholicism's public presence" online at http://www.catholicsinpublic-square.org/papers/fall2001commonweal/johnsonpaper/johnsonpaper.htm. For a review of various positions concerning the *sensus fidelium and Humanae Vitae* see D. Finucane, *Sensus Fidelium: The Use of a Concept in the Post-Vatican II Era* (San Francisco: International Scholars Publications, 1996) 379-401. I have defended the teaching numerous times, see particularly, *Humanae Vitae: A Generation Later* (Washington, D.C.: The Catholic University of America Press, 1991).

current authority as the authentic teaching of the magisterium will be lost at some moment later in the life of the Church, and that exhibits signs in the present moment that this final loss has begin to take place."[774] "Development" here does not mean discovering deeper and better understandings of a teaching or better justifications for a teaching, but means rejection of a teaching and replacement by another. Thiel states that, "Magisterial teaching that has not been received in belief and practice by a wide segment of the faithful, then, offers a more reliable, but still incomplete, criterion for judging when doctrine is currently in a state of dramatic development."[775]

To this criterion of "reception of the faithful" Thiel adds two further criteria for judging doctrines to be in a state of dramatic development: 1) when the magisterium is still in the process of providing theological argument for a teaching it signals that the teaching is not stable, and 2) when the theological argument does not prove convincing to a wide segment of Catholic theologians, the teaching is still developing. Thiel crystallizes these three criteria into one; a doctrine in the state of dramatic development (i.e., one that is likely to be proved as inauthentic in the future) is "magisterial teaching that one judges not to have been widely received by the faithful and that presents its teaching through theological argument that does not prove convincing to a wide segment of theologians."

Thiel uses the reception[776] of *Humanae vitae* as an example of a doctrine that is in a state of dramatic development. Although he is careful to state that he does not take polls as being the arbiter of who the faithful are who do or do not receive Church teaching, in fact his source for the claim that *Humanae vitae* has not been received by the faithful are polls that show that "a large percentage of Catholics do not practice the encyclical's proscription of artificial, preventive means of

---

[774] I am citing the online version of Thiel's article: http://www.womanpriest.org/traditio/thiel.htm.

[775] Thiel, "Tradition and Reasoning".

[776] The use of the term "reception" is variable in the theological literature. Thiel uses it here to refer to how the faithful have received a Church teaching. It also seems that "reception" can refer to the embracing in later magisterial documents of a teaching promulgated previously. See Francis A. Sullivan, S. J., *Creative Fidelity* (Eugene, Oregon: Wipf and Stock Publishers, 1996) 85-9. A classic treatment of the theory of reception is that by Yves Congar, "Reception as an Ecclesiological Reality," in *Election and Consensus in the Church*, ed. by Giuseppe Alberigo and Anton Weiler (New York: Herder and Herder, 1972), 43-68; he makes no mention of the faithful rejecting a moral teaching as an instance of "reception."

regulating births"[777] and his judgment that "few who practice 'artificial preventive means of birth control' would regard their actions as tragic."[778] He thus concludes that, "...*Humanae vitae's* prohibition of artificial, preventive means of birth control...has not found reception among a wide constituency of the faithful." He also finds abundance evidence that his other two criteria are met in respect to *Humanae vitae*.

Since my interest here is the sensus *fidelium*, I will respond in only the most cursory fashion to Thiel's claim concerning what we can conclude about the truth of *Humanae vitae* from the phenomena of magisterial theological argumentation in its favor and from the fact that many theologians do not find that argumentation persuasive. Let me briefly state that I believe the theological argument that is being provided for the teaching — and that argumentation is primarily Pope John Paul II's theology of the body, is, surprisingly, not defensive; that is, it seeks not so much to defend the teaching as to deepen our understanding why the teaching is true, so it does not appear to be the work of someone desperate to defend the indefensible. That theologians are not being convinced by the teaching is somewhat of a moot point since few of them have given due attention to John Paul II's theology of the body.[779]   Indeed, it is very difficult to locate scholarly critical

---

[777]Thiel cites a 1994 New York Times/CBS poll that found "that 98 [percent] of Catholics 19-29 years of age practice artificial birth control, 92 [percent] of those 30-44, 8 [percent] of those 45-64 and 72 [percent] of those 65 and older (The New York Times [1 June 1994]." "Tradition and Reasoning" footnote 8.**

[778]His use of the word "tragic" here is puzzling; one would expect to read "wrong" or "sinful".

[779]Typical is the essay by Christine E. Gudorf "Contraception and Abortion in Roman Catholicism" in *Sacred Rights*, ed. by Daniel C. Maguire (New York: Oxford University Press, 2003). The collection in which this article appears, edited by a Catholic theologian, purports to survey the views of major religions on the question of contraception. Gudorf's article reports on Roman Catholic teaching; she makes nary a mention of, let alone a response to, Pope John Paul II's views. Lisa Sowle Cahill in her *Sex, Gender and Christian Ethics* (Cambridge: Cambridge University Press, 1996) devotes a few pages to Pope John Paul II's defense of *Humanae vitae*. Her response is minimal; primarily she evaluates his view that each act of marital intercourse should be an act of "total self-giving" as being "a very romanticized depiction of sex." (203). It is telling that she lists no scholarly responses to the thought of John Paul II in her footnotes. The most extended response I have found is that by biblical scholar, Luke Timothy Johnson, "A Disembodied Theology of the Body: John Paul II on love, sex and pleasure," Commonweal, (Jan. 26, 2001) (online at: http://www.findarticles. com/cf_o/m1252/2_128/71578789/p1/article.jhtml). Surprisingly his critique is not directed towards John Paul II's use of scripture but towards his understanding of marital sexuality. For a response to Johnson, see Christopher West, "A Response to "A Disembodied Theology of the Body: John Paul II on love, sex and pleasure," online at: http://www.theologyofthe-body.net/articles/response_tlj.htm

[780]See my article, "The Stale and Stalled Debate on Contraception," in *Catholic World Report* (November 1993) 54-9. (available online at: http://www.aodonline.org/aodonline-sqlim-ages/SHMS/Faculty/SmithJanet/Publications/HumanaeVitae/StaleDebate.pdf).

responses to it.[780]   Furthermore, proportionalism, or revisionism, the moral theological system that has undergirded rejection of the Church's teaching on contraception, has arguably been rejected by the encyclical *Veritatis splendor*,[781] and thus the fact that proportionalists reject the teaching may have little force or relevance.

But I am not here to respond to the whole of Thiel's article;[782] rather I wish to examine at some length the view that the nearly universal practice of contraception by Catholics and their de facto widespread rejection of the teaching is a manifestation of the *sensus fidelium* and thus a criterion for judging the truth of the doctrine. The question I am addressing here is whether in our times the laity as a whole is the portion of the Church that is discerning correctly the movements of the Spirit in sexual matters or whether there is some subgroup of laity that more fully embraces and lives that faith that more rightly should be consulted. Certainly it would seem that the Church's teaching on marital sexuality is one of those areas where the *sensus fidelium* would count for a lot; and perhaps this is especially the case with regard to the Church's teaching on contraception since this is a matter about which Scripture does not speak explicitly.

This project requires us to establish what the *sensus fidelium* is; why it has any force in establishing Church teaching; what the limits of its authority are; what the *sensus fidei* [sense of the faith] is, and who the *fideles* or faithful are. We shall be looking at the work of John Henry Newman, whose thought has provided a touchstone for understanding the concept sensus *fidelium*. We shall supplement his understanding with citations from more recent magisterial documents, documents, as we shall see, which are in harmony with Newman's thought. We shall attempt to establish what role the *sensus fidelium* plays in the proper assessment of the status of the Church's condemnation of contraception. In the end, I am going to try to make the case that the *sensus fidei* [the sense of the faith], a term that will receive explication below, is to be found in that small group of Catholics who practice

[781]Aline H. Kalbian, "Where have all the Proportionalists Gone," *Journal of Religious Ethics* 30:1 (Spring 2002) 3-22 observes that since *Veritatis splendor* scholarly publication by proportionalists has been scarce.

[782]I believe the second half of his paper, arguing for "nonfoundationalism" is as problematic as his utilization of proportionalism; just as proportionalism has been repudiated in *Veritatis Splendor*, so has "nonfoundationalism" been repudiated by *Fides et Ratio*.

natural family planning when they need to limit their family size. I will not be arguing in a circular fashion, that is, that only those who accept the Church's teaching are proper judges of that teaching. Rather I shall be arguing that it is their faithfulness in other respects and their experience of "natural sex" (to be explained below) that are key elements in qualifying them as judges of the Church's teaching. That is, I shall be arguing that those who exhibit themselves to be faithful Catholics in respect to fundamental Church teachings (apart from the teachings on sexuality) and who have had some extended experience of what I identify as "natural sex" have the connatural sense both of the faith and of sex that enable them to be proper interpreters both of the faith and of sexual morality.

What is the sensus fidelium?

In an issue of the lay Catholic publication, the *Rambler*,[783] John Henry Newman defended the right of lay Catholics to criticize English bishops about the way they handled a practical matter. In doing so, he undertook to explain when and why it was appropriate for the laity to speak about Church matters:

> Acknowledging, then, most fully the prerogatives of the episcopate, we do unfeignedly believe, both from the reasonableness of the matter, and especially from the prudence, gentleness, and considerateness which belong to them personally, that their Lordships really desire to know the opinion of the laity on subjects in which the laity are especially concerned. If even in the preparation of a dogmatic definition the faithful are consulted, as lately in the instance of the Immaculate Conception, it is at least as natural to anticipate such an act of kind feeling and sympathy in great practical questions, out of the condescension which belongs to those who are *forma facti gregis ex animo*.[784] (*Rambler*, May 1959)[785]

Newman was referring here to the fact that Pius IX just five years earlier had taken into account the views of the laity in his decision to pronounce the dogma of the Immaculate Conception. He notes that if the Holy Father thought the opinion of the laity was

---

[783]I am following here the account of John Coulson in his introduction to John Henry Newman, *On Consulting the Faithful in Matters of Doctrine*, (Kansas City: Sheed and Ward, 1961). See also, Michael Sharkey, "Newman on the Laity," in the *Gregorianum* 68, 1-2 (1987) 339-346.
[784]Translation: "model for the flock".
[785]From the text available online at: http://www.newmanreader.org/works/rambler/contemporary5-59.html

worthy of consultation in reference to a point of dogma, it would be even more appropriate to consider their views in a matter of practical consideration.[786]

Due to a negative Episcopal response to his essay, in a subsequent issue of the *Rambler*, Newman provided an explanation of what he meant by consulting the faithful, in what has become known as his treatise: "On Consulting the Faithful in Matters of Doctrine."[787] Since the faithful had just been consulted in the establishment of the dogma of the Immaculate Conception, it might have been expected that Newman would have used that event as his illustrative example. But in his essay Newman chooses to use the role of the laity in the settling of the Arian heresy; he reports extensively on how in the fourth century the laity were responsible for the defeat of Arianism when nearly all high Churchmen had gone over to Arianism. He states that while he was "not denying that the great body of Bishops were in their internal belief orthodox; nor that there were numbers of clergy who stood by the laity and acted as their centres and guides," he was, however, boldly stating state that, "there was a temporary suspense of the functions of the '*Ecclesia docens*'.[788] The body of Bishops failed in their confession of the faith."[789] Newman seems to have three scenarios in mind where the *sensus fidelium*[790] would be useful:

1. in formulating an unformulated dogma; i.e., the Immaculate Conception;
2. in fighting heresy; i.e., in defense of the Nicene Creed against the Arians;
3. in determining the best policy for the Church to follow in Church/state affairs in respect to some concrete particular instance.

---

[786]Newman was referring to a controversy over how far the Church should cooperate with the state in matters of education

[787]Available online at: http://www.newmanreader.org/works/rambler/consulting.html ("Consulting")

[788]Translation: "teaching Church" or "magisterium."

[789]Newman, "Consulting."

[790]In Newman and elsewhere we also find the term *consensus fidelium* which seems generally to be used interchangeably with *sensus fidelium*. Edmund J. Dobbin, however, notes this difference "More strictly speaking, *sensus* [*fidelium*] refers to the active discerning, or capability of discerning, the content of faith, whereas consensus [fidelium] is the "consensual" result of that discerning." ("*Sensus Fidelium* Reconsidered," *New Theology Review* 2:3 (August 1989) 48–64). I am not so much concerned to distinguish these terms as to determine who are the faithful whose sense of the faith counts in judging the legitimacy of a doctrine or practice of the faith.

In these scenarios he does not include the case where the Church has constantly taught a doctrine and the faithful live in opposition to that doctrine.[791] At least from what he says about the *sensus fidelium*, it does not seem that he has in mind that the faithful might exercise a kind of "veto" over Church teaching manifested by nonadherence to the teaching. Benedict Ashley observes that historically Catholics have resisted many teachings of the Church: "There has often been a great deal of support for dueling and similar homicidal activities which the Church has condemned or at least sought to discourage. This is a good example of the fact that popular opinion, which approved such duels as noble and honorable, is of itself the *sensus fidelium* or the *vox Dei*, but requires to be instructed by the pastors of the Church witnessing authoritatively to the Gospel."[792]

Nor does Newman believe that the laity can always be trusted to discern what is compatible with the truth faith. Indeed he acknowledges that at various times, different elements of the Church will carry the burden of defending the faith:

> Then follows the question, Why? [Should the faithful be consulted] and the answer is plain, viz., because the body of the faithful is one of the witnesses to the fact of the tradition of revealed doctrine, and because their consensus through Christendom is the voice of the Infallible Church.
>
> I think I am right in saying that the tradition of the Apostles, committed to the whole Church in its various constituents and functions *per modum unius*,[793] manifests itself variously at various times: sometimes by the mouth of the episcopacy, sometimes by the doctors, sometimes by the people, sometimes by liturgies, rites, ceremonies, and customs, by events, disputes, movements, and all those other phenomena which are comprised under the name of history. It follows that none of these channels of tradition may be treated with disrespect; granting at the same time fully, that the gift of discerning, discriminating, defining, promulgating, and enforcing any portion of that tradition resides solely in the *Ecclesia docens*.[794]

Note that Newman recognizes that various parts of the Church are guardians of the faith at different times and also asserts that only the

---

[791]For a view of the *sensus fidelium* as a kind of veto over church teaching see, Daniel C. Maguire, "The Voice of the Faithful in a Clergy-dominated Church," in *Just Good Company*, a cyber journal online at: http://justgoodcompany.org/1.2/maguire.htm.
[792]Benedict M. Ashley, O.P., *Living the Truth in Love: A Biblical Introduction to Moral Theology*, (Alba House, 1996), 305.
[793]translation: "as one."
[794]"Consulting."

magisterium is ultimately charged with determining what is authentic Church teaching.

Although the *sensus fidelium* is just one source of truth, it can be a mark of the infallibility of a teaching, as Newman notes. This position is affirmed in Vatican II.[795] *Lumen gentium* speaks explicitly of the infallibility of the universal agreement of the faithful about some matter of faith or morals:

> The holy people of God shares also in Christ's prophetic office; it spreads abroad a living witness to Him, especially by means of a life of faith and charity and by offering to God a sacrifice of praise, the tribute of lips which give praise to His name (cf. Heb. 13:15). The entire body of the faithful, anointed as they are by the Holy One (cf. Jn 2:20, 27), cannot err in matters of belief. They manifest this special property by means of the whole peoples' supernatural discernment [*sensus fidei*] in matters of faith when "from the Bishops down to the last of the lay faithful" they show universal agreement [*universalem suum consensum*] in matters of faith and morals. That discernment in matters of faith [*sensu fidei*] is aroused and sustained by the Spirit of truth. It is exercised under the guidance of the sacred teaching authority, in faithful and respectful obedience to which the people of God accepts that which is not just the word of men but truly the word of God (cf. 1 Thes 2:13). Through it, the people of God adheres unwaveringly to the faith given once and for all to the saints, penetrates it more deeply with right thinking, and applies it more fully in its life. (*Lumen gentium,* 12; my emphasis)[796]

Note that the document does not speak of the *sensus fidelium* but of the *sensus fidei*. No definition of the term is given here but it is a phrase akin to John Henry Newman's *phronema* (to be discussed below); it is a kind of connatural instinct for discerning what is compatible with the revelation of the Gospel and what is not.[797]

---

[795]It is not a claim new to Vatican II; Francis A. Sullivan, S.J. cites passages from several revered theologians dating back to the second century who express this view, "The Sense of Faith: The Sense/Consensus of the Faithful," in *Authority in the Roman Catholic Church: Theory and Practice,* ed. Bernard Hoose (Aldeshot, UK & Burlington, Vermont: Ashgate Publishing, 2002): 85-93.

[796]"Constitution on the Church," *The Sixteen Documents of Vatican II,* intro by Douglas Bushman (Boston: Pauline Books and Media, 1999). The translation is that provided by the National Catholic Welfare Conference. Some find reference to the sensus fidei in *Dei Verbum:* "..Tradition, which comes from the apostles, develops in the Church with the help of the Holy Spirit. For there is a growth in the understanding of the realities and the words, which have been handed down. This happens through the contemplation and study made by believers, who treasure these things in their hearts (cf. Lk 2:10, 51) through a penetrating understanding [*intima intelligentia*] of the spiritual realities which they experience....(8)" from the Bushman edition of the documents of Vatican II.

[797]Here we are interested in the *sensus fidei* as empowered to judge doctrine but it should be noted that it has other powers as well. For instance, the Holy Father speaks of it as guid-

The clearest statement of what the *sensus fidei* is, is found in the *Gift of Authority,* a joint statement of the International Anglican-Roman Catholic Commission:

> In every Christian who is seeking to be faithful to Christ and is fully incorporated into the life of the Church, there is a *sensus fidei.* This *sensus fidei* may be described as an active capacity for spiritual discernment, an intuition that is formed by worshipping and living in communion as a faithful member of the Church. When this capacity is exercised in concert by the body of the faithful we may speak of the exercise of the *sensus fidelium* (cf. Authority in the Church: Elucidation, 3-4). The exercise of the *sensus fidei* by each member of the Church contributes to the formation of the *sensus fidelium* through which the Church as a whole remains faithful to Christ. By the *sensus fidelium,* the whole body contributes to, receives from and treasures the ministry of those within the community who exercise episcope, watching over the living memory of the Church (cf. *Authority in the Church* I, 5-6). In diverse ways the "Amen" of the individual believer is thus incorporated within the "Amen" of the whole Church.[798] (29)

The *sensus fidei* can be possessed by any member of the Church, laity, religious, and members of the hierarchy. When it guides the views of the faithful as a body what emerges is the sensus *fidelium.*[799]

Who are the *Fideles?*

Is being a baptized Catholic sufficient to qualify as one of the faithful who is to be consulted? Does one need to be a practicing Catholic? Does one need to believe the central dogmas of the Faith? Are there any other qualifying criteria?

---

ing the laity in "concrete choices" [See his Regina Coeli address of April 16, 1989; online at: http://www.vatican.va/liturgy_seasons/pentecost/documents/hf_jp-ii_reg_19890416_en.html]; the Catholic Catechism refers to the *sensus fidelium* as knowing "how to discern and welcome in [private] revelations whatever constitutes an authentic call of Christ or his saints to the Church. (67) (I am citing the online version: http://www.vatican.va/archive/catechism/p1s1c2a1.htm). The Holy Father speaks of the sensus fidei as being key in the process of inculturation, in determining what portions of a culture are compatible with the faith and which not (http://www.vatican.va/holy_father/john_paul_ii/speeches/1996/documents/hf_jp-ii_spe_18031994_address-to-pc-culture_en.html); the "Directory for the Application of the Principles and Norms of Ecumenism" speaks of the need to consult the *sensus fidei* (http://www.vatican.va/roman_curia/pontifical_councils/chrstuni/general-docs/rc_pc_chrstuni_doc_19930325_directory_en.htm)l

[798]available on line: http://www.vatican.va/roman_curia/pontifical_councils/chrstuni/documents/rc_pc_chrstuni_doc_12051999_gift-of-autority_en.html)

[799]Francis A. Sullivan discusses these terms and makes very much the same distinctions in his paper, "The Sense of Faith." See also Zoltán Alszeghy, S. J., "The *Sensus Fidei* and the Development of Dogma," in *Vatican II: Assessment and Perspectives: Twenty-Five Years After* (1962-1987) vol. 1, ed. by René Latourelle (New York: Paulist Press, 1988) 139-156.

> The more devout the faithful grew, the more devoted they showed themselves towards this mystery. And it is the devout who have the surest instinct in discerning the mysteries of which the Holy Spirit breathes the grace through the Church, and who, with as sure a tact, reject what is alien from her teaching. The common accord of the faithful has weight much as an argument even with the most learned divines. St. Augustine says, that amongst many things which most justly held him in the bosom of the Catholic Church, was the 'accord of populations and of nations.' In another work he says, 'It seems that I have believed nothing but the confirmed opinion and the exceedingly wide-spread report of populations and of nations.' Elsewhere he says: 'In matters whereupon the Scripture has not spoken clearly, the custom of the people of God, or the institutions of our predecessors, are to be held as law.[800]

Newman makes several remarks that shed some light on whom he would consider worthy to be counted among the faithful. In support of the practice of consulting the faithful, Newman cites a passage from a treatise by the Bishop of Birmingham written in support of the dogma of the Immaculate Conception:

Newman speaks here of "devout" Catholics and, as was noted earlier, he uses the conviction of the laity about the humanity of Christ during the Arian controversy to demonstrate the role that the fidelity of the laity can play in determining Church teaching. While Newman was adamant that the vast body of the laity opposed Arianism, he noted that the opposition was not unanimous: rather he acknowledged that "some portions of the laity were ignorant and other portions were at length corrupted by the Arian teachers," and that "there were exceptions to the Christian heroism of the laity, especially in some of the great towns."[801] Nonetheless "all or even the majority of the laity opposed Arianism."[JES1]

In speaking of what sort of laity Newman believes can be relied upon to preserve Church teaching in face of Protestantism, he states,

> What I desiderate in Catholics is the gift of bringing out what their religion is.... I want a laity, not arrogant, not rash in speech, not disputatious, but men who know their religion, who enter into it, who know just where they stand, who know what they hold, and what they do not, who know their creed so well, that they can give an account of it, who know so much of history that they can defend it. I want an intelligent, well-instructed laity; I am not denying you are such already: but I mean to be severe, and, as some would say,

---

[800]"Consulting."
[801]"Consulting."

exorbitant in my demands, I wish you to enlarge your knowledge, to cultivate your reason, to get an insight into the relation of truth to truth, to learn to view things as they are, to understand how faith and reason stand to each other, what are the bases and principles of Catholicism, and where lie the main inconsistencies and absurdities of the Protestant theory. I have no apprehension you will be the worse Catholics for familiarity with these subjects, provided you cherish a vivid sense of God above, and keep in mind that you have souls to be judged and to be saved. In all times the laity have been the measure of the Catholic spirit; they saved the Irish Church three centuries ago, and they betrayed the Church in England. Our rulers were true; our people were cowards. You ought to be able to bring out what you feel and what you mean, as well as to feel and mean it; to expose to the comprehension of others the fictions and fallacies of your opponents; and to explain the charges brought against the Church, to the satisfaction, not, indeed, of bigots, but of men of sense, of whatever cast of opinion.[802]

Here, Newman clearly states that the laity are not always reliable witnesses to the faith; he speaks of the time when they betrayed the Church in England and were cowards. In this passage, Newman identifies the faithful as those who know their faith; they are able to explain it and defend it and clearly also to believe it sincerely and live it.

What justifies consulting the faithful? What is the *sensus fidei*?

Newman says very little in the "On Consulting the Faithful" about why the laity have this gift of the *sensus fidei*, but what he does say is extremely helpful. He speaks of the *consensus fidelium* "as a sort of instinct, or *phronema*, deep in the bosom of the mystical body of Christ"[803] By way of explanation of *phronema*, he cites a passage from Father Perrone, the Jesuit theologian who promoted the role of the faithful in defining the Immaculate Conception:

The Spirit of God who directs and animates the Church, in becoming united to a human being, engenders a distinctively Christian sensitivity, which shows the way to all true doctrine. This common sensibility, this consciousness of the Church, is tradition in the subjective sense of that word. What, from that point of view, is tradition? It is the Christian mentality, existing in the Church and transmitted by the Church; a mentality, however, inseparable from the truths it contains, because it is formed out of and by those very truths.[804]

---

[802]J.H.Newman, *The Present Position of Catholics in England,* see online version: http://www.newmanreader.org/works/england/index.html

[803]"Consulting."

[804]Translation provided in an online version of the text, http://www.fordham.edu/halsall/mod/newman-faithful.html

This is all that Newman says about the *phronema* in "On Consulting the Faithful," but, as other scholars have observed, this *phronema* has "close affinity with his own teaching on the 'illative sense' involved in the assent of faith."[805] The word itself recalls what Aristotle and Aquinas spoke of as the virtue of prudence.[806] At this point I am going to let my deliberations be guided by the Aristotelian/Thomistic understanding.

Prudence is that virtue or *habitus* possessed by the person who has authentic and reliable knowledge of the reality to which some moral precept applies, as well as, of course, an understanding and acceptance of the precept as well. The understanding of the precept is not the understanding of the philosopher or the expert; it is the understanding that can be described as the acceptance of the truth of the precept as corresponding to the truth of reality. Aquinas's concept of connaturality is applicable here;[807] as an analogy we might speak of the horse trainer who knows horses so well that he can judge quickly when a horse is ill or out of sorts and knows how to remedy its condition; or the connoisseur of wine who can identify to what region and year a wine belongs. These individuals know a great deal about horses and wines generally and also of horses and wines in particular. The person who possesses prudence is one who has lived a virtuous life and has extensive knowledge of the realm of life in which he must make his moral judgment. The faithful spouse needs not only to know that adultery is wrong, but must know what presents a temptation to infidelity for him or herself, and also have the virtues to avoid or extricate one's self from such situations.

Connaturality is also reliable in matters of faith, but requires knowledge both of general principles and experience of relevant lived realities. That the bishops consulted the faithful about Mary's Immaculate Conception makes sense only if they believed that the faithful had an intimate knowledge of Mary acquired, one supposes, through having acquired a knowledge of Mary's role in salvation, mostly likely through instruction and through prayerful practice of Marian devotions.

[805]Dobbin, "*Sensus fidelium* Reconsidered, 56
[806]Dobbin, 57.
[807]Francis A. Sullivan also understands the *sensus fidei* to be equivalent to Aquinas' connaturality, "The Sense of Faith", p. 86.

The *sensus fidei* depends upon phronema, upon knowledge both of general principles and lived realities. So the question is, how do we know who possesses *phronema*? Who are the Catholic faithful who possess the sensus fidei in respect to sexuality?[808] Again, is being a baptized Catholic sufficient to qualify as one of the faithful who is to be consulted? Does one need to be a practicing Catholic? Does one need to believe the central dogmas of the Faith? As noted above, when the Church refers to "universal" agreement she does not mean unanimity of all believers. So, if we are to consult some subgroup, which subgroup of those who call themselves Catholic? What experience or knowledge of sex must be had by those who are to be consulted about matters of sexuality?

Donum veritatis (1990), the *Instruction on the Ecclesial Vocation of the Theologian,* addresses directly the question of the status of the opinion of the laity as manifestation of the sensus fidelium. It is worthy of being cited at some length:

> Dissent sometimes also appeals to a kind of sociological argumentation, which holds that the opinion of a large number of Christians would be a direct and adequate expression of the "supernatural sense of the faith".
>
> Actually, the opinions of the faithful cannot be purely and simply identified with the *"sensus fidei"*. The sense of the faith is a property of theological faith; and, as God's gift which enables one to adhere personally to the Truth, it cannot err. This personal faith is also the faith of the Church since God has given guardianship of the Word to the Church. Consequently, what the believer believes is what the Church believes. The *"sensus fidei"* implies then by its nature a profound agreement of spirit and heart with the Church, *"sentire cum Ecclesia"*.
>
> Although theological faith as such then cannot err, the believer can still have erroneous opinions since all his thoughts do not spring from faith. Not all the ideas which circulate among the People of God are compatible with the faith. This is all the more so given that people can be swayed by a public opinion influenced by modern communications media. Not without reason did the Second Vatican Council emphasize the indissoluble bond between the *"sensus fidei"* and the guidance of God's People by the magisterium of the Pastors. These two realities cannot be separated. Magisterial interventions

---

[808]Newman seemed to vacillate in sometimes equating the "faithful" with the laity and sometimes including priests among the faithful; in one passage he distinguished the "faithful" from priests and the episcopacy: "I mean...the 'faithful' do not include the 'pastors'" (Coulson, 65) in another he includes priests among the laity: "And again, in speaking of the laity, I speak inclusively of their parish-priests (so to call them), at least in many places" (Coulson, 110).

serve to guarantee the Church's unity in the truth of the Lord. They aid her to "abide in the truth" in face of the arbitrary character of changeable opinions and are an expression of obedience to the Word of God. Even when it might seem that they limit the freedom of theologians, these actions, by their fidelity to the faith which has been handed on, establish a deeper freedom, which can only come from unity in truth (no. 35).[809]

Several important points are made here: 1) the opinions of the Catholic community are not equivalent to the *sensus fidelium:* 2) it is only those who *sentire cum Ecclesia* (see below for an explanation of this term) that have the sensus *fidei;*[810] 3) the faithful can easily be swayed by trends of the time, which implicitly means that only those laity who understand what the Church teaches are reliable interpreters of the faith.

The phrase *"sentire cum Ecclesia"* illuminates what we are looking for. It would be wrong, I think, to understand *"sentire cum Ecclesia"* to mean "agree with the Church;" that would make an appeal to a *sensus fidei* circular — those who are to be consulted about Church teaching are those who accept Church teaching. Rather I believe *sentire cum Ecclesia* means something like "to think as the Church does," or that is, that the thoughts of such a thinker flow from the same source as the teachings — they flow from an acceptance of Christ and his teachings and from the guidance of the Holy Spirit. Such individuals need not be highly educated, to be sure, but would need to be in love with Christ and His Church, devoted to receiving the sacraments and other pious practices and to being instructed in the teachings of the Church.

The need for a laity that knows the faith is stated in many documents of John Paul II's pontificate. Early in his tenure as pope, John Paul II made this statement to the bishops of India upon their *ad limina* visit:

> In the community of the faithful — which must always maintain
> Catholic unity with the Bishops and the Apostolic See — there are

---

[809]See online version: http://www.vatican.va/roman_curia/congregations/cfaith/documents/rc_con_cfaith_doc_19900524_theologian-vocation_en.html

[810]Ormond Rush in his *"Sensus Fidei:* Faith 'Making Sense" of Revelation" *Theological Studies* 62 (2001) 231-261 extensively considers the *sensus fidei* as the possession of an individual believer : he states, "There is perhaps no more succinct definition of sensus fidei that this: *sensus fidei* is faith seeking understanding, interpretation, and application." I believe his definition does not exactly correspond to the sense it manifests in Church documents for he focuses largely on how the *sensus fidei* helps the individual believer understand the faith and apply it to his life rather than to the sensus fidei as a means of discerning what is compatible with the faith on a doctrinal level.

great insights of faith. The Holy Spirit is active in enlightening the minds of the faithful with his truth, and in inflaming their hearts with his love. But these insights of faith and this *sensus fidelium* are not independent of the magisterium of the Church, which is an instrument of the same Holy Spirit and is assisted by him. It is only when the faithful have been nourished by the word of God, faithfully transmitted in its purity and integrity, that their own charisms are fully operative and fruitful. Once the word of God is faithfully proclaimed to the community and is accepted it brings forth fruits of justice and holiness of life in abundance. But the dynamism of the community in understanding and living the word of God depends on its receiving intact the *depositum fidei;* and for this precise purpose a special apostolic and pastoral charism has been given to the Church. It is one and the same Spirit of truth who directs the hearts of the faithful and who guarantees the magisterium of the pastors of the flock. (my emphasis)[811]

Clearly the faithful are those whose faith has been nurtured, who have been taught the faith in its purity and integrity and who practice that faith. These are the ones who qualify as the faithful who possess the *sensus fidei.*

The above passage asserts that the opinions of the Catholic community are not equivalent to the *sensus fidei.* We find similar statements elsewhere. One of the clearest statements about the nature of and limits of the *sensus fidelium* appears in John Paul II's *Familiaris consortio* [1981] certainly directed towards the question of contraception. First the Holy Father acknowledges that the laity has a special power of discernment concerning "temporal reality" and then goes on to speak of those who are married as having a special charism concerning marriage:

This discernment is accomplished through the sense of faith, which is a gift that the Spirit gives to all the faithful, and is therefore the work of the whole Church according to the diversity of the various gifts and charisms that, together with and according to the responsibility proper to each one, work together for a more profound understanding and activation of the word of God. The Church, therefore, does not accomplish this discernment only through the Pastors, who teach in the name and with the power of Christ but also through the laity: Christ "made them His witnesses and gave them understanding of the faith and the grace of speech (cf. Acts

---

[811]May 1979; online version: http://www.vatican.va/holy_father/john_paul_ii/speeches/1979/may/documents/hf_jp-ii_spe_19790531_ad-limina-india_en.html; the Holy Father reiterated this claim a year later in his address to the bishops of Liverpool: http://www.vatican.va/holy_father/john_paul_ii/speeches/1980/may/documents/hf_jp-ii_spe_19800502_pastorale-liverpool_en.html

2:17-18; Rv. 19:10), so that the power of the Gospel might shine forth
in their daily social and family life." The laity, moreover, by reason
of their particular vocation have the specific role of interpreting the
history of the world in the light of Christ, in as much as they are
called to illuminate and organize temporal realities according to the
plan of God, Creator and Redeemer (no. 5).

And further:

> Christian spouses and parents can and should offer their
> unique and irreplaceable contribution to the elaboration
> of an authentic evangelical discernment in the various
> situations and cultures in which men and women live their
> marriage and their family life. They are qualified for this role
> by their charism or specific gift, the gift of the sacrament of
> matrimony.[812]

Yet, being married in itself is not sufficient to make spouses reliable
interpreters of the faith. *Familiaris consortio* responds to those who
argue that majority opinion constitutes the *sensus fidei*:

> The "supernatural sense of faith" however does not consist solely
> or necessarily in the consensus of the faithful. Following Christ,
> the Church seeks the truth, which is not always the same as the
> majority opinion. She listens to conscience and not to power, and
> in this way she defends the poor and the downtrodden. The Church
> values sociological and statistical research, when it proves helpful in
> understanding the historical context in which pastoral action has
> to be developed and when it leads to a better understanding of the
> truth. Such research alone, however, is not to be considered in itself
> an expression of the sense of faith.
>
> Because it is the task of the apostolic ministry to ensure that
> the Church remains in the truth of Christ and to lead her ever more
> deeply into that truth, the Pastors must promote the sense of the faith
> in all the faithful, examine and authoritatively judge the genuineness
> of its expressions, and educate the faithful in an ever more mature
> evangelical discernment (no. 5).

Clearly, *Familiaris consortio* holds that only the educated laity are
reliable interpreters of the faith.

In articles that deal with the *sensus fidelium*, the claim is routinely
made that a simple poll of Catholics would not serve to determine
what the *sensus fidelium* is about a given issue.[813]   After all, many

---

[812]John Paul II, *Familiaris consortio*, 5; I am citing from the online version: *http://www.
vatican.va/holy_father/john_paul_ii/apost_exhortations/documents/hf_jp-ii_exh_19811122_fa-
miliaris-consortio_en.html*

[813]Thiel, for instance, states: "Sociological findings may be helpful in locating teaching not
received by the faithful, but polling results alone cannot establish the extent of doctrinal
reception. In addition, there remains the theological issue of how one understands *Lumen*

claim to be Catholics who have not attended Church in years, who attend sporadically, or who believe very few of the key dogmas of the faith; witness such organizations as Catholic for Free Choice.   One reliable study gives this picture of the beliefs of Catholics; those polled were parishioners in Indiana and nationwide Catholics (numbers are percentages):[814]

	Pre-Vatican II (born 1940 or earlier)	Vatican (born 1941-1960	Post Vatican (1961-76)
The Catholic Church is the one true church. Strongly agree	58	34	30
It is important to obey Church teachings even when one doesn't understand them. Strongly agree.	38	24	11
One can be a good Catholic without going to Mass. Strongly agree.	26	32	45
Artificial birth control is "always wrong."	20	6	4
Premarital sex is "always wrong."	55	26	20

If the beliefs of parishioners constituted the *sensus fidelium* and thus are infallible, clearly much Church teaching would need to

Gentium's reference to 'the whole body of the faithful' in which infallibility resides. Does this phrase refer to the baptized, to practitioners of the faith, or more self-referentially to those who do indeed possess the unerring sense of the faith, however difficult it may be to determine its character or their number?" ("Tradition and Reasoning").   But see Philip S. Kaufman, *Why You Can Disagree and Remain a Faithful Catholic*, (New York; CrossRoad, 1992) who asks, "In our day, cannot carefully taken and carefully evaluated sociological surveys be a tool for determining that 'mind of the faithful'? (p.79).

[814] I have reproduced with some slight modifications for clarity the chart found in Dean R. Hoge, et al., *Young Adult Catholics: Religion in the Culture of Choice* (Notre Dame, IN: University of Notre Dame Press, 2001) p. 35; he is reporting on a study done by James D. Davidson, *The Search for Common Ground: What Unites and Divides Catholic Americans*, (Huntington, IN., Our Sunday Visitor, 1997) and Andrea Williamson and James D. Davidson, "Catholic Conceptions of Faith: A Generational Analysis," *Sociology of Religion* 57:3 (Fall 1996) 273-90.

change. The fact that those who are in the younger age groups are less likely to accept Church teaching across the board may be due to weak catechesis and failure to practice the faith and to the influence of the surrounding culture rather than inner sense of the faith.

If all those who identify themselves as Catholics or even all those who belong to parishes do not qualify as *fideles* possessing the *sensus fidei*, who does? I have found no proposed set of standards that might be used to discern who qualifies as the *fideles* who are to be consulted, as those who *sentire cum Ecclesia*.[815] Let me tentatively offer a few criteria that perhaps should be on any list by which we might discern who are those who *sentire cum Ecclesia:*

1) those who think missing mass on Sunday and Holy Days would be a serious sin;[816]
2) those who believe in the real presence of Christ in the Eucharist and who believe all the claims of the Creed;
3) those who know the basic duties of their faith (such as yearly reception of the sacrament of reconciliation if in a state of mortal sin);
4) those who support the work of the Church in some way such as through financial contributions and/or apostolic work,
5) those who practice some form of regular devotion, such as daily scripture reading, daily rosary or mass;

Let me for the moment call the individuals described above, those who sentire cum Ecclesia, the "SCEs"; since they *orare et vivere cum Ecclesia,* that is, they pray and live with the Church, it seems right to infer that they therefore *sentire cum Ecclesia.*

To be a SCE would be essential to being counted among the faithful to be consulted concerning the *sensus fidelium.* But as noted above, not only must one be a prayerful, practicing Catholic, one must

---

[815] Thomas Dubay, S. M., "The State of Moral Theology: A critical Appraisal," in *Readings in Moral Theology,* No. 3, ed. Charles E. Curran and Richard A. McCormick, S. J., (New York: Paulist Press, 1982), 332-63, gives a fairly vague set of criteria: "I would presume that both theology and common sense would reply [to the question who the faithful are] that "the faithful" are precisely that, namely, faithful. They are, it seems to me, those who accept the whole Gospel, who are willing to carry the cross every day, who lead a serious prayer life, who accept the teaching magisterium commissioned by Christ. We could hardly call faithful those who reject knowingly anything Jesus has taught or established." (353)

[816] For a survey of the views of "self-described" Catholics see Hoge, 208; 77% are you can "be a good Catholic without going to Church every Sunday;" 72 without accepting the teaching on birth control; 68% without obeying the hierarchy's teaching regarding divorce and remarriage; 53% without obeying its teaching on abortion. Only 8% of 20-39 years olds go to mass weekly and are active in the parish and another 42% attend two or three times a month but are not involved in a parish (71). See also, Kenneth C. Jones, *Index of Leading Catholic Indicators: The Church Since Vatican II* (St. Louis: Oriens Publishing Company, 2003).

also have some knowledge or experience of the reality which one is judging; that is, those who are to judge the truth of claims about Mary must be a practitioner of Marian devotions; one must possess *phronema* or connaturality about Mary. Possessing *phronema* about sex may be difficult in a culture where having multiple sexual partners before marriage is the norm, where divorce is widely practiced, for instance, practices at odds with what the Church teaches that natural law teaches about sexually. The *fideles* need to have had some knowledge or experience of authentic sexuality, i.e., a sexuality in keeping with natural law.

Knowledge of Natural Sex

Many propose that the Church's teachings on sexuality are suspect because they have been articulated largely by those who are celibates and who have not lived active sexual lives. It certainly is possible to challenge that claim since most of the most active advocates of the Church's teaching and the promoters of methods of natural family planning are married laypeople. Those who make this objection seem oblivious to the fact that many of those who defend the Church's teaching and who run the organizations that promote natural family planning are married.[817]   Is it true that only those who are married can pronounce upon the compatibility of contraception with the vocation of marriage? What kind of experience qualifies one to speak to any issue? Does one have to have been raped to understand that rape is wrong? To have been robbed to know that theft is wrong? The experience or knowledge required for *phronema* can be of different kinds. Indeed simply having direct experience of a reality is not sufficient to give one *phronema,* and lack of direct experience does not prohibit a kind of *phronema.* That is, those who have not been to war, may know a great deal about war because of what they have heard or read about war; because of their power of imagination; because of what they know about human nature. Some spouses who have been abused within marriage may know little about the realities of an authentic marriage. Those who have lived in a culture where severe injustice is

---

[817]Consider for instance the work of Dr. John and Lynn Billings, John and Sheila Kippley, Mercedes Wilson, William May, Germain Grisez, John Finnis, Joseph Boyle, Christopher West.

practiced may not have an accurate understanding of justice. What is necessary for *phronema* — of whatever kind or degree and however acquired — is that one's "experience" or "knowledge" of a reality must correspond to the truth of the relevant reality.

So who in the Catholic community are qualified to judge whether some teaching of the Church on sexual morality is in accord with the values of the Gospel? I have suggested above that it is not necessarily the case that individuals need to have direct lived experience of a reality in order to judge it accurately; that is, one need not have fornicated or committed adultery to know that these actions are immoral; thus one need not have had an experience of contracepted sex to be able to judge its morality or consistency with the values of the gospel.

Yet the fact is that most Catholics have experienced or at least been exposed to a wide variety of sex. In fact, presently it is somewhat difficult to find Catholics in their fertile years who have not had sex outside of marriage or who have had an extended experience of noncontracepted sex. Even many (likely most) of those who use natural family planning had premarital sex and contracepted.[818] It is important to keep in mind that most of those who use natural family planning have at one time contracepted but most of those who contracept have little experience of noncontracepted sex,[819] both their sex before marriage and their sex after marriage is dominated by the use of contraception or ultimately by sterilization.

Here I want to suggest that most sexually active Catholics presently do not have the kind of experience that would give them the *phronema* necessary to make them good judges of the Church's teaching on contraception. Certainly it is true that few have read, been taught, studied, or prayed about the Church's teaching on contraception.[820] It

[818]Mercedes Arzú Wilson, "The Practice of Natural Family Planning versus the Use of Artificial Birth Control: Family, Sexual and Moral Issues," *The Catholic Social Science Review* 7 (2002) 185-2111; available online; see the chart on p. 196. Another report of the study analyzed by the previous article is Andrew C. Pollard and Mercedes Arzú Wilson, "Correlates of Marital Satisfaction in a Sample of NFP Women," in *Integrating Faith and Science Through Natural Family Planning,* ed. by Richard J. Fehring and Theresa Notare, (Milwaukee, WI: Marquette University Press: 2004): 139-65
[819]Ibid.
[820]Avery Dulles, S.J., in his *"Humanae Vitae and Ordinatio Sacerdotalis:* Problems of Reception" in *Church Authority in American Culture: The Second Cardinal Bernardin Conference,* intro. by Philip J. Murnion (New York: Crossroad, 1999) observes, "...it is not surprising that the teaching on contraception and women's ordination is not universally welcomed. On the grassroots level it is not so much a question of dissent as of ignorance. To accept church

is well known that theologians largely rejected *Humanae vitae* and quite immediately upon its promulgation instructed the laity that they were free to reject its teaching.[821] Since few priests at the time[822] and perhaps even now accept the teaching, it can reasonably be assumed that it has rarely been taught in any fashion in the parishes or schools. Indeed, the bishops of the Philippines have acknowledged that they failed in their duty to teach the Church's teaching about contraception:

> It is said that when seeking ways of regulating births, only 5% of you consult God. In the face of this unfortunate fact, we your pastors have been remiss: how few are there among you whom we have reached. There have been some couples eager to share their expertise and values on birth regulation with others. They did not receive adequate support from their priests. We did not give them due attention, believing then this ministry consisted merely of imparting a technique best left to married couples.

> Only recently have we discovered how deep your yearning is for God to be present in your married lives. But we did not know then how to help you discover God's presence and activity in your mission of Christian parenting. Afflicted with doubts about alternatives to contraceptive technology, we abandoned you to your confused and lonely consciences with a lame excuse: "follow what your conscience tells you." How little we realized that it was our consciences that needed to be formed first. A greater concern would have led us to discover that religious hunger in you.[823]

In spite of the lack of instruction, perhaps most Catholics would know THAT the Church has taught that contraception is wrong but many would be confused about whether or not the Church

---

teaching one has to be exposed to credible presentations of it. Catholics who hardly know the doctrines of their church except through the fragmentary and often biased reporting of the secular media can scarcely be expected to assent in difficult cases."

[821]Karl Rahner, S.J. lent his considerable theological stature to this effort quite immediately upon the promulgation of Humanae vitae; see "On the Encyclical 'Humanae Vitae," in *Theological Investigations XI*, trans. David Bourke (New York: The Seabury Press, 1974): 263-87; originally in *Stimmen der Zeit* 182 (1968): 193-210; John Giles Milhaven announced *Humanae vitae* to be a dead letter in 1969 in "The Grounds of the Opposition to 'Humanae Vitae'," Thought 44 (1969) 343-57. For a collection of essays by prominent theologians justifying dissent, see *Contraception: Authority and Dissent*, ed. Charles E. Curran, (New York: Herder and Herder, 1969). For a concise history of the dissent against *Humanae Vitae*, see Megan Hartman, "*Humanae Vitae*: Thirty Years of Discord and Dissent,' online at http://www. catholicsforchoice.org/contraception/thirty.htm.

[822]Komonchak, "*Humanae vitae* and Its Reception:," p. 221 cites a study by Andrew M. Greeley that stated that only 29% of the "lower clergy" accepted the teaching; see Andrew M. Greeley, *Catholic Schools in a Declining Church* (Kansas City: Sheed and Ward, 1976), 153.

[823]From *Love is Life* by the Catholic Bishops' Conference of the Philippines issued Oct. 7, 1990 from section A; my source is the "Birth Control: What's Behind the Population Program" v. III, no. 12 published by the Documentation Service, p.7: Theological Centrum; 6th Floor, Quad Alpha Centrum Building, 125 Pioneer Street, Mandaluyoung, 1501 Manila Philippines.

still teaches that and how free they are to abide by the teaching or not. Few would be able to identify the reasons why it teaches that contraception is intrinsically evil.

But I not only want to say that most Catholics do not have sufficient understanding of the teaching to be able to have opinions about it that must be given much weight. Rather I want to make a bolder assertion. It is perhaps ironic that in an age where most people start acquiring sexual experience when they are young and when most experience a wide exposure to a variety of sexual activities through the entertainment world, not to mention through use of pornography, the pool of those who have an experience of what might be called natural sex may be dangerously small. It is plausible that very few Catholics have an experience of the true realities of sex. Yes, they have had lots of sex but few have had much if any experience of what the Church would call natural or real sex. Natural sex is sex that is meant to be an expression of committed love; it is sex within marriage and sex that is open to children — not just sporadically in a quasi-utilitarian way — but in a way in which children are seen to be the natural and good outcome of sexual intercourse and in which they would be understood as completing the marital commitment. I think it is arguable that perhaps even most people today do not first and foremost think of sexual intercourse as properly an expression of love. They began their sexual involvement quite young and frequently motivated more by curiosity and a desire for pleasure than motivated by the dynamics of love and affection. Likely most of the sexual relationships they had before marriage were initiated long before they could claim to have feelings of love for their sexual partner. Sex is largely seen as an act performed for the purposes of pleasure between individuals who experience an attraction for each other, or sometimes, between individuals who simply are available for sexual intercourse.[824] Such individuals often are nearly incapable of understanding what is meant by sex as an expression of love; they no more can appreciate such a reality than those who have only read comic books can inderstand what people are talking about when they speak of great literature, or

---

[824]It is, perhaps, unnecessary to support this claim, but a good place to start might be the article Benoit Denizet-Lewis, "Friends, Friends with Benefits, and the Benefits of the Local Mall," *New York Times Magazine* (May 30, 2004)

than those who have only drunk cheap wine can understand what those who have tasted the finest wines can be raving about.

Most Catholics have multiple sexual partners before marriage; they contracept before marriage and they contracept after marriage. They stop contracepting in order to conceive a child or two, and then many of them get sterilized.[825] The sexual beliefs and lives of most modern Catholics have been shaped much more by the culture in which they live rather than by their Church. They have never had a prolonged experience of a sexual relationship based on the understanding that sexual intercourse is only moral and good between those who have a lifetime commitment to each other based on love and who would welcome children as a natural result of the sexual act — something for which they should be prepared and which they should welcome.

Of course the question must be asked why Catholics rushed to use contraception in the first place. Certainly at one time, if only because contraception was not available, most Catholics did not contracept. Why did they embrace contraception? Part of the explanation would be that contraception was promoted as a kind of miracle solution to marital tensions; couples could now have spontaneous sexual relationships without the possibility of a pregnancy. Predictions were that marriages would be much happier once the fear of an unwanted pregnancy was removed from sexual intercourse. It was supposed that women would be happier in that they could pursue careers since they would not be so burdened by childcare. Families would also be happier because of the extra income.[826] The prospect of being able to have sex prior to marriage was seen (and still is largely seen) as a means of ensuring longer lasting marriages since the partners could discern their compatibility before marriage.[827] With such expectations, it is perhaps not surprising that so many turned to contraception. The fact that the doubling of the divorce rate coincided with the widespread use

---

[825] For a report on how many Catholics use contraception and NFP see http://www.ccli.org/articles/howmany.shtml and for data on the rate of sterilization see http://www.usccb.org/prolife/issues/nfp/cmrwin99.htm and http://www.cdc.gov/reproductivehealth/up_2320.htm

[826] For illuminating testimonies of couples who mostly abided by the Church's teaching on contraception before *Humanae vitae,* but who supported a change in Church teaching, see Michael Novak's *The Experience of Marriage* (New York: Macmillan Co., 1964).

[827] The greater frequency of divorce among those who cohabit is well documented. See for instance; http://www.cdc.gov/nchs/releases/02news/div_mar_cohab.htm and http://members.aol.com/cohabiting/

of contraception suggests that those promises may have been false.[828] Here is not the place to do a full consideration of the possible causes of the great increase in divorce but certainly the widespread use of contraception should not be ruled out (more about this below).

The willingness of Catholic couples to embrace contraception can be likened to the eagerness with which women were prepared to forgo breast-feeding and embrace bottle-feeding. Bottlle-feeding was promoted as healthy and efficient and sophisticated. And for a period of time bottle-feeding was more popular than breast-feeding,[829] but there has been a gradual return to breast-feeding as the health and psychological benefits have become more apparent.[830]

Although Catholics may have embraced contraception because it promised happier marriages, wouldn't we expect that those who had experienced natural sex prior to the use of contraception to have eventually noticed a diminution in the quality of their sexual experience once they began using contraception? Possibly they did, but failed to attribute it to contraception. I know of no studies that examine comparative satisfaction of sexual intercourse for those who have not contracepted for a period of time and then chose to practice contraception. On the other hand, we do have at least some information about the satisfaction of those who at one time contracepted and then adopted natural family planning,[831] and it overwhelmingly suggests that sexual satisfaction increased with the cessation of contraception and use of natural family planning.

We should also be open to the possibility that not all non-contracepted sex — even between the married — fully incorporates all

---

[828]For documentation on the connection between use of contraception and divorce, see Robert Michael "The Rise in Divorce in Divorce Rates, 1960-1974: Age Specific Components." *Demography* 15:2 (May 1978) 177-82; "Determinants of Divorce". In *Sociological Economics,* edited by Louis Levy-Garboua (London: SAGE Publications, 1979) 223-54.; "Why Did the U.S. .Divorce Rate Double Within a Decade?" *In Research in Population* (Greenwich: JAI Press, 1988) 361-99.

[829]For a history of the practice of breastfeeding, see Nancy E. Wright, "A Look at Breastfeeding: Past, Present and Future" http://www.breastfeeding.org/articles/alookat.html

[830]Among the benefits to breastfeeding are included, increased intelligence of the baby, increased protection from various diseases, decreased propensity to obesity, easier weight loss for mothers, decreased incidence of breast cancer: see http://www.babycenter.com/refcap/baby/babybreastfeed/8910.html

[831]Those who find personal testimonies to be a source of evidence and insight will find of interest: John Long, ed., *Sterilization Reversals: A Generous Act of Love* (Dayton, Ohio: One More Soul, 2001) and S. Joseph Tham, M.D., *The Missing Cornerstone* (Hamden: Circle Press, 2003).

the values of "natural sex." The Church understands sexual intercourse rightly experienced to be the expression of a committed lifetime union based on love and open to children as a great good, but that is not enough. "Natural sex", sex fully in accord with the goods of human nature, must also be sexual intercourse that flows not just from sexual desire but which is under the influence of the virtue of chastity. A significant level of chastity or self-mastery is required to ensure that acts of sexual intercourse are pursued as acts of expression of love and commitment and not just opportunities to experience sexual pleasure or release sexual tension. Perhaps few individuals have experience of sexual appetites governed by the virtue of chastity and thus free from lust.

Nonetheless there is some evidence that what I am calling natural sex is in fact more enjoyable sex and sex that leads to happier and longer lasting marriages. Many of those who use NFP have at one time contracepted and most of these testify that their marriages and sexual lives improved once they embraced NFP as their means of spacing or limiting children.[832] Very significantly, in contrast to the rest of the population whose divorce rate is rapidly approaching fifty per cent, they almost never divorce.[833]

In determining the sensus fidelium concerning contraception, I think sociological date can be very helpful. Indeed, I challenge theologians to take a very close look at the data that sociologists provide — not just the data of how many of those who are willing to assume the title of Catholic contracept and reject the Church's teaching on contraception, but the data of how happy and strong are the marriages of those who do accept and live by the Church's teaching; the data of the success of the marital relationships of those who contracept and the data indicating the damaging effects of contraception on our culture.[834]

Almost everyone currently has contraceptive sex before marriage. Those who remain virgins before marriage are small in number, but they are a group whose marriages are remarkably more stable than those who are not virgins.[835]Studies have shown for some time that those

---

[832]Wilson, "The Practice of Natural Family Planning."
[833]Wilson, "The Practice of Natural Family Planning."
[834]See, for instance, Lionel Tiger, *The Decline of Males*, (New York: Golden Books, 1991) as well as Wilson, "The Practice of Natural Family Planning."
[835]Edward O. Laumann et alii, *The Social Organization of Sexuality: Sexual Practices in the United States*, (Chicago: The University of Chicago Press, 1994), 503-5.

women who enjoy sex the most are Evangelical Protestants — women who more likely have been chaste before marriage and faithful within marriage. Consider this finding: "Women without religious affiliation were the least likely to report always having an orgasm with their primary partner — only one in five. On the other hand, the proportion of [Evangelical] Protestant women who reported always having an orgasm was the highest, at nearly one-third."[836] Although no data was given about the contraceptive practices of these Evangelical women, it is likely that they contracept at the same rate as the rest of the population. So would it be right to conclude that their lower divorce rate in spite of contraception indicates that use of contraception within marriage is not a threat to the marriage? It may be premature to draw that conclusion. Certainly their experience of sex may be better and their marriages stronger because they did not have sex prior to marriage; one might suppose they may be more able to be trusting of their husbands; they may benefit from not comparing their spouses to previous sexual partners or being compared to previous sexual partners; they experience at least one of the characteristics of natural sex; sex with someone with whom one has a lifetime commitment (those who cohabit and then marry seem to have a weaker commitment to their spouses.) I have not seen studies that show the comparative happiness of those who were virgins upon marrying and who contracepted after marriage with those who were virgins upon marrying and did not contracept after marriage, but it is not implausible that the second group would have even happier and more stable marriages. I propose these possible reasons: 1) the wives are not experiencing the bad physical and psychological effects of contraception; 2) the spouses do not need to interrupt the sexual act to put on a condom or insert a diaphragm; 3) the spouses appreciate the gift of fertility; 4) the spouses have attained the virtue of chastity or self-mastery; 5) the spouses communicate better and understand each other better; 6) they are open to more children and experience family life more fully. (Those who use NFP generally have more children than those who do not; not, evidently, because NFP is less reliable but because the spouses gain a greater respect for their fertility and want more children. In spite of the fact that having children puts a strain on

---

[836]Laumann, *The Social Organization of Sexuality*, 115.

marriage, those who have children have longer lasting marriages than those who don't).[337]

In the last year or so a new concern has shown up in popular publications; a concern with the phenomenon of sexless marriages.[838] These are marriages where the spouses have simply stopped having sex. No one has precisely identified the cause but the most commonly offered explanation is that the demands of double careers, household management, and raising children simply leave spouses too fatigued. Yet I know few people who have more demands made on them than mothers and fathers of large families, especially those who homeschool and reports are that love making among that group is very alive and well. Chemical contraceptives have as a side effect a reduced libido for the female, and may reduce the attractiveness of females to males,[839] so they may be a contributing factor to this diminished interest in sex among the married.

So, if I am correct about who belongs to the "faithful" who possess the *phronema* about sex that is necessary for the *sensus fidei* to do its proper work of discernment, it is a very small group of Catholics indeed.

Grex Parvus [The Small Flock]

Indeed, Newman certainly believes that it is sometimes the few who have the power to maintain fidelity to God in the midst of an attack on the faith. He states:

> Your strength lies in your God and your conscience; therefore it lies not in your number. It lies not in your number any more than in intrigue, or combination, or worldly wisdom. God saves whether by many or by few; you are to aim at showing forth His light, at diffusing "the sweet odour of His knowledge in every place:" numbers would not secure this. On the contrary, the more you grew, the more you might be thrown back into yourselves, by the increased animosity and jealousy of your enemies. (389)

---

[837]Carolyn Pape Cowan and Philip A. Cowan, *When Partners Become Parents: The Big Life Change for Couples* (New York: Basic Books, 1992); Jay Belsky and John Kelly, *The Transition to Parenthood* (New York: Dell, 1994); Tim B. Heaton, "Marital Stability Throughout the Child-rearing Years" *Demography* 27 (1990): 55-63; Linda Waite and Lee A. Lillard, "Children and Marital Disruption" *American Journal of Sociology* 96 (1991): 930-953.

[838]See for instance the cover story of *Newsweek Magazine*, "No Sex, Please, We're Married" (June 30, 2003).

[839]See Lionel Tiger, *The Decline of Males*, 36-39.

It is not giants who do most. How small was the Holy Land! yet it subdued the world. How poor a spot was Attica! yet it has formed the intellect. Moses was one, Elias was one, David was one, Paul was one, Athanasius was one, Leo was one. *Grace ever works by few; it is the keen vision, the intense conviction, the indomitable resolve of the few,* it is the blood of the martyr, it is the prayer of the saint, it is the heroic deed, it is the momentary crisis, it is the concentrated energy of a word or a look, which is the instrument of heaven. Fear not, *little flock,* for He is mighty who is in the midst of you, and will do for you great things.[840] (my emphasis)

Now the phenomenon of which he speaks in the above passage, the phenomenon of the effective witness of the few or even of the one, may not be what he means by the *sensus fidelium* or the *consensus fidelium.* It may in fact be another means by which the faith is preserved. Perhaps this should be called the *sensus fidei gregis parvi,* the sense of the faith of the small flock.

What this *sensus fidei gregis parvi* has in common with the *sensus fidelium* is that its worthiness as a test of legitimacy of doctrine or practice is not the authority of office or the extent of education or the worthiness of argument. What makes their witness powerful is that they believe and live the faith and also have an experience of the reality under question; they thus are in a position to have a nearly instinctual sense of what is or is not compatible with the faith.

As was noted earlier, in virtually every essay concerning the *sensus fidelium* the claim is made that a simple poll of those calling themselves Catholic does not suffice to determine the *sensus fidei.* Here I have attempted to identify some criteria that may be useful in determining who the *fideles* are. I have also argued that careful attention must be paid not only to what level of faith is possessed by those who would be numbered among the faithful but also the level of experience of the reality that is being judged. Currently most Catholics are sadly without the knowledge of the basics of their faith and also not fully faithful to the practice of their faith and that would disqualify them from being numbered among the *fideles.* It is also of no little importance that they are also without knowledge of the reality of sex that enables them to be able to be counted among those with *phronema* or connatural knowledge. There is within the Church a small flock, a *grex parvus,*

---

[840]Newman, "Duties of Catholics Towards the Protestant View," online at: http://www. newmanreader.org/works/england/lecture9.html

who know and live their faith; who have a knowledge both of the
sexual reality that involves fornication and contraception and of the
sexual reality that would confine sexual activity to marriage and finds
the procreative power of the sexual act to be a defining feature of that
act. It is of more than a little interest that this *grex parvus* affirms the
wisdom of the Church concerning sexual morality.

CHAPTER 14

THE ECCLESIAL VOCATION
OF THE THEOLOGIAN
IN CATHOLIC HIGHER EDUCATION

J. Augustine Di Noia, O.P.,
Undersecretary of the Congregation for the Doctrine of the Faith

IT SHOULD BE ADMITTED at the outset that the cosy juxtaposition of terms in my title, as much as they might reflect an ideal state of relations, do not fully correspond to the reality of the situation in which we find ourselves today.

1. Theology, theologians, and Catholic higher education: some disputed questions

For one thing, that the vocation of theologians is a properly ecclesial one has been and continues to be doubted, disputed or denied. Even if it is conceded that the theological profession entails a calling of some kind, it is supposed that this would be primarily an academic or intellectual vocation, involving overriding allegiances, not to a church or denomination, but to one's scholarly guild and the larger academic community. The code of free inquiry upheld by these communities is thought to exclude in principle the intrusion of non-scholarly considerations (such as creedal or dogmatic ones) and even more so the interference of representatives of non-academic communities (such as bishops or the Holy See) in the pursuit of the theologian's specific intellectual vocation. In this perspective, if the possibility of an ecclesial vocation were to be granted at all, then it would presumably have to be defined and expressed in ways that did not contradict the supervening obligations of a strictly academic or intellectual vocation.

Furthermore, that the theologian has a place in higher education is a proposition that has not been self-evident at any time in the past hundred years, and that remains in doubt among Catholic and non-Catholic educators alike. The issue here concerns not theologians qua theologians but the field of theology itself. It may come as something of a surprise — especially to Catholics thinking of the historic importance of theological faculties in the great universities of western Europe — that theology found its place in American higher education only relatively late, with difficulty, and at a moment coinciding with the ascendancy of religious studies. With or without an ecclesial vocation, the theologian's place in Catholic higher education at the present can hardly be said to be a secure one.

Finally, that institutions of higher learning could maintain recognizable — not to say institutional — bonds to the Catholic Church and still be true to their mission as modern research institutions has been and continues to be questioned by many, both within the Catholic Church and beyond it. Behind this doubt stretches a long history of which the period since the publication of *Ex corde Ecclesiae* is but the most recent phase. The view that church affiliation and academic integrity might be incompatible with one another has led many Catholic and Protestant institutions of higher learning over past century to weaken or dissolve the affiliations that bound them to their founding ecclesial communities. The pressure to pursue this course has perhaps been felt more acutely by Catholic higher education because the polity of the Catholic Church, in contrast to that of most other churches and ecclesial communities, is perceived to allow for a more direct involvement in the life of the Catholic campus. In the years since *Ex corde Ecclesiae*, it has perhaps become clearer that the issue here is not just the maintenance of a Catholic identity but also participation in Catholic communion. Disagreements about how to track the relationships between the Catholic college or university and the Catholic Church influence perceptions of the theologian's vocation, as well as judgments about his or her place in Catholic higher education.

It is clear then that, far from announcing the exposition of truths concerning which there is an undisturbed consensus in Catholic higher education in the United States, my title in effect introduces a set of disputed questions about which there are widespread and persistent doubts even within Catholic circles. In the form of powerful cultural assumptions, these doubts have influenced the actual shape of Catholic higher education in this country.

2. Catholic higher education and the ecclesiology of communion

The Church's teaching authorities, while cognizant of these doubts, cannot be said to share them. Consider higher education first. The Second Vatican Council reaffirmed the traditional Catholic view of the possibility and character of Church sponsorship of colleges and universities (in *Gravissimum educationis*). Following upon and implementing the conciliar teaching were two companion documents: *Sapientia Christiana* (1979), concerning the governance of ecclesiastically accredited institutions, and *Ex corde Ecclesiae* (1990), concerning all other Catholic institutions of higher learning. These apostolic constitutions laid out the different ways that ecclesial communion is embodied by Catholic institutions of these diverse types. The publication of *Sapientia Christiana* initiated a period during which American ecclesiastical faculties brought their own statutes into line with the new legislation, while in 2000 the United States Conference of Catholic Bishops' application of *Ex corde Ecclesiae* received official recognition by the Holy See.[841] What is more, within postconciliar teaching, theology and education have been regularly addressed by Pope John Paul II in his many discourses and encyclicals.

In the terms of the overall theme of this volume, the call to holiness and communion is central to understanding the confidence — one could as well say the absence of doubts — with which the Church advances her vision of Catholic higher education and the place of theology within it. The ecclesiology of communion is of fundamental importance in sustaining this confidence and in articulating this vision.

---

[841]United States Conference of Catholic Bishops, *Ex Corde Ecclesiae: An Application to the United States, Origins* 30 (2000), 68-75.

The gift of truth that we have received from Christ is this: to know that no one has ever wanted anything more than God wants to share the communion of his life with us. What Christ taught us and what we proclaim to the world is that the triune God invites all human persons to participate in the communion of the Father, Son and Holy Spirit, and with one another in them. Holiness is nothing less than the transformed capacity to enjoy this communion, and ecclesial communion is at root nothing less than Trinitarian communion.

This basic truth of Catholic faith unfolds in an ensemble of other truths about creation, incarnation, redemption and sanctification. The central truths of the Christian faith find their deepest meaning in the reality of Trinitarian communion. Everything created exists so that the Blessed Trinity could realize this plan of love. Through the incarnation and the paschal mystery, Christ enables creaturely persons to enter into the life of the uncreated Persons. In the Church, the Holy Spirit unites all those transformed in Christ and draws them into the communion of Trinitarian love. Ecclesial communion is nothing less than the beginning of our participation in the life of the Blessed Trinity.

Pope John Paul II has repeatedly described this communion as a "participated theonomy" which draws us into the communion of Trinitarian love in such a way that our full humanity is fulfilled and at the same time transcended. This theme, frequently reiterated in John Paul II's great encyclicals, is fundamental for developing a properly Catholic understanding of the place of education and scholarship in human personal, social and cultural life. In Christian faith, the human reality is not supressed but is fully realized. To embrace the First Truth and the Absolute Good who is God is not to accept constraints on human reason and desire, but to free them for their divinely willed destiny.

3. The Church's teaching and legislation regarding Catholic higher education are unintelligible apart from the ecclesiology of communion.

It is clear that a wide range of teaching activities is required if the Church is to be able to communicate the gift of truth she has received from Christ.[842] The institutional expression of these teaching activities has taken many different forms throughout Christian history. In the field of higher education the evidence for continuing a vigorous Catholic presence is indisputable. Far from experiencing any doubts about this possibility, the Church assumes as her rightful role the establishment of colleges and universities, and the maintenance of appropriate relations with them.

From a theological perspective, the genius of Catholic jurisprudence in this area arises from its underlying Christian humanism. As personal and social beings, the Christian faithful possess an inherent dignity and autonomy, which must be respected if ecclesial communion is to be realized. The reality of communion presupposes the reality of persons in communion and, in an ordered community like the Catholic Church, the reality of institutions in communion. It would be self-contradictory to invoke the ecclesiology of communion as grounds for infringing upon the autonomy rightly enjoyed by persons and institutions, and thus juridically protected, in the Catholic Church. The very notion of being in communion presupposes the integrity and autonomy, if also the interdependence, of the participants in ecclesial communion. The concrete expression of a series of relationships by its very nature affirms the proper autonomy and distinctive competencies of the persons and institutions enjoying ecclesial communion.

Although the grace of ecclesial communion is in the deepest sense an invisible reality, it is not an abstraction. Catholic tradition insists that it must take visible form in concrete communities and in their social and institutional structures. In the aftermath of the Second Vatican Council, the Church has invited Catholic colleges and universities to internalize the renewed ecclesiology of communion in the structures of their institutions, and in different ways depending on whether they are ecclesiastically accredited or not.

The historical record in the United States supports the conclusion that, given the political and cultural pressures favoring increasing secularization over the past hundred years and into the forseeable future, the Catholic identity of currently Catholic institutions of

---

[842]J. A. Di Noia, "Communion and Magisterium: Teaching Authority and the Culture of Grace," *Modern Theology* 9 (1993), 403-18.

higher learning is not likely to be sustainable without concrete juridical bonds between these institutions and the Church. Naturally, in developing its teaching and legislation in this area, the Holy See does not have only the situation in the United States in view. But the practical implications of an ecclesiology of communion, formulated with the whole Catholic Church in view, nonetheless have particular urgency in a situation where "the disengagement of colleges and universities from their Christian churches" has become endemic.[843] In his indispensable book on this topic, *The Dying of the Light*, Father James Burtchaell documented with considerable detail the informal arrangements by which hundreds of sincere and well-meaning faculty, administrators and church leaders of countless once church-related colleges and universities believed that they would be able to ensure the Lutheran, Presbyterian, Methodist, Anglican, and other denominational identities of their institutions.[844] Without the adoption of juridical provisions, and relying solely on the good will and sense of commitment of Catholic educators and bishops — as was strongly suggested by some — few of the currently Catholic institutions of higher learning in the U.S. are likely to remain distinctively and recognizably Catholic. Even with the adoption of something like the clearly stated juridical provisions of the USCCB Application, it may be that the secularizing trends will turn out to have been irreversible in some of the two hundred or more Catholic institutions of higher learning in the U.S.

Recent studies, including those by Father Burtchaell, Philip Gleason, John McGreevy, Philip Hamburger, and others, have made it possible to identify with greater precision the cultural and political forces operative in the relatively swift transformation that has occurred in Catholic higher education in the U.S. since the 1960s.[845] Significant anti-Catholic cultural assumptions, which in part contributed to

---

[843]Cf. James T. Burtchaell, *The Dying of the Light: The Disengagement of Colleges and Universities from Their Christian Churches* (Grand Rapids: Eerdmans, 1998).

[844]Ibid. On these themes, see also David J. O'Brien, *From the Heart of the American University* (Maryknoll: Orbis Books, 1994), and George Mardsen, *The Soul of the American University* (New York: Oxford University Press, 1994).

[845]Philip Gleason, *Contending with Modernity: Catholic Higher Education in the Twentieth Century* (New York: Oxford University Press, 1995); Philip Hamburger, *Separation of Church and State* (Cambridge, MA: Harvard University Press, 2002); Philip Jenkins, *The New Anti-Catholicism* (New York: Oxford University Press, 2003); John T. McGreevy, *Catholicism and American Freedom* (New York: Norton, 2003)

shaping public policy towards education, gave prevalence to the notion that church affiliation, most especially in the Catholic ambit, inevitably compromised the academic excellence, research capacity, and institutional autonomy of institutions enmeshed in such relationships. In addition, it was widely held that, because of their submissiveness to church authority, Catholics could never fully internalize the valued American traits of individual autonomy, and freedom of thought and expression, that would make for good citizens of the republic. In so far as they were not actively anti-religious, these forces favored the development of a broadly enlightened form of religiosity, free of ties to particular churches or denominations, and of the dogmatic and institutional commitments entailed by these ties. The impact of these cultural and political forces was aggravated after the Second Vatican Council, not only by the collapse of a distinctively Catholic culture, but also by the uncritical embrace of the secular culture (mistakenly thought to be warranted by the council's constitution, *Gaudium et spes*).[846] Catholic educators (and others) failed to recognize that the ambient culture, whose values they sought to embody institutionally, was not religiously neutral but often encoded with actively de-Christianizing assumptions.

The call to holiness and communion, reaffirmed by the Second Vatican Council and vigorously reasserted in the pontificate of Pope John Paul II, offers an opportunity for Catholic Church-related institutions of higher education in the U.S. to recover their distinctively Catholic identity, and embody it in clearly expressed communal bonds with the Church. With a tradition of academic excellence and freedom of inquiry stretching back to the medieval universities, Catholic higher education should courageously address the range of anti-Catholic and, increasingly, anti-Christian prejudices that seek to exclude Catholics and other Christians from participation in public life and from influence on public policy. According to the Second Vatican Council, Catholic universities aim to ensure that the Christian outlook should

---

[846]On American Catholic culture in the twentieth century, see Philip Gleason, *Keeping the Faith* (Notre Dame: University of Notre Dame Press, 1987), and William M. Halsey, *Survival of American Innocence* (Notre Dame: University of Notre Dame Press, 1980). On the impact of *Gaudium et spes*, see Tracy Rowland, *Culture and the Thomist Tradition* (London: Routledge, 2003). For a general view of Christianity and culture, see Kathryn Tanner, *Theories of Culture: A New Agenda for Theology* (Minneapolis: Fortress Press, 1997).

acquire "a public, stable and universal influence in the whole process of the promotion of higher culture" (*Gravissimum educationis* 10). As was true in the past, Catholic colleges and universities in the U.S. have an important contribution to make to the Christianization of American culture. George Lindbeck, the distinguished Lutheran theologian and astute observer of the Catholic scene, has written: "The waning of cultural Christianity may not be a good thing for societies. Traditionally Christian lands, when stripped of their historic faith, become unworkable and demonic . . . . Christianization of culture can be in some situations the church's major contribution to feeding the poor, clothing the hungry and liberating the imprisoned."[847] Catholic institutions of higher learning can play a central role in helping the Church, as well as other Christian communities, to monitor the impact of mass culture on the communication of the faith and the expression of Catholic and Christian life in western postmodern societies.

4. The place of theology in Catholic higher education

In addition to articulating a comprehensive vision of Catholic higher education, both conciliar and post-conciliar teaching consistently assigned a central role to theology and its cognate disciplines in Catholic higher education. Following upon *Gravissimum educationis* of the Second Vatican Council, the twin post-conciliar apostolic constitutions on higher education each assume that theology will find a place in the Catholic colleges and universities. As might be expected in a document that contains norms for ecclesiastical faculties and seminaries, Sapientia Christiana provides a complete picture of the curriculum of theology and its associated disciplines. But *Ex corde Ecclesiae* is no less explicit on the matter, even if it concedes that in certain situations nothing more than a chair of theology will be possible (*Ex corde Ecclesiae* 19). Both documents affirm that the primary focus of theology is to investigate and explain the doctrines of the Catholic faith as drawn from revelation. It is assumed that this study will be pursued in a spirit of true freedom of inquiry, employing appropriate methods, and acknowledging the derived character of the knowledge

---

[847]George A. Lindbeck, *The Church in A Postliberal Age*, ed. James J. Buckley (Grand Rapids: Eerdmans, 2002), 7. See also Aidan Nichols, *Christendom Awake: On Reenergizing Church and Culture* (Grand Rapids: Eerdmans, 1999).

sought and thus its dependence on divine revelation. Significantly, both documents ascribe important integrating functions to theology within the overall programs of Catholic colleges and universities, a traditional emphasis in the rationales for theology in almost all church-related higher education.

Studying these documents within the framework of Catholic history in Western Europe, one might well expect the legitimacy of theology's place in the curriculum of higher education to be self-evident. Indeed, as Cardinal Avery Dulles has noted, it is unrealistic not to include theology in the university curriculum since "the Church and the Catholic people legitimately expect that some universities will provide an intellectual environment in which the meaning and implications of the faith can be studied in relation to the whole realm of human knowledge."[848]

Nonetheless, for a variety of reasons, which are lately being subjected to more systematic study, the study of religion and theology did not enjoy an unchallenged place in the evolution of church-related, and indeed public, higher education in the U.S. Two brilliant books — D. G. Hart's on the history of Protestant rationales for the study of theology and religion and Philip Gleason's on the history of Catholic higher education in the twentieth century — give the topic the attention it deserves and at the same time provide fascinating reading for anyone interested in understanding the current situation of the study and teaching of religion and theology in American higher education.[849]

Hart and Gleason show that in the United States, throughout much of the nineteenth century, both Catholic and Protestant educators tended to view theology as a discipline that belonged in the seminary, not in the college or university. In church-affiliated Catholic and Protestant colleges, religious instruction was more likely to be seen as catechetical and moral formation than as properly theological inquiry. Later, with the emergence of the modern research university, Protestant educators struggled to legitimate teaching and

---

[848]Avery Dulles, *The Craft of Theology* (New York: Crossroad, 1992), 172.
[849]Gleason, *Contending with Modernity*, and D. G. Hart, *The University Gets Religion: Religious Studies in American Higher Education* (Baltimore: Johns Hopkins University, 1999), with extensive bibliography.

research in the Christian religion while at the same time downplaying the particular denominational entailments such teaching and research might otherwise involve. Catholic higher education in early twentieth century America tended to give a central role to religiously colored philosophical studies rather than to theology itself. Between the 1920s and the 1950s, neoscholastic philosophy played an influential role in curricular integration in Catholic colleges and universities and in the provision of the self-understanding that gave Catholic culture its shape. During this period, theology properly so-called, only gradually began to find a place in Catholic higher education, though kerygmatic, liturgical and Thomistic approaches remained in contention as Catholic educators strove to identify the kind of teaching that would be appropriate for undergraduates. Inevitably, both Protestant and Catholic curricula were influenced by the teaching of theology as conducted in their seminaries. For different but related reasons, neither Protestant nor Catholic university theology enjoyed the undiluted respect of the broader academic community. With the erosion of the hold of neo-orthodoxy in Protestant theology and the collapse of the neoscholastic synthesis in Catholic higher education, the 1960s were a time of crisis for both Catholic and Protestant theological and religious educators. The 1960s set in motion powerful cultural and educational trends that eventuated in the widespread (albeit unstable) prevalence of religious studies in Catholic, Protestant, and public higher education.[850]

In Catholic higher education, the displacement of theology by religious studies poses significant challenges. Frank Schubert's important study of this shift covers the crucial period 1955-1985 and demonstrates the steady move away from courses engaging in appropriation of the Catholic tradition toward courses in the history, anthropology and sociology of religion.[851] While admitting areas of overlap between theology and religious studies, most scholars

[850]See Patrick W. Carey and Earl Muller, eds., *Theological Education in the Catholic Tradition: Contemporary Challenges* (New York: Crossroad, 1998); Patrick Carey, "College Theology in Historical Perspective," in Sandra Mize and William Portier, eds., *American Catholic Traditions: Resources for Renewal* (Maryknoll: Orbis Books, 1996), 242-71; Susan M. Mountin, "A Study of Undergraduate Roman Catholic Theology Education, 1952-1976," Ph.D. diss., Marquette University, 1994; Pamela C. Young, "Theological Education in American Catholic Higher Education, 1939-1973," Ph.D. diss., Marquette University, 1995.
[851]Frank D. Schubert, *A Sociological Study of Secularization Trends in the American Catholic University* (Lewiston, Maine: Edwin Mellen Press, 1990).

acknowledge the fundamental difference in perspective represented by the approaches to religious realities in these diverse fields. Whereas theology takes the claim to truth made by the sources of Christian revelation as its framework, the field(s) of religious studies systematically bracket the claims to truth made for contending religious traditions. For theology, revelation provides the principles for inquiry, and the truth of Christian doctrines is the basic assumption for this inquiry. For religious studies, the world's religions present a richly diverse set of texts, institutions, rites, and other phenomena, which are studied employing a range of humanistic and social scientific methodologies.

In Catholic colleges and universities where this shift is complete and likewise unchallenged, it is difficult for theology to maintain its integrity and finality as *fides quaerens intellectum*. Apart from any other secularizing pressures that might be operative in the midst of predominantly religious studies departments, theology itself can easily yield to the methods and perspectives of the study of religion. As we shall see shortly, the transformation of theology into a branch of religious studies makes it nearly unintelligible to claim for theologians any properly ecclesial vocation or even connection with the believing community.

5. The ecclesial vocation of the theologian

What must be surely regarded as among the most significant official documents on the place of the theologian in the Church appeared in 1990. It was prepared by the Congregation for the Doctrine of the Faith and was confidently entitled "The Ecclesial Vocation of the Theologian."

Although the documents of the Second Vatican Council mentioned theology and theologians at various points — perhaps most notably in the Constitution on Divine Revelation (*Dei Verbum*, 23-24), the Constitution on the Church (*Lumen gentium*, 23), and the Decree on Priestly Formation (*Optatam totius*, 12, 14-16), the council did not make this theme the focus of an extended treatment.[852] Given the

---

[852]For a helpful discussion of conciliar teaching regarding theology, see Anthony J. Figueiredo, *The Magisterium-Theology Relationship: Contemporary Theological Conceptions in the Light of Universal Church Teaching* (Rome: Gregorian University Press, 2001), 211-37; for the historical background and setting, 167-237; for the relations between bishops and theologians in the United States, 287-342.

impact that the council had on the work of theologians, this may come as something of a surprise — all the more so perhaps, since, as Cardinal Ratzinger has noted, it was "the great blossoming of theology between the world wars which made the Second Vatican Council possible."[853] After the conclusion of the council the continuing contribution of theologians was institutionalized in a remarkable way when Pope Paul VI established the International Theological Commission in 1969.[854]

The CDF Instruction reflects the Church's renewed consciousness of the centrality of the role of the theologian in her life. Reprising significant elements of the Catholic tradition, as articulated in conciliar and post-conciliar teaching, the Instruction forcefully argues that the theologian's vocation is a properly ecclesial one and, as in the case of Catholic colleges and unversities, that the bonds of ecclesial communion implied by this relationship can be expressed juridically. In the terms of the overall theme of this volume, the CDF Instruction may be taken as a robust reminder that the call to holiness and communion comes to theologians at least in part through the mediation of their ecclesial vocation precisely as theologians.[855]

At the start of his splendid book, *The Shape of Theology*, Father Aidan Nichols, O.P., asks the question: "What sort of person must I be in order to become a theologian?" — to which we might well add, "and in order to continue being one."[856] This, in effect, is the arresting question posed by the CDF document. In addressing this question, the Instruction takes up in turn the divine gift of truth, the vocation of the theologian, and the role of the magisterium. Under its consideration of the role of the magisterium, the Instruction gives extended attention to the problem of theological dissent.[857]

---

[853]Joseph Ratzinger, *Nature and Mission of Theology* (San Francisco: Ignatius Press, 1995), 66. See also K. H. Neufeld, "In the Service of the Council: Bishops and Theologians at the Second Vatican Council," in R. Latourelle, ed., *Vatican Council II: Assessments and Perspectives II* (New York: Crossroad, 1988), 74-105.

[854]Michael Sharkey, *International Theological Commission: Texts and Documents 1969-1985* (San Francisco: Ignatius Press, 1989).

[855]For post-conciliar teaching on theology, see Figueiredo, 239-86.

[856]Aidan Nichols, *The Shape of Theology* (Collegeville, MN: Liturgical Press, 1991), 13.

[857]This discussion of dissent is perhaps the most complete to be found in any official Catholic document. For the setting of this discussion , see Figueiredo, 232-3; 254-60. It could be noted here that, for a Catholic theologian, the situation of being in dissent from Catholic doctrine is essentially an anamolous one and should not be allowed to frame the treatment of the ecclesial vocation of the theologian.

But what is particularly noteworthy, in Cardinal Ratzinger's view, is that the Instruction begins, not with the magisterium, but with the gift of divine truth. Indeed, the Instruction's Latin title is Donum veritatis, "the gift of truth." Because theology is not simply an "ancillary function" of the magisterium, we need to locate the theologian and the work of theology in the broader context of the life of Church, precisely as she is the locus of a truth which she did not generate but which she received as a gift. At the center of this truth is the person of Jesus Christ who reveals the divine desire to draw us into the communion of Trinitarian love and, moreover, who enables us to enjoy this communion. The function of the magisterium is to guard and teach this truth in its entirety, which the Church received as a gift and is bound to hand on. For this reason, according to Cardinal Ratzinger, the Instruction "treats the ecclesial mission of the theologian not in a duality of magisterium-theology, but rather in the framework of a triangular relationship defined by the people of God, bearer of the *sensus fidei,* the magisterium, and theology."[858] In different ways, therefore, both the magisterium and theology are servants of a prior truth, received in the Church as a gift.[859]

Perhaps the most important contribution of the Instruction is to have secured in this way what Cardinal Ratzinger calls the "ecclesial identity of theology"[860] and, correspondingly, the ecclesial vocation of the theologian. In the words of the Instruction itself: "Among the vocations awakened ... by the Spirit in the Church is that of the theologian....[whose] role is to pursue in a particular way an ever deeper understanding of the Word of God found in the inspired Scriptures and handed on by the living Tradition of the Church ....[which he does] in communion with the Magisterium which has been charged with the responsibility of preserving the deposit of faith" (*Donum veritatis,* 6) The theological vocation responds to the intrinsic dynamic of faith which "appeals to reason" and "beckons reason ... to come to understand what it has believed" (no.6). In this way, "theological science responds to the invitation of truth as it seeks to understand

---

[858]Ratzinger, *Nature and Mission of Theology,* 104-5.
[859]See Di Noia, "Communion and Magisterium."
[860]Ratzinger, *Nature and Mission of Theology,* 105.

the faith" (no.6).   But the theological vocation also responds to the dynamic of love, for "in the act of faith, man knows God's goodness and begins to love Him ... [and] is ever desirous of a better knowledge of the beloved" (no.7).

The gift of truth received in the Church thus establishes both the context for the vocation and mission of the theologian, and the framework for the actual practice of of the discipline of theology. This ecclesially received truth, as articulated in the deposit of faith and handed on by the magisterium, constitutes not an extrinsic authority that poses odious limits on an inquiry that would otherwise be free but an intrinsic source and measure that gives theology its identity and finality as an intellectual activity. Hence, as Cardinal Ratzinger asks, "Is theology for which the Church is no longer meaningful really a theology in the proper sense of the word?"[861] Examined independently of the assent of faith and the mediation of the ecclesial community, the texts, institutions, rites and beliefs of the Catholic Church can be the focus of the humanistic, philosophical and social scientitic inquiries that together constitute the field of religious studies. But Christian theology is a different kind of inquiry. Cut off from an embrace of the truth that provides its subject matter and indicates the methods appropriate to its study, theology, as the Church has always understood it, loses its specific character as a scientific inquiry of a certain type.[862] Its precise scope is to seek the intelligibility of a truth received in faith by the theologian who is himself a member of the ecclesial community that is, as Cardinal Walter Kasper has said, "the place of truth."[863]

The theologian is thus free to seek the truth within limits imposed, not by an intrusive external authority, but by the nature of his discipline as such. As the Instruction points out: "Freedom of research, which the academic community holds most precious, means an openness to accepting the truth that emerges at the end of an investigation in which no element has intruded that is foreign to the methodology corresponding to the object under study" (no.12). Theology cannot "deny its own foundations," to use the words of Cardinal Dulles; the acceptance of the authority and Scripture and doctrines in theology is

[861]Joseph Ratzinger, *Principles of Catholic Theology* (San Francisco: Ignatius Press, 1987), 323.
[862]See J. A. Di Noia, "Authority, Dissent and the Nature of Theological Thinking," *The Thomist* 52 (1988), 185-207.
[863]Walter Kasper, *Theology and Church* (New York: Crossroad, 1989), 129-47.

"not a limitation but rather the charter of its existence and freedom to be itself."[864] The freedom of inquiry proper to theology is, according to *Donum veritatis*, the "hallmark of a rational discipline whose object is given by Revelation, handed on and interpreted in the Church under the authority of the Magisterium, and received by faith. These givens have the force of principles. To eliminate them would mean to cease doing theology" (no.12). The principles of theology, as we noted earlier, are derived from revelation, and constitute the discipline as such. In accepting them, the theologian is simply being true to the nature of his subject, and to his vocation as a scholar in this field.

These elements of the Instruction's account of the theological vocation are ferociously contested in today's academy, largely on the basis of what Lindbeck has called the "individualistic foundational rationalism" which shapes the deepest cultural assumptions of modernity.[865] But the Church has a solid, well substantiated, and historically warranted rationale for its account of the nature of theology as an intellectual discipline of a particular sort, and of the responsibilities of its practitioners. In the present circumstances, we need to make this case without apology. It is central to the convictions of the Catholic Church, and indeed of the Christian tradition as such, to give priority to a theonomous rather than to an autonomous rationality. It so happens that certain postmodern intellectual trends have begun to advance what Alasdair MacIntyre calls the traditioned character of all rational inquiry[866] and Lindbeck calls the socially and linguistically constituted character of belief. This intellectual climate is, to a certain extent, more favorable to the defense of the priniciple of theonomous rationality that is crucial for the Catholic understanding of theology. But it must be recognized that the basis for this understanding is itself a properly theological one that is rooted in fundamental Christian convictions about the gift of truth and its reception in the ecclesial community.[867]

---

[864]Dulles, 168.

[865]Lindbeck, 7.

[866]Alasdair MacIntyre, *Three Rival Versions of Moral Theology* (Notre Dame: University of Notre Dame Press, 1990). See especially the essays by Jean Porter, Stephen P. Turner and Terry Pinkard in Mark C. Murphy, ed., *Alasdair MacIntyre* (Cambridge: Cambridge University Press, 2003).

[867]See Lindbeck's *The Nature of Doctrine* (Philadelphia: Westminster, 1984). For an excellent overview, see Bernhard A. Eckerstorfer, "The One Church in the Postmodern World: Hermeneutics, Key Concepts and Perspectives in the Work of George Lindbeck," *Pro Ecclesia* Vol. XIII, No. 4 (Fall, 2004): 399-423.

The Church embodies her understanding of the nature of theology and of the ecclesial vocation of the theologian by granting to both the discipline and its practitioners a role in Catholic higher education according to the principles of the ecclesiology of communion, which we considered earlier.

According to *Ex corde Ecclesiae* and Sapientia Christiana, the standard theological disciplines include: sacred Scripture, dogmatic theology, moral theology, pastoral theology, canon law, liturgy and church history. Those teaching these disciplines are invited to make a profession of faith and oath of fidelity in order to express the derived character of these disciplines and the ecclesial space they inhabit. These formulas in effect allow the scholar to express a promise to respect the principles of his or her field as well as the personal communion of the theologian with the Church. Viewed in this light, theological disciplines and their practitioners are in a situation analogous to other disciplines and to scholars in other fields that are supervised by professional societies, by peer review, and by a whole range of certifying and accrediting bodies who maintain the standards within these fields and the credibility, which they rightly enjoy among the general public.

In addition, the Church offers a canonical mission to theologians teaching in ecclesiastical faculties, and a mandatum to those teaching in all other institutions of higher learning. Although both the canonical mission and the mandatum have provoked controversy, the necessity of the canonical mission is perhaps better understood within the context of ecclesiastically accredited faculties. Here, I will confine my remarks to the mandatum. [868]

The nature of the mandatum referred to in *Ex corde Ecclesiae* is best understood in the light of the Second Vatican Council's decree on the laity: "Thus, making various dispositions of the apostolate according to the circumstances, the hierarchy enjoins some particular form of it more closely with its own apostolic function. Yet the proper nature and distinctiveness of each apostolate must be preserved, and the laity must not be deprived of the possibility of acting on their own accord.

---

[868]For helpful discussions of the canonical mission and the *mandatum*, see Figueiredo, 185-87; 253-54; 374-80.

In various church documents this procedure of the hierarchy is call a "mandate" (*Apostolicam actuositatem*, 24). While the mandatum has a different juridical character from the canonical mission of professors teaching in ecclesiastical faculties as required by *Sapientia Christiana*, both express in a concrete way the ecclesial identity of the theologian. According to canonist Father Reginald Whitt, the above-mentioned mandate "refers to those apostolic activities that remain activities proper to the laity in virtue of their baptism yet joined closely to the apostolic ministry of the bishop." A Catholic professor of theology in a Catholic university is thus considered "as one of the faithful engaged in the higher education apostolate entitled and required to obtain endorsement from the competent hierarch."[869]

In requiring the mandatum (and, for that matter, the canonical mission) the Church acknowledges that the Catholic theologian pursues his or her inquiries under the light of revelation as contained in Scripture and tradition and proclaimed by the magisterium. In seeking the mandatum, the individual theologian gives a concrete expression to the relationship of ecclesial communion that exists between the Church and the Catholic teacher of a theological discipline in a Catholic institution of higher learning. The acceptance of the mandatum does not make the pursuit and recognition of truth a matter of obedience to authority: as we have seen, it is not that the doctrines of the faith are true because the magisterium teaches them, but that the magisterium teaches them because they are true. It is the Catholic conviction that the truths of faith point ultimately to nothing less than the First Truth itself, whose inner intelligibility constantly draws the inquiring mind to Himself. The acceptance of the mandatum by a theologian is simply the public affirmation and social expression of this fundamental Catholic conviction.

---

[869]D.R. Whitt, " 'What We Have Here is a Failure to Communicate': The Mind of the Legislator in *Ex Corde Ecclesiae*," *Journal of College and University Law* 25 (1999), 790.

Conclusion

We have considered the ecclesial vocation of the theologian in Catholic higher education in a volume devoted to the teaching of the Second Vatican Council and the legacy of Pope John Paul II. We began with a series of doubts, but we end on a note of confidence. Surely, if the example of John Paul II teaches us nothing else, it should teach us confidence in the inherent attractiveness of the Christian faith, and, in particular, the Catholic vision of higher education and of the vocation of the theologian. While the assumptions of the ambient culture will not always be friendly to it, this vision nonetheless deserves to be presented fully and without compromise. Indeed, because the call to holiness and communion originates not with us but with Christ, our hearers deserve from us a confident and unapologetic invitation to share a vision of human life that finds its consummation in the divine life of Trinitarian communion. Nothing less will do.

The Influence of Biblical Studies on Ecclesial Self-awareness Since Vatican II, a Contribution of *Dei Verbum*

Rev. Francis Martin

One of the key themes of Pope Paul VI, in his Encyclical, *Ecclesiam Suam* is that of self awareness: "We think it is a duty today for the Church to deepen the awareness that she must have of herself, of the treasure of truth of which she is the heir and custodian and of her mission in the world."[870] Essential to that effort is the message of *Dei Verbum* §21, which speaks of this "treasure of truth" as being found in a unique manner in the Sacred Scriptures:

> The Church has always venerated the divine Scriptures just as she venerates the body of the Lord, since, especially in the sacred liturgy, she unceasingly receives and offers to the faithful the bread of life from the table both of God's word and of Christ's body... For in the sacred books, the Father who is in heaven meets His children with great love and speaks with them; and the force and power in the word of God is so great that it stands as the support and energy of the Church, the strength of faith for her sons, the food of the soul, the pure and everlasting source of spiritual life. Consequently these words are perfectly applicable to Sacred Scripture: "For the word of God is living and active" (Heb. 4:12) and "it has power to build you up and give you your heritage among all those who are sanctified" (Acts 20:32; see 1 Thess. 2:13).

I would maintain that it only in recovering for our own day access to the mystical bread of the word of God that we will achieve

---

[870]Paul VI, *Ecclesiam Suam* (Washington, D.C.: National Catholic Welfare Conference, 1964), §18.

that self awareness which will enable us to bear witness to the world of the wonders God has worked for the whole human race. I wish in this study to concentrate on §12 of *Dei Verbum* because we find there, in an unmistakable manner, the challenge issued to theologians of the Bible to avail themselves of all the resources provided by modern critical historiography while at the same retaining the approaches of faith that have nourished the Church for two millennia. Accordingly, my study will have two parts. In the first part, I point to the challenge posed by the document which sets forth the need to use modern historical and literary methods in order to grasp the intention of the human author while at the same time reading and interpreting the Scripture *"eodem Spiritu quo scripta est."*[871] In the second part I will propose some lines of thought that respond to the challenges and lacunae uncovered in the previous analysis

PART ONE:
THE HISTORICAL AND LITERARY TASK

The Latin title of Chapter 3 of *Dei Verbum* is: *De Sacrae Scripturae Divina Inspiratione et de Eius Interpretatione.* I will look briefly at §11, which speaks of inspiration and then reflect on §12 dedicated expressly to the topic of interpretation. The last paragraph in the chapter, §13, reflects with Tradition on the condescension of God and concludes with a traditional theme to which we will return.

Inspiration: Paragraph §11

The document wisely eschews discussion of the "mechanics of inspiration" and contents itself with a series of statements that serve to establish a theological space within which to set forth the mystery of the divine authorship of the Sacred Writings, their canonical status, the fact that God employed human authors who freely used their own powers and abilities and are truly authors. At this point there follows a statement whose full import has yet to be realized:

---

[871]"In the same Spirit in which it was written." For a discussion of this phrase, to which I will return, see Ignace de la Potterie, "Interpretation of Holy Scripture in the Spirit in Which It Was Written," in *Vatican II: Assessment and Perspectives. I,* ed. René Latourelle (New York: Paulist, 1988), 220-66.

> Therefore, since everything asserted by the inspired authors
> or sacred writers must be held to be asserted by the Holy Spirit,
> it follows that the books of Scripture must be acknowledged as
> teaching solidly, faithfully and without error the truth which God,
> for the sake of our salvation, wanted, put into the sacred writings.

The paragraph concludes with a a modified form of the Vulgate's rendering of 2 Timothy 3:16-17: "And thus, all Scripture (is) divinely inspired and useful for teaching, for disputing, for correcting, and for training in justice: that the man of God be fully formed and prepared for every good work."

The Human Authors: The First Theme of §12

After having asserted that the human authors writing as true authors, "consigned to writing everything and only those things which God wanted," and that this activity "transmits without error the truth which God, for the sake of our salvation, wanted put into the sacred writings," the Council Fathers had now to explain how the Sacred Text is to be interpreted. One of the primary purposes of the latter section of §11 had been to rescue the discussion about inerrancy from its previously fruitless debates by introducing the concept of *veritas* which God, *nostrae salutis causa*, wished to communicate. This eliminates many of the problems of the inerrancy debate and allows a simple acknowledgement of the inaccuracies, historical, textual, and so forth that appear in the Sacred Text.[872] This same notion of the mode of expression now underlies the ensuing discussion of literary genre, culture, etc., in the attempt to understand the human authors on their own terms.

> However, since God speaks in Sacred Scripture through men in
> human fashion, the interpreter of Sacred Scripture, in order to see
> clearly what God wanted to communicate to us, should carefully
> investigate what meaning the sacred writers really intended, and
> what God wanted to manifest by means of their words.

---

[872] At times there are discrepancies between the present state of our historical knowledge and the statements in the Sacred Text. Thus the worldwide "census" under Caesar Augustus in Lk 2:1, the discrepancy in dating between Dan 1:1 and the Chronicle of King Nebuchadnezzar regarding the siege of Jerusalem, etc. There are also mistaken attributions: Mk 27:9 names Jeremiah while in fact the text adduced in regard to Judas' death is Zech 11:12.

The opening lines of paragraph §12 place the accent on grasping what "the sacred writers really intended." This introduces a cardinal principle already enunciated by St. Athanasius and quoted in *Divino Afflante Spiritu:*

> Here, as indeed is expedient in all other passages of Sacred Scripture, it should be noted, on what occasion the Apostle spoke; we should carefully and faithfully observe to whom and why he wrote, lest, being ignorant of these points, or confounding one with another, we miss the real meaning of the author.[873]

This basic rule governing the interpretation of all texts takes on a particular importance when the interpreter is removed linguistically, culturally and geographically from the text he or she is studying. Nevertheless, there is a danger in this manner of expression and it lies in the two dimensions of the verb "to intend." The work of establishing cultural sympathy can result in a reasonably successful attempt to understand the correct tenor of the author's work, what he "intended to say." However the statement is about something and that too is what the author intends; his mind intends some reality, some aspect of being and interpreting his text includes participating in the knowledge that the author is communicating. Take for instance the following statement:

> But for men like Kelvin, Crookes and Roentray, whose research dealt with radiation theory or with cathode ray tubes, the emergence of X-rays violated one paradigm as it created another.[874]

Someone in Morocco (or Chicago) could report quite correctly to his audience what Thomas Kuhn intended to say in this statement without having any notion of what he is talking about, without, that is, participating in the intention of Kuhn's mind, and grasping the object of his thinking. One telling expression of this truth is found in a phrase of Martin Luther: "The one who does not understand the reality cannot draw the meaning out of the words."[875] The paragraph that describes the historical work of the exegete is well expressed and deserves to be cited in full here:

---

[873] *Contra Arianos* I, 54; PG 26, col. 123 (DAS §34). The phrase translated "real meaning" (*alēthinēs dianoias)"* also evokes nuances of "real understanding" of the author.
[874] Thomas S. Kuhn, *The Structure of Scientific Revolutions,* ed. Otto Neurath, *International Encyclopedia of Unified Science* (Chicago: Chicago University Press, 1970), 93.
[875] "Qui non intelligit res non postest sensum ex verbis elicere." *Tischreden,* WAT 5,26, n.5246.

> To search out the intention of the sacred writers, attention should be given, among other things, to "literary forms." For truth is set forth and expressed differently in texts which are variously historical, prophetic, poetic, or of other forms of discourse. The interpreter must investigate what meaning the sacred writer intended to express and actually expressed in particular circumstances by using contemporary literary forms in accordance with the situation of his own time and culture. For the correct understanding of what the sacred author wanted to assert, due attention must be paid to the customary and characteristic styles of feeling, speaking and narrating which prevailed at the time of the sacred writer, and to the patterns men normally employed at that period in their everyday dealings with one another.[876]

It is impossible to exaggerate the benefit that has accrued to the study of the Sacred Page and thus to the Church by the correct application of the methods described in this paragraph. We must bear in mind the earlier statement of this document, which speaks of the *oeconomia revelationis* taking place *"gestis verbisque intrinsece inter se connexis"* (§2). In this context we may say that in order to participate more fully in the reality mediated by the words — *intentio* understood metaphysically — it is of great importance that we grasp what, in terms of his own context, the author "wants to say" — *intentio* understood psychologically. I will return to this important point later in the discussion.

There are many examples of ways in which historical, literary and philological research has served to clarify the intention of the author thus illuminating the teaching of the Sacred Text in ways that have led to significant advances in theology. One small example will suffice. Romans 5:12 has always been crucial for an understanding of the relation between Adam's sin and humankind's sin and death. Yet, a key expression in the verse has eluded understanding. The text reads as follows in the Revised Standard Version: "Therefore as sin came into the world through one man and death through sin, and so death spread to all men because all men sinned." The last four English words represent the Greek: *eph' ho pantes emarton*, and these words have

---

[876]Note the number of times the notion of the intention of the author is invoked here: *"Ad hagiographorum intentionem eruendam,"* attention must be paid to literary forms; the interpreter must investigate what the author *"exprimere intenderit et expresserit;"* finally, due attention must be paid to common styles of speech in order to attain a correct understanding of what the sacred author *"scripto asserere voluerit."*

received about eleven interpretations.[877] With the electronic capacity to examine the phrase in extant Greek literature, the possibilities have been reduced to two: "inasmuch as all have sinned," or, "with the result that all have sinned." In either case, though with different nuances, the teaching of the verse asserts both the causality of Adam in regard to human sin and death and the fact that this causality expresses itself in the sinning of each individual person. This is extremely important in the development of the Church's teaching on original sin.

The Divine Author: The Second Theme of §12

The second section of §12 begins with a long sentence whose opening phrase changes the direction of thought and is followed by statements that point successively to the fact of the canon of Scripture, the Tradition of the Church, and the "analogy of faith." This sentence is then succeeded by remarks regarding the Magisterium and the way in which biblical interpretation both serves this function and is subject to it:

> But, since Holy Scripture must be read and interpreted in the same Spirit in which it was written, in order rightly to draw out the meaning of the sacred texts, no less diligent attention must be devoted to the content and unity of the whole of Scripture, taking into account the living Tradition of the entire Church and the analogy of faith.
>
> It pertains to exegetes to work according to these rules in order to understand and expound more profoundly the meaning of Sacred Scripture so that the judgment of the Church might mature, as it were, by preparatory study. For all of what has been said about the way of interpreting Scripture is subject finally to the judgment of the Church, which carries out the divine commission and ministry of guarding and interpreting the word of God.

Three procedures are listed in this text as part of reading and interpreting Holy Scripture in the same Spirit in which it was written, and these are necessary "in order rightly to draw out the meaning of the sacred texts." There is first, attention "to the content and unity of the whole of Scripture," what may be called "canonical criticism." There is secondly, an account of "the living Tradition of the entire Church."

---

[877]See Stanislaus Lyonnet, "Le sens de eph' ho en Rom 5,12 et l'exégèse des Pères grecs," *Biblica* 36 (1955): 436-56.; and especially Joseph Fitzmyer, Romans. *A New Translation with Introduction and Commentary*, ed. William Foxwell Albright and David Noel Freedman, *Anchor Bible* 33 (New York: Doubleday, 1992), 413-17.

This must refer to the Fathers and Liturgies of both East and West as well as the living faith practice of the members of the Church. And finally, there is *"analogia fidei,"* a traditional phrase which emphasizes the fact that, not only is the Bible a whole with a multifaceted but consistent message, but also each part of the Sacred Text must be understood as compatible with others in the Canon, indeed as deriving from and contributing to an understanding of the whole.

Reading the Scripture in the Spirit in which it was written means first acknowledging that "no prophecy of scripture is a matter of one's own interpretation, because no prophecy ever came by the impulse of man, but men moved by the Holy Spirit spoke from God" (2 Pet 1:20-21). Aquinas sums up the rhythm that leads from original revelation to interpretation. The fact that the transmission and reception process is much more complex than the ancients thought does not detract from the solidity of his understanding:

> After the level of those who receive revelation directly from God, another level of grace is necessary. Because men receive revelation from God not only for their own time but also for the instruction of all who come after them, it was necessary that the things revealed to them be passed on not only in speech to their contemporaries but also as written down for the instruction of those to come after them. And thus it was also necessary that there be those who could interpret what was written down. This also must be done by divine grace. And so we read in Genesis 40:8, "Does not interpretation come from God?"[878]

Aquinas also considers that all the authors of the New Testament were prophetically endowed because they could correctly interpret the Old Testament: "They are also called prophets in the New Testament who expound the prophetic sayings because Sacred Scripture is interpreted in the same Spirit in which it is composed."[879]

The first consequence, then, of the fact that Scripture is written by the Holy Spirit and must be read and interpreted in the same Spirit

---

[878] *Summa Contra Gentiles* 3,154.

[879] *Ad Romanos* (on Rom 12:8) Marietti ed. §978. For the background of this principle see Ignace de la Potterie, "Interpretation of Holy Scripture in the Spirit in Which It Was Written." We find in that study this text from Origen describing the responsibility of a bishop or priest: "To learn of God by reading the divine Scriptures and by meditating on them with great frequency, or teach the people. But he must teach what he has learned of God, not from his own heart or any human sense, but what the Spirit teaches" (In Lev. Hom 6,6 [*Sources Chrétiennes 286,297*], text is on p. 225 of de la Potterie's study.

is that "no less diligent attention must be devoted to the content and unity of the whole of Scripture." Such a manner of so reading and interpreting has been instinctive for most of Christian history. It suffices to look at any patristic writing to experience this: any part of Scripture may be invoked to shed light on another part. With the advent of historical study and increased attention to the author and the author's intention the tendency has been to consider a book or part of a book as an isolated entity. Thus, we have the modern phenomenon of studies devoted to "the theology of Jeremiah" or Mark, or Deutero-Isaiah, etc. There are other procedures that are not as useful, and in fact, are wrong. These consist in trying to determine a more primitive layer of composition, attempting to discern its theological direction and then attributing to the final and more "orthodox" redaction a different direction. The orientation of most of this work is to consider that the "orthodox" layer was superimposed upon a more primitive and less exclusive view. The multiplicity of opinions resulting from this procedure is evidence enough of its shaky foundation and it often betrays a theological bias on the part the investigator.[880]

In reaction to this atomizing and pluralizing understanding of the Scriptures there has been a return to the more instinctive manner of considering the totality of the text. This return seeks to retain what has been gained through attention to the individual authors and books but to integrate this with "the whole of Scripture." I am, of course, speaking of the approach linked with the name of Brevard Childs which concentrates in a reflective way on the Canon as whole as mediating the divine message by holding all its parts in an overarching unity in diversity.[881] Though the insight is extremely important there remain weaknesses in Childs' approach. Some of these come from a lack of

---

[880]I have discussed this more at length in my review of *Christology, Controversy and Community. New Testament Essays in Honor of David. R.Catchpole*, ed. David Horrell & Christopher M. Tuckett. Supplements to *Novum Testamentum* XCIX. (Leiden: Brill, 2000) in *Catholic Biblical Quarterly* 64, 3 [2002] 608-610. For an example of this procedure that finds irreducible diversity in the New Testament see Carolyn Osiek, "The Family in Early Christianity: 'Family Values' Revisited," *Catholic Biblical Quarterly* 58, no. 1 (1996): 1-24.

[881]See Brevard Childs, *The New Testament as Canon: An Introduction* (Philadelphia: Fortress, 1984), Brevard Childs, *Biblical Theology of the Old and New Testaments. Theological Reflection on the Christian Bible* (Minneapolis: Fortress, 1992). See as well C. Theobald, ed., *Le Canon des Écritures. Études historiques, exégétiques et systématiques, Lectio Divina 140* (Paris: Cerf, 1990).

an understanding of magisterium, some from the sheer vastness of the historical information that has to be integrated, and some from a lack of philosophical insights, e.g. analogy, that could help in portraying the transposition process by which the various components of the final text have been formed into a whole.[882] A good description of this process is given by Bernard Lonergan who uses the term "sublation," where I prefer "transposition" because of the distance it allows us from Hegel. Lonergan writes:

> What sublates goes beyond what is sublated, introduces something new and distinct, yet so far from interfering with the sublated or destroying it, on the contrary needs it, includes it, preserves all its proper features and properties, and carries them forward to a fuller realization within a richer context.[883]

The canon is both a work of Tradition and its inspired expression. Surrounding the canon of Scripture, and bearing it along, is the whole life of the Church; and the exegete must place himself within this movement in order to take "into account the living Tradition of the entire Church." As surprising as it may seem, there is hardly any philosophical reflection extant on the nature of what we call tradition.[884] A recent study by Jorge Gracia can serve as an effective beginning.[885] Gracia's main contention is that tradition is action. The action must be voluntary, intentional, repeated by members of social groups and significant for their identity. To the observation that, at least in the Roman Catholic view, Tradition should have verbal content Gracia replies:

> Accordingly, when Roman Catholics talk about beliefs as constituting a tradition, for example, they can be taken to be referring to the very actions of believing rather than to certain doctrines or to their textual formulation... what counts in religious faith is the very actions of believing in which people engage and,

---

[882]For a treatment of some of these problems see Paul R. Noble, *The Canonical Approach: A Critical Reconstruction of the Hermeneutics of Brevard S. Childs* (Leiden: Brill, 1995).
[883]Bernard Lonergan, *Method in Theology* (New York: Herder & Herder, 1972), 241.
[884]Though see the study by Kenneth Schmitz, "What Happens to Tradition When History Overtakes it?," 59-72.
[885]Jorge J.E. Gracia, Old Wine in New Skins. *The Role of Tradition in Communication, Knowledge and Group Identity, The Aquinas Lecture 2003* (Milwaukee: Marquette University Press, 2003). One should also consult George F. McLean, *Hermeneutics, Tradition and Contemporary Change,* ed. George Mclean, *Cultural Heritage and Contemporary Change. Series I, Culture and Values Volume 30* (Washington, D.C.: The Council For Research in Values and Philosophy, 2003).

second, ontologically it is such actions that exist – doctrines exist only insofar as someone hold them.[886]

The advantage of this statement is that is places liturgy and the whole of Christian living at the very heart of Tradition. It should be completed by the nuanced work of Yves Congar, for instance,[887] and I should point out that the very soul of Tradition is to be found in the action of the Holy Spirit by which those divine realities "handed on" (*tradere*) are rendered present, accessible and life giving.[888] I cite Gracia here because his work serves to highlight exactly what can be lacking in modern historical study of the Scriptures, particularly when the action of the Holy Spirit in the past and in the present is methodologically excluded. Tradition may also simply be described as *sacra doctrina*. The term, *sacra doctrina,* is an analogous expression that applies to many facets of that activity by which God manifests and communicates himself and a knowledge of his plan because only in this way can we know the reason why we were created and set our lives in that direction. It includes, on the part of God, an original activity of self-manifestation which culminated in Jesus Christ who is the revelation of God and the source of that divine gracious activity by which we can attain the end to which God has freely called us. The subject of this activity is the Church whose prophetic function, exercised principally through the Magisterium, consists in preserving the authenticity of what has been and is being "handed on" by the Holy Spirit. By extension, the term *sacra doctrina* applies to all the derivative human acts, initiated and sustained by the Holy Spirit, by which this originating activity is perpetuated and made available, in many forms, to subsequent generations of God's people.[889]

The last "rule" to be mentioned by the document is *"analogia fidei,"* the analogy of faith. The term is found in Rom 12:6 (*analogia tes pisteos*) preceded by *metron pisteos* (measure of faith) in Rom 12:3. Both expressions seem to refer to testing prophecy to determine its genuineness, and the "faith" referred to is rather the faith of other

---

[886]Gracia, *Old Wine in New Skins.* p.94.
[887]Yves Congar, *Tradition and Traditions. An Historical Essay and a Theological Essay,* trans. Micahel Naseby and Thomas Rainborough (New York: MacMillan, 1967).
[888]DV 8 and CCC 78
[889]For a fuller discussion of this see Francis Martin, "Sacra Doctrina and the Authority of its Sacra Scriptura in St. Thomas Aquinas," *Pro Ecclesia* 10, no. 1 (2001): 63-75.

prophets (see 1Cor 14:29-33). However since a norm was already involved even in this type of charismatic faith, it was not long before the term took on the overtones of "corresponding to the overall teaching of the Church" specifically the Creeds. Later still, the expression also referred to the analogical relation between what is known naturally and what is revealed.[890] The *Catechism of the Catholic Church*, commenting on this passage of *Dei Verbum* defines the analogy of faith this way: "By 'analogy of faith' we mean the coherence of the truths of faith among themselves and within the whole plan of Revelation" (CCC §114).

One of the most important expressions of this analogy of faith is found in the Canon itself. Attention to this fact would have prevented the tendency in much historical critical investigation to understand the "pluralism" of the New Testament to be a conglomeration of conflicting views that would entitle one to continue the centrifugal movement in several new directions.

The final two sentences of §12 speak of the relationship between exegetical work and the teaching office and function of the Church. The first sentence urges exegetes to work according to the "rules" just elaborated so that the judgment of the Church "might mature." A good example of such collaboration can be seen in the way the documents of Vatican II are the fruit of the biblical, liturgical, patristic and theological work of the previous 150 years, especially that of the *Ressourcement* movement. The final sentence enunciates the principle that the Church has the divine mandate and ministry of preserving and interpreting the Scriptures and other efforts are subject to the authority of the Church's judgment. This principle is well expressed by Thomas Aquinas: "Faith adheres to all the articles of faith because of one reason (*medium*), namely because of the First Truth proposed to us in the Scriptures understood rightly according to the teaching of the Church (*secundum doctrinam Ecclesiae*)."[891]

---

[890]See Leo Scheffczyk, "Analogy of Faith," in *Sacramentum Mundi. An Encyclopedia of Theology*, ed. Karl Rahner et. al. (New York: Herder and Herder, 1968), 25-27.
[891]*Summa theologica*, 2-2,5,ad 2. For a judicious account of how the Church asserts the meaning of a biblical text see Maurice Gilbert, "Textes Bibliques dont l'Église a Défini le Sens," in *L'Autorité de l'Écriture*, ed. Jean-Michel Poffet (Paris: Cerf, 2002), 71-94.

PART TWO:
THE CHALLENGE OF INTEGRATION:
THE TENSIONS

The directive of the first part of *Dei Verbum* §12 that the exegete should employ historical and literary methods in order to grasp what the author intended, and that of the second part that this be done in a genuinely theological manner, has proved challenging to Catholic and other biblical studies. In this part of my study I wish to point out the tension created in modern Catholic biblical studies despite some significant contributions and then suggest some lines of theological and philosophical effort that can aid in effecting a more satisfactory integration, one that will serve the Church in responding to the Lord's call to holiness.

The tension between the first and second aspects of what is described in DV can be attributed, I would propose, to the fact that the methods enthusiastically encouraged and embraced were not sufficiently considered in the light of their philosophical presuppositions. I wish first to look at the study of history and the use of what is called the Historical Critical Method, though it is in fact a medley of methods. Then I wish to look briefly at the understanding of knowledge and language that must be operative in the interpretative effort.

History

It is a commonplace to point to the inaugural address of Johann Philipp Gabler at the University of Altdorf, March 30, 1787 as the occasion for a program-setting distinction between biblical and dogmatic theology (the title of his address) and the restriction of biblical theology to historical considerations.[892] At one point in his address he states:

> There is truly a biblical theology, of historical origin, conveying what the holy writers felt about divine matters; on the other hand there is a dogmatic theology of didactic origin, teaching what each theologian philosophizes rationally about divine things, according to the measure of his ability or of the times, age, place, sect, school and other similar factors.

---

[892]For an English translation and commentary see John Sandys-Wunsch and Laurencde Eldrege, "J.P. Gabler and the Distinction between Biblical and Dogmatic Theology: Translation, Commentary, and Discussion of His Originality," *Scottish Journal of Theology* 33, no. 2 (1980): 133-58.

Gabler goes on with all the enthusiasm of an Enlightenment style Christian[893] to speak of the need to "gather carefully the sacred ideas and, if they are not expressed in the sacred Scriptures, let us fashion them ourselves from passages that we compare with each other." After speaking of the historical and philological distance that must be traversed in order to understand the sacred writers, the author goes on to describe how the ideas thus derived must be weighed to see whether they are "truly divine, or rather whether some of them, which have no bearing on salvation, were left to their own ingenuity." Then, finally, the genuine message thus obtained "can then be laid out as the fundamental basis for a more subtle dogmatic scrutiny."[894] Gabler's program effectively separates the very things that DV §12 hopes will be integrated, with historical study as a theological undertaking. Underlying this program one can find most of the fallacies that have characterized the historical critical method since its inception. They are well summed up by Brian Daley in a recent article:

> "[H]istorical reality" — like physical reality — is assumed to be in itself something objective, at least in the sense that it consists in events independent of the interests and preoccupations of the scholar or narrator, something accessible through the disciplined, methodologically rigorous analysis of present evidence such as texts, artifacts and human remains... As a result, modern historical criticism — including the criticism of Biblical texts — is methodologically atheistic, even if what it studies is some form or facet of religious belief, and even if it is practiced by believers. Only "natural, inner-wordly explanations of why or how things happen, explanations that could be acceptable to believers and unbelievers alike, are taken as historically admissible... So God is not normally considered to count as an actor on the stage of history, God's providence in history, the divine inspiration of Scriptural authors and texts, even the miracles narrated in the Bible are assumed to be private human interpretations of events, interior and non-demonstrable, rather than events or historical forces in themselves.[895]

---

[893]Consciously or unconsciously Gabler is following in the footsteps of Baruch Spinoza: "The rule for (biblical) interpretation should be nothing but the natural light of reason which is common to all – not any supernatural light nor any external authority." (*Tractatus theologico-politicus*, 14). For a more protracted consideration of the move toward a "closed system" interpretation of Scripture see Francis Martin, "Critique historique et enseignement du Nouveau Testament sur l'imitation du Christ," *Revue Thomiste* 93 (1993): 234-62.
[894]All translations are from the article mentioned in the previous note.
[895]Brian Daley, "Is Patristic Exegesis Still Usable?," *Communio* 29, no. 1 (2000): 185-216.

That such is the case can be seen from the statements of some of the biblical scholars themselves. Let this text from Rudolf Bultmann stand for many that could be adduced:

> The historical method includes the presupposition that history is a unity in the sense of a closed continuum of effects in which individual events are connected by the succession of cause and effects. (This continuum) cannot be rent by the interference of supernatural, transcendent powers, and that, therefore, there is no "miracle" in this sense of the word.[896]

Many scholars have intuitively overcome the atheism inherent in the historical critical method and the results of their work have been successful to a greater or lesser degree. However, the restrictions placed on them by the orientation of the method itself have made a genuine integration of their work with attention to the present action of the Holy Spirit, the whole of the canon and the tradition, the analogy of faith, and the teaching of the Magisterium something yet to be accomplished.[897]

There is no doubt that the development of a critical historiography has been of immense help in understanding aspects of the biblical text, and has raised history to the rank of an authentic discipline. The positivistic bias of the historical critical approach, however, has produced something akin to the results one can find in the physical sciences lamented today by many scientists themselves: we fail to account correctly to ourselves as to what we actually do when we know, and thus falsify the process and the results.[898] I would suggest that, in regard to history we must look more closely at what we do when we intuitively "adjust" the results of the historical critical method. Only in this way can we move from the inassimilable presuppositions of the historical critical method to a genuine theological integration of the invaluable work of critical historiography. The faith instinct leads believing exegetes to take account, though as yet imperfectly, of

---

[896]I owe this reference to the more complete discussion in Alvin Plantinga, "Two (or More) Kinds of Scripture Scholarship," *Modern Theology* 14, no. 2 (1998): 243-77.

[897]I have been referring to Christian, particularly Catholic, scholars but the same understanding of the limitation can be found among Jewish scholars. See the remarks by Jon Levenson, *The Hebrew Bible, The Old Testament, and Historical Criticism. Jews and Christians in Biblical Studies* (Louisville: Westminster/John Knox, 1993).

[898]One could consult the works of Michael Polanyi, viz., Michael Polanyi, *The Tacit Dimension* (New York: Doubleday, Anchor Books, 1967) and Michael Polanyi, *Personal Knowledge. Towards a Post-Critical Philosophy* (Chicago: University of Chicago Press, 1958).

the mystery of Christ, the center of history, and to understand time and the temporality of events in a manner that includes, at least less superficially, an awareness of the interior and vertical dimension of events. Thus, to borrow a famous book title, we must look at Christ and Time, though these will be understood in a different way than that of the author, Oscar Cullman.

Christ

Much modern philosophy, particularly Catholic philosophy, has moved away from the mental abstractions and fascination with practical reason that characterized the Enlightenment to a deeper understanding of the concrete. By "the concrete" here I mean the actually and uniquely existing individuum as distinct from the particular, which is but one instance of a class or category. Such a move is in the direction of biblical thought since it is in the direction of giving primacy to that revelation of Being that has taken place in history.[899] For, as Aquinas points out, God is present to his creation in three ways. He is present as cause of all that is, he is present as the object of knowledge and love in those human beings whose level of existence has been raised or intensified by grace, and he is present personally through the grace of union in the covenant between his eternal Word and the elect humanity of Jesus.[900]

By positing a Divine Person within the limits of historical existence Christianity necessarily claims that all history ultimately finds its meaning in relation to him. Thus we answer affirmatively the question once posed by Jean Nabert: "Do we have the right to invest one moment of history with an absolute characteristic?"[901] This does not imply that there is no such thing as a history with its own existence and intelligibility: if human existence were not something "other" the Incarnation would not be union but absorption. The medievals appreciated the fact that Israel's history was more closely bound to the plan of the Incarnation than that of other people. Thomas Aquinas, in

---

[899]For an excellent treatment of this point see Martin Bieler, "The Future of the Philosophy of Being," *Communio* 26 (1999): 455-85.
[900]*Summa Theologiae* (ST) 1, 8, 3, c and ad 4 where he mentions the *singularis modus essendi Deum in homine per unionem* which he will consider in ST 3, 2.
[901]J. Nabert, *Essai sur le mal* (Paris: Presses Un. De France, 1955), p. 148.

answering the objection that the judicial precepts of the Jews should not receive a figural interpretation any more than that of other people, responds in this way:

> The Jewish people were chosen by God in order that Christ be born of them. Therefore it was necessary that the whole state (*status*) of that people be prophetic and figural as Augustine says in *Contra Faustum* (22,4). And for this reason even the judicial precepts handed on to that people are more figural than the judicial precepts handed on to other peoples. And thus even the wars and actions of that people are expounded mystically but not the wars and actions of the Assyrians or Romans even though they were by far better known among men.[902]

Because of Christ's death and resurrection the very essence of human existence has been modified and thus there will come a moment when all of history reaches the goal set for it by God. Thus, there is a history that is more intimately linked to Christ and his Body and yet this history is placed within the movements and actions of all history. Enlightenment history tends to look at agents rather than subjects and thus restricts its enquiry to a level of causality that, because it seems to imitate that of the physical sciences, has no interior and no genuinely human dimension. But this is not history. History is the action of human subjects and thus necessarily has an interior dimension, what Jean Lacroix calls the "interiority of history."[903] And what Henri de Lubac can refer to as the "S/spiritual dimension of history."

> God acts within history, God reveals himself within history. Even more, God inserts himself within history, thus granting it a "religious consecration" which forces us to take it seriously. Historical realities have a depth; they are to be understood spiritually: *historika pneumatikôs*... and on the other hand, spiritual realities appear in the movement of becoming, they are to be understood historically: *pneumatika historikôs* ... The Bible, which contains revelation, thus also contains, in a certain way, the history of the world.[904]

---

[902]ST 1-2,104, ad 2

[903]Lacroix, using the ancient Christian understanding of "mystery" as the divine and Christological dimension of history resumes, and I give here the complete text cited above in Chapter --- (Imitation): *"Un temps sans mystère, si meme on pouvait le concevoir, serait un temps vide, strictement linéaire. Le mystère est ce qui ouvre la temporalité et lui donne sa profoundeur, ce qui introduit une dimension verticale : il en fait le temps de la révélation et du dévoilement. Ainsi acquiert-il sens."* (Jean Lacroix, *Histoire et Mystère* (Tournai: Castermann, 1962), 7.

[904]*Catholicisme. Les aspects sociaux de Dogme chrétien* (Paris: Cerf, 1938, 1941) 119. Translation, is from ; emphasis is in the text.

This reality of history introduces us into a totally different understanding of time. Rather than a mechanical process moving from past to present and measured by production and progress, history, with the Body of Christ at its center, is a mystery of presence.

The mystery of the presence of Christ obliges us to look at expanding what we usually understand by analogy and participation. Gregory Rocca, paraphrasing Cornelio Fabro, states: "[P]articipation is especially the ontology of analogy and analogy is the epistemology and semantics of participation."[905] Participation is usually divided into predicamental and transcendental. In predicamental participation two realities are said to participate in the same notion: one may be the exemplar of the other. In transcendental participation one reality (God) possesses something *totaliter* ("Whatever is totally something does not participate in it but is essentially the same as it.")[906] while another reality shares in that something but not essentially. Here there is efficient causality in addition to exemplar causality. Participation in this case involves a dependence in being between the first reality and the second. As the phrase cited above indicates, this second type of participation is the "ontology of analogy," allowing God's being to be correctly though inadequately spoken of on the basis of those perfections in creatures which participate, through God's efficient causality, in something of which he is the ineffable exemplar.

In the light of the Incarnation a new dimension of reality is made available to humanity. I would wish to call this "economic participation." Just as transcendental participation is an ontological reality now seen because of the revelation of creation, so economic participation is an ontological reality because of the Incarnation. Israel's possession of a covenantal relation to YHWH, as Aquinas noted, is unique in the whole of the history of religion. This must be taken seriously. The covenant relation is itself based upon and expressive of acts of God in time, in history, and, as, we have seen, these events participate in a proleptic manner in the mystery of the Incarnation, and in its own

---

[905]"Analogy as Judgment and Faith in God's Incomprehensibility: A Study in the Theological Epistemology of Thomas Aquinas" (Ph.D. Thesis, Catholic University of America, 1989) (UMI Dissertation Services: Ann Arbor, 1994) 537. Rocca is condensing the thought of Cornelio Fabro, *Participation et Causalité selon S. Thomas d'Aquin* (Louvain: Publications Universitaires de Louvain, 1961) 634-40.

highpoint in time: the death and resurrection of Jesus. There is thus an economic participation in which all God's acts in human history are related to the supreme act, the cross, which realizes and is, *"totaliter,"* the economic action of God, the exemplar and instrumental efficient cause of all the other acts.

It is my contention that this dimension of economic participation, the fact that the events and persons, "the wars and actions" of Israel share proleptically but metaphysically in the reality of Christ is the basis for the ancient understanding of the "spiritual sense" of the OT. Within the parameters of the historical critical method such a thing is impossible. The best that can be achieved is the discovery of a certain resemblance between events or personages on the basis of some type of "intertextuality." But this is far from the notion of history that takes the Incarnation seriously, to say nothing of the sovereign action of God in all of creation. This latter point is clearly elaborated in an early discussion of the "spiritual sense" by Thomas Aquinas:

> Things are so ordered in their working out, that from them such a signification (*talis sensus*; i.e. *sensus spiritualis*) can be derived which is from him only who governs all things by his providence and this is God alone... Therefore, in no branch of knowledge forged by human effort can there be found, properly speaking, anything but the literal signification (*sensus*) except only in this Scripture whose author is the Holy Spirit and for whom human beings are instruments as it is written: "my tongue is the pen of a swiftly writing scribe." (Ps 44:2 [Vg]).[907]

In concluding this section, I would like to suggest that part of what is needed in our search for an integration of historical methods and a theological understanding of the word of God is a deeper and more adequate understanding of the Christological dimension of history. This, ultimately, is a work of faith, penetrating to the interiority and direction of the events to which critical historiography gives us, as it were, a parallel and important exterior understanding. To quote Aquinas once again: "[Theology] has for principles the articles of faith which, by the infused light of faith, are per se evident (*noti*) to one having faith; [they function] in a way like the principles naturally placed (*insita*) in us by the light of the agent intellect."[908]

---

[906]Thomas Aquinas, *Sententiae libri Metaphysicorum* 1.10.154
[907]*Quodlibeta* 7,16. I plan to publish a study on the Spiritual Sense shortly.
[908]I *Sent. Prol.* a 3, sol 2, ad 2.

Time

I wish now to look at some aspects of the mystery of time and suggest that, once the transcendent dimension of time is rescued from the modern study of history, the possibility of the integration we are seeking is more attainable.[909] For modern history time is succession, a dubious and uneven march toward an indeterminate future. The study of history, now capable of genuine reconstruction and insight, records this march. As we have seen, it resolutely eschews any consideration of transcendence, any search for a causality that exceeds the forces, and resources of what is fundamentally, a closed system.[910] I would propose that we use the term "temporality" to describe the nature of human existence: temporality includes succession in a vision of presence. I derive this understanding from St. Augustine. Insisting that the way to an understanding of eternity and transcendence lay in a conversion of life that rendered accessible an experience of Being, Augustine describes the fruit of his own conversion: "And in the flash of a trembling glance my mind came to That Which Is. I understood the invisible through those things that were created."[911] From this came an understanding of eternity as not being endless changelessness but rather infinite presence. This gives rise to an appreciation of the intrinsic reality of the *individuum* to which I referred earlier, not as a particular instance of a class but as a unique reality receiving its identity from a relation to its Creator.[912] God, the Creator, who is Eternity, is necessarily present in the action of sustaining all that is.[913] Augustine, responding to the opinion that, since God's will to create is eternal, creation itself must be eternal, answers in this manner:

> People who take that line do not yet understand you, O Wisdom of God and Light of our minds. They do not yet understand how things which receive their being through you and

---

[909]In the lines which follow, I am indebted to two studies delivered at a Symposium held at the Intercultural Forum of the John Paul II Cultural Center and to be published soon. I am grateful to their authors to be able to utilize their material: Kenneth Schmitz, "The Ingathering of Being, Time and Word and the Inbreaking of a Transcendent Word," (forthcoming), Matthew Lamb, "Temporality and History: Reflections from St. Augustine and Bernard Lonergan," (forthcoming).

[910]The relation between this view and the pre-Christian pagan view of reality can be seen in the study by Robert Sokolowski, *The God of Faith and Reason. Foundations of Christian Theology* (Notre Dame, IN: University of Notre Dame Press, 1982).

[911]*Confessions* 7,17. Translation by Matthew Lamb.

[912]I refer the reader to Kenneth Schmitz, "Created Receptivity and the Philosophy of the

in you come into existence; but their heart flutters about between
the changes of the past and future found in created things and an
empty heart it remains... [If they consider] they would see that
in eternity nothing passes, for the whole is present (*sed totum esse
praesens*) whereas time cannot be present all at once (*nullum vero
tempus totum esse praesens*).[914]

In this deceptively simple presentation we have the way to
recover transcendence in regard to human existence. Temporality,
the proper mode of creation's existence, is not just succession; it is
succession with the dimension of presence. In this sense *tempus*,
is intrinsic to creation: "God, in whose eternity there is no change
whatsoever, is the creator and director of time...the world was not
created in time but with time."[915] To understand, therefore, time as
intrinsic to creaturely existence[916] and not an exterior and neutral
"container" for the changes of the past and future is to advance toward
an understanding of history that includes what Jean Lacroix has already
referred to as its "mystery." Augustine and many others have pointed
to this dimension of the events narrated in the Bible. The "mystery"
is the eternally present Christological dimension of the events of
salvation history as this moves through the succession of "before and
after." The meaning is to be found, not in the exterior comparison of
texts, but in the interior recognition of economic participation. Let
two patristic texts suffice out of a countless number that could be
adduced. "Holy Scripture, in its way of speaking, transcends all other
sciences because in one and the same statement while is narrates an
event it sets forth the mystery."[917] The two words "event" and "mystery"
refer in turn to the literal sense, the event, and then the same event as
it is now seen to have been a participated anticipation of the mystery
of Christ. Augustine has much the same to say; "*In ipso facto* [the
event itself], *non solum in dicto* [the text of the OT], *mysterium* [the
plan of God revealed in Christ] *requirere debemus.*"[918]

Concrete," *The Thomist* 61, no. 3 (1997): 339-71.
[913]See note 911 above.
[914]Augustine, *The Confessions*, ed. John E. Rotelle, trans. Maria Boulding, vol. I/1, *The Works of St. Augustine* (Hyde Park, NY: New City Press, 1997). The passage is 11,11.
[915]*De Civitate Dei* 11,6, translation is that of M. Lamb. "Cum igitur Deus, in cuius aternitate nulla est omnino mutatio, creator sit temporum et ordinator... procul dubio non est mundus factus in tempore sed cum tempore."
[916]While succession, an aspect of time, is clearly present in material creation, created spirits also have succession in that they go from potency to act.
[917]Gregory the Great, *Moralia* 20,1 (PL 76,135): "*Sacra Scriptura omnes scientias ipso locutionis suae more transcendit, quia uno eodemque sermone dum narrat gestum, prodit mysterium.*"
[918]*On Psalm 68* (PL 36,858).

One last consideration will conclude this reflection on integrating historical study and authentic exegesis through a deeper understanding of time. Some practitioners of the historical critical method point to the great advantage we now have in being able to establish a "parallel narrative interpretation," as it were of the events narrated in the Bible. There are NT exegetes who have used this approach to great effect by trying to reconstruct through critical historiography an event in the life of Jesus and then tracing the inspired interpretative activity of the Gospel writers.[919] Generally, however, as I have said, the tendency is to use the reconstructed event as the norm against which the biblical narration is measured

If we take the NT manner of narrating seriously, then we must acknowledge that the parallel information we can obtain by historical study is always to be at the service of seeking to follow the inspired narrative techniques of the biblical authors. What we have is an action of God in history, in this case in Christ, interpreted by an action of God in the composition of the subsequent tradition and its Scripture. This is what *Dei Verbum* (§2) meant by describing the "economy of revelation" as taking place *"gestis verbisque intrinsece inter se connexis"* so that "the works accomplished by God in the history of salvation, manifest and confirm the teaching and the realities signified by the words, while the words proclaim the works and bring to light the mystery contained in them."[920] It is precisely here that I think we must acknowledge a failure of historical study. Rather than seek to understand more deeply what DV has already urged us to do: "To search out the intention of the sacred writers, attention should be given, among other things, to "literary forms." What is the "literary form" of the Gospel narratives, which are recounting past events as they exist now in the transformed humanity of Christ? What is the literary form of the Exodus accounts, which, based on the memory of a people and seeking to mediate the experience of God's action in

[919]I am thinking, for example of Ignace de la Potterie, "The Multiplication of the Loaves in the Life of Jesus," *Communio* 16 (1989): 499-516, René Latourelle, *The Miracles of Jesus and the Theology of Miracles*, trans. Matthew J. O'Connell (New York: Paulist Press, 1988).

[920]This teaching is admirably summed up by Hans Urs von Balthasar; "The gradual clothing of the events within the folds of Scripture is not only an inevitable drawback (because the people of the Orient of that time did not know, in fact, an historiography in the modern understanding of the term), but assuredly also this corresponds unqualifiedly to a positive intention of the Spirit."Hans Urs von Balthasar, "Il Senso Spirituale della Scrittura," *Ricerche Teologiche* 5 (1994): 5-9. Cite is from p.7.

the history of Israel, have a particular mode of narrating that is apt to effect just this mediation? This is surely a different question, one that can only be approached with faith and sensitivity to the authors, redactors, and storytellers etc. who were moved by the Holy Spirit to mediate an event whose actual "historical" existence can hardly be pieced together.[921] A more complete answer to this type of question would involve an understanding of the role of "memory" in the forming of an interpreted event. Once again we return to the fact that the proper dimension of human existence and of salvation history is not mere succession but succession and presence. This is the mystery; it is the mode of biblical address and it should be the mode of authentic exegesis

CONSIDERATIONS FOR
FURTHER DEVELOPMENT

We have seen that at the very center of temporality is the Word, the Word made flesh. In dying and rising again, this Word, Jesus Christ, has now in principle, brought all creation to its perfection. This reality, however, must work out in the world of succession — the world was created with time — and then at some point all creation will reach its goal:

> Then the end will come, when he hands over the kingdom to God the Father after he has destroyed all dominion, authority and power. For he must reign until he has put all his enemies under his feet. The last enemy to be destroyed is death. For he "has put everything under his feet." Now when it says that "everything" has been put under him, it is clear that this does not include God himself, who put everything under Christ. When he has done this, then the Son himself will be made subject to him who put everything under him, so that God may be all in all. (1 Cor 15:24-28).

Now, just as temporal existence can have a penultimate and partial intelligibility but never an independent intelligibility, so too, thought and language possess the twofold levels of intelligibility. And just as

---

[921]For this reason, though the approach is not always nuanced I recommend the study by Ronald Hendel, "The Exodus in Biblical Memory," *Journal of Biblical Literature* 120, no. 4 (2001): 601-22. I have treated Pentecost as a "paradigm event" in Francis Martin, "Le baptême dans l'Esprit; tradition du Nouveau Testament et vie de l'Eglise," *Nouvelle Revue Théologique* 106 (1984): 23-58.

a non-transcendent understanding of history will ultimately distort history itself, so too a non-transcendent understanding of knowledge and language will ultimately distort the reality it seeks to grasp. Space does not allow a complete treatment of these notions, though they are essential to the philosophical and theological bridge building necessary to bring together modern exegesis and revelation.   I will merely point out how such a bridge building might proceed and leave to another study a complete development.

Knowledge and Transcendence

Aquinas says of the interior light of reason that it is itself a "certain participation in divine light;" it is, in fact "nothing else but the imprint of the divine light in us."[922] This is expanded in his commentary on the Johannine Prologue:

> We can understand, "And the life was the light of men," in two ways. We can consider the light as an object, only viewable by men, because the light can be seen by a creature endowed with reason, since only such a nature is capable of the divine vision, as it says in Job 35,11: "He taught us rather than the beasts of the earth, and made us wise rather than the birds of the heaven." For, while animals know some things that are true, only man knows truth itself.
>
> The light of men can be considered as something participated in. For we could never see the Word or the light itself except by participating in that which is in man himself, namely the superior part of his soul, that is, intellectual light. This is what is said in Ps 4,7 [LXX/Vg]: "The light of your face is sealed upon us," that is the light of your Son who is your face, the means by which you are made manifest.[923]

The light spoken about is the capacity to receive reality, transpose it to the level of intelligibility and name it.   The ancient philosophers appreciated the "divine" quality of such a capacity but had to consider it something "borrowed" by a human being, rather than as actually part of his psychosomatic constitution. It was left to Aquinas to correct Avicenna, a devoted disciple of Aristotle on this point, and to posit the intellectual soul as indeed the form of the

---

[922] *ST* I,12,11, ad 3; ST I-2,91,2.
[923] Thomas Aquinas, *Super Evangelium S. Joannis Lectura* (Rome: Marietti, 1952). For a development of this notion see D. Juvenal Merriell, *To The Image of the Trinity. A Study in the Development of Aquinas' Teaching, Studies and Texts 96* (Toronto: Pontifical Institute of Medieval Studies, 1990).

body.[924] The anthropological consequences of this are enormous, and affect our understanding of what it is we do when we know.

In the very first article of *De Veritate* Aquinas, who is asking the question *"Quid sit veritas?"* discusses the relation of being to the intellect. He makes the following statement:

"Assimilation is the cause of knowledge."   And again,

> True (*verum*) expresses the correspondence (*convenientia*) of being to the knowing power (*intellectus*), for all knowing is produced by an assimilation of the knower to the thing known, so that assimilation is said to be the cause of knowledge (*assimilatio dicta est causa cognitionis*). Similarly, the sense of sight knows a color by being informed with a species of the color...
> As we said the knowledge of a thing is a consequence of this conformity (*ad quam conformitatem, ut dictum est, sequiter cognitio rei*); therefore it is an effect of truth, even though the fact that it is a being is prior to its truth (*Sic ergo entitas rei praecedit rationem veritatis; sed cognitio est quaedam veritatis effectus*).[925]

"knowledge of a thing is a consequence of the conformity of thing and intellect." And since truth is precisely the "assimilation of the knower to the thing known," it follows that "knowledge is a certain effect of truth." We may call the conformity or assimilation of the knower to what is known "ontological truth" and the knowledge that follows from this "epistemological truth." A person is already modified by being or a being before he can articulate the conformity established through what Maritain calls "the basic generosity of existence."[926] Beings give themselves to us and modify us, thus establishing us in truth whose effect is knowledge.

The "Copernican Revolution" effected by Kant has served to invert this whole understanding of truth and knowledge. Conformity is now between what is considered and the mental structure of the human being considering it. This conviction has, consciously or unconsciously, been the basic conviction of thinkers since the 18th

---

[924]See Anton Pegis, "Some Reflections on Summa Contra Gentiles II, 56," in *An Etienne Gilson Tribute*, ed. C.J. O'Neill (Milwaukee: Marquette University Press, 1959), 169-88.
    [925]Because this is a controverted text, I give the omitted part here: The first reference (*comparatio*) of being to the intellect, therefore, consists in its agreement with the intellect (*ut ens intellectui correspondeat*). This agreement is called "the conformity of thing and intellect" (*adaequatio rei et intellectus*) and in this conformity is found the formal constituent of the true (*et in hoc formaliter ratio veri perficitur*), and this is what the true adds to being, namely, the conformity or equation of thing and intellect (*conformitatem seu adaequationem rei et intellectus*).
    [926]Jacques Maritain, *Existence and the Existent* (New York: Doubleday, 1957) 90.

century, and it explains the non-transcendence of the horizons within which the study of history and of text interpretation are carried out.   It has been precisely the work of Edmund Husserl to move metaphysical and epistemological thought out from this "ego-centric predicament" to a position that retains Kant's awareness of the subject but reinstates the priority of the real in the act of knowledge. This is not the place to develop this, but I refer the reader to the work of Robert Sokolowski who has made such a valuable contribution in clarifying and advancing the work of Husserl.[927]

> One of phenomenology's greatest contributions is to have broken out of the egocentric predicament, to have checkmated the Cartesian doctrine. Phenomenology shows that the mind is a public thing, that it acts and manifests itself out in the open, not just inside its own confines...By discussing intentionality, phenomenology helps us reclaim a public sense of thinking, reasoning, and perception. It helps us reassume our human condition as agents of truth.[928]

The challenge remaining in Catholic philosophy is to integrate the traditional metaphysical understanding of knowledge to be found in the Tradition, especially in the thought of Aquinas, with the work of modern philosophy especially that of Husserl as well as that of Gabriel Marcel and others. As this integration is effected, we will be able to elaborate a genuinely Christian epistemology and thus bring the fixation with texts and words out of its impasse into a place of integration and revelation. We will understand, that, in human knowing and communicating "words are revelatory not representational."[929]

Language

I have already offered elsewhere a brief critique of some modern understandings of language.[930] I wish here merely to offer a very few

---

[927]See, among others, Robert Sokolowski, *Introduction to Phenomenology* (New York: Cambridge University Press, 1999), Robert Sokolowski, *Eucharistic Presence. A Study in the Theology of Disclosure* (Washington, D.C.: Catholic University of America Press, 1993), Robert Sokolowski, "Semiotics in Husserl's *Logical Investigations*," in *One Hundred Years of Phenomenology*, ed. D. Zahavi and F. Stjernfelt (Boston: Kluwer Academic Publishers, 2002), 171-83.

[928]"Robert Sokolowski, *Introduction to Phenomenology* (New York: Cambridge University Press, 1999), 12.

[929]I owe this phrase to Robert Sokolowksi in a private conversation.

[930]See Francis Martin, "Feminist Hermeneutics: Some Epistemological Reflections," in *This is My Name Forever: The Trinity and Gender Language for God*, ed. Jr. Alvin F. Kimel (Downers Grove, IL: InterVarsity Press, 2001), 108-35.

words of reflection on the human depth of language, the very medium of our thought and communication, and to indicate how language too is a certain participation in the Word.[931]   To take the teaching on inspiration seriously means to understand that, in some mysterious way, the Word enters into a culture and a linguistic grid: he becomes "flesh" in language. This traditional theme was echoed in *Dei Verbum* itself:

> Just as this spoken word cannot according to its own nature be touched or seen, but when written in a book, and, so to speak become bodily, then indeed is seen and touched, so too is it with the fleshless and bodiless WORD of God; according to its divinity it is neither seen nor written, but when it becomes flesh, it is seen and written. Therefore, since it has become flesh, there is a book of its generation.
>
> You are, therefore, to understand the scriptures in this way: as the one perfect body of the WORD.[932]

For the words of God, expressed in human language, have been made like human discourse, just as the word of the eternal Father, when He took to Himself the flesh of human weakness, was in every way made like men (§13)

Origen often sounded this theme:

> Though there be many participated truths, there is but one absolute Truth which by its own essence is Truth, namely the Divine Being itself, by which Truth all words are words. In the same way there is one absolute Wisdom, raised above all, namely the Divine Wisdom by participation in whom all wise men are wise. And in the same way the absolute Word by participation in whom all who have a word are said to be speaking. This is the Divine Word, which in Himself is the Word raised above all.[933]

There is much work remaining in order to elaborate a Christian theology of language, but it is necessary in order to complete the integration I have been describing in these pages. It will not be done without a deep sense of the "poetic" quality of language, the fact that it reveals rather than represents. The beginnings of such a theology

[931] I refer the reader to the excellent study by Olivier-Thomas Venard, "Esquisse d'une Critique des 'Méthodes Littéraires'," in *L'Autorité de l'Écriture*, ed. Jean-Michel Poffet, *Lectio Divina. hors série* (Paris: Cerf, 2002), 259-98.

[932] Origen, fragment of the *Commentary on Matthew* (PG 17, 289 AB), and fragment of a *Homily on Jeremiah (PG* 13, 544C). To be found in Hans Urs von Balthasar, ed., *Origen. Spirit and Fire. A Thematic Anthology of His Writings* (Washington: The Catholic University of America Press, 1984), Pages. See also Hugh of St. Victor: "The Word of God comes to man everyday, present in the human voice." (*The Word of God* , I,2-3 [*Sources Chrétiennes* 155,60])

[933] Aquinas, *Super Evangelium S. Joannis Lectura.*

are implicit in the writings of some of the Fathers and Medieval theologians I have cited here.

CONCLUSION

We have been considering some aspects of the contribution of *Dei Verbum* to the holiness of the Church and her self-awareness. I have concentrated on the way in which this document describes the manner in which the Sacred Scriptures are to be read and interpreted. We have been immensely helped by the historical and linguistic work that has been done in the last century or so, but it remains for us to overcome the intrinsic shortcomings of these methods in order to bring into full flower all that they can contribute to that movement of the Church, gathered to celebrate the Liturgy or receiving a visit of the Word in contemplating him in the Sacred Text. The philosophical work is great but it can be done in the energy of faith that calls reason out beyond itself to heights it could never have suspected. Then, we will be partakers of the Mystery, that is mystics in the profound Christian sense of the term, in union with and sharing intimately in the cross and resurrection of Jesus Christ, the Word in whom all history, knowledge and language find their ultimate source. Allow me to conclude with these words of Henri de Lubac who knew their truth experientially:

> [S]ince Christian mysticism develops through the action of the mystery received in faith, and the mystery is the Incarnation of the Word of God revealed in Scripture, Christian mysticism is essentially an understanding of the holy Books. The mystery is their meaning; mysticism is getting to know that meaning. Thus, one understands the profound and original identity of the two meanings of the word mystique that, in current French usage, seem so different because we have to separate so much in order to analyze them: the mystical or spiritual understanding of Scripture and the mystical or spiritual life are, in the end, one and the same.[934]

---

[934]Henri de Lubac, "Mysticism and Mystery," in *Theological Fragments* (San Francisco: Ignatius, 1989), 35-69.

CHAPTER 16

Living Communion in the American Political Community: Catholicism and the Democratic Prospect

George Weigel

NINETEEN HUNDRED YEARS AGO, the anonymous author of the *Letter to Diognetus* spelled out the distinctive character of the Christian engagement with public life in these terms:

Christians are, in other words, resident aliens in any political community; Christians live "in the world" in a somewhat unsettled condition. The world, as Christian orthodoxy understands it, is the stage of God's action in history and an arena of moral responsibility. But this world is also an antechamber to the Christian's true home, which is "the city of the living God" (Heb. 12.22). There is one, Christian orthodoxy; but there are many ways of being a Christian-in-the-world. In some circumstances, Christians will be more comfortably "resident;" in other situations, the demands of faith will require that Christians be more defiantly "alien," even risking the charge of being "sectarian" (which can be a synonym for "faithful").

> Christians are not distinguished from the rest of humanity by country, language, or custom. For nowhere do they live in cities of their own, nor do they speak some unusual dialect, nor do they practice an eccentric life-style...But while they live in both Greek and barbarian cities, as each one's lot was cast, and follow the local customs in dress and food and other aspects of life, at the same time they demonstrate the remarkable and admittedly unusual character of their own citizenship. They live in their own countries, but only as aliens; they participate in everything as citizens, and endure everything as foreigners. Every foreign country is their fatherland, and every fatherland is foreign. They marry like everyone else, and

367

have children, but they do not expose their offspring. They share their food but not their wives. They are 'in the flesh,' but they do not live 'according to the flesh'. They live on earth, but their citizenship is in heaven. They obey the established laws; indeed in their private lives they transcend the laws.[935]

Christians are "resident aliens" because of their unique situation in time as well as their unique reading of "the world". For Christians are a people both in time and ahead of time. Christians are the people who know, and who ought to live as if they knew, that the Lord of history is in charge of history. Christians are the people who know how the world's story is going to turn out, because Christians know that salvation history is the world's story read in its proper depth and against its appropriately ample horizon.

Christians know how the world's story is going to turn out because Christians know and bear witness to the fact that, in the power of the Spirit, God and his Christ will be vindicated. Or, to recall a phrase that got a lot of attention some years ago, Christians know all about "the end of history" – and have known about it for almost two millennia. Christians know that, at the end of history, the world's story, which is anticipated in the Church's story, will be consummated in the Supper of the Lamb, in the New Jerusalem whose "temple is the Lord God the Almighty and the Lamb" (Rev. 21.22). Christians know that the world's story will be fulfilled beyond the world, in that true city, the "dwelling of God...with men," where God will "wipe away every tear from their eyes, and death shall be no more, neither shall there be mourning nor crying nor pain anymore, for the former things have passed away" (Rev. 21.3a, 4).

1. Ideas with Consequences

These convictions have had a crucial impact on the civilization of the West, the current debate over the preamble to the European Constitution notwithstanding. For the Christian proclamation of the Lordship of Christ and the Fatherhood of God is, at the same time, a refutation of the claims to godliness, to ultimacy, that might be made by any other power. Because God is God, Caesar is not God. Because

---

[935] See *The Apostolic Fathers*, 2nd ed., trans. J.B. Lightfoot and J.R. Hammer, ed. and rev. by Michael W. Holmes (Grand Rapids: Baker, 1989).

Caesar is not God, Caesar cannot occupy every inch of "public" space in the world. Because Caesar is not God, Caesar's reach into our lives is limited. Indeed, because God is God and Caesar is not God, Caesar cannot reach into that part of us that is most deeply and constitutively human, that part of us which encounters the Mystery through which we say, "I believe in God, the Father Almighty, creator of heaven and earth..." According to the classic teaching of the Church, it is only in the Spirit that we are empowered to say "Abba, Father!" (Rom. 8.15). That affirmation and that acclamation imply that within every human being there is a sanctuary of conscience or personhood into which the state's writ does not run.

Christian faith, in other words, implies pluralism. The radical demands of Christian faith disclose a world in which our absolute obligation to one final (eschatological) sovereignty, and the communal expression of that obligation in the Body that is the Church-in-the-world, have public consequences. Christian faith, by relativizing all other claims to our allegiance, helps create the personal and social space in which we can fulfill our duties to the lesser sovereignties (family, profession, voluntary association, the state) with legitimate claims upon us; and Christian faith helps us fulfill those obligations without absolutizing, or making an idol of, those other, lesser sovereignties. The Church's commitment to a God beyond history helps make pluralism possible in history.

The Christian insistence that God is God and Caesar is not God has shaped the history of the West for two millennia. It profoundly shaped one of the world's great civilizations, that of the Christian Middle Ages, whose prototypical "civil society" was a kind of pre-school for democracy. It contributed to the evolution of modern political theory in various ways. In our own time, the Christian refusal to burn incense to a modern idol was instrumental in bringing about the collapse of European communism. And, as the Church and the world enter the third millennium of Christian history, the Christian commitment to the world that is mediated through an eschatological distance from the world makes Christians good citizens of any state that does not fancy itself God. Indeed, being "resident aliens" allows Christians to give an account of their commitment to American democracy that is far thicker than many of the other accounts offer in American public life today.

In American Christianity, no Church or ecclesial community has a thicker account of democracy, or a more penetrating critique of real existing democracy, than the Catholic Church, thanks to the Second Vatican Council and the magisterium of Pope John Paul II.. A review of contemporary Catholic teaching on democracy will bring the account and the critique into clearer focus.

2. The Catholic Case for the Democratic Experiment

Faced with the charge by Puritan and nativist bigots that there was a fundamental incompatibility between Catholic faith and democratic politics, U.S. Catholic leaders from John Carroll on insisted that no such incompatibility existed. They were right to do so, for there was no such incompatibility. Yet the fact remains that it took the universal Church more than a century and a half to effect a development of social doctrine in which democracy was something the Church defended and promoted, not simply something the Church's teaching authority tolerated.

Understanding why that was the case requires us to get beyond a Whig view of modern political history. Nineteenth and early twentieth century liberal polities in Europe were rarely good for the Catholic Church, because liberalism, on the Continental model, invariably brought state-enforced secularism, or state attempts to control the Church, in its wake. Continental liberalism was frequently intolerant liberalism, and that intolerance lasted long after the French Revolution's Reign of Terror; indeed, it was more than one hundred twenty years after the Terror that a liberal French administration summarily shut down France's Catholic schools, in the first decade of the twentieth century. Similar situations obtained in other parts of Europe, most especially including the Italy of the *Risorgimento*. These were not the circumstances in which the teaching authority of the Catholic Church could have reasonably been expected to take a benign view of the democratic project. Real existing democracy was too often bad news for the Church.

There was one, great exception, however: real existing democracy created circumstances in which the Catholic Church in the United States flourished, retaining the loyalty of a working class lost to the Church in Europe. The fact of that American exception, coupled with three other factors – the rise of totalitarian power in Europe, the development of the Church's social doctrine (with special reference to the definition of the principle of subsidiarity in *Quadragesimo anno*), and the development in Europe of a Catholic theory of democracy to underwrite the program of nascent Christian Democratic parties in the end-game and immediate aftermath of World War II – eventually compelled a re-examination of Catholic political theory that reached a watershed moment at the Second Vatican Council.

Here, the crucial text was not *Gaudium et spes* (which in fact has very little to say about democracy *per se*) but *Dignitatis humanae, the Declaration on Religious Liberty. Dignitatis humanae's* definition of religious freedom as a fundamental human right was the crucial move in developing a Catholic theory of democracy. Why? Because religious freedom has both a personal and a public meaning. Its personal meaning can be stated in these terms: Because human beings are persons who have an innate capacity for thinking and choosing and an innate drive for truth and goodness, freedom to pursue that quest for the true and the good, without coercion, is a basic human good. The integrity of this innate quest for truth and goodness, which John Paul II called the "interior freedom" of the human person, is the good to be protected by that human right we call the right of religious freedom. Put in a slightly different way, the right of religious freedom is an acknowledgment, in the juridical order, of a basic claim about the defining elements of human being-in-the-world. As the Council fathers put it, religious freedom means that "all men are to be immune from coercion on the part of individual or of social groups and of any human power, in such wise that in matters religious no one is to be forced to act in a manner contrary to his beliefs."[936] Therefore religious freedom can be considered the most fundamental of human rights, because it is the one that corresponds to the most fundamentally human dimension of human being-in-the-world.

---

[936] *Dignitatis humanae*, 2.

This personal or "interior" meaning is what most people understand by "religious freedom." Yet "religious freedom," rightly understood, also has a public meaning. For religious freedom, protected in law and cherished in culture, is a crucial aspect of civil society; religious freedom is a basic condition for the possibility of a *polis* structured in accordance with the inherent human dignity of the persons who are its citizens. The right of religious freedom establishes a fundamental barrier between the person and the state that is essential to a just *polis*. The state is not omnicompetent, and one of the reasons we know that is that, in acknowledging the right of religious freedom, the state gives juridical expression to the fact that there is a *sanctum sanctorum*, a privileged sanctuary, within every human person, where coercive power may not tread.

In *Gaudium et spes,* for example, the bishops of the Second Vatican Council describe conscience as "the sanctuary of man, where he is alone with God whose voice echoes in him."[937] This affirmation of the sanctuary of conscience is not to be understood in relativist terms as endorsing a putative "right to be wrong"; nor did the Council fathers have in mind some "right to do wrong," based on the individualist notion that a human being has the right to think whatever he likes, and to behave accordingly, simply because he thinks it. The free man of conscience is also and always obliged to listen to the "voice of God" – the voice of truth – echoing within him. Thus John Paul II notes that the dialogue of conscience is always a dialogue "with God, the author of the [natural moral] law, the primordial image and final end of man."[938] Religious freedom, in other words, is not dependent on epistemological skepticism or indifferentism. And the state, by acknowledging the "prior" right of religious freedom, also acknowledges its own inability to write or edit the script of the dramatic dialogue that takes place within the sanctuary of human conscience.

The right of religious freedom includes, as the Council taught, the claim that "within due limits, nobody [should be] forced to act against his convictions in religious matters in private or in public, alone or in

[937] *Gaudium et spes*, 16.
[938] *Veritatis splendor*, 58.

association with others."[939] This claim is also helpful in establishing that distinction between society and the state that is fundamental to the democratic project. In both theory and practice, democracy rests upon the understandings that society is prior to the state, and that the state exists to serve society, not the other way around. Social institutions have a logical, historical, and one might even say ontological priority over institutions of government. Among the many social institutions that have persistently claimed this priority are religious institutions; the Catholic expression of this conviction was given classic form by Pope Gelasius I (492-496).

Thus the public dimension of the right of religious freedom is a crucial barrier against the totalitarian temptation, in its royal absolutist, Leninist, or "mobocracy" forms. Some things in a democracy – indeed, the basic human rights that are the very building blocks of democracy – are not up for a vote, in the sense that their truth cannot be measured by majority acquiescence. This, in turn, reminds us that democratic politics cannot be not merely procedural politics; democracies are substantive experiments in self-governance whose successful working-out requires certain habits (virtues) and attitudes in addition to the usual democratic procedures. The public meaning of the right of religious freedom reminds us of this, in and out of season. And that is why the right of religious freedom is a crucial part of the architecture of democracy for unbelievers as well as believers, for the secularized U.S. new-class elite as well as for the 90 per cent of the American people who remain stubbornly unsecularized. Religious freedom reminds us what democracy is.

Dignitatis humanae was thus a crucial moment in the Catholic Church's engagement with the modern democratic project. Absent a genuinely Catholic theory of religious freedom, there could be no Catholic theory of democracy. Conversely, with *Dignitatis humanae*, the Catholic Church embraced "the political doctrine of ... the juridical state ... [i.e.] government as constitutional and limited in function – its primary function being juridical, namely, the protection and promotion of the rights of man and the facilitation of the performance of man's native duties" – as John Courtney Murray, SJ, one of the

---

[939] *Dignitatis humanae*, 2.

intellectual architects of *Dignitatis humanae,* put it.[940] The juridical or constitutional state is ruled by consent, not by coercion or by claims of divine right. The state itself stands under the judgment of moral norms that transcend it, moral norms whose constitutional and/or legal expression can be found in bills of right. Moreover, religious freedom, constitutionally and legally protected, desacralizes politics and thereby opens up the possibility of a politics of consent. Where, in the modern world, could such constitutionally regulated, limited, consensual states be found? The question, posed, seemed to answer itself: in democratic states.

Thus the path to an official Catholic affirmation of democracy was cleared, and the obligatory ends of a morally worthy democratic polis specified, in Vatican II's development of doctrine on the matter of the fundamental human right of religious freedom.

3. The Catholic Human Rights Revolution

Dignitatis humanae had other, perhaps unanticipated, public consequences. Its affirmation of religious freedom, coupled with Pope John XXIII's defense of basic human rights in the 1963 encyclical *Pacem in terris,* helped energize what I have called elsewhere the "Catholic human rights revolution," which would have important consequences for public life throughout Latin America, in east central Europe, and in east Asia. Pope John Paul II deepened and intellectually extended the Catholic human rights revolution during the quarter-century of his pontificate by explicitly connecting it to the democratic revolution in world politics, and then by undertaking a searching critique of democratic theory and practice on the edge of the third millennium.

It is interesting to remember that the pope who effected this decisive extension of Catholic social doctrine never lived under a fully democratic regime (inter-war Poland having been something of a truncated democracy, especially after 1926). Yet in a sense his intense interest in questions of democracy reflects his experience in Poland, where the "parchment barriers" (as James Madison would have called them) of Communist constitutions illustrated how important it is that

---

[940]John Courtney Murray, SJ, "The Issue of Church and State at Vatican II," *Theological Studies* 27:4 (December 1966), p. 586.

rights be secured by the structure of governmental institutions, as well as by the habits and attitudes of a people. The totalitarian assault on human rights in the twentieth century was, paradoxically, a prod to the extension of the Catholic thinking about democracy. .

In the first ten years of his pontificate, though, John Paul II also had to contend with various theologies of liberation, and it was in his dialogue with liberation theology that the new Catholic "theology of democracy" began to take distinctive shape.

Whether liberation theology represents a genuinely distinctive phenomenon in Catholic history, or merely the old Iberian fondness for altar-and-throne arrangements in a unitary state moved from right to left on the political spectrum, is an intriguing question. In any event, and while liberation theology was and is more complex than what has typically been presented in the secular media, the sundry theologies of liberation have tended to share a pronounced skepticism, at times verging on hostility, toward what they consider the bourgeois formalism of liberal democracy. Thus by the early 1980s these theologies had taken a sharply different path, in defining the nature and purposes of public Catholicism, than that taken by the papal magisterium.

In an attempt to close this widening breach between official Catholic social teaching and the theologies of liberation, the Congregation for the Doctrine of the Faith issued two documents on liberation theology, one in 1984 and the other in 1986. The 1984 *Instruction on Certain Aspects of the "Theology of Liberation,"* issued by the Congregation with the Pope's personal authority, acknowledged that liberation was an important theme in Christian theology. It frankly faced the overwhelming facts of poverty and degradation in much of Latin America and argued that the Church has a special love for, and responsibility to, the poor. But the Instruction rejected a number of key themes in several theologies of liberation: the tendency to locate sin primarily in social, economic, and political structures; the class-struggle model of society and history and related analyses of structural violence; the subordination of the individual to the collectivity; the transformation of good and evil into strictly political categories, and the subsequent loss of a sense of transcendent dimension to the moral life; the concept of a partisan Church; and an "exclusively political interpretation" of the death of Christ.

For our purposes here, though, the most crucial passage in the 1984 Instruction was this:

> One needs to be on guard against the politicization of existence, which, misunderstanding the entire meaning of the Kingdom of God and the transcendence of the person, begins to sacralize politics and betray the religion of the people in favor of the projects of the revolution.[941]

Against the pluralist dynamics of classic Catholic political theory and the teaching of *Dignitatis humanae,* the theologies of liberation seemed to be proposing a return to the altar-and-throne arrangements of the past – this time buttressed by the allegedly "scientific" accomplishments of Marxist social analysis. With this new monism came, inevitably, the use of coercive state power against individuals and against the Church. The politics of consent was again being threatened by the politics of coercion. The theologies of liberation were frequently presented as expressions of Vatican II; in fact, on this crucial point, the theologies of liberation rejected a key element in the social teaching of the Council.

In the 1986 *Instruction on Christian Freedom and Liberation,* the Congregation for the Doctrine of the Faith pushed the official Roman discussion even further toward an open endorsement of the moral superiority of democratic politics:

> ... [T]here can only be authentic development in a social and political system which respects feedoms and fosters them through the participation of everyone. This participation can take different forms; it is necessary in order to guarantee a proper pluralism in institutions and in social initiatives. It ensures, notably by a real separation between the powers of the State, the exercise of human rights, also protecting them against possible abuses on the part of the public powers. No one can be excluded from this participation in social and political life for reasons of sex, race, color, social condition, language, or religion...[942]

The politicization of the Gospel – its reduction to a partisan, mundane program – and the resacralization of politics were decisively rejected by the 1984 Instruction. The 1986 Instruction taught that participatory

---

[941]Congregation for the Doctrine of the Faith, *Instruction on Certain Aspects of the "Theology of Liberation,"* [1984], 17.

[942]CDF, *Instruction on Christian Freedom and Liberation* [1986], 95.

politics was morally superior to the politics of vanguards, whether aristocratic or Marxist-Leninist. The link between these themes and the positive task of democracy-building was made in late 1987 by John Paul's second social encyclical, *Sollicitudo rei socialis.*

4. The Case for Participation

Sollicitudo's portrait of the grim situation of Third World countries was based on a more complex historical, social, and economic analysis than could be found in the encyclical. It was written to commemorate, Paul VI's *Populorum progressio* (1968). Where Paul tended to assign primary (some would say, virtually exclusive) responsibility for underdevelopment to the developed world, John Paul II argued that responsibility for the condition of the world's underclass was not unilinear. For the development failures of the post-colonial period certainly involved "grave instances of omissions on the part of the developing countries themselves, and especially on the part of those holding economic and political power."[943] In a more positive vein, John Paul II extended the Catholic human-rights revolution in explicitly political-cultural terms, teaching that sustained economic development would be impossible without the evolution of civil society: "the developing nations themselves should favor the self-affirmation of each citizen, through access to a wider culture and a free flow of information."[944]

Yet the enhanced moral and cultural skills of a people, important as they were, were not enough, the Pope continued. "Integral human development" could not take place if the peoples in question remained the vassals or victims of inept, hidebound, ideologically rigid, and/or kleptocratic dictatorships. Thus, true development required that Third World countries "reform certain unjust structures, and in particular their political institutions, in order to replace corrupt, dictatorial, and authoritarian forms of government by democratic and participatory ones."[945] In short, in *Sollicitudo rei socialis,* the formal leadership of the Roman Catholic Church reconfirmed its support for the democratic

---

[943] *Sollicitudo rei socialis,* 16.
[944] *Sollicitudo rei socialis,* 44.
[945] *Sollicitudo rei socialis,* 44 (emphasis added).

revolution in world politics. As John Paul II wrote in *Sollicitudo,* addressing this striking phenomenon of the 1980s,

> This is a process which we hope will spread and grow stronger. For the health of a political community – as expressed in the free and responsible participation of all citizens in public affairs, in the rule of law, and in respect for the promotion of human rights – is the necessary condition and sure guarantee of the development of the whole individual and of all people.[946]

Sollicitudo thus brought Catholic social doctrine into congruence with Catholic social practice during the first decade of the pontificate of John Paul II. Whether the locale was El Salvador, Chile, Nicaragua, Paraguay, Poland, the Philippines, South Korea, or sub-Saharan Africa, John Paul II was, throughout the 1980s, a consistent voice of support (and, in Poland, the Philippines, and Chile, far more than that) for replacing "corrupt, dictatorial and authoritarian forms of government" with "democratic and participatory ones."

As for criticism that his preaching on behalf of human rights and democracy constituted an unbecoming interference in politics, the Pope, en route to Chile and Paraguay in 1987, had this to say to a reporter who asked him about such carping: "Yes, yes, I am not the evangelizer of democracy, I am the evangelizer of the Gospel. To the Gospel message, of course, belong all the problems of human rights, and if democracy means human rights it also belongs to the message of the Church."[947] From religious conversion, to moral norms, to institutions and patterns of governance – the Pope's sense of priorities was clear. So, too, was the connection between Catholic social teaching and the democratic revolution then unfolding dramatically throughout the world.

5. A Critique From "Inside"

Even as this development of the Church's thinking unfolded, it was clear that the papal magisterium had not become an uncritical or naive celebrant of the democratic possibility. As John Paul II made clear during his pastoral visit to the United States in 1987, democratic societies have to remind themselves constantly of the moral standards

---

[946] *Sollicitudo rei socialis,* 44.
[947] Cited in *New York Times,* April 6, 1987.

by which their politics are meant to be judged. The Pope put it this way, speaking, in Miami, of the United States:

Among the many admirable values of this country there is one that stands out in particular. It is freedom. The concept of freedom is part of the very fabric of this nation as political community of free people. Freedom is a great gift, a blessing of God.

> From the beginning of America, freedom was directed to forming a well-ordered society and to promoting its peaceful life. Freedom was channeled to the fullness of human life, to the preservation of human dignity, and to the safeguarding of human rights. An experience of ordered freedom is truly part of the history of this land.
>
> This is the freedom that America is called upon to live and guard and transmit. She is called to exercise it in such a way that it will also benefit the cause of freedom in other nations and among other peoples.[948]

Thus did the Bishop of Rome endorse the moral intention of the American democratic experiment in categories reminiscent Lord Acton's postulate that freedom is not a matter of doing what you want, but rather having the right to do what you ought.[949]

This line of development in the magisterium of John Paul II displayed a particular sharp edge, of course, in the Revolution of 1989 in central and eastern Europe: a political revolution that was, as the Holy Father has insisted, made possible by a moral revolution, a revolution of conscience and of the human spirit, in the countries of the old Warsaw Pact. The experience of 1989 and the struggles of democracies both old and new in the 1990s, in turn, drove the social doctrine of the Church under John Paul II into a new reflection of the philosophical and moral foundations of democracy.

The Church's encounter with democracy, from the days of Gregory XVI and Pius IX to the present, can be described as a process of transition from hostility (Gregory XVI and Pius IX) to toleration (Leo XIII and Pius XI) to admiration (Pius XII and John XXIII) to endorsement (Vatican II and John Paul II). From the early 1990s on, endorsement has been complemented by what I would call

---

[948] See Origins 17:25 (September 25, 1987).
[949] The Pope returned to this Actonian theme in his 1995 pastoral pilgrimage to the United States; see his homily at the papal Mass at Camden Yards and his remarks at the Cathedral of Mary Our Queen in Baltimore, October 8, 1995.

internal critique. Prior to the Council, the Church was speaking to democracy from "outside"; since the Council, the Church has, in a sense, spoken to democracy from "within" the democratic experiment as a full participant in democratic life, committed, through its own social doctrine, to the success of the democratic project.

To describe the relationship in these terms is by no means to subordinate the Church to politics; it is to note, however, that as the Church's understanding of democracy has evolved, so has the Church's understanding of itself vis-à-vis democracy. Because of the teaching of the Council and John Paul II, an "exterior" line of critique has given way to an "interior" critique. Far from being a neutral observer, and without compromising its distinctive social and political "location," the Church now believes that it speaks to democracy from "within" the ongoing democratic debate about democratic prospect.

John Paul II developed this "internal line" of analysis – which arguably constitutes the world's most sophisticated moral case for, and critique of, the democratic project – in a triptych of encyclicals: *Centesimus annus* (1991), *Veritatis splendor* (1993), and *Evangelium vitae* (1995).

In *Centesimus annus,* John Paul defined the "free society" as a pluralist triad composed of a democratic political community, a free economy, and a vibrant public moral culture – and the last, the Pope insisted, was the key to the entire edifice. Thus John Paul forthrightly challenged the notion, prominent in the American academy and in certain intellectual circles in post-Communist east central Europe, that democracy was necessarily hollow in its philosophical core, so that the democratic project could be reduced to a matter of legal and political procedures. As he wrote:

> Nowadays there is a tendency to claim that agnosticism and skeptical relativism are the philosophy and the basic attitude that correspond to democratic forms of political life. Those who are convinced that they know the truth and firmly adhere to it are considered unreliable from a democratic point of view, since they do not accept that truth is determined by the majority, or that it is subject to variation according to different political trends. It must be observed in this regard that if there is no ultimate truth to guide and direct political activity, then ideas and convictions can easily be manipulated for reasons of power. As history

demonstrates, a democracy without values easily turns into open
or thinly disguised totalitarianism.[950]

The last word stung. Surely, critics asked, the Pope was not
suggesting that the democracies, which had defended freedom from
two twentieth century totalitarianisms, risked becoming exemplars of
those evil systems? That was exactly what John Paul was suggesting,
but with a crucial difference. A new and subtle form of tyranny was
encoded within those secularist and relativist ideologies that tried to
banish transcendent moral norms from democratic political life. If
a democracy did not recognize the reality of such moral norms and
their applicability to public life, then conflicts within that democracy
could only be resolved through the raw exercise of power by one group
— exercising its will through legislation, judicial fiat, or more violent
means — on another. The losing faction would, in turn, think that
its basic human rights had been violated. And the net result would
be the dissolution of democratic political community. There was a
new specter haunting, not just Europe, but the democratic world as
a whole: it was the specter of Weimar Germany, a splendid edifice of
finely-calibrated democratic institutions built on wholly insufficient
moral-cultural foundations. The only way to exorcize that specter,
John Paul was suggesting, was by re-linking democracy and moral
truth.

The question of the relation between truth and democracy,
and the papal critique of the idea of the merely procedural republic,
continued two years later in *Veritatis splendor* [1993] – which is not a
"social encyclical," of course, but rather a lengthy reflection on the
current situation of Catholic moral theology and an authoritative
prescription for its authentic renewal. Nonetheless, John Paul II was at
pains to draw out at some length the public implications for democratic
societies of one of the encyclical's key teachings: namely, that there are
"intrinsically evil" acts, acts that are always and everywhere wrong,
irrespective of circumstances or the intentions of the individuals.

John Paul argues that the reality of objective evil is a public
truth with public consequences. The "truth," in this instance, is that

---

[950] *Centesimus annus*, 46.

there is a moral logic "hard-wired" into human persons, which we can discern through a careful reflection on human nature and human action. And that "truth" is, in turn, a crucial component of the inner architecture of civil society and democracy. Why? Because, the Pope suggests, the foundations of democratic politics can be secured only when society possesses a common moral "grammar" that disciplines and directs the public debate about public life. Truth and freedom, in short, have a lot to do with each other; and so do truth and democracy.

John Paul intensified his "internal critique" of the democratic project in *Evangelium vitae,* his 1995 encyclical on the "life issues" of abortion and euthanasia. If *Centesimus annus* opened the question of truth and democracy, and *Veritatis splendor* specified the ways in which moral truth sets the cultural foundations for sustainable democratic societies, *Evangelium vitae* discussed several of the ways in which "real existing democracies" can betray their own core values, setting in motion processes that lead to their decay and, ultimately, to their dissolution

John Paul recognized that "decisions that go against life" – i.e., decisions to take an innocent human life through abortion or to terminate a life through euthanasia – often reflect "tragic situations of profound suffering, loneliness, a total lack of economic prospects, depression, and anxiety about the future." These circumstances can mitigate "subjective responsibility and the consequent culpability of those who make ... choices which in themselves are evil." But that has always been the case. What is different, indeed ominously different, today is that these choices "against life" are being described as "legitimate expressions of individual freedom, to be acknowledged and protected as actual rights." [951] Wrongs have become rights.

The modern quest for freedom, in the politics of nations and in the social witness of the Church, has frequently been articulated in the language of "human rights." Now the Pope argues, a decisive turning point has been reached, and the entire edifice of freedom has been jeopardized in consequence:

---

[951] *Evangelium vitae,* 18.

The process which once led to discovering the idea of "human rights" – rights inherent in every person prior to any Constitution and State legislation – is today marked by a surprising contradiction. Precisely in an age when the inviolable rights of persons are solemnly proclaimed and the value of life is publically affirmed, the very right to life is being denied or trampled upon, especially at the more significant moment of existence: the moment of birth and the moment of death.

On the one hand, the various declarations of human rights and the many initiatives inspired by these declarations show that at the global level there is a growing moral sensitivity, more alert to acknowledging the value and dignity of every individual as a human being, without any distinction of race, nationality, religion, political opinion, or social class.

On the other hand, these noble proclamations are unfortunately contradicted by a tragic repudiation of them in practice. This denial is still more distressing, indeed more scandalous, precisely because it is occurring in a society which makes the affirmation and protection of human rights its primary objective and its boast. How can these repeated affirmations of principle be reconciled with the continual increase and widespread justification of attacks on human lives? How can we reconcile these declarations with the refusal to accept those who are weak and needy, the elderly, or those who have just been conceived? These attacks go directly against respect for life and they represent a direct threat to the entire culture of human rights.[952]

When democracies use the language of "rights" as a tool to justify laws permitting objectively evil acts – indeed, when those objectively evil acts are described as "rights" – more has been lost than precision of language; something has happened to the character of democratic practice. That defect of character quickly shows up in public policy. As the contemporary American experience illustrates, democracies, when they abandon the central moral principles that give meaning to self-governance, begin to take on some of the attributes of tyrannies. For when those moral principles are abandoned or traduced, says John Paul II,

---

[952] *Evangelium vitae*, 18.

The State is no longer the "common home" where all can live together on the basis of principles of fundamental equality, but is transformed into a tyrant State, which arrogates to itself the rights to dispose of the life of the weakest and most defenseless members, from the unborn child to the elderly, in the name of a public interest which is really nothing but the interest of one part. The appearance of the strictest respect for legality is maintained, at least when the laws permitting abortion and euthanasia are the result of a ballot in accordance with what are generally seen as the rule of democracy. Really, what we have here is only the tragic caricature of legality; the democratic ideal, which is only truly such when it acknowledges and safeguards the dignity of every human person, is betrayed in its very foundations....

To claim the right to abortion, infanticide and euthanasia, and to recognize that right is law, means to attribute to human freedom a perverse and evil significance: that of an absolute power over others and against others. This is the death of true freedom.[953]

It may seem to some a harsh judgment. But examples of this process of democratic decay are not hard to find in the contemporary United States. When, for example, judicial ukase and congressional legislation combine to prevent pro-life Americans from exercising their free-speech rights, or when pro-life Americans are required by law to provide tax support for procedures that they deem to be grave moral evils, then consciences are being coerced by force in a way that threatens the integrity of the democratic experiment. Democracy is also imperiled when certain misconstrued "rights" become the pretexts for circumventing the normal legislative processes of democratic government by handing over all power on issues of life and death to "shadow governments" such as courts, regulatory agencies, and professional associations, which by their nature are less open to scrutiny, and less susceptible to change by democratic persuasion.

If a single sentence could sum up the main thrust of this new "internal critique" of democracy in the social magisterium of John Paul II, it might be this: Culture is "prior" to politics and economics. After *Sollicitudo rei socialis*, John Paul II became markedly less interested in the old structural questions of politics and economics (democracy vs. *ancien regime* vs. totalitarianism; capitalism vs. socialism vs. the

---

[953] *Evangelium vitae*, 20.

"Catholic third way"). Those questions, the Pope seemed to suggest, had been largely answered. If, under the conditions of modernity, you want a free and prosperous society that protects basic human rights while advancing the common good, you choose democracy and the market (or, in the Pope's preferred phrase, the "free economy"). The really interesting and urgent questions today have to do with culture – with the habits of heart and mind that make democracy and the market work to promote genuine human goods.

Thus Catholics in the United States will continue to be "resident aliens, as Christians in every polity have been for two millennia. Given the tendency of the Supreme Court to declare the imperial autonomous Self as the *telos* of American democracy, it is not unlikely that the stress for faithful Catholics will be on the "alien" side of the "resident alien" equation for the next several decades. What can sustain Catholics in their determination to strengthen the moral-cultural foundations of American democracy?

When he addressed the U.N. General Assembly on October 8, 1995, John Paul II defined himself as a "witness to hope," a fine phrase that I adopted as the title for the Pope's biography. Hope for John Paul was never a matter of optimism. As I came to know him, Karol Wojtya was neither an optimist nor a pessimist, for these are matters of optics, of how things look and of how we look at things – and that can change from day to day. There were a lot of optimists in the United States on the evening of September 10 who had become pessimists by the following night. Hope is a sturdier reality than optimism. Hope is a virtue, indeed a theological virtue, and Christian hope rests on the foundation of Christian faith. That, certainly, is how John Paul II understood the sources of his own hope for a springtime of the human spirit. Speaking at the rostrum of the U.N. in 1995, he said:

> As a Christian, my hope and trust are centered on Jesus Christ....Jesus Christ is for us God made man, and made part of the history of humanity. Precisely for this reason, Christian hope for the world and its future extends to every person. Because of the radiant humanity of Christ, nothing genuinely human fails to touch the hearts of Christians. Faith in Christ does not impel us to intolerance. On the contrary, it obliges us to engage in a respectful dialogue. Love of Christ does not distract us from interest in others, but rather invites us to take responsibility for them, to the exclusion of no one...Thus...the Church asks only to

be able to propose respectfully this message of salvation, and to be able to promote, in charity and service, the solidarity of the entire human family.[954]

There are deep, one might even say "cosmic," ironies in our times. A century that witnessed the proclamation of the death of God was in fact the century of the death of the gods who failed. None of the false gods who were worshiped in the twentieth century — gods who called men to slaughters of unprecedented proportion — were able to drive from history the paralyzing fear that hung, like a funeral pall, over the trenches of France in late 1914 and then drifted down the decades, blighting the lives and destinies of four generations. Being on "the right side of history" didn't expel the demon of fear from Lenin's communists and Lenin's political heirs; it gave greater scope to evil, from the execution chambers in the Lubyanka basement to the frozen wastelands of the Siberian mines. Racial determinism and its presumed sense of biological superiority didn't exorcize the demons that created German National Socialism; living out its fears, the master race laid waste to Europe from the Atlantic to the Urals. The therapeutic society explained fear away, which worked only for a while, or medicated it into oblivion, legally or illegally.

Now we are afraid again, as a fear- and hate-driven irrationality, marrying nihilism to a variant of an ancient religious tradition to form another manifestation of the culture of death, stalks the earth. Now we are afraid again, as the day draws ever nearer when we have the capability of remanufacturing the human condition by manufacturing human beings. Now we are afraid again, as the noble experiment of American democracy is redefined as a question of the constitutional protection of perversions described as "needs."

Christian hope, as displayed by John Paul II, does not deny fear; on the contrary, moral realism requires us to recognize that fearsomeness. No, Christian hope transforms fear by an encounter with Christ and his Cross, the place where all human fear was offered to the Father, making it possible for us to live beyond fear.

That kind of fearlessness — Christ-centered fearlessness — is what John Paul II embodied in a singular way. That is the kind

[954]John Paul II, Address to the Fiftieth General Assembly of the United Nations Organization [1995], 17.

of fearlessness that is indispensable for Catholics rebuilding the moral foundations of the American house of freedom. Speaking truth to power in the face of the *mysterium iniquitatis* in its multiple manifestations is, as Thomas Merton once wrote, more a matter of the "language of *kairos*" than the "language of efficacy" — although we must be as efficacious in our argumentation as our wits allow. Still, as "resident aliens" grateful for and committed to the genuine freedom on which the Anmerican democratic experiment rests, we do not sing "we shall overcome" so much as "This is the day of the Lord, and no matter what happens to us, He shall overcome."[955] Because of that, we just might have a chance. In any event, the hope that rests on faith demands that we give it a try.

---

[955]Cited in Gordon Zahn, "Original Child Monk," in *Thomas Merton on Peace*, edited with an introduction by Gordon C. Zahn (New York: McCall, 1971), p. xxix.

CONTRIBUTORS

Author of the Foreword

HIS EMINENCE ADAM CARDINAL MAIDA, Archbishop of Detroit, was ordained a priest for the Diocese of Pittsburgh, PA in 1956. He holds a S.T.L. from St. Mary's Seminary's, Baltimore; a J.C.L. from the Pontifical Lateran University, Rome and a J.D. from Duquesne Law School. He has taught theology at LaRoche College in Pittsburgh and civil law at Duquesne School of Law. From 1984-1990, he was the Bishop of Green Bay, WI, and from 1990 to the present, he has been the Archbishop of Detroit, MI.

Editors

REV. STEVEN BOGUSLAWSKI, O.P. is the Rector/President of the Dominican House of Studies in Washington, D.C. and the director of the John Paul II Cultural Center. He served as the Dean of Studies (2001-2003) and Rector/President of Sacred Heart Major Seminary in Detroit, MI (2003-2006) and has taught at Providence College. He was ordained a priest for the Province of St. Joseph for the Order of Preachers in 1987. He holds a B.A. and a M.A. from Providence College; a S.T.B. and a S.T.L. from the Dominican House of Studies in Washington, D.C.; and the degrees of M.A., M.Phil and Ph.D from Yale University in biblical studies. He has published a number of scholarly articles and is the author of Thomas *Aquinas on the Jews: Insights into His Commentary on Romans 9-11* (Paulist Press, 2008).

DR. ROBERT FASTIGGI is Professor of Systematic Theology at Sacred Heart Major Seminary in Detroit, MI, where he has taught since 1999. Prior to coming to Sacred Heart, he taught for 14 years at St. Edward's University, Austin, TX. Dr. Fastiggi holds a B.A. in religion from Dartmouth College and a M.A. and Ph.D. in theology from Fordham University. He is the author of *The Natural Theology of Yves de Paris* (Scholars Press, 1991); *What the Church Teaches about Sex: God's Plan for Human Happiness* (Our Sunday Visitor, 2008); and the co-author (with José Pereira) of *The Mystical Theology of the Catholic Reformation* (University Press of America, 2006). He is also the general editor of the English edition of Denzinger-Hünermann's *Enchiridion symbolorum definitionum et declarationum de rebus fidei et morum* [40th ed.]

(Ignatius Press, forthcoming) and the executive editor of the electronic edition of the *New Catholic Encyclopedia* (Cengage Learning and The Catholic University of America Press).

Authors of the 16 chapters

Chapter One: Trends in Ecclesiology

HIS EMINENCE AVERY CARDINAL DULLES, S.J. was ordained a priest for the Society of Jesus in 1956 and elevated to the College of Cardinals in 2001. He holds a S.T.D. from the Pontifical Gregorian University and has published twenty-one books and numerous articles. Cardinal Dulles has taught at Woodstock College, the Catholic University of America and Fordham University, where he now is the Laurence J. McGinley Professor of Religion and Society. He has served on the International Theological Commission and is currently an advisor to the Committee on Doctrine of the U.S Conference of Catholic Bishops.

Chapter Two: Christ, the Light of the Nations: The Church, His Spouse and Helpmate

HIS EMINENCE ANGELO CARDINAL SCOLA has been the Patriarch of Venice since 2002. He was ordained a priest in 1970 and a bishop in 1991. Along with Hans Urs von Balthasar and Henri De Lubac, he was an original founder of the international journal, *Communio*. He has taught at the University of Fribourg in Switzerland, the John Paul II Institute for the Study of Marriage and Family in Washington, D.C. and the Pontifical Lateran University in Rome, where he served as Rector. Cardinal Scola has published five books, numerous articles and is a member of the Congregation for Clergy, the Pontifical Council for the Family and the Pontifical Council for the Laity.

Chapter Three: Christ, the Measure for the Inculturation of the Gospel; His Church, the Universal Sacrament of Salvation

HIS EMINENCE FRANCIS CARDINAL GEORGE, O.M.I., Archbishop of Chicago, was ordained a priest in 1963 for the Oblates of Mary Immaculate. He holds a Ph.D. in philosophy from Tulane University in New Orleans, LA and a S.T.D. from the Pontifical University Urbaniana in Rome. Cardinal George served as vicar general of the Oblates of Mary Immaculate for 12 years. In 1990, he was named the Bishop of Yakima, WA, and in 1996, the Archbishop of Portland, OR. In 1997, he became the eighth Archbishop of Chicago and was elevated to the College of Cardinals in 1998. The author of numerous articles, Cardinal George has taught at five different universities and is a member of the Congregation for Divine Worship and Discipline of the Sacraments and the Congregation for the Evangelization of Peoples.

Chapter Four: Officium signa temporum perscrutandi:
New Encounters of Gospel and Culture of
the New Evangelization

REV. RICHARD SCHENK, O.P. was ordained a priest in 1978 for U.S. Western Province of the Order of Preachers. He holds a Dr. Theol. from the University of Munich (Ludwig-Maximilians-Universitaet) and a S.T.M. from the Dominican Order. Fr. Schenk's career includes 23 years of research and teaching in Germany and 11 years as a professor of philosophy and theology at the Dominican School of the Graduate Theology Union in Berkeley, CA. He has published the critical edition of Robert Kilwarby's *Quaestiones* on the fourth book of the *Sentences* and has served as the Director of the Intercultural Forum for Studies in Faith and Culture of the Pope John Paul II Cultural Center, Washington, D.C.

Chapter Five: The Eucharistic Liturgy as the Source
and Summit of the Church's Communion

FR. JEREMY DRISCOLL, O.S.B., is a monk of Mt. Angel Seminary, St. Benedict, Oregon. He holds a S.T.D. from the Pontifical Atheneum, Sant'Anselmo, and he teaches at both Mt. Angel Seminary in Oregon and Sant'Anselmo in Rome. Fr. Driscoll is the author of two books on the fourth century monk, Evagrius Ponticus, and numerous articles on the liturgy.

Chapter Six: Exploring the Identity of the Bishop
through the Theology of Disclosure

MSGR. ROBERT SOKOLOWSKI is a priest of the Archdiocese of Hartford, CT. He holds a Ph.D. in philosophy from Louvain University in Belgium and has taught at the Catholic University of America since 1963. Among his many books are *God of Faith and Reason, Eucharistic Presence* and *Introduction to Phenomenology.*

Chapter Seven: The Petrine Ministry and the
Indefectibility of the Church

DR. ROBERT FASTIGGI [see above]

Chapter Eight: Pastores Dabo Vobis: Establishing
an Ecclesial Culture for the Clergy

Most. Rev. Allen H. Vigneron was ordained a priest of the Archdiocese of
Detroit in 1975. He holds a S.T.L. from the Pontifical Gregorian University
and a Ph.D. in philosophy from the Catholic University of America. Bishop
Vigneron worked for the Secretariat of State in Vatican City for three years,
and he served as the Rector/President of Sacred Heart Major Seminary in
Detroit from 1994-2002. Ordained a bishop in 1996, he became the Bishop
of Oakland, CA in 2003.

Chapter Nine: The Renewal of Religious Life:
Strengthening the Trinitarian
Communio of the Church

Rev. Gabriel O'Donnell, O.P., S.T.D. is the Academic Dean at the Dominican House of Studies in Washington, D.C. He is also the Postulator for the
Cause of Fr. Michael J. McGivney, the founder of the Knights of Columbus.
He is a board member and past president of the Society for Catholic Liturgy.

Chapter Ten: Disciples in the Midst of the World:
Collaboration of the Lay Faithful in
the Sacred Ministry of Priests

Dr. Peter Casarella is Professor of Catholic Studies at DePaul University in
Chicago. He has also taught at the Catholic University of America and the
University of Dallas. He holds a B.A., M.Phil and Ph.D. from Yale Univer-
sity. Dr. Casarella is the co-editor of *Christian Spirituality and the Culture of
Modernity: The Thought of Louis Dupré* (Eerdmans, 1998) and *Cuerpo de Cristo:
The Hispanic Presence in the U.S. Catholic Church* (Crossroad, 1998). He has
also edited a book on the thought of Nicholas of Cusa with CUA Press and
has published numerous articles and book reviews.

Chapter Eleven: The Family: Sign of Communion in the New Evangelization

DR. CARL ANDERSON holds a B.A. in philosophy from Seattle University and a J.D. from the University of Denver. He worked for the President of the United States from 1983 to 1987 and was a member of the U.S. Commission on Civil Rights. From 1983-1998, Dr. Anderson taught as a visiting professor of family law at the John Paul II Institute for Marriage and Family in Washington, D.C. and the Pontifical Lateran University in Rome. Since October 2000, he has been the Supreme Knight of the Knights of Columbus. He is a member of the Pontifical Academy for Life, the Pontifical Council for the Laity and the Pontifical Council for the Family. In addition, he serves on the Board of Trustees of the Catholic University of America and the Basilica of the National Shrine of the Immaculate Conception.

Chapter Twelve: The Authority of Women in the Catholic Church

DR. PIA FRANCESCA DE SOLENNI holds a B.A. from Thomas Aquinas College in CA and a S.T.D. from the Pontifical University of the Holy Cross (Santa Croce) in Rome. Her thesis on "Integral Feminism in the Light of St. Thomas' Philosophy" received the 2001 award for the best dissertation of the pontifical academies. Dr. de Solenni has worked for the Family Research Council in Washington, D.C. and has been an adjunct professor for the Notre Dame Graduate School of Christendom College in Arlington, VA. She is the author of many articles for Catholic journals and is the director of Diotima Consulting.

Chapter Thirteen: Humanae Vitae and the Sensus Fidelium of a Contraceptive Culture

DR. JANET E. SMITH holds the Michael J. McGivney Chair in Life Ethics at Sacred Heart Major Seminary in Detroit, MI. She received her Ph.D. from the University of Toronto and taught for nine years at the University of Notre Dame and twelve years at the University of Dallas before joining the faculty of Sacred Heart in 2001. Dr. Smith is the author of *Humane Vitae: A Generation Later* (The Catholic University of America Press, 1991); the editor of *Why Humanae Vitae Was Right* (Ignatius Press, 1993) and the co-author (with. Christopher Kaczor) of *Life Issues, Medical Choices: Questions and Answers for Catholics* (Servant Books, 2007). She is in her second term as an advisor to the Pontifical Council for the Family.

Chapter Fourteen: The Ecclesial Vocation of the Theologian
in the Setting of Catholic Higher Education

VERY REV. J. AUGUSTINE DI NOIA, O.P. was ordained a priest in 1970 and earned his Ph.D. from Yale University. He has taught at Providence College and the Dominican House of Studies in Washington, D.C. Fr. DiNoia is the former editor-in-chief of *The Thomist* and the past executive director of the Secretariat for Doctrinal and Pastoral Practices of the USCCB. He is the author of *Diversity of Religions: A Christian Perspective* (CUA Press, 1995) and *Turn to God the Father* (St. Anthony Messenger Press, 1998). He has been a member of the International Theological Commission, and, since 2002, he has been the Undersecretary of the Congregation for the Doctrine of the Faith.

Chapter Fifteen: The Influence of Biblical Studies on
Ecclesial Self-Understanding Since Vatican II

REV. FRANCIS MARTIN is a priest of the Archdiocese of Washington, D.C. and a member of the faculty of the Dominican House of Studies in D.C. He holds a S.T.L. from the Angelicum and the S.S.L. and S.S.D. from the Biblicum in Rome. In addition to his teaching at the Dominican House of Studies and Sacred Heart Major Seminary, Fr. Martin has taught at the Catholic University of America; Franciscan University of Steubenville, Ohio; and the École Biblique et Archéologique Française in Jerusalem. He has held the Chair of Catholic-Jewish Theological Studies at the John Paul II Cultural Center in Washington, D.C. and the Adam Cardinal Maida Chair in Sacred Scripture at Sacred Heart Major Seminary. Fr. Martin has published eight books and approximately 300 articles. Among his books is *The Feminist Question: Feminist Theology in the Light of Christian Tradition*. (Eerdmans,1994).

Chapter Sixteen: Living Communion within American Polity

GEORGE WEIGEL holds a M.A. in theology from St. Michael's College, University of Toronto and eight honorary doctorates. He has written or edited eighteen books, the best known of which is his biography of Pope John Paul II, *Witness to Hope* (HarperCollins, 1999). Mr. Weigel has taught at St. Thomas Seminary School of Theology in Kenmore, WA and is presently a Senior Fellow of the Ethics and Public Policy Center, Washington, D.C. He is a frequent contributor to many journals and a much-sought-after commentator on Catholic issues.

INDEX

Gregory the Great, St.: 356
Gregory XVI, Pope: 377
Grex parvus (the small flock): 317-318
Guardini, Romano: 21

Hamer, Jerome, O.P.: 229
Hegel, G.W.F.: 345
Heidegger, Martin: 58, 94
Hierarchy (of the Church): 8, 9
Hobbes, Thomas: 62, 63, 66
Holiness (of the Church): 4, 5
Hormisdas, Pope: 162-163
Humanae salutis: 49, 76, 82
Humanae vitae: 291-293, 310
Husserl. E.: 189-191, 361

Ignatius of Antioch: 10, 152
Immaculate Conception: 295-296, 299, 301-302
Immaculate Heart of Mary Sisters of Los Angeles: 211
Inculturation: 14
Indefectibility of the Church: 147-186
Inerrancy of Scripture: 339
Infallibility (of the Church): 159, 178-179, 182
Infallibility (of the Pope): 179, 181-182
Inspiration (of Scripture): 339, 362
Interpretation (of Scripture): 342
Inter insignores, 281, 284, 287, 288
Irenaeus, St.: 118, 152, 162

Jefferson, Thomas: 63
Jerome, St.: 153-154
John Chrysostom, St.: 154, 278
John Paul II, 1, 5,14, 15, 16, 18, 25, 37, 49, 50, 61, 64, 99, 109, 112, 184-185, 196, 203, 206-209, 220, 240, 249, 250, 255, 258, 265, 268, 269, 270, 274-275, 279, 288-290, 293, 304-305, 321-322, 336, 368-369, 372, 375-384
John XXIII: 49, 50, 75, 78, 79, 170, 372, 377
Jonas, Hans: 71
Justin Martyr, St.: 118

Kant, Immanuel: 58, 62, 66, 94, 360-361
Kasper, Walter Cardinal: 6, 221, 237-238, 332
Kierkegaard, S: 23, 34
Kingdom of God: 15, 16
Komonchak, Joseph: xii, 3, 5, 7, 77, 221, 223, 291
Kuhn, Thomas S.: 340
Küng, Hans: 3, 12, 158-160, 165, 169, 182-183

Lacroix, Jean: 352, 356
Laity, vocation of: 215-263
Lakeland, Paul: 9, 234
Lateran V: 90
Latin America: 95, 96, 372-373
Lay ecclesial ministry: 217-219
Lenin, V.: 384
Leo I, Pope St.: 154, 180, 185
Leo XIII: 158, 166-167, 173, 377
Letter to Diognetus: 365
Letter to Families (of John Paul II): 265, 272-273
Liberation theology: 373-374
Libertarianism: 266
Lindbeck, George: 59, 326, 333
Literary forms (of Scripture): 341
Local Churches: 5
Locke, John: 63
Lonergan, Bernard: 345
Lubich, Chiara: 258

Lumen gentium: 2, 10, 15, 18, 20, 22 29, 35, 37, 51, 108, 109, 131, 132, 151, 158, 168, 169, 171, 174, 182, 184, 205, 230, 231, 233, 235, 237, 239, 298
Luther, Martin: 224, 340

Machiavelli: 140
MacIntyre, A: 333
Madison, James: 372
Magisterium: 47, 97, 102, 150, 165, 179, 240, 342, 345, 346, 350
Marcel. Gabriel: 361
Marchetto, Bishop Agostino: xii
Maritain, Jacques: 130
Martin I, Pope: 155
Martin,Francis: 278
Marx, Karl: 266
Marxism: 43, 143, 374
Marian profile of the Church: 250-252, 255-256, 258-261
Maritain, Jacques: 360
Mary (Blessed Virgin): 26, 27, 28, 29, 31, 32, 33, 34, 41, 45, 136, 140, 186, 251, 254, 282-283, 288-290
Maximus the Confessor, St.: 155-156
McBrien, Richard: 3,15
McGrath, Bishop M.: 83, 95, 96, 97
Merton, Thomas: 385
Messner, Reinhard: 182-183
Metz, J.B.: 95, 104
Michael Palaeologus (Byzantine Emperor): 163
Mill, J.S.: 143
Moeller, Charles: 85-88
Möhler, J.A.: 21, 229
Mühlen, C.H.: 35
Mulieris dignitatem: 243, 279
Murphy, F.X.: 53
Murray, John Courtney, S.J.: 371
Mystical Body of Christ: x, 156, 230, 231, 259

Nabert, Jean: 351
Natural Family Planning (NFP): 315-316
Nazism: 266
Neoplatonism: 129
New Evangelization: 98
Newman, J.H.: 21, 60, 72, 73, 74, 150, 153, 215, 294-302, 317
Nichols, Aidan, OP:330
Niebuhr, Reinhold: 104
Nietzsche, Friedrich: 17, 37, 62, 66, 143, 266
Novo millennio ineunte: 288

Ordination to the priesthood (reserved to men alone): 281, 285
Ordinatio sacerdotalis: 184, 281, 285, 288
Orientalium Ecclesiarum: 158, 170
Origen: 362
Original sin: 342
Orthodox (Eastern): 149, 172
Oxford Movement: 21

Pacem in terris: 76, 79, 372
Pascal. Blaise: 17, 19, 78
Paschal Mystery: 209
Passaglia, Carlo: 21
Pastores dabo vobis: 187-200
Pastores gregis: 7, 11, 12
Pastor aeternus (of Vatican I): 158, 166, 182
Patriarchal Sees: 157-158
Paul VI: 1, 14, 50, 76, 203, 206, 221, 244, 245, 337, 375
Pentarchy, the: 156
Perfectae caritatis: 201, 205
Perfect society (Church as): 172-174
Perrone, G: 172, 301